LET YOURSELF BE LOVED

Let Yourself Be Loved

The Life and Letters of Will Jenks

William J. Kane

SYREN BOOK COMPANY

SAINT PAUL

Most Syren Book Company books are available at
special quantity discounts for bulk purchases for sales promotions,
premiums, fund-raising, and educational needs. For details, write

Syren Book Company
Special Sales Department
2402 University Avenue West, Suite 206
Saint Paul, Minnesota 55114.

Published by
Syren Book Company LLC
2402 University Avenue West
Saint Paul, Minnesota 55114

Printed in the United States of America on acid-free paper.

ISBN 0-929636-18-X

LCCN: 2003116323

*To order additional copies of this book
see the order form at the back of the book or Amazon.com.*

Dedicated
To the memory of Will's parents
Ella Cronin Jenks and Orra Mack Jenks
and
Two of his most enduring friends
Reverend Patrick J. Cummings, S.J.
and
Reverend Francis J. Hart, S.J.

Contents

The Letters of Will Jenks

Preface

WE'VE ALL MET PEOPLE WHO HAVE HAD AN INFLUENCE ON OUR LIVES and, if we're lucky, we've met a few who have made us better human beings. One such man in my life was Will Jenks. Upon becoming president of the College of the Holy Cross in July 1970, I began a friendship with Will Jenks that thrived on a steady flow of correspondence back and forth between the Jenks' home in the Midwest and Worcester, Massachusetts. It proved to be a friendship that, until Will's death in 1989, was an immensely rich source of inspiration and encouragement for me.

"Talent," said Goethe, "builds itself in stillness, character in the stream of the world." Will Jenks had both strong character and multiple talents. He formed them by dividing his time between a driving activity, manifested in his prodigious reading and letter writing, and the contemplative solitude of one afflicted with chronic quadriplegia due to polio.

A voracious reader whose intellectual interests ranged from world renowned theologians to politicians to literary writers, Will Jenks acquired a breadth of knowledge far beyond what most people achieve in a life time. The power of his spoken and written words, the compelling force of his language and the depth of his faith never failed to inspire those with whom he conversed. He knew well that in some mysterious way the Kingdom of God is already among us, and that the more fully human one becomes, the more God is taking hold.

Bill Kane, a college classmate and close friend of Will, has provided us with a moving and detailed account of the life of this giant of a human being from the summer of 1951 when Will contracted polio until his death thirty-eight years later in December 1989. It is an emotional story that provides deep insights (medical and otherwise) into Will's painful and lonely journey through denial, anger, bargaining, depression and finally to acceptance.

The late French Jesuit paleontologist and philosopher, Father Pierre

Teilhard de Chardin, S.J. (1881–1955) taught that one of the tricks in life is to convert everything into good. He makes reference to a stone. If you're a sculptor and you have a block of stone that has a scar in it, you must work with what you have and use that scar to make it part of whatever it is you're going to produce that's beautiful. What student has better grasped Teilhard's insight than Will Jenks? Can there ever have been a man who endured misfortune with such good grace or learned to accept it so triumphantly, so heroically?

Among Will's loving friends was numbered Father Patrick Cummings, S.J., a faculty member at the time in the Department of English at the College of the Holy Cross. It was Father Cummings who fashioned an unusual but tremendously effective priestly apostolate by writing daily letters to Will during the first year of his illness when he was confined to hospitals, and then a letter every other day until his death—an estimated 3,300 letters and a million words over a period of eighteen years! It was in large part, I suspect, the content of these letters that gave hope to Will Jenks and enabled him to transcend his suffering and to embrace the mystery we call God—to "allow himself to be loved."

(Rev.) John E. Brooks, S.J.
October 15, 2003
Feast of St. Theresa of Avila

Acknowledgements

IT SHOULD NOT BE UNEXPECTED, I BELIEVE, THAT MY FOREMOST expressions of appreciation should be to Will Jenks. Without his life, a story of devastation and deliverance attended by courageous ambition, exemplary endurance and a potent intellect, I and those who knew him would be less for that loss. His acceptance of the sudden deprivation of his ability to move physically came slowly, but it was complete and without reservation.

The story of Will's life and of the sacrifices of those who loved him could not be told without the active participation of many of his family and friends.

In that company, John Mack Jenks is preeminent for his time, interest, accessibility, and responsiveness. He made available to me, without restriction, his earlier work compiling the histories of the Jenks and Cronin families. His sons, William P., John C., and Charles D. Jenks provided insights into living with their uncle that only young nephews would remember. "Anyone who wants ice cream, raise their hand!"

In a like fashion, James Edward Jenks and his wife Carol and their daughter Karen spoke of Will in generous interviews.

The Cronin cousins, especially Patricia Ann, now Sister Teresa of Christ the King, O.C.D., Mary Lou Murphy, and Judith Krugman provided correspondence from Will as well as answers to my many questions.

Father Lawrence J. Moran and Madelyn Bussing Hendrix, two of Will's closest friends from Dana, graciously made available the largest portion of letters and spent many hours in conversation in person and by phone. Two other friends from the Dana days were Liz Helt Gavin and Clarabell Beard Mishler, and they related stories from earlier happenings around Dana. Ann Gerstenbrand, Will's neighbor and his morning helper, and Dr. Dudley S. Childress, leader of the Northwestern University Rehabilitation Engineering Program, provided special insights into Will's talents and abilities.

Dr. Robert C. Munson, Jr. made available, with brother John's permission, office records and recollections of the medical issues upon which he and Will worked. The Medical Records staff of Condell Memorial Medical Center were similarly accommodating.

The Archives of the College of the Holy Cross, under the direction of Mark W. Savolis, '77, and assisted by Lois Hamill and Joanne Carr, provided essential material, particularly the correspondence to Rev. Francis J. Hart, S.J., and to Rev. John E. Brooks, S.J., as well as background information and photographic records of the College, its faculty and its student body.

Barbara Plumhoff was a cheerful and invaluable transcriptionist, and I received important assistance from my daughters, Kathleen Kane, '84, and Patricia Kane. My wife, Elizabeth, who loved Will and who received his love, lovingly supported this endeavor from the beginning.

My editors Mary Coons and Deanna Lackaff collaborated with Ralph Watkins of LifePath Histories in refining my efforts.

Don Leeper, trusted tutor, Wendy Holdman, fashioner of the format, and Kyle Hunter, cover designer—all of Syren Book Company—made the production process straightforward and enjoyable.

To those named and many unnamed that helped, I extend my sincere gratitude, yet I remain responsible for those errors which escaped my final review. Mea culpa!

Introduction

MY FRIEND WILL JENKS, A MIDSHIPMAN ASSIGNED TO THE USS SHAN-
non, completed an eight-week cruise from Norfolk to Copenhagen, Lisbon
and Guantanamo Bay, Cuba in June and July of 1951. When he returned
to Chicago, he was looking forward to his sophomore year at Holy Cross
College in Worcester, Mass. where he was an NROTC scholarship student.
He never made it; as a matter of fact, he was nearly dead by Labor Day,
September 3, 1951, saved only by the use of a Drinker respirator, known in
those days as an "iron lung."

This is the story of his life, of what he called "an ideal boyhood," a savage
attack of poliomyelitis which left him quadriplegic, completely paralyzed in
four limbs, and with severely weakened breathing muscles, followed by his recovery from "the slough of despond" to a life committed "to an involvement
in human affairs that few able-bodied Holy Cross graduates can match."

Despite the year in hospitals, which began in August 1951, Will remained a quadriplegic until his death. However, he did not give in to his
despair; he gathered his wits about him, sorted out his very few choices, and
encouraged by letters from his Holy Cross English professor, he resumed
his intellectual, emotional, and spiritual growth. He set about creating a
unique curriculum—heavily weighted in literature, history, philosophy,
and theology—while maintaining a discriminating familiarity with current
events and thinking.

Once he gained his footing in an intellectual sense, he experienced an
emotional and finally a spiritual rebirth. This recovery enabled him to move
gradually from the sidelines into a fully competitive position where he proved
himself a capable computer programmer employed by a forward-thinking
Fortune 500 company.

In this era it is unlikely that anyone in a nation with a polio vaccination
program will suffer such a stunning onslaught from polio, but there are

xiii

millions of us who can learn from the lessons Will Jenks taught. That is the motivation and justification for this story.

When he learned that Holy Cross would award him an honorary Doctor of Humane Letters degree in 1975, Will wrote, "After three or four days the numbness passed and made way for confusion. In some ways unearned honor is harder to accept than undeserved humiliation. It took long thought and probing conversation to understand the why of it: I was to be a symbol of the College's belief in the regenerative power of love, a mystery perhaps expressed in the amended biblical prayer, 'The Lord gives and the Lord takes away. Blessed be the name of the Lord.' For the Lord then gives again and what he gives is the love of others to make up what is lacking . . . Fate left me poor, love made me rich. And that truth is worth proclaiming."

Whenever Will said something was worth doing, I listened and remembered his words. Will had discovered that love enriched him in a way that changed his life, and he believed that it was an insight to be shared and spread.

He enunciated it most memorably in a remarkable address four years later before 1200 Holy Cross alumni and their spouses. "Sooner or later everyone of us will be made to feel flawed, inadequate, powerless. And there is no defense against it. Believe me, the humiliation is devastating."

Will's message carries a wisdom, which is universally applicable to adults of all faiths. Those believers who have heard of God's unconditional love for us will be impressed by the victorious life Will achieved. His prescription is clearly rewarding for those of us afflicted with physically and psychologically crippling diseases and for those caregivers of such disabled individuals. But all of us should learn the lesson before we need to apply it; our lives would be fuller and happier absent such burdens or not. Will said that "Asking for help or understanding in small things will prepare us for the day when we must ask for help and understanding in larger things."

Will Jenks was a unique person; he was the sanest, saintliest and smartest person I have ever personally known. He was the sanest because he could separate the reality of his immobile limbs from the potentiality of his nimble intellect.

He was the saintliest because he lived and died by the Prayer of St. Francis of Assisi; he learned that only by surrendering would he gain his freedom and eternal life.

He was the wisest because he was better read and understood more of life than any of his degreed contemporaries, and he could solve tough, real-life problems of every sort lovingly, quickly, and reasonably.

The second and larger portion of this book is the presentation, in whole or part, of a few hundred of Will's letters to family, Holy Cross faculty, and his friends. A Jesuit with whom Will corresponded told him, "You are a Scribe that even the Evangelists would envy." These letters revealed the author's mind, heart, and soul. His intelligence, charm, humor, style, determination, and sincerity shine in these selections, as they would in his letters to other fortunate recipients. His genuine tenderness and obvious joy expressing his ideas and sentiments with the use of a clothespin, unorthodox as it is, can be easily appreciated.

How did I get involved? It started with our essentially identical backgrounds; we grew up in urban settings surrounded by extended families, were trained in parochial primary and secondary schools, and we chose the same curriculum, which put us together in Freshman Section E of the Class of 1954 at the College of the Holy Cross. That meant we took Latin, English, Math and Religion, our core studies, in the same classroom together. As an NROTC student, Will took Naval Science while I selected a pre-med program. We routinely ate at the same table in the dining hall and we played pick-up, half-court basketball games together. I found him a happy, intelligent classmate whom I came to know better than anyone else of the Class of 1954 did.

Because I had polio in 1949, which earned me a ten-week hospitalization, followed by another ten weeks of essentially house arrest and home physiotherapy sessions, I had an instantaneous empathy and understanding for Will once I heard of his polio plight. Later, we both admitted having learned much from the polio experience, though the cost-benefit ratios were very different for each of us. I learned that I wanted to be an orthopaedic surgeon, and Will learned to be the most amazing person I ever met.

In 1953 I visited Will at his rural home outside Dana, Ind., where his parents had always planned to retire, and learned firsthand of his sorrowful situation, both physical and emotional. In 1968 I was one of the first of our class to see and realize what a transformation had been achieved in those fifteen years in his mind, his attitude to life and the world, and his will.

By 1973 both of us had moved into Chicagoland; he and his mother northwest and my family and I southeast—to a mere 20 miles apart as the crow flies. We saw much more of each other; most visits were social, but some were medical. I connected him with Dr. Childress who made life much easier and more enjoyable for Will with his electronic devices, especially the battery-powered wheelchair guided by Will's own 'sips and puffs.' Will changed my life too by showing through example what disabled people can accomplish with determination, patience, and acceptance, but more importantly, how individuals without major impediments can better their lives by conquering their own fears.

On three occasions, Holy Cross delegated me to bring special expressions of its love for him. In each instance, he initially wanted to deflect the college's esteem and regard, but ultimately he rose to the occasion because of his inner transformation. In each instance, after the fact, he was pleased when he realized what the acceptance meant not only for him but also, more importantly, for the college.

During his final illness, he asked me to help him gauge any possible medical options available. He also called upon me to insure that his end-of-life preferences be followed. Prior to our conversation that day, he had also instructed his physician as to his directives. On the last day of his life, Will and I spoke privately wherein he expressed his great faith in his Lord and Savior and the promise of eternal life.

At various later times, written and spoken words honored Will Jenks, Doctor of Humane Letters, and an extraordinary human being.

At the outset I recognize how preferable it would have been for Will to have written his autobiography, but as Will's mother or mine would have taught us, "If wishes were horses, beggars would ride." At one point he did write of such a literary notion but in a totally dismissive fashion. He also told our class at our 35th reunion that "to tell the truth, I find nothing remarkable about the everyday Will Jenks." Because 'beauty is in the eye of the beholder,' this is one time Will's vision failed him.

The Life of Will Jenks

3 July 1982

Dear Mrs. Beard,

When I was a kid I knew that time hurried up in the summer and slowed down during the school year. The days on the farm went so fast it hardly seemed worth the trouble to unpack our bags, because we would be headed back for the city before we ran out of clean socks. That's how I saw things as a kid . . . One time the three of us boys went camping down in the woods. We packed the tent and our sleeping bags and our groceries on Thunder's back and set out for the unexplored wilderness of the south woods. Naturally, we pitched the tent in the worst possible place, right next to the creek at the lowest spot on the farm. The mosquitoes ate us alive, and when we tried to escape them inside our sleeping bags the heat almost smothered us. As soon as we ate our Wheaties we headed for home . . .

Love, Bill

CHAPTER ONE

A Sense of Place

THE GREAT DEPRESSION FOLLOWING THE MARKET CRASH OF 1929 WAS particularly harsh, persistent, and stubborn, lasting to the start of the Second World War. In October, 1929, the New York Times Industrials Index stood at 452, and in July, 1932, had fallen to 58. A share of U.S. Steel had sold at $262 in 1929 and at $22 in 1932, and one share of General Motors fell from $73 to $8. Foreign and American depositors began a gold run on the banks and, by 1932, over 5,000 U.S. banks had folded. Unemployment, which was 3.2 percent in 1929 rose to 24.9 percent in 1933 and was climbing. In 1932, the Dow Jones Industrials hit its Depression-era low of 41.22. During this year alone, nearly 20,000 businesses went bankrupt and 21,000 people committed suicide.

The implications of the Depression included general instability, pessimism, poverty, unemployment, unrest, isolation and, for many, the lack of care and love. From many perspectives it wasn't the choicest of times in which to be born, but natural events usually overcome economic calamities, and so into this era infants made their way.

Likewise, into these troubled times William Henry Jenks made his debut. Born at Chicago's Norwegian-American Hospital at 9:30 P.M. on Friday, March 18, 1932, and weighing eight pounds, one ounce, he was the second of Ella and Mack Jenks' three sons. His boyhood was seemingly typical on first glance; however, on closer review, it was much better than average for a boy born in Chicago in early 1932.

Mack Jenks was a teacher who still had a job, and Will's mother, who also had been a Chicago public school teacher, chose to stay at home caring for Will and his older brother John Mack, and later, his younger brother James Edward.

Despite his apparent security and at least a decade's seniority in the school system, Mack must have felt uneasy. The Chicago Board of Education owed its teachers $20 million and consequently pledged real estate to obtain a loan to repay part of its debt. In New York City, over 300,000 children could not attend school because of unavailable funding. On the positive side of the ledger, Bill's parents, both college graduates and experienced in the education of the young, were clearly devoted, loving, and intensely dedicated to their family's welfare. And, they had a good family home in which to live.

Ella's parents, Peter and Catherine Cronin, had purchased an upper/lower duplex around 1928, where Ella and her brother, Dominic, resided with their parents. It was commonplace then for unmarried adult children to live at home until marriage. For example, Mack Jenks, soon to be Ella's husband, and his brother Roy, both teaching high school, lived with their widowed mother, Susan, until Mack and Ella married on June 29, 1929. The newly-weds then occupied the upper floor of her parents' house while Dominic and his parents continued living on the first floor.

John M. Jenks, Mack and Ella's firstborn, was born January 8, 1931. His maternal grandmother Catherine Conway Cronin, died thirteen months later, and the second son, William H. Jenks, was born three weeks later. James E. Jenks was born February 6, 1934, the third son of Mack and Ella.

Dominic married Marion Boerste on June 3, 1933 and then they moved into the first floor apartment together with Dom's dad, Peter, who worked up until 12 days before his death on November 23, 1934. Dominic C. Cronin Jr., Dom and Marion's first child, was born August 31, 1934, followed by a brother, Charles E., November 30, 1935. The five boy cousins grew up in an extended family relationship, and the closeness of their ages led to life-long bonds and rapport between them.

For the first dozen years of his life, Bill lived in an Irish Catholic neighborhood, essentially a village. The widely extended "support system" of caring neighbors, schoolmates, acquaintances and even strangers, kept children in check and out of serious trouble. The social structure was not based on mean-spirited tattling, but on the benevolent hope of behavior change; the seemingly ubiquitous forces of right, law and order were a deterrent to the temptations of wrong, sin and chaos, especially if one's father was a retired U.S. Army officer, still involved in teaching military science to Junior ROTC students. Thus, while Mack Jenks was considered a gentle father, no one was about to test the nature of his discipline, especially if there might be a discrepancy in stories.

Bill Jenks ('Jinks' to his grade schoolmates), his brothers and cousins had another big advantage over most other boys aside from having four reliable near-the-same-age companions living in the same house, and that was the Jenks' family farm just south of Dana, Indiana, 170 miles south of Chicago. This was a happy annual summer retreat to a comparatively primitive house (no electricity or indoor toilets during their early years) and a farm with barns and live-in tents along with horses to ride or drive, other farm animals, and a bunch of relatives and friends who dearly loved the five boys. The net effect was that it was part of the wholesome boyhood which Bill, in his later years, judged to have been "ideal." The subsequent experiences of his life would indeed influence Bill's assessment of his youth; nevertheless, to most observers, despite the Great Depression years, Bill Jenks did have an "ideal" boyhood.

More than 20 years later, Bill recalled in a letter, dated 18 Aug 1977:

Dear Mrs. Beard,

The same mail that took away my last letter to you brought the *Clintonian* with the 1947 social item from Tennessee Valley: "Mr. Roy Jenks of Bono and Mr. Mack Jenks and son Jim of Chicago were dinner guests of Mr. and Mrs. Ordie Beard Wednesday evening." When I showed it to John's boys they wanted to know why he and I weren't invited. I told them we were still up in the big city, working long and hard, while their Uncle Jim was down on the farm, riding our pony. That old news item brought back memories of the many beautiful meals we ate at your table. You were as generous with invitations as you were with food, and your cooking was fit for a king's banquet. So many of our boyhood delights were made possible by the Beards. They were enjoyed then; they are valued now. Repeated thanks for having been so kind to us . . .

Love, Bill

- Mrs. Beard was a neighbor who loved the Jenks boys and enjoyed cooking for them. "*Clintonian,*" the weekly newspaper based in Clinton, IN, also covered the Dana news. In 1947, John was 16, Will was 15 and they both had summer jobs keeping them in Chicago, while Jim was only 13, so he escaped to the farm.

3 July 1982

Dear Mrs. Beard,

. . . Now that I'm a grown-up I know better. Time takes its time during workhours and speeds up as soon as it's quitting time. That's the only explanation I can figure out for getting so little done when Mr. Walgreen isn't paying me. Otherwise I would have written this letter when I first thought abut writing . . . The Fourth of July is the day Jim and Carol decided to celebrate Nancy's birthday, so this year I tried to think of what I wanted for my tenth birthday. I remembered the little green tent Aunt Mimi gave me when I was about that age, and I asked Jim to sound her out about having a tent. She's already planning to take it to the farm for an overnight camping trip. Maybe a few passers-by will see it and remember the old days, when there were two tents out in front. The green tent never turned a drop of water, but it was fun even in the rain . . . Say hello to all your family. The Jenks boys send their prayers and their love and their lasting thanks for so many joyful memories . . .

Love, Bill

- Bill's younger brother Jim and his wife Carol adopted Nancy, a child from Korea, whom they estimated was then 2 or 3 so July 4, 1982 was celebrated as her 10th birthday. Aunt Mimi's tent "never turned a drop of water," which meant it leaked like a sieve.

Overlaying Bill's secular social system was the influence of the Catholic Church in the person of the teaching nuns and brothers, priests, pastors and, progressively more remotely, the bishops, cardinals and the Pope. For outsiders it may have seemed uncomfortably controlling, but for most Catholics it was considered helpful, reliable and comforting. The Church in that era defined the envelope of its tolerance—and for the young in years or maturity, there were clear limits of behavior, whether from the religious implications or the societal consequences of misbehavior.

The Baltimore Catechism covered the basic tenets in a soft-covered 144-page tract. Learning it was no great problem; there was a rhythm and meter to the questions and answers which facilitated memorization. Many of the responses are still retrievable, 60 years later. In the parochial grade schools, one had eight years to learn what were perceived as the fundamentals of the Faith, except, of course, if you were going to be a priest—and that took another 12 or 20 years depending on whether you were "going diocesan or Jesuit." There was no lack of fire and brimstone either; the eschatology taught during those years emphasized the judicial and punitive aspects of the afterlife, with graphic descriptions of what was meant by eternity.

Students for self-serving motives often exaggerated the tough discipline meted out in the Catholic schools. But even if there were the occasional use of the yard stick on the palms or backs of the boys' hands, later there was a strange sense of pride and welcome relief that the chastening was done and over with, which meant no time-consuming sentence, like staying after school or writing out a prescription for proper behavior 250 times. Or— worse yet—notifying parents of the transgression and requiring they come to school to discuss it. Parents believed there was an incalculable amount of benefit derived intellectually, socially, and spiritually in the parochial grade and high school classrooms and playgrounds of the 1940's and 50's.

In a 1973 letter to Fr. Hart at Holy Cross, Bill wrote, "Recently I read *Leaving Home*, a novel by and about a product of Regis H.S. . . . For anyone raised in the Irish-Catholic 'ghetto' during the Depression the story stirred memories. There was a sameness to the experience, whether in Brooklyn, Chicago, or Haverhill, and gave us a sense of identity denied to the culturally assimilated post-war generation. As with most things human, that is our strength and our weakness . . ." [Regis was a Jesuit school which was in

Manhattan, though many of its students were from Brooklyn where I grew up; Fr. Hart's boyhood was in Haverhill, MA]

Bill Jenks attended kindergarten at Budlong School, and then advanced to Our Lady of Angels for grade school, where he became an altar boy and choirboy. The Jenks family moved in November 1943 to suburban Park Ridge, on the northwest edge of Chicago, and Bill transferred to St. Paul of the Cross School, where the Sisters of Mercy taught.

Bill earned one of two Honor Medals in a class of thirty grade school graduates and won a merit scholarship to Fenwick High School where his older brother went. Naturally, he chose to go there too. In the fall of 1946, Bill began high school, taught by the Dominican Fathers as well as lay faculty members. He prospered in his studies, wrote for the school newspaper and, by his own testimony, only shined the bench for the basketball team, which won the Chicago city championship his senior year.

In a moment of biographical recollection, Bill related his long list of employment experiences from age twelve onward: caddying (which he believed violated the spirit and the letter of the Thirteenth Amendment), in-house mail delivery man, newspaper delivery boy, catalogue palletizer, and Jack-of all-chores down on the farm—milker, sweeper, hefter, painter and rounder-upper.

During his high school senior year, Bill learned he had won a full NROTC (Naval Reserve Officer Training Corps) scholarship to college. He had the option of choosing any college (with an NROTC unit) which accepted him. The scholarship obliged him to take Naval Science courses, drill a few hours a week, wear a midshipman's uniform to those activities and to go on summer cruises or land-based training assignments and, ultimately, spend a pre-set number of years on active duty in the Navy or Marines in return for the four-year educational scholarship. He chose the College of the Holy Cross, and the College of the Holy Cross welcomed him.

Dec. 7, 1950

Dear Tom,

Every letter from home tells that you would like to come up and play football. This is good news, both for those who want a good football team, but especially for me as I need someone to back me up on the fabulous tales of Fenwick, Chicago, and the Middle West . . . I know you'll like it up here. The guys are good guys. The priests are good guys. The food is good . . . I'll see you during Christmas holidays, and we can discuss anything that might interest you.

Will Jenks

CHAPTER TWO

Holy Cross: A Community of Family

WILL JENKS WAS A BRIGHT, BUBBLY, OPEN FELLOW. STANDING ABOUT 6′1″ and 190–200 pounds, he was a handsome guy—blue eyes, light brown hair worn short—with clear skin that was susceptible to a ruddy flush during exertion on the basketball court. A frequent smile and ready laugh complemented the 18-year-old's good looks, as did his NROTC uniform. He was a mesomorph, while the majority of us were ectomorphs. The gals would have fallen all over him.

He was well liked by his classmates, and the two he planned to room with in sophomore year, John O'Grady and John Weimer, were definitely good people and thinkers; they wouldn't have chosen Will unless they thought highly of him.

On September 19, 1950, a sunny and mild Tuesday, 505 young men enrolled as freshmen at Holy Cross. Distance and travel were more influential factors in the choice of colleges then than is true today. Consequently, the overwhelming majority of this class was from New England and the Mid-Atlantic States, and most were graduates of Catholic high schools.

Being from Chicago made Will unique as most of us were from Atlantic seaboard states. Aside from coming from a big urban area, he fit the notion of an All-American Boy.

What prompted Will Jenks to select Holy Cross is uncertain, although it didn't take long to become a school booster to the extent that during the fall semester he sent Tom Carstens, a good friend who was a year behind him at Fenwick High School, a strong letter of encouragement recommending Holy Cross as a college choice. Tom followed his advice, and the two continued their friendship through the next 39 years.

Another unanswered question is why, once at Holy Cross, "Bill," as his family knew him, would change to "Will." He continued calling himself Will in his dealings with the class and the college, with occasional exception, yet he continued to use "Bill" virtually all of the time with his family and pre- and post-college friends. Apparently changing one's first name to a more pleasing one was a common family trait evidenced by his father (Orra) Mack Jenks, his mother Ella aka "Ellen" or "Helen" Jenks, a cousin (Catherine Marie) "Sue" Cronin, and the grandfather for whom he had been named (William) Henry Harrison Jenks. Whether known as Bill or Will, it mattered little to family or friends. [From his college days onward, I will refer to him as Will.]

Will's confessed lack of ability in basketball was not evident to the East Coast high school grads who played him, what with his Midwestern, rambunctious and rough-house approach to Holy Cross intramural basketball during the 1950–51 school year. Despite being captain of the Campion Hall team, he could not lead them to a single victory during the entire season. It was one of Will's rare unhappy memories of his freshman year at college. While I didn't play intramural ball against him, I remember playing half-court (three-on-three) with or against him. He was a rough and tumble player, typical of the Big Ten approach in those years when basketball was very physical. He wasn't a mean player, but I remember Fr. Charley Cronin saying that Will once fouled out of a game in six minutes, meaning almost a foul a minute.

Earlier in September, all incoming freshmen received the following letter from Fr. Francis J. Hart, S.J., Student Counsellor. It was written in a spirit that warranted not only our parents', but also our own affirmation.

COLLEGE OF THE HOLY CROSS
WORCESTER, MASSACHUSETTS

Office of the Student Counsellor   September 1, 1950

Dear William:

While browsing through some old editions of the *Purple*, the
monthly magazine published by the students, I came across an editorial addressed to a Freshman Class. The thoughts obtained therein
are as pertinent to the Freshmen of 1950 as they were to the Freshmen of yesteryear, so I'm sending it to you for your consideration.
Read it over before you leave home to register as a Crusader
at the College on the Hill.

The most important course at Holy Cross is not listed in the catalogue
nor are the grades attained in it listed in the quarterly reports—except
indirectly. It is a course more or less exclusive to boarding colleges and
it is extremely practical as it will do a great deal to determine whether
you will be what is rather loosely called a "success" in life, or just
another entry in the lists of mediocre citizens known as "the average
man." This important, but indefinite course could be listed as:

The Theory and Practice of Life Management; Being on Your Own.
Seven days per week for two semesters. Four year course.

The great majority of Freshmen who come to Holy Cross are "on
their own" for the first time, and the reaction to the new freedom is
an excellent test of how the individual stands up when the props of
the affectionate guidance of home life are removed. The Freshman
is not hazed or harassed here, but he is certainly deprived of much
support and attention, and finds himself judged strictly according to
what he is himself without any of the astigmatism of family devotion. It is a good laboratory test to indicate what a person is made of
and how he will make out in the stern competition of later life.

Of course, Holy Cross, along with West Point and Annapolis, is
rather unique among the colleges of the country in its curtailment of
student liberty, but enough of it remains to enable a lightweight to

wreck himself very soon if he so chooses. The college cannot dictate your use of time, (Cf. the old gag re the horse and the water), nor can it choose your friends, your ideals, your tastes, your amusements or your neckties. Discipline is external—life management is internal.

It is a trite but startling thought that in college one is daily fashioning the man that is to be. That is what makes it forgivable to moralize on the importance of paying a great deal of attention to being in college what we want to be at forty-five. Usually—if one is given to that sort of thing—we picture ourselves at that remote stage as successful, urbane, healthy, endowed with considerable charm and intellectual power, cultured of speech, suave of manner—a man of parts. And yet, if at this stage we have not begun to shape up somewhat according to that picture, our chances of being like that are about as remote as are those of a young milk-wagon horse of winning next year's Kentucky Derby.

The horse can't do much about it. We can.

The incoming Freshman has four years ahead of him that will be very decisive in shaping his mature stature morally, mentally, physically, socially and financially. At the end of them he will have sunk more definitely into the category of mediocrity or raised himself definitely above the average. The opportunities are here.

And the important thing is that it is up to him. From now on he is calling the plays.

Don't regard this letter as a lecture, but just as an exchange of ideas between two Holy Cross men. You have received and will receive plenty of advice as a Freshman. The suggestions given you by the wisest of all counsellors—your parents—may be summed up as follows—that whatever was taboo around home is still on the blacklist while you are away at school. That is a fairly safe rule to follow.

May God bless you with success and happiness during your Freshman year.

Sincerely yours,
(Rev.) Francis J. Hart, S.J., Student Counsellor

For boarding students, dormitory rooms were assigned in advance either through the incoming students choosing their own roommates or by the college making up the usual threesomes and then assigning the trio to one of the freshman rooms. As over 30 of us from my high school were starting here, it was easy to choose roommates; and so, Johnny Wines, Jim Watson and I, all from St. Francis Xavier High School in Manhattan, lived in Wheeler 405 during our freshman year. The college assigned Will Jenks to Campion Hall, a small frame building at the eastern end of the campus.

It was a very different era back then; no alcohol on campus and no girls in our rooms. The two Jesuit priests living on every dormitory corridor assured that the theme of the college acting *in loco parentis* ["in the place of the parent"] was followed studiously. As a matter of fact, I believe that most of the class was taken aback that freshmen rooms really were to have lights out on weekday nights by 10:30 P.M., and that there were usually two corridor checks each evening. If you were not in or around your room, your roommate would advise the good father where you were, e.g., at Dinand Library, singing in a Glee Club concert or attending a lecture or play on campus. Classrooms in the dorm buildings became study halls in the evenings and it was possible to study there after "lights-out." If you were to be off campus during a weekday evening for a legitimate purpose—i.e., dinner with visiting family members or attendance at a sporting or artistic event—then prior notification and permission was required from Father Jeremiah Donovan, S.J. or Father Eugene McCarthy, S.J., who managed the office of the Dean of Discipline. Any "spur of the moment" travels were expressly discouraged, so anticipated overnight absences over a weekend had to be approved by Thursday noontime. These restrictions on our mobility may appear severe by today's standards, but as underclassmen then we were not allowed to have an automobile on campus. That was not a major problem for many of us as most came from families that were happy to have one car and very few freshmen would have been given a car—even a clunker—for high school graduation; nor were many of the class flush with extra cash. We may have been only freshmen but we got the message—"your college loves you so much that it wants to have you around all the time." More importantly, we were all in the same boat, and there was an "espirit de corps" that allowed us to gripe or boast, as the occasion required, about the draconian rules and regulations that, we were told, were second to none, except perhaps West Point and Annapolis.

The ready availability of the sacraments of Penance and the Eucharist was a feature of campus life that we silently appreciated and valued, and only later were able to acknowledge publicly in a louder voice, i.e., that the sacramental life of the College, aided and abetted by the presence of the Jesuit priests, was the essential element of the College of the Holy Cross, the *sine qua non*, which distinguished it from other schools and most of us knew it, both then and now. Recently, Rev. John E. Brooks, S.J., '49, President Emeritus of the College, reported that an estimated 110 Jesuit priests lived and worked on campus during the years the Class of 1954 was on campus.

Attending morning Mass was compulsory three days a week; Monday, Wednesday and Friday for the freshmen and sophomores and the other three weekdays for the upper classmen. With attendance taken, if you didn't sit in your assigned seat you were marked absent. Picking up too many such marks would "campus" you for a weekend. This meant checking in at the Dean of Discipline's office so regularly during the non-sleeping hours of Saturday and Sunday that absenting oneself for more than a few hours from the campus was effectively prevented. This continued for another decade until 1962 when the Vatican ruled that the compulsory obligation to attend weekday Mass be discontinued.

The Jesuits established the College of the Holy Cross in 1843, three centuries after the Society of Jesus had been founded by Ignatius Loyola, and formally recognized as a religious order by Pope Paul III in 1540. The Jesuits' prime functions were defending and propagating the Faith via preaching, teaching, and spiritually consoling the faithless. Within a few years of the Society's beginning, the rapid growth of new members emphasized the need for educational excellence of the clerical recruits as well as of lay students being admitted to the curriculum. Dissatisfied with the syllabus at secular universities, Ignatius, in 1551, requested a new plan of studies, the "Ratio Studiorum." Nearly 50 years after its first appearance, the "Ratio" was further codified and sanctioned by the Society. It was characterized by "progressively more difficult classes, individual progress through the course, competition as a stimulus for learning, frequent holidays and opportunities for sports, and personal mentoring relationships between teachers and students." (Rev. A.J. Kuzniewski, S.J., *Thy Honored Name*, pp. 6–7) Further, the goal was the student's intellectual, emotional, and spiritual development in a "personal relationship with God." The classical humanities, the philosophy of

Aristotle, and the teachings of St. Thomas Aquinas were the fundamentals to prepare the graduate with the knowledge and charity with which to serve society as an active Christian. The full program required 14 years beginning at 10 years of age—five years of humanities, three of philosophy and the natural sciences, and six of Holy Scripture and theology, as well as classes taken contemporaneously in mathematics and science.

The teaching methods included: prelection, wherein the teacher read, translated, and explained the foreign language text, followed by students emulating the professor's presentation, using their own skills and talents; disputation which involved debate and argument to encourage mental agility and quickness; and competition for class ranking, which was fostered to encourage pupils' extra efforts. There were rules promoting rivalry, and the professors were instructed in classroom decorum so that their comments would elevate not only the students' vocabulary and rhetoric, but also their religious character.

Over the ensuing centuries, the Jesuits became noted for the success of their educational regimen that was ascribed to its responsiveness and adaptivity to the needs and interests of the students. By 1950, the Ratio implemented at Holy Cross was limited to four years, and while basically the curriculum was really a major in philosophy, ethics, theology and religion, there were course selections in the humanities and, for pre-professional students, in the physical and social sciences.

The institution's goal was inscribed on the frieze of the Dinand Library, "UT COGNOSCANT TE SOLUM DEUM VERUM ET QUEM MISISTI JESUM CHRISTUM," which translates to "That They Might Know You, the One True God, and Jesus Christ, Whom You Have Sent."

By the mid 20th Century, Holy Cross had earned a high, if not the highest, ranking in the educational subset of Catholic liberal arts colleges in America. As a student at St. Francis Xavier High School in New York City, also a Jesuit school, I gave little thought to attending any but a Jesuit college when I reached that point in my scholastic career. I recall being encouraged by the Jesuit faculty at Xavier to consider Holy Cross as the first choice for my collegiate career. It was obvious to me and my parents that the Jesuits at Xavier ranked Holy Cross at the top. I applied and was accepted after an interview with Fr. Leo A. Shea, S.J., Dean of Freshman and Sophomores and Dean of Admissions. He didn't hesitate to note that Geometry was "Plane" and not "Plain" as I had (mis)spelled it on my application.

Classes, homework, extracurricular activities, spectator and participatory sports, plus a slate of organized social events both on and off campus, kept us busy and reasonably content and satisfied.

While academic competition was real it was not worrisome, oppressive, nor uncharitable; cooperation and assistance were readily offered between roommates and classmates, and there would be no hesitancy responding to a request for help. However, cheating, plagiarism, or letting someone else do your work was extraordinarily rare for a variety of reasons. First, the professors—Jesuit or lay—knew us better than we knew ourselves; most core sections were about 30–34 in size, so any aberrant and isolated stroke of unpredictable and inexplicable excellence would have been readily spotted by the teacher, whom we respected, not only for their knowledge and understanding of the subject matter, but also for their understanding of their students. They were judged as experienced education professionals, and while we spotted, enjoyed, and publicized their idiosyncrasies, we didn't underestimate their own keen powers of observation. As students, we also had a bond of solidarity and communion with the rest of our class, and exposure for cheating causing loss of reputation and status was not worth the risk. We knew too that, of course, there would be little if any mercy, if caught. Lastly and most importantly, we knew it was wrong to cheat or lie; to do so would have been fouling ourselves and showing an adolescent immaturity, which we wished to outgrow.

Dividing the incoming class into sections was relatively simple. The administration created an algorithm whereby curriculum choices of the incoming freshmen held certain weights and priorities. The students were further subdivided within common choices according to what appeared a combination of a high school transcript, the academic reputation of their high school, and finally the high school's letters of recommendation.

For example, I chose a pre-medical curriculum leading to a Bachelor of Arts (A.B.) degree; The Honors Program required Greek for the first two years. As I hadn't taken Greek at Xavier, I preferred to continue with mathematics during the first two college years. Clearly, the faculty considered Greek more prestigious than mathematics for why else would the Honors Program require Greek in order to be eligible for that title on one's diploma? It was also recognized that freshmen who selected the A.B. curriculum with Greek rather than Math were accorded a higher position in the pecking order of class assignments since they were in sections 1-A, 1-B, 1-C and 1-D. Those selecting Bachelor of Science tracks were assigned to sections further into the alphabet, probably beginning around 1-H, as 1-E, 1-F and 1-G would have been for the A.B. Math sections. For me to select Greek would have meant taking four languages for two years (English, Latin, Greek and German), and pragmatically I believed that two more years of advanced Math would be more reasonable, valuable and desirable than two years of beginning Greek. The second and last choice I ever exercised at Holy Cross was taking German. That was the totality of my options! German rather than French, and Math rather than Greek, in the AB Math (Pre-Med) curriculum. I was assigned to section 1-E where all of us were taking Math in the AB track with Math, History or English majors as well as the pre-law, pre-medical and pre-dental students. We all took Latin with Father Paul F. Izzo, English with Father Patrick J. Cummings, Religion with Father Leo A. O'Connor, and Math with Professor Vincent O. McBrien. Those four courses formed the backbone of our academic corpus as section 1-E. The remaining course work was specific to our career choices; I took Inorganic Chemistry, and Will took NROTC. Will was a bright guy, but 1-E was a bright class; he and I placed in the middle.

A major component of class 1-E's curriculum was memorization, and the premier effort was memorizing *The Hound of Heaven,* by Francis Thompson. Father Cummings would perennially provide his freshman English class with the anecdote about a politically well-known personage who, when asked what she thought of *The Hound of Heaven,* had responded that it was one of the best dog stories she had ever read. We knew it wasn't a dog story, but a poem about God—a poem that has been described as "one of the great, if not the greatest, lyrical poems in the English language." Rev. John F. Quinn, S.J., in an interpretive commentary, *I fled Him, down the nights and down the days,* best sums up the poem's theme in one sentence. "Though the allegorical title may at first sight seem almost irreverent (God, the heavenly hound, pursuing the fugitive hare, the soul), yet this metaphor really brings out with more telling force even than the comparison of the Good Shepherd and the lost sheep, the insistent, unrelenting search of God after the soul that is flying from his love and service." Father Quinn quotes the essayist John Freeman, "The poem is a striking instance of the co-existence of the two sincerities—the personal and the artistic; the joint activity of the two motives—one spiritual and one poetic."

The members of the section memorized the one hundred and eighty-two lines with greater or lesser ease, understanding, and recall. Would that Father Quinn's commentary and annotations had been available to us in 1950–51! As it was, bits and pieces of the poem have remained with the members of 1-E over the ensuing decades. It was a rite of passage, memorizing that entire poem, but the fullness of understanding Father Cumming's rationale for selecting it did not come until much later for most class members; but much sooner for some.

The secondary aspects of our first year were just that—secondary. The dorms were clean, institutionally attractive, and reasonably quiet. Food was better than satisfactory, served family style to two groups of six at each table with a set tradition of whoever began the main course on one evening would be the last of the six the next evening. We had a student-waiter for each 12-man table, and his hustle was a prized trait. Table manners, attire (coat and tie if you were coming from or going to class), and consideration for others were likely slightly better than what was tolerated at our own homes as we were all susceptible to peer pressure, and wanted to rise in the group for selfish as well as altruistic motives. Conversation was steady and usually light.

Our time was spent mainly in the classroom and on homework. An A.B. Pre-Med class load was 18 hours plus four hours of inorganic chemistry lab. Will's class load would have been approximately the same plus drill time for the NROTC. There were plenty of campus organizations to join; some intellectual, like debating or writing for the weekly paper or literary magazine; music was well covered with the marching band, the glee club and a dance band; athletics ranged from intercollegiate through intramural to completely informal such as three-on-three half-court basketball with spectator sports available through the year, both home and away.

Visiting lecturers and performers as well as collegiate dramatics, Outing Club trips and weekly movies assured us of more than enough entertainment. Some social events were organized and others random; there were reports of more seats of higher learning per capita in Worcester than in any other U.S. city except those built around a university; e.g., College Station, TX and Texas A. & M.

We bellyached about any and everything without convincing ourselves or anyone else that we had it that badly. Besides, we dared not carry on too long or too loud for fear of being labeled a "whiner." And so our first year in college proceeded.

The author of our class history, written for the 1954 yearbook *Purple Patcher,* described us as: "The men who were born in the bootprints of the depression, but who never came to know its poverty. We are the men who watched the Great World War from the front row of the corner movie house with a bag of popcorn in our hand and a cap pistol in our pocket, men who played commando and counter-spy, and rarely noticed the gold-starred flags in the windows . . . We are the men who shut ourselves up in Holy Cross to seek the education we had as heritage, and to live in the gaiety we claimed as birthright. We are the men, who, as the years crept by, awakened to the world we never knew, and realized that, in it, we were unimportant figures leading very important lives. And this awakening we valued as an education in itself, and began to cling dearly to the Catholic principles we knew could never fail us in any world."

Rereading those lines 50 years later bring a slight smile at the mild hyperbole of being "men" at 17 or 22 years of age, and the strength of our religious faith. Granted, most of the '54 graduates were Catholic "men" in the fullest sense, but their post-baccalaureate pathways were not always straight and narrow.

"Ah! Is Thy love indeed
A weed, albeit an amaranthine weed,
Suffering no flowers except its own to mount?
Ah! Must—
Designer infinite!—
Ah! Must Thou char the wood ere Thou canst limn with it?"

excerpt from "The Hound of Heaven" by Francis Thompson

CHAPTER THREE

A Savage Attack

WITH OUR FRESHMAN YEAR COMPLETE BY JUNE 1, 1951, MOST OF US
had gone home to work over the summer at hundreds of available jobs. Those
in the NROTC saw shipboard duty or were dispatched on Marine Corps
assignments.

Will Jenks' summer cruise aboard the USS Shannon docked at Norfolk,
Virginia where he and fellow classmate/shipmate Paul J. Otis disembarked.
They boarded a train for Chicago where Paul stayed a few days with the
Jenkses before continuing westward to his own home. Will wasn't home a
week before the right flank pain, which he had experienced during the cruise,
flared again. He checked into St. Francis Hospital in Evanston, Ill. seeking
pain relief; fortunately, a stone which had been lodged below the kidney in
the right ureter passed with a urologist's aid into the bladder and then to
the outside. Although now painfree, the ordeal indicated that Will, at 19
years old, was a 'stone-former' regardless of normal diet and activity. This
may have been a family trait, as during one of Will's future hospital stays
his admission work-up noted that his father, Mack, had a history of kidney
problems as well.

Upon discharge from St. Francis, Will rejoined his two brothers. They
were the relocation crew organizing the Jenks household move from Park
Ridge to the family's new address six miles south of Dana, Ind. The Jenks

boys referred to the house as "the place," but at $25 a month rent, it would suffice. As Uncle Roy had been living in the ancestral farm homestead outside of Dana since retiring in 1939, Mack had elected to rent a house as near as possible to the farm.

The three brothers arrived in Dana the weekend of August 18, 1951 and after moving in immediately got to work baling hay. Saturday, August 25, was a long and very hot working day, yet Will managed a refreshing swim late that afternoon before a double date with John, his older brother. Sunday following Mass, Will and younger brother Jim joined some pals in town where they played basketball for more than two hours in 105° heat.

That evening, Mack, and his three sons enjoyed a movie in Dana. Since John had driven to town, Mack offered Will the chance to drive home, but Will demurred uncharacteristically, saying he wasn't feeling up to par.

Around 2 A.M. on Monday, August 27, Will awoke with a high fever accompanied by a painful spasm in his right arm. He called to his mother, who after checking on him sent John to town for Dr. Dorothy Lauer. By the time John and the family doctor arrived, muscle weakness was already clear-cut in Will's right arm, forearm, and hand. Completing her exam, Dr. Lauer ordered the family to transport Will immediately to Union Hospital in Terre Haute, 25 miles away. Her physical findings suggested an early, yet reasonable diagnosis: polio.

With Bill loaded into the family car, Mack and John drove to Terre Haute as urgently as possible. A million thoughts must have raced through Will's mind as the car sped along country highways. With his first year of college behind him and summer near end, he was looking forward to his sophomore year. His anticipation was never realized; his sophomore year was not to be.

By the time Will was examined in the E.R., detectable weakness in his left upper limb was evident. An examination of his cerebrospinal fluid would clinch the diagnosis. Before the day ended, he was displaying signs of paralysis in the muscle groups of all four limbs, and worse, his muscles of respiration.

For those old enough to have experienced those years and hale enough to remember them, the summers of the 1940's and early '50s were full of fear and worry for families with children and adolescents. For young people of that era, there were maximal restrictions during school vacations. "Stay out of crowds" meant not going to movies, swimming pools and playgrounds.

"Don't get overtired or overheated" meant cutting back on all of the competitions that drove summertime activities, whether organized or spontaneous.

In those years, maternal admonitions had more heft and immediacy than the well-known predictions that "your eyes will stay that way if you keep crossing them" or "if you keep on cracking your knuckles, plan on getting arthritis." Despite knowing of a paralyzing illness causing an epidemic among children and young people, youngsters of that time were not overly concerned. While the paralysis known as poliomyelitis might be serious and possibly fatal, it was not common, and teenagers, in particular, considered themselves virtually invulnerable and robustly healthy; consequently, their fears were dim and distant.

But for the parents, it was more frightening. How could one ignore what was reported? The *New York Times,* for example, ran a day-by-day box score listing the numbers of proven cases in New York City. Alternatively, it seemed that despite the exceptional news coverage, there weren't many that were severely affected. It seemed almost a shame to continuously harp about its dangers.

Public health officials took to the airways, newspapers, and billboards warning of a disease called polio (acute anterior poliomyelitis) or, more popularly, infantile paralysis. The centuries-old historical record of poliomyelitis is itself discontinuous and uncertain. What is certain however is that it was known as the only common cause of sudden paralysis in a previously healthy infant or youngster. That clue alone would have been sufficient to provide a traceable medical identity, but the historical chase has turned fruitless as the ancient descriptions were so fragmentary as to fail to clearly indict poliomyelitis as the cause of the muscular weakness. While there were recognized examples of crippled or atrophic limbs dating from pre-Christian times the evidence that they were absolutely due to poliomyelitis was usually insufficient to satisfy medical historians.

Polio was, and still is, a disease with fascinating and oftentimes confusing aspects. Failure to vaccinate causes the uncommon case even today. With different levels of clinical intensity, it involves various tissues in the body, but causes damage to only one type of cell, progressing through four sequential stages.

Paralysis from polio was not described in detail until the end of the 18th century; there is no reliable record of a polio epidemic before 1800, whereas there has been an exceptional increase in polio outbreaks beginning about 1900. This led to the notion that polio was a "new" infection. The alternative theory was that poliomyelitis did date to prehistoric times, but that it was a reflection of changing patterns of community behavior with improvement in sanitation and hygiene during the 19th and 20th centuries, which altered its clinical appearance not only in regard to the spread of the viral agent which causes polio, but also the post-exposure immunity to the same virus. The thrust of this concept is that the poliomyelitis virus in pre-Christian times and in the first nineteen centuries of the post-Christian era was basically ubiquitous, that is, an infectious agent which was omnipresent and highly contagious within a population. Since one exposure confirmed life-long immunity even after a sub-clinical or asymptomatic infection, virtually the entire community would eventually have been exposed to the virus, mildly infected with it, and actively immunized against it. Two consequences of the active immunization were that first the host population harboring the virus would diminish, and secondly, the population thereby escaped the later, more severe or paralytic attacks. In addition, earlier era newborns were nearly universally breast-fed and benefited from colostrum, the high caloric, high protein fraction of breast fluid present for the first few days after birth. Colostrum contains maternal antibodies and white blood cells, which would provide partial, passive immunologic and cellular protection to the infant against various infectious agents including polio, until the baby developed sufficient immune competence to actively respond to infectious agents and thus gain active immunity for itself.

During the late 1800's, the medical focus centered almost entirely on the paralytic effects of polio and the appearance and function of a paralyzed sufferer previously beset by polio. This gradually changed during the early 20th century when the focus shifted to the recognition that the disease was a wide-spread, highly contagious, viral infection affecting the youngest in the greatest numbers, but also affecting, to a lesser extent, adolescents and adults. The inverse relationship between the age of the patient and the symptomatic incidence rate for a given age group suggested to epidemiologists that the development of immunity was secondary to a non-clinical or asymptomatic exposure or infection. Fortunately, this virus, found throughout the populated world, caused many more asymptomatic infections than cases characterized by symptoms or physical findings. The ratio of asymptomatic to symptomatic patients far exceeded 100–1, and a single, unrecognized exposure immunized the individual against later, more severe forms of the disease. This fact became the key to solving the problem of how to prevent symptomatic or paralytic polio.

The spread of the virus may be airborne or by direct contact with an infected human, the only natural host for the three polio virus species, of which Type I is the most likely to cause paralysis and is responsible for most epidemics. The mouth is the virus' most common entrance portal settling in the lymphoid tissue of the mouth and throat, the tonsils and adenoids, and then passing into the intestinal tract. Here the virus multiplies rapidly within days unless the body's defenses overwhelm and beat back the infectious organisms. In a few individuals, small amounts of the virus are carried via the blood stream to the spinal cord and, to a lesser extent, certain parts of the brain; these are the only important sites of virus-induced pathology. The spinal cord motor neurons which are the cells responsible for the electric signal transmission to the extremity and external torso muscles, causing them to contract, are the main sites of destruction. Less likely sites are the motor neurons of the medulla, the anatomically most inferior portion of the brain, which connects the upper brain with the spinal cord, and which is responsible for the swallowing, speaking, and diaphragmatic breathing muscle function. Medullary polio carries a graver prognosis and a higher mortality rate because of the functions which can be affected. The higher portions of the brain, such as the cerebral cortex, can be minimally involved and may be inflamed by the virus temporarily leading to meningeal signs such as headache and fever, but cell death does not occur.

The sites and intensity of the virus' neural destruction determine the location and severity of subsequent muscular paralysis. For all intent and purposes, each motor neuron is responsible for a specific set of muscle fibers. Once that neuron is destroyed and cannot send out its usual electrical signals, those muscle fibers stop functioning and ultimately wither away undergoing atrophy, the harshest example of the observation from nature, "use it or lose it." Regrettably, as yet there is no known specific therapy against this virus nor cure for the motor neurons once they are destroyed. They have no ability to regenerate or replace themselves as do the cells of other organs destroyed by other infections, and there is essentially no functional muscle fiber restoration, although the body will attempt to overcome these contractile losses by strengthening neighboring intact motor units (the neuron and the fibers under its control) or by sending new nerve branches from surviving motor neurons to whatever viable muscle fibers survive.

One other consequence of the polio attack, independent of the number of musculoskeletal residua, is the activation of the body's immune mechanisms consisting of both cellular responses and the creation of antibodies, specifically designed to thwart the polio virus. In the vast majority of initial exposures, the virus is quickly overcome and the involved individual is provided a life-long immunity against future polio infections by the virus species responsible for the first attack. There are still the two other polio virus species, which could account for the very rare occurrence of an immune-competent individual, that is, someone able to produce immunological resistance to a foreign organism, being subjected to a second attack of polio.

In summary, the first stage of an encounter with polio can be "a minor illness," either asymptomatic altogether or a short-lived period of fatigue, sore throat, fever, headache, diarrhea, nausea and/or vomiting without central nervous system involvement. Alternatively, a "major illness" involves the central nervous system with severe headaches, a stiff neck and muscle pain. This could present as a form of meningeal inflammation from which complete recovery could occur, or it could progress to paralysis and weakness of various muscle groups. From an epidemiological standpoint in the pre-vaccine era, the "minor illness" was deemed to be more than 100 times more common than the "major illness."

The second chronological stage of a polio attack is the period of recovery stretching from a few days with the least severe involvement, to many years, particularly in infants or youngsters with extensive or severe paralysis.

The third stage is one of stable impairment when the plateau of maximum recovery from the acute period of most severe paralysis has been achieved, and any reconstructive surgery to alleviate deformities or to perform muscle-tendon transfers has been completed. For most, this stage extends through the patient's life.

Unfortunately, for about a third of afflicted patients, particularly the most severely impaired, there is a fourth stage, called post-polio syndrome (PPS). Patients with PPS present with additional weakness and muscle wasting, increased fatigue and lethargy, and developing joint and muscle pain, which results in deteriorating function. The length of time from the onset of the acute illness to the appearance of the post-polio syndrome symptoms averages three to four decades. PPS was first recognized by Jean Charcot, a brilliant French neurologist in the late 19th century, who theorized that the years-long accumulated overuse would lead to fatigue of both affected and unaffected muscle groups causing new weakness, or that the damage caused in the disease's first stage might render the spinal cord pre-disposed or vulnerable to another assault. Over the next century, PPS garnered minimal attention as most of the medical field's attention was directed at developing preventive vaccines or altering the acute phase so that permanent deformities and impairments would be minimized. It was not until after 1980 that the syndrome even received its name. In *Managing Post-Polio,* edited by Dr. Laura S. Halstead, M.D., and Naomi Naierman, M.P.A., Dr. Halstead reports on a Center For Health Statistics retrospective survey in 1987, which estimated that at that time, approximately 640,000 living Americans had had paralytic polio.

For patients who had required respiratory assistance in the iron lung during the initial phase of the disease, there was the specter of the PPS again weakening the muscles of respiration, the muscles which move the rib cage, to the point where the patient again needs ventilatory assistance. The prognosis, however, was not especially promising.

Dr. D. Armin Fischer, Chief of the Pulmonary Service at Rancho Los Amigos Medical Center in Downey, California, which became a world-famous center for the treatment of polio victims, wrote in the journal *Orthopedics* in 1985 that "the polio patients who develop late respiratory failure and require tracheostomies were often observed to decompensate with what appeared to be a lower respiratory tract infection. Some, however, seem to gradually lose their respiratory reserve with increasing levels of CO_2 retention." Dr. Scott F. Davies, a 1970 Holy Cross graduate, pulmonary disease specialist, and Chief of Medicine at Hennepin County Medical Center in Minneapolis, believes most post-polio patients "seldom regain lost function once the syndrome has forced them back into the respirator." Davies has used the iron lung in dozens of patients with chronic respiratory insufficiency, including patients with PPS.

About the mid-20th century, prior to the introduction of the first successful vaccine, the polio incidence rates in the United States were approximately 40,000 cases per year. In 1952, due to an increase in reporting accuracy,

60,000 cases were recorded; a third were paralytic while 3,000 patients died of the disease, yielding an overall mortality rate of 5 percent but a mortality rate of 15 percent amongst the paralytic cases of that particular year.

There were some other interesting epidemiological findings during the last epidemic years in the United States. For example, the disease had no geographic predilection for either urban or rural settings; males were afflicted slightly more commonly than females; the middle and upper socio-economic classes were more commonly subject to paralytic polio, presumably because the lower socio-economic class populations would, in the face of more crowding and poorer sanitation, have been exposed to the virus at an earlier age when the resultant illness was generally milder and the lifetime immunity would still have developed. There was no clear-cut racial epidemiologic differences, though access to care may have caused a bias in terms of mortality rates.

Additionally, it was noted during the epidemics around the mid-20th century that factors predisposing to serious neurologic damage included older age, recent inoculations (especially with the diphtheria, pertussis, tetanus vaccines), pregnancy and physical exertion leading to fatigue at the time of the central nervous system phase. Mortality rates in this country ran at 1–4 percent of the pediatric paralytic patients, but rose to 10 percent or more of the adult paralytic patients or younger patients with medullary disease.

Unfortunately, there was and still is no exact therapy or treatment for paralytic polio patients aside from bed rest, mild pain relievers, and application of hot moist packs three or more times a day during the stage of painful muscle spasm, followed by gentle passive range of motion to the affected limbs. Sister Elizabeth Kenny, an Australian nurse, opposed the concept of using plaster casts as rigid immobilization of the involved limbs during the early disease stage process. She developed a regimen of hot pack application and physical therapy, which avoided the stiffened joints brought on by the plaster casts.

The research efforts of thousands of scientists and clinicians through the latter portions of the 19th century and the first half of the 20th century to find a vaccine finally bore fruit in 1955. The work of Dr. John F. Enders of Boston, devoted to the behavioral study of viruses, and specifically their cultivation and replication in chicken eggs was a major step to success. Subsequently, Enders and two colleagues, Drs. Thomas H. Weller and Frederick C. Robbins, won the Nobel Prize in 1954 for this work.

Dr. Jonas E. Salk, building on the earlier research, perfected a killed virus vaccine, which could be used for mass human immunization. This vaccine required an initial series of injections and later booster doses. After field trials, its general use release was announced on the tenth anniversary of Franklin D. Roosevelt's death, April 12, 1955. It was Roosevelt, who at the age of 39, lost the function of both his lower extremities to polio, but who, in 1937, as President, helped create the National Foundation for Infantile Paralysis—later called the March of Dimes. This Foundation and Roosevelt's political power and personal prestige were major factors in the discovery of the polio vaccine.

In 1962, the oral, live but attenuated or weakened virus, vaccine developed by Dr. Albert B. Sabin was ready for general use. Sabin, who like Salk had also attended New York University's College of Medicine, reduced the virus' capacity to paralyze without reducing its capacity to immunize the recipient. The Sabin vaccine has been considered immunologically superior and logistically simpler to use, and therefore has become more widely utilized throughout the world, though currently there is a plan to use both vaccines in this nation, to increase effectiveness and safety. The Sabin vaccine is deemed the reason for the virtual global eradication of poliomyelitis aside from the very rare cases seen because of failure to vaccinate the entire population.

Within a quarter century following the Salk vaccine introduction, and the subsequent usage of Sabin vaccine, there was no case of paralytic polio caused by a wild, live virus in the United States. The Centers for Disease Control and Prevention, in Atlanta, GA, reported in March of 2002 that the world was close to being polio-free, with fewer than 600 cases reported in 2001.

CHAPTER FOUR

360 Days and 180 Degrees

SIMILAR TO A BELLOWS, THE CHEST CAVITY DRAWS AIR INTO THE LUNGS then pushes it out. When both of the major muscle groups responsible for respiration contract, the chest cavity expands creating sufficient negative pressure so that air moves into the lungs obliterating the partial vacuum in the space between the chest walls and the lungs; after a moment, the muscles of respiration relax and the chest cavity gets smaller so that the air is pushed out of the lungs. These two phases comprise one respiration. Because Will's respiratory muscles were becoming paralyzed, he was gradually losing the ability to breathe. Clearly, this was a lethal problem. Dr. Stewart Combs, Will's physician, was determined to keep Will Jenks alive.

Therefore, he and the Union Hospital staff set Will up in what is called the "iron lung." The machine is not a replacement for the lungs; rather it replaces the paralyzed muscles of respiration, which is why it's more correctly called a "respirator." The patient is placed in an airtight compartment, except for his head and neck, then the atmospheric pressure inside the compartment is lowered and raised by a pulmotor, and the entire system works to draw air, or a mixture of air and oxygen, into the lungs.

Despite being in the respirator within hours of admission, Will was "critical," as the possibility of his death was becoming more probable. He received Extreme Unction, the sacrament of the last rites, shortly after arrival and twice again over the course of his ensuing hospitalization.

Will required 24-hour-a-day observation by the hospital staff who were assisted by family members. Once in the iron lung with respiratory failure, a number of serious needs required this constant surveillance. The first would be to maintain an open airway from his nose and mouth through his throat into his windpipe or trachea. If pulmonary secretions accumulated and plugged one of the main airways, it would reduce lung function, which in turn would decrease the oxygen level of the blood. Simultaneously, carbon dioxide would not be efficiently removed from the blood.

A second consequence would be that the plugged portion of the lung would be more likely to become infected leading to pneumonia. This would cause more secretions, which would cause more plugging of adjacent air tubes resulting in a vicious death spiral. Will could not effectively clear these tubes himself as his own cough mechanism was markedly weakened by his paralyzed respiratory musculature; one function, which the iron lung could not perform, was coughing for the patient. Therefore, the need for outside assistance. To keep a patient's airway system clear, it was necessary to rely on mechanical suction via a flexible rubber or plastic tube, which entered the throat either through the nose or mouth, and passed carefully between the vocal cords into the trachea, and into the left or right bronchus in an effort to withdraw mucus or phlegm, which could be blocking the airway. It was not comfortable, but it was critical.

During these frightening days, there was also the worry about either a respirator motor failure or, worse, an electrical power outage affecting the entire hospital. The Drinker respirator (named for its inventor) could be operated manually if an emergency arose, but it was hard work that would reportedly exhaust a person after a half-hour of manually pumping the bellows back and forth, especially at the prescribed rate and at the correct negative pressure.

But these weren't the only concerns. Since Will couldn't move himself, someone else had to so that he would not develop pressure sores. Because

Will had not lost his sensation, he could still appreciate superficial touch, pain, and temperature. While paraplegics and quadriplegics who have also lost protective sensation secondary to complete spinal cord lesions due to trauma or other spinal cord pathology are at greater risk for pressure sores, they can still occur in a severely paralyzed polio patient. This meant Will would be repositioned at least every four hours, night and day. In the confines of the respirator with just two "port-holes" on each side to provide entry for nursing hands, it was often easier to slide the platform out of the respirator, reposition the patient in a stable way with pillows and blanket rolls on one side or the other, or occasionally prone, although this was not very comfortable for any prolonged period of time.

John Jenks stayed with his brother on a number of evening shifts. He was helpless except to watch Will, give him a drink when requested, and make certain the respirator kept working. Nurses would stop periodically as well to attend Will. John recalls that during the first few weeks at Union Hospital, Will was "touch and go" due to his breathing difficulties.

Another consequence of the respirator is that the patient's talking becomes cadenced; the patient would need to synchronize his speech to the expiratory phase of the cycle. Both the patient and attendants learned to adjust their conversations accommodating the timing of the respirator.

After John returned to the University of Michigan for his junior year in mid-September 1951, Ella would write him with updates. She told of Will receiving "hot packs" to his limbs in accordance with the Sister Kenny regimen. To provide the heat, squares or rectangles of heavy wool, the consistency of horse blankets, would be steam-cooked in double boilers called hydrocolators. Excess water was wrung out, then the hot and damp squares wrapped around the affected limbs. John remembers the process as described by his mother in a letter as "not particularly comfortable"—a classic example of Midwestern understatement due to the initial intense heat until they cooled and the body tolerated the temperature. Hot packs were followed by the physiotherapist performing passive range of motion of the affected limbs.

This program's major benefit was that the joints did maintain their passive mobility that otherwise would have slowly diminished. It did nothing for their active motion because neither the killed anterior horn cells in the spinal cord nor the muscles innervated by those cells gained any appreciable benefit from the hot packs followed by passive motion. The treatment's unattractive

feature was that the packs were quite hot on the skin of the torso and the upper and lower extremities—at least for the first two or three minutes—then
as they cooled enough, the skin acclimated to them. The packs would be re-
heated once or twice more over twenty or so minutes, and then a daily session
of physiotherapy would follow, though, hot-packing could be undertaken as
often as three or four times a day. A secondary effect of these hot packs is that
they would heat up the entire body. During hot and humid summer days, in
the period when air conditioning was not commonplace, even in hospitals,
the patient's discomfort increased substantially.

Fifty days into treatment at Union Hospital, and with his general condition somewhat improved, Will was transferred to the isolation ward of Robert
Long Hospital on October 16, 1951. This larger facility, part of the Indiana
University Medical Center (IUMC) in Indianapolis, was felt to have greater
experience and resources for treating polio patients. Upon his admission to
Robert Long, Dr. Maura J. Lynch personally notified Ella Jenks that Will was
"in a critical condition," according to his medical records. The admission
diagnosis was: "Post-poliomyelitis with complete flaccid quadriplegia."

Twice, once in October and again in January, when Will was in a coma,
the Jenks' were summoned because of his dangerously deteriorating status.
Ella and Mack had been dutifully making the arduous three-hour round trip
from Dana to Indianapolis twice a week for the two-hour visiting sessions
on Wednesdays and Sundays to be with their son. Jim, then a Dana High
School senior, recalled that when Will was "critical" his parents would stay
at a nearby boarding house for three to four days at a time to save themselves
from the repetitive travel. Because Jim was under 18, hospital rules prohibited
him from visiting at all, though once Will was moved to IUMC he would
visit on Sundays by saying he was 18. During the 1950s, most hospitals routinely discouraged young visitors, and with the heightened polio epidemic
and fear of contagion in children, parents did not strongly protest these
visitation restrictions.

In addition to the standard orders for "critical" patients with "flaccid
quadriplegia" requiring the Drinker respirator, Will also required zinc
oxide paste and lanolin cream twice daily and later he would be seen by the
dermatologists for dermatitis of his chest and abdomen, as a consequence of
the hot packs. The metaphor in *"Must thou char the wood ere thou canst limn
with it?,"* in which Thompson asks if God must purify the soul before it can

serve a divine purpose just as wood must be burned to charcoal before it can serve an artistic purpose, became a reality for Will.

A month later, on November 18, Dr. Millis recorded that Will was "now out of respirator 20½ hrs/day. Time out being increased 15 min each day. Receiving packs and PT. Progressing satisfactorily." The language of medicine frequently requires explanation. Dr. Millis opines that Will is progressing satisfactorily because when compared to his critical status a month ago, now he is in much better condition. This may be a variation of the "First, view with alarm, then point with pride," school of medical communications. He is being weaned from the respirator and his therapy is continuing; but I would surmise that Dr. Millis and the attending physician knew that with each passing day with no detectable improvement in Will's muscle activity, they were increasingly doubtful of any improvement. Time was running out. There were no significant signs of neuromuscular improvement at this juncture, but that's not a message the medical staff would want to convey to Will, either explicitly or implicitly. First, they couldn't be absolutely certain, even though they may have been approaching medical certainty, that he would not improve; and secondly, no physician wanted to deprive any patient of hope, especially one who hadn't yet reached his 20th birthday. If hope were removed, the will to live and fight on would wither. Even young physicians knew that "the cure was in the patient"; the patient may die in spite of having the will to live, but without the will to live, death was soon to arrive.

By December 9, Will was out of the respirator 24 hrs a day and "ready to be transferred from isolation to the open ward when he is ready." His chart notes read on the 18th, "kept on this ward because of the extent of his paralysis, as nursing care on open ward would not be equal to what he is receiving now." This bears remembering when his 51-year-old mother and, to a lesser extent, his 66-year-old father take over his care at home despite no change in the "extent of his paralysis," and that Will was still requiring so much care that he couldn't be moved to a standard hospital station!

This period in January 1952, demonstrated best what those later physicians found amazing, that before the explosion of the new medical diagnostics and therapies of later years, this patient toughed it out and was able to survive major setbacks such as will be described below.

With the advent of a new year came new problems. On January 15, 1952, Will developed abdominal distention and pain, vomiting, and an elevated white cell count, a sign of inflammation of some sort. An x-ray showed a stone in his left kidney and another in the right ureter, just above the urinary bladder. He was given gastrointestinal suction to relieve the distention and after having been out of it for 41 days was put back in the respirator to reduce the exertion of his breathing. The next day Will had blood in his urine, the white cell count was still higher, and a x-ray called an intravenous pyelogram (IVP) pinpointed the right ureteral stone. On the 17th, the urologists examined his bladder with a cystoscope, and inserted a tube into the right ureter anticipating it would provide drainage of urine from above the blockage caused by the stone, and perhaps eventually allow the stone to pass into the bladder where it could be more easily removed. On the 19th, Will's temp spiked to 104° F, and antibiotics were begun after a urine culture for bacteria was obtained. That day, Dr. Black wrote that Will "tolerates only few minutes of breathing for himself."

On the 21st, Dr. Black notes the continued "distention; his serum potassium level was so low that intravenous replacement of potassium chloride was started," and he could "tolerate less than 1 minute out of respirator today." On the next day's note (1–22–52), Will's condition is judged "extremely critical." The stones in the kidneys and urinary tract, caused by the leeching of calcium and phosphorus from his immobile skeleton, were affecting many different systems, including the gastrointestinal and pulmonary as well as his overall metabolism.

The next chart note on the 23rd reports: "Pt. complains of feeling cold and a throbbing headache." His temp again reached 104° F, his pulse up to 160, blood pressure at 150/90, which was high for Will, and his urine cloudy. These findings were grim.

What was going on here? The answer is that while Will Jenks was medically known as a 'polio quadriplegic,' what is not so well known is that that diagnosis was simply the first of a chain of interconnected events which followed upon the destruction of the anterior horn cells of the spinal cord by the polio virus. The death of those cells led to paralysis of all four limbs, hence 'quadriplegia,' and the muscles of respiration, thereby requiring a mechanical respirator. Medically, the loss of active motion caused "disuse atrophy" of the skeleton, and the flushing out of calcium phosphate salts into the blood stream whence they precipitated from the dissolved form into the insoluble form in the urine which created stones in the kidneys. The stones could block the urinary tract and lead to infection of the urine, which would involve kidneys, ureters, and bladder, and the infection could even spread into the blood stream, causing septicemia (blood poisoning). This would trigger intra-abdominal inflammation, which in turn, shuts down the normal activity of the intestines, leading to distention, nausea, vomiting, and failure to retain and absorb the various chemical components needed for the body and its organs to maintain a stable internal chemical environment. The infection originating in the genitourinary tract and the likely bacteremia led to the elevated temperature, which in fact, was the body's defense mechanism brought about by the need to increase its metabolism in its effort to combat the bacterial invasion with the production of antibodies and white cells, causing the elevated peripheral white cell count. The increased metabolism required the diversion of energy sources from other activities. In Will's case, it decreased his ability to breathe independently even after being out of the respirator 41 days, so that he could only "tolerate less than 1 minute out of the respirator." The abdominal distention caused by accumulated gas produced by the intraintestinal bacteria also made it more difficult for the diaphragm to push down the abdominal organs so that more air could be taken in by the lungs. In short, the mechanical respirator was needed again.

Will was fatigued by the effort of breathing, by fever sapping his energy, by nausea, and by some chemical imbalances. It is no wonder he had a "throbbing headache" to top it off. The fever may have also aggravated his skin rash, which hospital records blamed on the hot packs. Will was in the throes of a multi-system failure and was in "a critical condition." His parents were again called to his bedside.

Many, many years later Will was examined and evaluated by physicians in various specialties, and they all marveled at his durability and staying power considering the multi-organ system difficulties he had faced—neurological, muscular, pulmonary, skeletal, genitourinary, gastrointestinal, metabolic, hematologic, cardiac, dermatologic—and overcome throughout his life. Although a falling domino effect on various organ systems recurred a number of times in his life, this was a typical step-by-step version of one such episode.

On January 25, 1952, Dr. J.H. Matz, from the Urology Service, performed a cystoscopy (an exam of the bladder using a cystoscope), and a catheter was passed 12 inches into the ureter above the bladder meeting no obstruction.

The urine was fairly clear and flowed freely. The blockage seemed to have spontaneously relented.

The following day Will felt "much improved" and there was no abdominal pain, tenderness, or distention. Pseudomonas bacteria grown from the earlier urine culture were identified as the bacterial source for the urinary tract infection. Within two days, Will was taking and retaining fluids by mouth and the IV was discontinued. He had no complaints and no abdominal distention. Another critical episode had passed.

It was a short-lived reprieve; distention and vomiting resumed on the 28th. A barium swallow followed by an x-ray was done to see if there was a gastrointestinal tract obstruction. It indicated a partial block of the first section of the intestines, a condition called "superior mesenteric artery syndrome" where that vessel pinches off the intestine as the duodenum passed across the abdominal aorta from right to left. One therapeutic approach would be to simply "wait and watch" carefully, while the other was to surgically explore and loosen the vascular pincer causing the partial obstruction. Fortunately, Will was successfully managed without surgical intervention.

Dr. Black wrote an off-service note on February 12th stating Will had "spent most of past month in respirator." It was added "he has a stone in rt. kidney pelvis and many stones in left kidney. He has done well for the past week and eats regular diet. He has now been out of respirator for 4 days. Attitude excellent." While Dr. Black describes his attitude as excellent, this probably was an example of Will feigning toughness on the outside despite a troubled psyche. He was nearly twenty and not "allowed" to cry. He had spent nearly six months in hospitals, at death's door more than once, and now he was plagued by kidney stones. Imagine the emotions churning inside his very capable and thoughtful head! Boredom, loneliness, anger at his plight and the Almighty, plus fear for his future must have ruled his thoughts. Early on there was the muscle pain, then the discomfort of the hot packs four times a day, followed by the ache during the daily passive range of motion exercises to his flail limbs. Spending hours upon hours upon days upon weeks locked in the iron lung, as helpless as an infant for food, fluids, and hygiene must have eroded the spirit of this nineteen-year-old.

And there were so few visitors. His parents would come for the twice-weekly two-hour sessions, but John was at Ann Arbor and Jim in school on Wednesdays and already fibbing about his age to visit on Sundays. It was frightful. At times the entire scene would get to the doctors and nurses too; it was tougher the younger they were, it seemed, while the more senior staff appeared to weather the stormy elements more easily.

As the year wore on with no signs of movement returning to his limbs; they considered trying braces, but just getting them on would be a chore for two.

The kidney stones continued making their presence known; in addition to the exquisite pain, they were causing infections, fevers, and various secondary consequences, like intestinal obstructions and pulmonary problems causing regression back to full-time use of the iron lung. Nearly a month later he was out of the respirator completely though he had a vital capacity, which is the volume of air that can be expelled from the lungs from a position of maximal inspiration through maximal expiration, of only 800 cc, which was about 16 percent of normal for a 20-year-old male of 6'1". Later in his life this figure would improve to 1250 ml, still only 25 percent of normal. He had barely enough to sustain him in quiet activity, and virtually no reserve if he developed any sort of intrinsic lung problem, such as pneumonia, pulmonary congestion due to cardiac failure, or a pulmonary embolus, all of which would further deprive him of a portion of his functioning lung tissue.

In March, he had three more episodes of fever, chills, and flank pain—leading to surgical removal of four stones from the right kidney on April 7. But symptoms recurred a week later, and a dye study showed urine leakage from the right kidney, but no evidence of gross infection, so no further surgery was performed. Later evidence showed the leak had healed spontaneously.

Will could sit upright by late May, and a trial of leg braces was recommended. Unfortunately, he demonstrated little useful ambulatory ability without a great deal of assistance, and could not independently achieve any mobility, such as rolling over in bed. It is unlikely the orthopaedic service had high expectations or anticipated that Will would ever walk unassisted even with braces or crutches based on the earlier evaluations of his muscle "involvement." But no one, I suspect, would have denied Will the opportunity to try his best in order for him to gradually recognize the full meaning of his paralysis—something, he later wrote, which took him years to fully comprehend, and even longer to accept.

During the summer of '52, the hospital occupational therapy staff taught Will to hold a stick between his teeth to strike the keys on an electric typewriter; this was to become his 'open sesame.' Later he would comment that "typewriter ribbons would substitute for vocal cords," an exaggerated figure of speech since his vocal cords produced beautiful words and thoughts, despite many early post-polio years when most of his thoughts were, by his own admission, disheartening and humiliating.

By August, the possibility of discharge brought Will some hope and uplift. The rumor came true late that month. Will returned to Dana by ambulance because his endurance was still suspect for a 75-mile car trip. Only one year ago, this tall, 190-pound male was strong and robust; now Will Jenks weighed 110, having gained back some weight from his low of 100.

8 Dec. 1970

Dear Madelyn,

I've been sitting here trying to decide whether or not it would be worth the trouble to go insane. The prospect of having a psychiatrist listen to my gripes against the world is compellingly attractive, but with my obsessively rational middle-class mind-set I'm deferring my decision until I can check my Blue Cross policy to see if I'm covered for fractured psyche . . . The thing that scares me is that this stupid sequence keeps recurring, and instead of getting better it gets worse. I have these volcanic rages against everyone from God down to Spiro Agnew for leaving me out in the cold. Then I resolve that conflict by reordering my whole inner world—values, affections, intentions, everything; it seems imperative that I should start a whole new existence based on doing only those things that will earn me recognition. I convince myself that caring for people who happen to be close at hand prevents me from making contact with the Great World Out There, where my efforts would automatically be appreciated, where I can participate in something IMPORTANT . . . Just when it seems that I am ready to embark on my new career as a hard-headed whatever, I make the fatal mistake of looking back on the world I'm about to leave behind and a new wave of confusion washes over me. I think of those whose lives and love have taught me the truths that have given me a hold on this precarious situation. A whole new struggle begins and whether through laziness, cowardice, or humility I argue myself back to where the last cycle started—accepting what may or may not be my fate. If I had some assurance that this is the life God planned for me—passivity, meaninglessness, silence—I might be able to endure it, but I can't escape the idea that I should do something. That's what keeps the wheel turning . . .

Thanks for listening to my sad story. Will

CHAPTER FIVE

Conquering the Slough of Despond

ON AUGUST 22, 1952, FIVE DAYS SHORT OF A YEAR SINCE HIS ILLNESS began, Will returned home to face the future as best he could. His 51-year-old mother and 66-year-old father surrendered their lives to his care. Granted, some concessions were made—no bed turning every four hours—but just getting him ready for the day involved an hour or more of chores, including bathing, shaving, medications, nursing care, dressing him, and using a hydraulic lift to bring him from the bed to his wheelchair, and then moving him to his desk. Eating meant being fed a spoonful or forkful at a time. Initially, glass straws were utilized for drinking and swallowing medications, but these were fragile. In one of his earliest available letters, Will typed a thank-you note to Walter Collins, his first cousin, and his wife Virginia, who were among his first out-of-town [Lee's Summit, MO] visitors.

Sept 18, 1952

Dear Walter and Virginia,

You cannot imagine my surprise and delight when your most useful gift arrived. To say they are useful is an understatement, for they far surpass the glass tube. In two weeks we had broken four glass ones, and when yours arrived, I was drinking from a broken one. I accused Mom of trying to feed me ground glass. At least there is no worry of that now.

Since you returned home there have been no foreign visitors. A few of the local acquaintances have dropped in to discuss the corn crop or watch our TV which we got only yesterday. On Friday nights Raymond and his gang come out to show movies. It sure is nice of him to travel that distance and stay up that late just so I can have some diversified entertainment. The brothers and dog have gone back to school. We'll probably miss the dog more than the boys, since we saw a bit more of him. He'll probably write as much too . . . If anything exciting happens I'll faint first and write you second.

Again, many thanks for the gift. Come back to see us again. But don't wait five years.

Your cuzzin, Will

- Walter was the son of Mack's twin sister, Ora, and 21 years older than Will. The gift to which Will refers presumably was a package of plastic or paper straws to help Will drink safely.

• "Raymond and his gang" refers to Raymond Gosnell, married to Jessie Miller, daughter of Aunt Elsie Jenks Miller and Mort Miller; the Gosnells lived with their two children in Summit Grove, 15 miles south of Dana.
• Note that he calls himself "Will" at the letter's closing. Later on, in writing to Walter he routinely calls himself "Bill."]

Mack and Ella had continued putting on Will's leg braces daily in what was to be an impossible effort to help him walk until four months later, when it was recognized by patient, parents and physicians as a futile labor, exhausting and unproductive. At night, readying him for bed was a similarly long process. Their dedication was unwavering; there was more than one hero in the Jenks household.

Coming home must have been both a source of elation as well as of distress. Joy came in finally leaving the hospitals where he had been so ill that he had been given the last rites on three occasions. Encouragingly, Will was now considered well and strong enough to manage without around-the-clock health care professionals. What was discouraging however was the unspoken medical team's observation and Will's gradual realization after the one-year hospitalization that there was little likelihood of improvement in the paralysis affecting his arms and legs. He couldn't avoid recalling that just over a year ago he had been a midshipman in the United States Navy sailing the Atlantic, looking forward to his college sophomore year, back at Holy Cross rooming with two of his best friends, Jack O'Grady and Jack Weimer, and the adventures and elation of young adulthood.

He had lost virtually all muscle mass. His skeleton had lost not only its mineral content, but also the protein matrix. Will Jenks was now physically just a shell of his former athletic self. Understandably, he unavoidably focused his future on the immobility of his limbs, the atrophy of not only his muscles but also of his horizons, and the genuine fear of the unknown. What else could go wrong? He could breathe but with only a fourth of his expected lung capacity. The stones had damaged both kidneys, and his skin was burned and blemished by the hot packs. He had been rendered vulnerable and helpless, requiring artificial respiration for months. His spirit had been battered by the turn of events; his life, as he had once imagined it, was over; it was gone.

He was, by his own admission, deep in despair. Only sleep brought relief from the incessant realization of his plight. It is probably valid to compare the psychological stresses Will felt to those confronted when facing death. Dr. Elizabeth Kubler-Ross, in her book *On Death and Dying*, divides the process into five stages: denial and isolation, then anger, followed by bargaining, next depression, and finally, acceptance. However, she also writes that hope runs through all stages, even for "the most accepting, the most realistic patients." John Jenks recalls conversations with his brother indicating Will was indeed moving through exactly those stages while coming to grips with his condition. He himself confessed to having sunk into a "slough of despond" before accepting "the situation." Years later he says, "sooner or later every one of us will be made to feel flawed, inadequate, powerless."

There is, however, no doubt that there was one factor during his first year of illness which was of enormous benefit to Will and his family. When he took so ill, Holy Cross was notified that he would not be returning to school. Will also had a letter sent a letter to Fr. Pat Cummings telling him of his plight. Fr. Cummings had not only been Will's English professor, but also had become his good friend and confessor. Fr. Cummings was always available as a counselor, listener, advisor, or confessor, whether in his confessional halfway down the right side of St. Joseph's Chapel during weekday morning Mass, just strolling about campus, standing outside his classroom door, or in the O'Kane parlor.

Receiving news of Will's severe polio, Fr. Cummings immediately began a personal letter writing campaign to his young friend—daily letters during the year in the hospitals, and every other day for the rest of his dedicated life—an estimated 3,300 letters and a million words over his remaining eighteen years. During those years he came out to visit Will four times. Few knew of these labors of love by this self-effacing priest and friend until many years after his death when Will would confide that this dedicated friend "helped lead me out of the woods." John says Fr. Cummings' letters were not read to Will, but rather positioned with rubber bands or paper clips on a mirrored panel positioned over Will's face so he could read them privately while lying supine with his head outside the iron lung. Later, once out of the respirator, they would be placed on a table in front of him. The protocol was at Will's request sustaining the spirit of privacy and confidentiality that existed between them. That that was the type of a relationship which was sought by the two is strengthened by the fact that none of Fr. Cummings' letters to

Will—not one—was saved. It is also true that Fr. Cummings destroyed all of Will's letters. When Fr. Pat died, his room and contents, as is traditional, were surveyed by the Rector of the Jesuit Community at Holy Cross and if meaningful letters were found, they would have been preserved in the college archives, where Will's letters to other faculty are. I assume that as Will credits Fr. Cummings with "saving" him, those letters, filled with encouragement, spiritual insights and perduring love were meant only to be read and felt by the man to whom they were addressed.

John has said his brother wasn't a collector; he didn't have the space nor the ability to file his correspondence himself, and it's unlikely he would ask his parents to do so in addition to everything else they did for him. It simply may be that the Cummings-Jenks letters were, by mutual agreement and for appropriately lofty and reasonable motives, destroyed bilaterally.

Fr. Cummings, by virtue of his persevering dedication and love for Will, taught his pupil a far greater lesson than he ever did in the classroom. He brought to life the truth of *The Hound of Heaven,* the truth of the unconditional love of the Lord, Jesus Christ, and the truth of what Will could accomplish, despite flail limbs, by accepting the gifts of Faith, Hope, and Love.

In his first months home, Will practiced typing with his newly learned skill of grasping a wooden clothespin, and later a long dowel, with his teeth. Next, with his surviving neck and jaw muscles, he would peck out one letter at a time on an electric typewriter. He would also use longer metal wands with a rubber eraser tip positioned on the end to turn book pages and later to move his correspondence cards onto the typewriter's roller bar. At first someone had had to insert his paper or cards, but he soon became adept enough to slide the 3½″ x 6″ cards from the stack across the top of his typewriter, onto the roller bar, and to reinsert it when the first side was finished. Later on, he mastered drawing with a pen gripped between his teeth, adding whimsical cartoons to his notes.

It also was during this time that he began his curriculum—prose, poetry, drama, philosophy, theology, psychology, sociology, history, current events and thought-provoking periodicals provided by near and distant libraries postage-free to the disabled homebound. His theological reading, which he routinely referred to in his letters to Fr. Moran, his pastor, included all of the following: Paul Tillich, Edward Schillebeeckx, Thomas Merton, H. Richard and Reinhold Niebuhr, Karl Barth, Avery Dulles, Hans Kung, Gustavo Gutierrez, Karl Rahner, Paul Ricoeur, Jon Sobrino, Rosemary Redford Ruether, Teilhard deChardin, Soren Kierkegaard, Rudolph Bultman and Dietrich Bonhoeffer. He did not refer to these authors as if he were putting on a "purple patch," but rather in the words of one song; "it's just a thing I do." He also honed his fondness for games and puzzles of all types—crossword, verbal, and mathematical—as well as devising them himself. Words, printed and typed, were the coin of his exchequer, and he learned to use them easily, comfortably, and unostentatiously.

Initially, when Will asked his father for the dictionary so he could check the spelling or meaning of a word, "The General," as his sons called him, would want to know what word was stumping him. But Will would hold out for the dictionary, believing that seeing the word and its varied meanings would more forcefully impress his memory. He could now begin cultivating his communication skills.

Madelyn Bussing Hendrix, who was six years younger than Will and whose mother, Agnes, was a good friend of Ella's, recalls that "after Will got polio, he was so thin across the shoulders. But his personality was fantastic. He never felt sorry for himself; not one time did I ever hear him complain. No one ever did, I don't think. Anybody who was depressed would go see him because he could boost you up in no time flat. He was a very caring person. The first memory I have of him," she continues, "was the day I was sitting out on our porch. Jim and Bill and their friends were in our house. They all came out, jumping off the porch rather than walking down the steps, except for the last boy, who walked down the steps. That was Bill . . . and that night he got polio."

With brothers Jim and John back at college, the house was lonelier. There weren't many surprise visitors during the autumn of 1952; but there were unwelcome problems. On October 4, 1952, following four days of spiking a fever, and reaching 104° on the third day, Dr. Lauer referred Will back to IUMC. He had lost his appetite, was feeling feverish, ill, and again complained of right flank pain. Hospital admission work-up notes categorized his upper extremity paralysis as "complete," his lower extremities had only "faint movements" and he had "some respiratory paralysis." He was characterized as a "cheerful, cooperative" patient "unable to walk or use his arms," but "able to sit in a wheelchair if helped."

Since no mention was made of braces or other assistive devices, it is assumed that that therapeutic trial had been discontinued. Diagnosed with a chronic urinary bladder infection and multiple stones detected in the right kidney, Will again required surgery. The stones, which had had been removed just six months earlier; had re-formed. This time surgeons inserted a tube through his flank allowing for daily kidney irrigation in an attempt to reduce future stone formation and infection.

Will's life was not all gloom however, and fortunately he was good humored. There were some incidents which, retrospectively at least, provided some comic relief. Will told of the time in the early summer of 1953 when he ended up on the floor during a bed-to-chair transfer. The hydraulic lift was equipped with two wide canvas straps, one passed behind the knees and the other behind his upper back and under the armpits, onto a pair of bars attached to the hydraulic lift frame. But the lift was designed only to work within certain heights—mainly to move a person from a bed to chair and back, not to lift a person from the floor. Mack and Ella lacked the combined strength to get Will up onto his chair or his bed, and there he lay. Mack phoned Jim, who was back from Notre Dame and working for the summer telling him that he was needed at home to help lift his brother from the floor, but on the way home, Mack also wanted Jim to stop and pick him some "Rough-Cut Granger" as he was out of pipe tobacco! Will laughed heartily whenever he told that anecdote of how he learned where he ranked on the priority list.

That August I hitchhiked out to Dana via Indianapolis. One bit of unfortunate luck was that Indiana Bell Telephone was on strike so I couldn't contact the Jenks family to see if I'd be welcome, but I set out from New York City anyway. I was well received, and Will and I spent our time gabbing about school, our classmates, the faculty, and other usual topics of two young guys. Regrettably, the next day he was going back to IUMC to be admitted.

My own run-in with polio in 1949 hadn't prepared me for what I saw. I had seen polio cause paraplegia, but I was shocked when I saw Will's gaunt face and stock-still arms in long-sleeved shirts with his hands and fingers splayed on the ends of the arm rests, and his shoes positioned on the foot plates of the wheelchair. That was due to the polio, but his face showed something else was going on. It was then he told me about the kidney stones, which prompted his return to IUMC.

What I did realize was that two years after the onset of his polio, Will wasn't going to get any "return," and the extent of his paralysis was devastating. It was, however, something that neither of us broached. It seemed he didn't want to burden me with his problem, and if it was a topic he wished to avoid I wasn't going to bring it up. At 20 years of age, I confessed complete naiveté with the nuances of a major tragedy, but I believed that this was one.

Because John had graduated the previous June from the University of Michigan, he was working at a bank in Detroit. Jim, who had just finished his first year at South Bend, was home and gave me the grand tour of Dana. I remember Mrs. Jenks as being much like my own mother, ready to make a visitor comfortable and Mr. Jenks being reserved and quiet. Having been born and raised in Brooklyn, I knew little about farming, and I think Will enjoyed answering my elementary questions about pollination or what kind of beans they were growing.

The next morning the four of us drove to Indianapolis. It was Tuesday, August 11, 1953, and Will was admitted to IUMC for the removal of two more stones under general anesthesia, and discharged home August 20.

In late September he was seen at IUMC's physiotherapy outpatient clinic where his medical records noted, "there has been a strong desire to go to Warm Springs." [This was the Georgia spa and therapeutic facility used and made famous by President Franklin D. Roosevelt for treatment of his own polio-stricken legs.] Dr. Martz, the staff physician, didn't encourage this plan for Will since the "recent muscle analysis was consistent with others, demonstrating a flail quadriplegia," indicating no improvement in the "polio status quo," nor in the "renal complications." A compromise was reached whereby a "medical summary of this entire case would be sent to Warm Springs to let their staff make this decision." Will's "strong desire" is a further example of Kubler-Ross' observation that hope runs through all stages. Will never went to Warm Springs. Among other things, the repetitive muscle analyses, showing no evidence of change over two years, may have finally led Will and his parents to recognize that the prognosis for meaningful improvement in his muscle function was poor, even at Warm Springs.

His kidneys continued forming stones faster than the urologists could remove them, which led to yet another IUMC admission in early November only 10 weeks after his most recent stay. Will ran a septic course with temps over 104 degrees, which gradually responded to antibiotics, and increased fluid intake and analgesics. On November 11, four more stones were removed from the right kidney. Will had a slow recuperation and was not allowed home until December 1.

The last notation in his IUMC medical files was dated March 25, 1954 when the tube to his kidney was changed. He had been doing relatively well since December and was scheduled for a return follow-up visit in late May.

About the same time the class of 1954 received their diplomas from Holy Cross, Will Jenks took his leave of the Indiana University Medical Center.

The tube to the kidney, however, was a mixed blessing. Will turned to Terre Haute urologist Dr. John Humphrey, a former football All-American at Purdue University, for his continued care. The tube would need changing every two months and whenever it became accidentally displaced.

Recognizing their isolation, the Jenkses decided to move from their rented rural home that November into a rented house in town to be closer to friends and conveniences. This proved an immense advantage for Will as he had an enormous sense of community, which he capitalized on by tutoring high school youngsters and writing for the town's weekly newspaper. Now located in the center of Dana, he became a magnet for those seeking conversation, information, and companionship. He soon learned that despite his paralysis and some daunting associated medical problems that he still had his intellect and his will, both of which were to be strengthened to amazing degrees in the years ahead.

Gradually accepting the new hand of cards he had been dealt, Will initially struggled with what to do next. Having always possessed a competitive nature, he knew he needed a plan. Never short of ideas, his imagination spawned them both original and acutely focused; and from his ambition emerged a healthy resolve to achieve and compete, in a meaningful fashion, in the mainstream against talented rivals. He had to do that for his own sake; his self-esteem and self-regard required that he set his sights on such a goal. But where would he find the competition? His last group of reasonable and worthwhile competitors—contenders for excellence who could raise his own standards of excellence—were his college friends. He couldn't compete against people he didn't know or admire; his former classmates also provided him with information about their own activities, jobs and lives through the class letters so he could keep track of them. They would unknowingly serve as one benchmark of his progress. He would also serve as his own benchmark over time with concessions only in the physical sphere. It was quite a task he envisioned, but he felt he was up to it. As he created this strategy, he believed this could be his pathway out of his despair.

Will continued his education, and through the library system, he maximized this opportunity. Liz Helt, a neighbor who first met him when she was four or five years old, reports that once she grew older she stopped by the post office weekly to pick up and return as many as six or eight books for him from distant libraries, including New York City's. Father Cummings, in addition to his spiritual and psychological counseling, would undoubtedly have ideas, suggestions, and inspirations for Will's curriculum. English literature classics and the translations of French, German, and Russian novels, intermingled with texts of the historical foundations of America, Europe, and Eastern lands, would be followed by Bible studies and the writings of philosophers. Not only did Will study the past; he demonstrated a wide-ranging hunger for the literature, politics, sports, and personalities of the current day. Later, both Fr. John E. Brooks, S.J. of Holy Cross and Fr. Lawrence J. Moran, Will's pastor at Dana, would direct him into theological tomes. This was work; it was unassisted by classmates taking the same course, and was never regularly recognized by external approvals such as exams or class presentations. William Henry Peter Jenks' education was a solitary journey. He realized that if he were to accomplish anything at all, it would require a good mind educated in the liberal arts, and an earnest striving. As he looked back on what he was accomplishing, his mood would rise. A tiny bit of optimism grew, and his outlook broadened accordingly.

In 1960 his parents purchased a two-story white frame home, also with a front porch. That feature alone, I believe, helped Will extricate himself further from his earlier despair. Being outdoors in decent weather gave a passerby the chance to say "hello," and stop to visit.

Will was especially fond of Liz Helt. She and her parents visited the Jenkses when they lived south of town and later when Liz went to her grandmother's, who lived across the way from the Jenkses, for piano lessons, she would call out "hi" to Will when he was in his chair on the porch. She confirmed that the local bar "often called upon Will to settle trivia questions" and "his word was good enough to settle the dispute." Liz also recalls that in the mid-60's, with his "great sense of comedy and of irony" he and her father discovered Sartre and Camus. The two men enjoyed debating philosophy despite Will's devout Catholicism and her father's agnosticism. "They got along famously," Liz said.

Will Jenks had a quick wit and healthy sense of humor, which is evidenced in hundreds of letters he wrote over the years. Liz recalls some of his antics with the following examples.

It was Will who introduced Liz, her brother Dan, and their cousins to J.D. Salinger's *Franny and Zooey*. "There's one part of the book where a brother and sister are earnestly talking about performing 'for the fat lady;' they eventually learn that 'the Fat Lady' is Christ himself," explained Liz. "Most of my family that went to church went to the local Methodist Church, as did Mack. And church floats and farm equipment were always a big part of Dana's Fall Festival Parade. So one year, when no one had any ambition or ideas, Will suggested that we get a big white balloon and tow it behind a float, with a sign 'The Fat Lady' . . .

"I attended DePauw University, where my mother, aunt, several cousins, grandfather, and great-grandfather—who quit to join the Civil War—had gone. I think we both thought I was going to get in, because he convinced me to answer the question on the application, 'What do you hope to develop in college?' with 'My existential perspective and my meager bosom.' I think I mailed that without parental supervision," she wrote. "While at DePauw, Will wrote me a long letter every week, typed out with the stick with the eraser on it, using the typewriter . . . By letter, I introduced him to the girls on my floor and some of them took up corresponding with him. When we brought friends home from college, we'd always introduce them to Will; sometimes from vacation to vacation he would remember them and recall the conversations when they met again. For quite a while, my brother and I had many people convinced that there was no better place to know or be from than Dana."

And so it was during the '50s, '60s and into the '70s; in addition to tutoring, Will wrote a weekly column for the newspaper, managed the farm, and extended his reading and typing correspondence with a grand plan.

He continued his correspondence with Fr. Cummings and later began one with Fr. Francis J. Hart, S.J., also at Holy Cross. Will's first cousin, Patricia, now named Sister Teresa of Christ the King and a cloistered Discalced Carmelite nun in Des Plaines, IL, began writing Will, who responds, "You have to admire my versatility. I have never spelled the name Teresea [sic] the same way twice." [29 Nov 1962]

Mary Lou Cronin, Sister Teresa's next younger sister, also earned Will's

letters by sending her own reports of life as a high school student at Marywood
Academy followed by St. Mary of the Woods College near Terre Haute. Reading his letters to various recipients, Will's different style, tone, or inflection
for each correspondent becomes obvious. There is wisdom, humor, common
sense, opinion, and in all of them, good writing, love and affection. They are
usually conversational and recount the events of his recent life in Dana with
its "copyrighted script for exquisite boredom."

By 1961 he was also asked to serve as secretary for the Holy Cross class
of 1954, which he readily accepted. He was easily up to this task, and it
strengthened his lines of communication to his classmates. Receiving notes
and cards from his mates, he fashioned the bits and pieces of news into an
entertaining class report two or three times a year. It represented yet another
link forged back to what he referred to as "the happiest year of my life," his
freshman year at college.

Uncle Roy Jenks, a lifelong bachelor, died on Halloween, 1963, less than
a week before his 85th birthday. He willed his quarter share of the farm to
Will, a generosity that would keep the land in the Jenks' family, and add to
Will's income.

In late 1965, Dr. Veatch, also a urologist and an associate of Dr. Humphrey,
informed Will that he concurred with his partner's earlier opinion that Will's
right kidney, now causing more trouble than its worth, should be removed.
Just after New Year's 1966, the two urologists performed the surgery.

Jim Jenks recalls that the nephrectomy was expected to take about 2½
hours, but due to the heavy scar tissue around the kidney, it lasted eight
hours. Dr. Humphrey admitted it was one of the toughest surgical dissections
he had ever performed. It wasn't too easy for Will either, in part resulting
from postoperative problems due to the prolonged surgery and anesthesia,
but on top of that, Will developed a severe allergic reaction to one of his antibiotics. All in all, he was hospitalized for over three weeks. Jim also reports
that his parents disclosed that Dr. Humphrey never sent Will or them a bill.
"He was a heck of a guy," Jim says of Humphrey. Like many of the physicians
who cared for Will, I believe his pro bono kindness was a sign of personal and
professional appreciation of Will's character in the face of his fate.

No sooner was Will home than "the General" suffered "three consecutive seizures last Thursday, and even though the attacks did no perceptible
physical damage, they worsened his mental deterioration . . . he is completely

bedfast . . . Mom now bears the load of work and worry for two total losses."
[Mary Lou Cronin—5 Feb 1966]

My own father died in February 1966 and Mack Jenks died in August of
the same year. Later Will wrote me of both fathers: "I offer you my sympathy
for your loss in the death of your father. Since it could hardly have been by
accident that your father set the mark of a good man on his son, I think it's
safe to assume that he was joyfully received into the company of Christ at his
death. In any case, he and those who mourn his absence will have my prayers
for their present needs. You will appreciate the honesty of my sympathy when
I tell you that my father, too, died recently—Aug 21. A cerebral stroke put an
end to four days of dying, eighteen months of increasing helplessness, almost
a decade of decline, and more than eighty years of life. For us the period of
his physical and mental erosion was a time of grief. Death itself robbed him
of little except the power to breathe. God rest his beleaguered soul." [Bill
Kane—22 Oct 1966]

Will's memory for dates was impressive. In a 1973 letter to Fr. Hart, he
writes of Mack Jenks. "Seven years ago today my father died. With time
we have forgotten the distressing erosion of his last eighteen months and
have learned to remember him as a man of verbal agility, supple wit, courtly
manners, and random erudition. Almost fifty years older than his three
sons, and not of our faith, he was not a 'dad' in the storybook tradition,
but he was a good and patient man and he gave us the freedom to become
men . . . " [Fr. Hart—21 Aug 1973]

In early June 1968, when I was a full-time staff surgeon at the University
of Minnesota Hospitals, I accompanied four senior orthopaedic surgery residents to northeastern Indiana where an orthopaedic product manufacturer
was headquartered along with its production facilities. We flew the 500 miles
from Minneapolis on the company's twin-engine plane to tour and see how
orthopaedic implants were designed, manufactured, and tested. The trip
was planned to give the four residents, who were finishing their residency
training, a site-visit that would fine-tune their future orthopaedic practices.
Dr. John H. Moe, Chief of Orthopaedic Surgery, had approved the one-day
jaunt and thought it might be desirable if a staff member went along; thus,
I was asked.

I told the corporate representative who organized the trip that since I
had previously seen the facilities, I'd prefer spending that portion of the day

visiting Will in Dana. I intended to rent a car, drive to Dana, and return in time for supper with the group. The rep explained it was six hours round-trip by car and would make more sense if I flew thereby allowing more time with Will. I finally agreed.

I was the sole passenger on the 40-minute hop southwest to Danville, IL, where Will had dispatched two high-schoolers to meet me at the airport for the 20-mile ride south to Dana. I asked the two pilots, who had given me very VIP treatment, if they wanted a ride into Danville, which was much larger than Dana, but they declined preferring instead to "hang out" at the airport until I returned.

Will and I had a terrific visit for about four hours, some of which was spent out on the front porch. People would pass by, greet Will, be introduced to me, spend a few minutes in conversation, and then take their leave. Mrs. Jenks prepared lunch for the two of us, and I showed her and Will recent pictures of my wife Betty and our five children.

Jim came from his classes (a master's degree program at Indiana State University at Terre Haute) about mid-afternoon, and the three of us took a short sightseeing tour: the farm, the 1847 homestead, and Dana. En route back to Danville, Will inquired if I would ask the pilots to tip their wings as they took off. I replied that I'd rather not make them feel obligated to do something they maybe shouldn't. He said he understood my concern and dropped the subject as we slowly made our way onto the tarmac. Jim and I maneuvered Will into his wheelchair so that he could continue enjoying the light breezes of the gorgeous summer day.

The two pilots came out of the flight operations office to greet us, and I made the introductions. They quickly sized up Will's status, for which I had prepped them earlier. Promptly they and Will were engrossed in a lively conversation. It was heartwarming to see how within fifteen minutes these two men, skilled in their specialized work, were clearly impressed with this man in a wheelchair, and his talent for warm and good-humored conversation. As banter was exchanged, one of the pilots spotted thunderhead clouds forming in the direction we were heading, and the five of us knew it was time for departure. The pilots laid their hands briefly on Will's shoulders as a way to say good-bye, and went to the plane. I hugged him around his neck and our cheeks touched. I told him he was amazing and that I'd keep in touch. Jim and I shook hands as Will relaxed in his chair prepared to watch our take-off.

I did not mention Will's request to the pilots as I buckled myself in alongside a starboard side window, as I knew Will and Jim would be to the right of us watching as we took off. Moments later after taxiing to the head of the runway and a run-up of each engine at the north end of the field, both engines revved up, the brakes were eased, and we began moving.

Picking up speed, the plane's nose lifted, and we were airborne. Just as we were opposite the Jenks men about 30 or 40 feet above the runway, I felt a quartet of strong wing tilts to the right and to the left, and then back to the right and to the left, followed by a normal climb. What a salute! How magnificent that the two pilots knew what great courage was when they saw it, even for just a few minutes, and intuitively saluted Will with their aircraft. Rubbing stray tears from my eyes, I felt exhilarated in knowing such an extraordinary human being.

After landing, I thanked them for their winged salute to my friend, at which they replied that Will was pretty special and deserved it. It wasn't until some time later that I told Will I hadn't asked the pilots to do what they did; their spontaneous gesture was a sign of how they felt about him.

Reliving the day's events, I was utterly impressed in the change I had seen in Will. He looked far healthier than on my first visit fifteen years earlier. His face was ruddy, eyes clear, and his disposition was cheery, laughing, and assured. This wasn't someone who was uncertain about himself or his talent. Of course, there was no change in his physical limits, but that was the most remarkable aspect of his personality change. The grimness and sadness he had previously exuded when I saw him in the summer of 1953 was partially due to the pain and illness caused by the right kidney, but more than that was the palpable realization that back then his paralysis seemed to influence virtually his every thought and idea. Not so, now! It was as though he knew he was quadriplegic, but it didn't matter or, if it did, it didn't matter very much. It's like everyone knows the color of their eyes; they're just there, and not something that affects the way we go about our daily routine. And that was what I saw in Will that wonderful June day in 1968. Maybe he had passively grown accustomed to his paralysis or perhaps he had elected to put it to one side actively; but he would not allow it to take him over. It was a powerful transformation of his psyche and spirit.

Additionally, it was clear that he had absorbed a tremendous amount of knowledge in the course of his education. He didn't wear his erudition on his sleeve, but it became apparent that he had a great range to his information—philosophies, politics, poetry, people—and one could run the alphabet with like examples. More than just recall, however, were his abilities to analyze and synthesize new and different concepts.

Will Jenks had taken his mountain of melancholy and transformed it into a molehill.

23 Apr 1971

Dear Madelyn,

*Father [Moran] and I had one of our usual elevating discussions on the subject
of friendship yesterday. Which is to say we buried the reality under a mountain
of abstractions. My later, less lofty thought was this: our friendship is like three
vines growing together, holding each other up in the climb for the sun, so
intricately interwoven that it is impossible to imagine each alone. And the truth
is that alone each would only wander over the ground in search of the shared
strength and weakness of love . . .*

Bill

5 Nov 1971

Dear Madelyn,

*Tomorrow is the third anniversary of the mission of mercy that delivered me out
of the slough of despond into the garden of delight—or out of range of the bridge
club's shrill ecstasies and into the company of an enchanting woman . . .*

Bill

CHAPTER SIX

The Three Musketeers

IT WAS ON THAT JUNE 1968 TRIP THAT WILL TOLD ME ABOUT HIS NEW
pastor, Father Lawrence J. Moran, an energetic 40-year-old, who introduced
himself to Will on Sunday, August 27, 1967, shortly after becoming the new
pastor of St. Joseph Church in Rockville and of Immaculate Conception
Church in nearby Montezuma, and a man who became one of the most
important influences in Will's life.

Fr. Moran became acquainted with his new parishioners through informal house calls. Not long after first meeting with Will, he began frequent

visits to the Jenks household, as he quickly recognized how intelligent Will was and the two were on the way to a great friendship with stimulating yet challenging conversations and debates.

In a letter to Mary Lou Cronin, dated 18 Sept 1967, Will wrote, "This marked his second visit in two weeks, which put him one-up on his predecessor, who stopped by once in ten years. Father pretended that he came for 'inspiration and stimulation,' and since my back issues of *Playboy* were out of sight I felt free to play the role of backwoods philosopher and all-around good guy. I tried, with little success, to dazzle him with some of Tillich's theology. Unfortunately, he assumed that the ground rules permitted cross-examination, so my erudite pose quickly dissolved." [Mary Lou Cronin and a couple of her pals at "Woods" anted up the subscription cost for a year of *Playboy* for Will's 35th birthday in 1967.]

From the pulpit one Sunday, Fr. Moran sought assistance in the parish office. Madelyn Bussing Saxton called him and subsequently became the church secretary working only on Fridays as she had another job in nearby Newport the other four days of the week.

One of Fr. Moran's directives after arriving at the new Dana parish was to construct a new Catholic church. From the pulpit, he announced his plans to form a parish council to meet this initiative and invited those interested to submit their names. Will Jenks threw his hat into the ring unsure of what to expect, but confident in what he could contribute. Balloting for the eight-person council ended in a tie, with Fr. Moran casting the tie-breaking vote. Will described the election process in his 20 Feb 1968 letter to his cousin Mary Lou Cronin:

"Unlikely as it may sound, I had an important engagement Sunday afternoon. I had to sit in at the first meeting of the two-parish council, a board of eight elected by the people at Montezuma and Rockville. The irony of the matter lies in the fact that I had recommended the complicated voting procedure to insure proportional representation from both places, confident that the system would preclude my election. (I'm not at all certain that the ballots determined the cast of characters. Father Moran had little faith in the wisdom of the weighted vote: number your choices 1 through 8, first choice gets 8 points, second 7, etc.) Anyhow, the parish bulletin noted that Jay Benton, a Bussing son-in-law now recuperating from a heart attack, had tied with me for eighth place and I had won the toss. (As Willy Loman would say, "I'm liked, but I'm not *well*-liked.") The meeting Sunday afternoon offered a preview of future confusion. Since everyone else seemed reluctant to open discussion of our purpose I, the least of the brethren, grabbed the ball and ran with it. That saved us time, even if it earned me some ill will. The meeting damnnear foundered at one point, when one of the guys made a token nomination of Rockville's perennial Mr. Fix-it to be chairman of the group. Predictably this clown took the suggestion literally, as an imposition rather than an honor (to be declined, self-deprecatingly), and chose the occasion to vent his spleen against every pastor since 1940, all of whom had shoved every dirty job on him. The embarrassment nearly suffocated us. When Father had squirmed halfway out of the situation I nominated the guy all of us wanted in the first place, and he won by acclamation. The rest of the deliberations went smoothly.

"Monday the council had another gathering, this time to eat supper with Archbishop Biskup, who was in Rockville for confirmation . . . Madelyn Bussing Saxton chauffeured me to Rockville, since she was on the kitchen committee. My colleagues unloaded me and hauled me into the rectory, where the archbishop greeted us cordially and without pomp . . . I was stuck in a corner, with Madelyn at the controls, but I managed to butt into the conversation from time to time. When the meal was over and the discussion got around to the problems of the parish the bishop was treated to a classic example of Hoosier insouciance. The same guy who turned down the chairmanship interrupted again and again with irrelevant anecdotes, reminiscences, and trivialities, and two others couldn't resist the temptation to join him. When the supper broke up and everyone else busied himself with confirmation chores I listened to the bishop as he outlined his position on theological controversy. What he had to say seems to bode ill for the avant garde. Our tete-a-tete lasted fifteen minutes. He did all the talking. So I wasn't excommunicated . . . Bye. Bill"

Will and Father Moran subsequently developed an easy and close friendship over the next six years. The two became confessor and penitent, mutual confidants and devoted friends. In a March 1968 letter to Mary Lou, Will illustrated the tempo of that friendship:

"Father Moran came by yesterday with the Bread and stayed for a Lenten lunch. I didn't needle him about his alliterative allusions (illusions) . . . Father is a great guy and a real Christian, but he's too easily impressed. After I sent him an irreverent post card he was fully convinced that I should write a column for a paper, and when I wrote again asking him to get me a job as sports writer for *Osservatore Romano* he was ready to wheel me to the office of *New Yorker* magazine." [M.L. Cronin—1 Mar 1968. "*Osservatore Romano*" is the Vatican's official newspaper.]

Being on the parish council meant not only participating in meetings to run the old church and to plan and organize the construction of the new one, but also the preparation, production, and marketing of crullers! Crullers were the chosen medium by which St. Joseph parishioners participated in an entrepreneurial way in the Parke County Covered Bridge Festival. The annual event attracted tens of thousands of visitors during the colorful leaf-turning autumn season to travel through the 38 bridges standing in 1971. Will's contribution was mainly enthusiasm, cheerleading, and writing the lyrics to post-Cruller-Time celebratory poems and songs when the profits were added to the general funds of the church.

Madelyn explained that Will was responsible for taking and sending out all the council meeting notes. "He did a lot of work during the time we were building the church. He even contacted the guy at the University of Illinois to see if he would build the church."

During those parish council years, Father Moran, Madelyn Bussing Saxton, a mother of three going through a difficult divorce, and Will became the Three Musketeers in the "all for one, one for all" fashion, each bringing different perspectives, experiences, minds and spirits to the trio. Together, the three formed the task force nucleus to build the new church.

Will's future notes to Fr. Moran and Madelyn were often addressed to and signed with the appropriate Musketeer initials; "P" standing for Porthos, "D" for D'Artagnan, and "A" for Athos, in the person of Madelyn, Will and Fr. Moran, in their assumed guises of the Three Musketeers.

Father Moran had a notion that Will should visit Lourdes, the site of the apparitions of the Blessed Virgin Mary to a 14-year-old girl named Bernadette Soubirous in 1858. The shrine is known for miraculous recoveries of well-ness, documented by a medical board of physicians that pointedly excludes Catholic doctors. Fr. Moran's hope was that Will, with his unshakeable faith and belief in the Infinite Love of His Lord, Jesus Christ, would be an ideal candidate for one of those miracles. When confronted with Father's idea, Will dismissed it, slightly dismayed that his loving, priest-friend did not, in turn, recognize the level of Will's acceptance of his fate.

Father Moran encouraged Will to write for publication; Will tried to define for Father what the limits of Father's reasonable responsibilities are, and both supported Madelyn during the trying years of a marriage she knew must end, yet still reluctant to accept such a result. As the only female of the Musketeer trio, Madelyn brought her own beauty to the two celibates.

Although Will and Madelyn had known each other for more than 15 years, their friendship strengthened and deepened the greatest during this time. "Bill had a huge impact on my life," Madelyn has admitted. "He had an impact on everybody's life, but he really had one on mine because I had three kids, was without a husband, and didn't make that much money. He was so good with my kids, wrote them letters; they thought the world of him. He was a father figure to them. Bill was an emotional lifesaver for me, and I think I was more or less a lifesaver for him. We complemented each other that way."

Once Will's vehicle was equipped with an electric lift which enabled Madelyn by herself to get him into and out of the car, the two began to socialize within a platonic relationship. "It just changed his life," recalled Madelyn. "We'd go out to eat, to movies, and to the drive-in. Bill loved to go out to eat. He said if his brother took him to a smorgasbord, for example, he'd just pile food onto his plate. He told me how nice it was that I asked him what he wanted and how much. 'I'm used to these guys who just put something on the plate and it doesn't make a difference what it is,' he would tell me."

Madelyn portrayed Will's father as a slightly absent-minded professor and described a typical meal. "He'd [his father] be reading a book in German and might give Will a bite of food and then 15 minutes later he might give him another bite. Or, he might give him 10 bites in a row, real quick." Contrasting that scenario with how his buddies would just pile anything and everything onto a plate, it's easy to understand why Will enjoyed having meals with Madelyn so much.

Unable to pinpoint how their relationship evolved, Madelyn recalled it as "just one of those things. I listened a lot, but our friendship just sort of clicked from the beginning. He liked to write and I liked to read." She was, however, able to offer some interesting insights into Will's psyche and sense of humor.

"When I would leave on vacation, he would draw a plane caricature with a tailing cloud, which said 'welcome back Madelyn.' So, one time when he was on a trip, I put that on his house in big letters almost two feet high saying 'welcome home Bill.' We did things like that.

"He was as comfortable talking to the town drunk as he would the president of the United States," she continued. "He never saw anybody he didn't like except my ex-husband. He just talked to anybody. I remember taking him to a high school football game in nearby Clinton shortly after he returned home from the hospital that first year he got polio. I had unloaded him from the car and as I was pushing him toward the stadium, the visiting team's school bus pulled up with the team. As they jumped off the bus, every one of them was staring at Bill. He immediately called out to them, 'I'd look too if I were you. We played Clinton last week and look what happened to me!' He had such a great sense of humor."

His feelings about their friendship were echoed in a note he sent to her on 15 Feb 1970. "I have only begun to learn what you have to teach, but for the chance to learn, you are thanks in my prayers. (I try not to figure out why God let me stumble into your life. Let it be counted one of His more inscrutable mercies.)

He often told Madelyn she was both complex and subtle, and that it was a struggle and joy to understand her.

On 29 June 1970 he typed, "From you I have learned patience (with myself), courage (with my cross), humility (in the face of forgiveness), confidence (in the certainty of grace), joy (in the presence of beauty), and, I hope, love (in response to love). I have none of these gifts in great measure, but if it weren't for you—and by Tracy's reasoning, polio—I would be a stranger to the best things life has to offer." [Tracy is Madelyn's daughter, born in 1962.]

Will Jenks had his great memory to accompany his quick wit. In a note dated Feb. 4, 1971, he mentioned to Madelyn, "by my rough calculations, Saturday, Feb. 6 at 4:17 A.M., I have spent half my life sitting and half standing. As my butt often complains, standing is better. . . ."

In his 16 June 1973 letter to Fr. Moran, after completing his parish council term of office, he wrote, "Whether in the alien mode of speech or in the familiar mode of print I can't think of words to say thanks for the past six years. Others have encouraged me not to be less; you've prodded me to be more. The doubts and fear that kept me even more confined than my paralysis have vanished. I now know that the world is for the most part friendly to those who try to do good. Your reckless FAITH and limitless love were your strongest arguments, just as your life is your most eloquent—and most entertaining—sermon. Thanks for caring."

On July 7, 1969 one of Will's staunchest and loving friends, Father Patrick J. Cummings of the Society of Jesus, died within days of his last letter to Will. The letters had begun on a daily basis immediately upon Father's hearing Will had been devastatingly assaulted by polio. Once Will was back home, Fr. Cummings' letters continued every other day for seventeen years—letters buoying, prodding, succoring and inspiring Will. Good with dates, Will recognized how close Fr. Cummings' ordination, Saturday, June 22, 1929, was to his parents' wedding—Saturday, June 29, 1929—and how much he loved and owed the three of them.

With Fr. Cummings' passing, Rev. Francis J. Hart, S.J., of Holy Cross became Will's most consistent College correspondent. After spending 54 years as a member of the Holy Cross faculty, and faithfully writing to Will for more than 30 years, Fr. Hart would ultimately depart this world on February 3, 1986.

As much as Will would later come to enjoy traveling and sightseeing, he was initially quite cautious about the prospect, given his physical disabilities and the limits they imposed. In 1970 after his first wife Virginia died Walter Collins invited Will to Lee's Summit, MO for a week on the pretense of giving Ella a well-deserved vacation. Will found the idea daunting however. "I'm afraid the ride out would leave me punchy for a few days. Besides, I have so many physical necessities—bed board, foot board, hydraulic-lifter, etc.—that we'd be confronted with a major logistics problem in relocating my equipment. I'm enthusiastic for the original idea, though, and I'm sure it will work out well." [W. Collins—27 April 1970]

It did, eventually. Since Will couldn't get to Walter's place, Walter came to Dana the summer of 1970 along with his pontoon boat on a trailer having driven over 400 miles from his home outside Kansas City. He organized a Wabash River day cruise, inviting Jim, Carol and Karen Jenks, along with Ella and Will.

Walter remarried in January 1971, and by year-end he bequeathed his one-eighth share of the Jenks' family farm to Will. Now, with the quarter share willed from Uncle Roy, Will owned three-eighths of the farm. On January 5, 1972 he told Walter and his new wife, Florence, "My mind is no closer to finding words for the thanks I owe than it was two weeks ago but at least it can give shape to good wishes on your first anniversary . . . If Heaven will do as much to make your life worry free as you have done for my mother and me, you will live all your days in serenity."

In the summer of 1972 John Jenks and his sons had driven through the West to Los Angeles, meeting up with Will who arrived there by plane. They made a road tour of the West Coast from Tijuana to San Francisco, including Anaheim's Disneyland, before Will flew home while the others made the long return journey by car.

It's likely Walter countered Will's 1970 concern about the car ride across Illinois and Missouri with a plan for Will to fly to Kansas City in 1970, because in a letter dated 20 Sept 1972 to Walter and Florence, Will responded, "You have grounds for complaining that I discriminated against you in accepting John's invitation to fly to California after having refused yours to fly to Lee's Summit. But I plead extenuating circumstances: two years ago I was reluctant to try anything out of the ordinary, mostly because I could imagine ten thousand inconceivable calamities, any one of which would hurt, hinder or humiliate. In all honesty, the boat trip on the Wabash went a long way toward exorcising my cowardice . . . When I found out that reality's obstacles are not nearly as formidable as imagination's, I relaxed and enjoyed myself. With that reassuring experience behind me, I managed to overcome my timidity about flying—not so much about flying as about boarding the plane."

While Will likely suspected in 1972 that his brother John's marriage was under stress and that its breakup might impact his mother and him, there wasn't much he could do about it. Little did he know his days in Dana were now numbered. One day in early 1973, John called to discuss with his mother and Will his imminent divorce and his predicament insofar as the two older boys chose to live with him. [Carolyn later consented to Charley also living with John so he could grow up with his brothers.] John now needed to provide a stable home life for them despite his frequent out-of-town business travels. He invited his mother and Will to consider moving from Dana to Chicagoland to help provide that stability for Bill–16, John–14, and Charley–9, and felt this proposed situation could be a win/win for all.

There were several advantages to a move, but it would be a tough decision leaving the friends—the very dear friends—of Dana behind. Will recognized that he could assist his nephews with their schooling, even type some assignments, and be an active guide for their behavior, as well as their learning. In turn, they could help with his care, and ease the burdens of their grandmother, now 72, who had soldiered on, taking care of him all alone, from the onset of Mack's debilitation, at least, and in truth for the major part of Will's care the past 20 years. Will also needed to realistically envision what his options would be were his mother to become disabled if they remained in Dana. If John wanted to assume the responsibility for Will, then it was an offer that really could not and should not be refused.

24 Oct. 1975

Dr. Dudley Childress
c/o Ben Hur Motor Works

Dear Dudley,

I wish the accompanying check had three more zeroes to underwrite the good work you and your co-conspirators do. The technologies you focus on the physics of every problem seem magical to the Neolithic mind, but the honest compassion that allows you to see the human problems implicit in your work eases my Luddite anxieties and makes me grateful for minds still in touch with their heart.

Unsippable thanks to everyone . . . for new freedom and dignity.

Irreversibly, Bill

CHAPTER SEVEN

Sip & Puff Agility

ON GOOD FRIDAY, 1973, JOHN LOCATED A HOUSE BETWEEN MUNDElein and Long Grove, IL which would provide wheelchair accessibility. In late May, Will saw his home-to-be for the first time, and in a card to Fr. Moran, he described it and a few of the anomalies of modern society in a typically Will Jenks tone.

1 June 1973

Angel Guardian—

Having reconnoitered my next waystation, I can fearlessly predict that my disintegration will take place amid Nordic splendor. The owner-and-builder of the house must be the reincarnation of a Viking Bob Rambusch. [Bob Rambusch was a member of the parish council and an advocate for the use of wood, lots of wood, in the new church.] The interior abounds in natural woods—floors, walls, trim, beams. An entire wall of the family room is stone. Warm-yet-rich, rich-yet-simple, simple-yet-noble, noble-yet-and-yet-and-yet. The immediate neighborhood achieves the suburban dream of distance, privacy, and conspicuous consumption. And of course, Chicago—the idea—depressed me as soon as living things gave way to concrete and homo erectus disappeared in favor of homo propel-litus. It is a gross perversion of right reason (if you'll excuse a quaint expression) for seven million people who need to live together to insist on living apart. Until city folk recognize the automobile as their common enemy their hopes for a livable city will be futile and even demented . . .

D.

Less than a week after moving in on June 21, he sent a critique of his new parish, in both the spiritual and architectural senses.

27 June 1973

N. Ab Sentia—

One Sunday was enough to give me a reading of Santa Maria del Popolo. If apathy weren't so miasmic among the pew-fillers, I'd try to organize a coup and kidnapping to remedy the situation. (There's evidence the parish may be in schism from Rome. We asked to be given envelopes and received an equivocal answer.) From the general inertia of the congregation and the elusiveness of the priest, I would guess that SMdP could use a transfusion of the spirit of St. Joe's or, better, the transplanting of St. Joe's pastor and office staff. Billy Jim and Bob Rambusch would attribute the torpor to the design of the church, which is aptly called 'the big red barn.' No doubt it was built cheaply—brick veneer, block-and-panel interior, laminated beams, acoustical tile ceiling, rectangular shape; but the overall effect is dispiriting. The pews in the rear half of the church might as well face the other way, because they offer no eye contact with the altar. Singing somehow evaporates before it can blend with other voices, and that disconcerting experience defeats even so intrepid a soloist as WHPJ. In all, an unpromising situation. I can only hope my verdict is premature . . . Read the *Criterion's* change-of-address roster, I'm glad you survived the cut . . . P. might take up with an anvil salesman if both of us abandoned her . . . Start laying plans for an excursion to Mundelein. Like the London fog, you are mist . . .

D.

• The *Criterion* is the diocesan paper and it carried the list of new assignments for the diocesan priests, as of July 1.

Will's first impressions turned out to be right on target, but it was his mother, according to John, who suggested they change parishes a few years later because she felt SMdP was too big and impersonal. They had first attended St. Mary's in Fremont Center in March 1975 and eventually became parishioners there. Will taught Confraternity of Christian Doctrine (CCD) at SMdP but decided to transfer his efforts to St. Mary's beginning September 1977. He then wrote Fr. Moran about his new CCD work that he wasn't sure "if this is the job for me" because "the theological bias was decidedly to the right" and "the 'philosophy' statement" and "the rules for students could have been written . . . in 1942—or 1842, for that matter." [L.J. Moran—15 Sept 1977]

After John and Carolyn's divorce was final, John invited Will to accompany him on Bell & Howell's annual incentive trips; e.g., Acapulco in 1974, followed yearly by the Bahamas, Puerto Rico, Hawaii and Florida. Although travel presented challenges and special needs, Will embraced the opportunities presented. He wrote a tongue-in-cheek article about the Acapulco trip, which led a B&H marketing manager to suggest he try his hand at writing creative marketing material for them; Will tried, but felt this wasn't his best element. Travel reports though were right up his alley as wonderfully illustrated with his Acapulco piece.

IT HAPPENED IN ACAPULCO
—BUT WE APOLOGIZED

For the citizens of Acapulco February 28, 1974, was a day that will
live in infamy or at least in perplexity. On that fateful date a band
of frost-bitten refugees—some from such cold-oppressed climates
as Los Angeles and Miami—sought asylum in that tropical haven,
where summer winters. Lax security and Latin compassion allowed
the turistas to enter Mexico, and for the next five days Acapulco had
to live with that mistake.

The invading gringos were in fact management people and their
wives—or brothers or amigos—from the Business Equipment
Group of Bell & Howell, ordinarily sedate, hard-working Americans
whose jobs and homes keep them wholly occupied and preoccupied.
But on holiday from responsibilities they became the Katzenjammer
Kids, the Barnum and Bailey Circus, and the Mormon Tabernacle
Choir. No one was likely to confuse them with a United Nations
Agricultural Commission.

The first embrace of the sun-drunk afternoon hinted that the plane
had been rerouted to heaven. But would St. Peter insist on inspect-
ing the baggage? The bus ride into town raised new doubts about
destination, whether Acapulco or eternity. It is a curious fact of
Mexican life that hurry is restricted to the highway, a try-out camp
for French Connection stunt drivers.

Having taken shelter in a humble wayside inn, the International
Plaza, some members of the B&H party made their way to the
hotel's dreaded moat, an extension of the pool separating the thirsty
from the potable of their choices. Desperate men were seen to
wrestle crocodiles that blocked their way, with the loser expected
to sign the tab. For the less venturesome there was a thatched hut
supplied with such native drinks as piña colada, a hollow pineapple
transfused with its own rum-reinforced juice and decorated like an
exotic jack-o-lantern. With its mottled skin and bristly leaves the
head bore a strong resemblance to a Marine Drill Instructor. One

ex-leatherneck, having drained several, stood at rigid attention for
an entire afternoon, waiting manfully to be dismissed.

Off-campus diversions lured men and women down to the sea
in ships for big-game fishing, out to the links for a round of golf,
or out onto the clay for a few fast sets of tennis. The fishing fleet
brought back one sailfish, one dolphin, and one shark, but the
sharks almost evened the score by nearly taking home a fisher-
woman who fell overboard in the excitement of hooking the
dolphin. The golfers, only slightly demoralized by the perpendicu-
lar terrain, flailed away into the twilight hours and quit merely
because the burros pulling their golf carts had to be refueled. Two
racketeers returned from their first afternoon on the courts claiming the doubles championship of Latin America. The language
barrier prevented them from learning the names of the vanquished
foes or their reason for stringing their rackets with palm fronds
instead of catgut or nylon.

Shopping in the local specialty shops or in the public markets
aroused the acquisitive instincts of the visiting Americanos, who,
as one observer remarked, seemed intent on gathering together all
the trinkets used in the purchase of Manhattan Island. Haggling—
mortal combat over the current status of supply and demand—was
carried on in numb-tongued high school Spanish and José Jimenez
English. It is testimony to the indomitable spirit of commerce that
goods and money changed hands to the mutual satisfaction of hag-
gler and haggled.

Two shoppers, fearful of being stranded downtown during the
three-hour siesta, gave up hope of attracting a taxi and accepted a
bid of 30 pesos for a ride back to the hotel in a 1960 pick-up truck.
St. Christopher came out of retirement to oversee the journey, and
in time the truck pulled into the driveway of the hotel. The door-
man, un hombre of imposing Spanish dignity, spied the coughing,
rattling clunker and frantically began waving it off, as though it were
a kamikaze plane trying to return to its home carrier. When at last he
recognized the smiling passenger clutching the livestock racks as one

of the crazy contingent he relented, cursing his ancestors for having lost that war with America.

To satisfy the tourists' hunger for culture, Acapulco welcomed non-believers to the Friday night services at the Temple of the Aztec Flyers. There the loyal devotees of the earth goddess reenacted ancient fertility rites, over the protest of the local chapter of Planned Parenthood. With choreography borrowed from a junior high musical, a line of acolytes danced themselves into a subdued frenzy, whereupon four of them, taking care to cross themselves, shinnied up a 115 ft phallic symbol. At the very moment the god of death plunged a dagger into the heart of a bare-breasted maiden the four pole-sitters, sparklers grasped in each hand, began to spiral earthward at the end of a rope wound 33 times round the top of the pole. As if that were not thrill enough, eight second-string chicos leaped aboard two giant propellers and pinwheeled themselves into ecstasy. Altogether it was a religious experience, and unlike the worship of the major denominations, it lasted only 20 minutes. In a creative afterthought, one of the B&H spectators went backstage and offered 20 pesos for the sacrificial remains. The remains herself countered with an exorbitant figure, and so the work of mercy stalled over price.

Saturday morning all hands reported aboard the good ship Fiesta for a cruise of Acapulco bay and the Pacific shoreline. Kept in constant awe by the mountaintop shrines—Dolores del Rio's home, Jack and Jackie Kennedy's honeymoon cottage, John Wayne's fortress, the sea-farers eventually relaxed to the undulating rhythm of the waves and the pulsating beat of the ship's combo. But when the paid performers took a break, the ad hoc entertainment committee seized the piano and the microphone and the in-house madness got underway. Mild-mannered Clark Kent's phone booth transformations would have passed unnoticed in the pandemonium of the Fantail Follies, where a shy, inarticulate boy suddenly oozed suave and turned into Bert Parks; where a sweet little Irish lady threw off her inhibitions and put on a naughty Gracie Fields song; where a placid, spectacled father-of-the-year type let the piano cast a spell over him and change him into Steve Allen; where a brisk, business-minded executive made room for another self and was instantly recognized as Fred Waring. To make things still more tumultuous the entire cast lunged into a bedlam of folk-dancing that ended with bodies strewn across the deck like drop-outs at an orgy.

There are other lively memories: the farewell banquet, with its tantalizing peek at next year's target and the deft reminder of the real world that awaited the sojourners' return; the birthday tribute to the mock chocolate cake, which was a year-old that very day, as one wag told it; the glee club's early morning ouster from the dining room and its temporary residence in the lobby, where it disoriented passers-by by singing Christmas carols; the mournful listing of daily casualties struck down by the perverse Montezuma; the final adios to the Plaza and its 'muy simpactico' people; and the painful realization that but for Adam and Eve, life could be like that the other 360 days of the year. Que lastima!

The above account was written by an interloper on the Acapulco expedition, with fond recollections of the thousand kindnesses of new friends.
                                                              —*Bill Jenks*

Happily, Will's move to Chicago had provided a serendipitous solution to some of his basic needs in the person of Dudley S. Childress, a professor of Electrical Engineering and also Orthopaedic Surgery as well as co-director of the Northwestern University Rehabilitation Engineering Program (NUREP), located in the Rehabilitation Institute of Chicago. I spoke with Dudley and inside of a few months he and his talented team, especially John Strysik, were hard at work engineering an environmental control system for Will.

More than a year of research and fabrication was required, but this innovative system allowed him—via sipping or puffing on a tube—to place and receive phone calls, turn lights on/off, operate a radio and other electronic devices, plus much more. Childress' brainchild provided Will Jenks with newfound independence all by way of sips and puffs.

Meanwhile, Will continued his letter correspondence with Madelyn

Bussing Saxton after his move to Illinois; however, now with his new environmental control system, he could also talk to her on the phone. Madelyn never enjoyed writing as much as Will, and now he was just a phone call away!

By spring of 1974 Will was proficient with his new control system. He wrote to Margaret Pfrommer, whom he had heard was in the same predicament as he. She worked as a receptionist at NUREP after she had been one of the first to test the sip-and-puff environmental control or pilotage system.

During the '74 summer, Dudley told Will that the sipping and puffing guidance system could be adapted to a battery-operated wheelchair if he could bear some of the expenses. Never hesitant to make himself the butt of a joke or anecdote, Will wryly responded:

17 Aug 1974

Dear Dudley:

God must have intended me for a friar. I find it hard to screw up sufficient courage to spend large sums of money. Until last week I could rally no motives, either economic or hedonistic, for investing in a look-ma-no-hands perambulator. But fate rescued me from that quandary by locating a dirty book store only an amp or two down the road. So now there is reason, if not justification. I've decided to go ahead with the project, drought or no . . . Bill

Not only was Dudley his great and liberating benefactor, but he and Will also shared similar world views and a motivation to "do good."

More than a year of research and fabrication was needed before Will got his chair in October; but he soon became an accomplished driver, and even gave command performances of his newly acquired abilities. But more importantly, Childress' brainchild provided Will Jenks with joyful mobility and independence, a huge leap forward in his self-directed quest for a more meaningful life as more and more physical barriers tumbled away.

19 November 1975

Dear Father Hart,

Two weeks after I got my chair I went back to Northwestern Rehab Engineering to perform tricks for visiting dignitaries, the Madame Jehan Sadat, wife of the Egyptian President, Nancy Kissinger, wife of Henry, Eleanor Daley, wife of Hizzoner da Mare, and Sen. Chuck Percy, best friend of Sen. Chuck Percy. Actually, my turn in the extravaganza lasted 90 seconds. I said little more than hello—goodbye to Madame Sadat, so you can imagine my surprise—not to say chagrin—when the *Clintonian*, the closest thing to a Dana paper still in business, published an account of my long, fascinating conversation with the lovely lady. If Egypt has a clipping service I may find my way into Madame Sadat's scrapbook—under false pretenses . . .

In November of 1975, about the same time Ella had cataract surgery, Will began selling plastic sheeting for the Porter Film Co. Cold calling on prospects was not fun during the daily one or two hours he was competing in a tough commercial venture. The speaker phone with its echo tone distinguishable from a regular phone mouthpiece led one prospect to state he wouldn't speak to anyone using a speaker phone because he didn't know who else was in the room; Will didn't dare tell him it was just his mother and the cat! Being a part-time salesman was not the road to glory or riches, but that wasn't the point, was it? However, it was another step forward in his lonely competition—the Will of the present versus the Will of the past.

In the time not devoted to sales, correspondence, or reading, and while waiting for his new chair, Will assisted his family with their typing! In a letter to Fr. Moran he explained his delay in writing as "wasn't entirely a matter of waiting. I used several typing hours doing two long business letters for John and copying two book reports for Johnny."

On February 7, 1976, Will fell from his hydraulic lift while John was lifting him into his van. He sustained a significant concussion and for a considerable number of months lost his senses of smell and taste, but fortunately no broken bones. Follow-up neurological consults and imaging studies allowed for a conservative, non-interventional approach. Fortunately, too, his enjoyment of fine dining returned after a year once both his taste and smell recovered. Most importantly, however, was that he suffered no brain injury and only a short period of amnesia for the afternoon of the accident.

The bulk of 1976 proceeded uneventfully until September when Tom Carstens, Fenwick, '51, and Holy Cross, '55 successfully nominated Will to a three-year-term as trustee at their high school alma mater. Fenwick High School's acknowledgement of his value as an advisor surely was a point of pride for Will.

Ella continued over the next two years as primary caregiver with additional support from John and the nephews, until the young men left home for col-lege—Billy at Kansas, class of '79, Johnny at Holy Cross, '81, and Charlie at Kansas, '86—and subsequently began their own careers living in Kansas City, KS or Chicago. As John's promotions and new executive responsibilities at Bell & Howell's Phillipsburg division necessitated out-of-town travel and long workdays in Chicago, and with Ella's energy ebbing, it made sense to hire additional caregivers to assist Will despite his increased self-sufficiency with the environmental controls and the mobility of his new chair.

The first of four, Willard Tonyan, who also had had polio, was a 67-year-old retired farmer. "Despite muscle weakness on his right side, Willard hefts me about when hefting is needed, and he usually has me at my desk by nine o'clock. Mom is relieved, grateful and almost carefree," Will wrote Fr. Hart in 1978 shortly after Willard was hired.

In mid-1979, Will wrote Walter and Florence Collins that Willard "had to take time out to tend to a complex of ailments—shortness of breath, swollen legs, a hiatus hernia. Luckily, Willard had a friend who recently retired, and he took over without missing a beat. "He [Frank Taggart] talks loud and long, but he's faithful and conscientious." In his September 6 letter to Fr. Hart, Will noted that Willard "hospitalized for lack of oxygen in his blood, died this week."

Claudia Greenlee followed as caregiver, starting in November 1980, and assisted Will for more than seven years. Her own children grown, she showed great kindness to him, and he reciprocated with special cards celebrating the anniversaries of her hire date and her birthdays. The following note was his way of expressing gratitude for all that Claudia did for him.

4 Nov 1983

Dear Claudia,

Three years is not just a span of time; it is one of the dimensions of
a gift. The other two dimensions—the depth of caring, the height of
joy—yield no numbers, but the heart knows the size. What thanks
can there be for so full a gift? The answer must be to accept it,
delight in it, use it as it was given, in freedom. My joy is my thanks.
Let my smile say daily what my mind cannot find means to say
yearly.

Love, Bill

Madelyn Bussing Hendrix recalls how good Claudia was about taking
Bill places and doing things with him, just as she and Bill had done during
the "Dana" years. "Bill was not the type of man who needed to be in a social
situation or surrounded by people, but he was not a loner either. He enjoyed
life, good food, and visiting people and places. Claudia even came to Dana
to visit Bill's grave about a year or two after he died," Madelyn said. "She
stopped by my house, as Bill must have told her where I lived, and I took
her to the cemetery."

Will's last caregiver was his next door neighbor, Ann Gerstenbrand, wife
and mother of a young family, who cared for him his final two years of life.
She was an efficient and able provider, and if Will needed her during the
night for an emergency, he needed only to call her via the sip and puff tube
located near his mouth and connected to his phone via the environment
programmer. Her five daughters—Tracy, Vanessa, Katrina, Shannon and
Anne—became good pals with Will, passing notes in his mailbox, at pizza
parties and when sharing evenings together with a bowl of popcorn. Shannon, the second youngest, would frequently eat breakfast with Will.

Charlie Schmidt and Will Warner, partners of the non-profit venture, Lift,
Inc., a placement service of sorts, were working with companies willing to
train and hire individuals with significant physical impairments. After some
prompting by Margaret Pfrommer, Will contacted Lift, Inc. He interviewed
for a full-time computer programmer position, passed the preliminaries, and
in October 1979, began the learning program. Six months later the Walgreen

Company hired Will. He had competed successfully with the able-bodied despite his quadriplegia. This was a major milestone in Will Jenks' solitary quest to be a valued and productive employee. Now earning a competitive salary [$30,000 in 1984 and $37,000 in 1988], he also had health insurance coverage, no small matter for someone with his medical history. His brother, John wrote of his work: "One cannot overstate how meaningful this job was to Will. It not only provided him with a sense of financial independence, but it was a vehicle to additional contacts with the outside world. Though Walgreen placed a computer terminal on-line in his bedroom which allowed him to work without leaving the house, he typically traveled to work two days each week primarily because it gave him the opportunity to mix socially with his fellow workers. The job also enhanced his image of self-worth, as the completed projects made him feel like a contributing member of society." Will remained on the job until his death.

A hip fracture historically has been an accurate indicator of diminished well-being. Thus, on February 2, 1979 when Ella broke her hip, despite surgical repair, the fall appeared to trigger a significant physical decline, and intermittently, her cognitive abilities were also markedly affected. During one of John and Will's visits with their mother in the nursing home where she was rehabbing, Ella confided, "I'm on my way out, boys." Approximately two months after her fall—April 9—her prediction came true.

Ella Jenks lived her life with saintly endurance, patience, self-sacrifice, and confidence in God's love. She devoted herself to Will's extraordinary needs, never faltering in that mission, for 27 years. She was laid to rest beside Mack Jenks outside Dana, in the village of Bono, near the house where the Jenkses first resided after retirement. Ella's best friend, Agnes Bussing, Madelyn's mother, died less than a year after Ella, in March 1980, and the two bridge partners were reunited.

Liz Helt Gavin, a Ph.D. in classical studies from Indiana University and one of Will's long-time friends and correspondents, moved from Dana shortly after her marriage, to Chicago where she taught English literature at the Illinois Institute of Technology. In 1980, after moving to the northern suburbs, she and Will formed a monthly book club of about twelve members. Recalling Will and the club, Liz said, "He was probably the center of our book club. We always made an evening out of it—dinner at the host's house (sometimes thematic), then a discussion. One Halloween, probably two or three years before he died, when he was supposed to host it, he ended up in the hospital the Tuesday or Wednesday before. I went to visit him and he was quite down about having to skip the book club. So I went to the head nurse and told her of Will's and my long friendship, the book club, how very nice and polite and cultured we all were—and got her permission for all of us to visit, food, beer and wine included, for two hours that Saturday night. I remember it was some eerie story— *The Turn of the Screw* maybe—so we just turned off all the lights so we wouldn't be reminded it was a hospital room, lit a few candles and carried on . . ."

Much as he was dedicated to the book club, Will was not above playing a practical joke on it. Liz tells how Will and Alicia, "the two most resounding Catholics" in the group, conjured up a bogus thesis that the multiple stops made by Huck Finn and Jim were Twain's allegorical Stations of the Cross. "Their earlier conspiratorial preparation was quite convincing until they gave it up," Liz said fondly of Will. "He had a great sense of comedy and of irony."

The book club proved to be an enjoyable, yet stimulating intellectual outlet for Will. "Despite—or because of—the absence of long-term goals or commitments, there ensued more than eight years of animated discussions, good friends and memories . . . The group did not change materially over the years until Bill's death," said Liz.

May 1974

Peerless Peers:

Ah, to be in Worcester now that spring is there. Or again, what is so rare as three days in June? The 20th reunion offers us Worcester in June, almost more than the heart of man dare dream of. It also promises a return to the scene of our own springtime, when the world was green with hope. Most of all, it brings together friends who are too distant or too busy to keep old loyalties alive. As a salutary side-effect, a reunion makes it possible for men now several years removed from the college to appreciate what has been done and what needs to be done to keep Holy Cross among the best of the liberal arts colleges. What better investment of time? There is still time . . .

Will

CHAPTER EIGHT

The 20th Reunion

IN NOVEMBER 1973, THE UNIVERSITY OF MINNESOTA FOOTBALL TEAM was scheduled to play Northwestern University's Wildcats at Dyche stadium in Evanston, IL. If the weather cooperated, the field, within sight of Lake Michigan, was a great venue for football and its wide pedestrian ramps were quite wheelchair-accessible. What a great fall outing for Will and an excuse for a mini-reunion of some nearby 1954 classmates! Betty and I invited Paul and Claire Rollins and Jack and Audrey Rutherford. Will too was looking forward to the get-together and the game.

Paul and Claire picked up Will, and they and the Rutherfords gathered at our place. The four football fans went to the game and the three wives spent the afternoon on a leisurely stroll to the lakefront, as the weather was perfect for a football game or a walk sunny with mild temperatures. Libations and appetizers were available when everyone reconvened at our home, after the visitors won, while conversations and laughs about the game and our lives came easily.

That evening for the first time, Paul, Jack and I considered that Will might be willing to join us at the 20th reunion the following June. Will's vitality and his energy despite his paralysis impressed them, and we three agreed that it was doable. Will, we learned, was indeed up for it, and plans were underway.

Will returned to Holy Cross for the first time since June 1951. The weather held up beautifully for the three-day event, as did Will. Classmates and spouses, all of whom wanted to share in his charisma, and experience his smile, constantly surrounded Will who seemed oblivious to his physical status. He amazed people, when, with only a quick glance at their faces, he would greet them and connect them to an occupation, hometown, or to their children.

Will had developed into a spectacular conversationalist and, in part, it was his ability to put people at ease which made everyone else a better conversationalist. Within moments people unfamiliar with quadriplegia lost their fluster and were suddenly swept into a dialogue untouched by any sign of hesitancy or pity—only enthusiastic and unself-conscious chatting between peers.

Many classmates instinctively offered a right hand to him, but when this prompted no response that hand would withdraw and be replaced with a stroke to Will's shoulder or a touch to the top or side of his head. It was a caress offered in a somewhat sudden and awkward recognition of what Will dealt with. The word "quadriplegia" carried less impact than seeing and interacting with a quadriplegic. For many, that weekend reinforced in graphic detail what Will had endured for twenty-three years; what he had—what he had missed—and what would never change.

Will absorbed facts and data relying only on his memory, which had been transformed and honed since leaving school. He met his dear friend, Father Hart, who had also directed the intramural sport programs in which Will had participated. Father Hart, his primary connection to Holy Cross after Father Cummings' death in 1969, sent college periodicals and newspaper clippings with other miscellaneous bits of school happenings. Father Brooks, now president of the college, found time to make his acquaintance, and Will spent private prayer time at Father Cummings' grave.

Friday night extended well into Saturday morning for most of us, including Will who showed impressive endurance and stamina. Saturday brought the all-class picnic, a late afternoon liturgy followed by a happy hour and dinner in Kimball Dining Hall. Singing, joking and catching up on the lives of classmates filled the later evening hours.

After Mass and breakfast Sunday morning, we had to break the special spell and return to reality. We had enjoyed ourselves immensely and Will was a large part of that; he left an indelible imprint on many memories, an imprint of courage, good humor, strength, and perseverance. We vowed to return for the Silver Anniversary Reunion in 1979.

Will summarized the weekend events in an amazing tour de force class letter from memory.

1974 REUNION RUNDOWN

To The Re- and Dis-United, Greetings and Condolences!

Yea, verily, it was the best of times, as all the survivors will attest. At least 54 '54 men came back to Holy Cross for all or part of the extended weekend. Some of them never actually set foot inside the college gate; they devoted themselves to an endless search for old haunts paved over by the freeway or shut down by the board of health. The rest of us, though, wandered the familiar goat paths of the Hill, reliving, reviewing, or revising the memories that drew us back. For some it was a pilgrimage. As GEORGE FARGIS explained, it puts a man in touch with the wellsprings of strength and happiness to return to his college. For others it was the weekend of long-dormant dreams—full of song and laughter and lesser vices without the awkward limitations of time and money. The only disappointment was the absence—unexcused and inexcusable—of so many classmates who could have made it even better. It was agreed that those of us who attended the 20th would be apostles for the Reunion five years hence, the Silver Anniversary gathering. So make plans for June 1979. Or prepare to be shanghaied.

Everyone who had been away for the full 20 years had to be overawed by the changes on the Hill. There are now 22 buildings; in our day there were eleven. And one of the newer structures is the Henry Hogan Campus Center, which has replaced the cafeteria, the pool hall, and the Fenwick auditorium with some measure of adequacy—

in the same sense that the Taj Mahal adequately replaces a pauper's grave. If the face of the campus has changed dramatically the faces of classmates have changed appallingly, appreciably, or not at all. An ad hoc jury of two, POKARDAS CHATANI and I, picked ED ROBINSON as the guy who has given time the slip most adroitly. He must have been in cold storage since graduation. And it's not cosmetic effect. Ed won the alumni golf tournament . . . JOE CORRY ran a close second. He stays young working with the carefree kids at the U of Wisconsin. Joe says Madison has become so tranquil he wears his flak jacket only on Che Guevera's birthday . . . Instant recognition also greeted BOB DALURY, who seems to find the South American climate salubrious. Next year, though, he will be summoned back to reality, the good ole USA, where age is bound to catch up with him . . . JACK KEENAN and MARK FOLEY belong to that rare breed of men who grow better looking with the years. Somewhere along the way Jack learned to smile, and he no longer looks as though he intends to leave spike marks on your face. Jack's a Worcester attorney . . . Mark, having shed 30 lbs and let a hair stylist redesign his head, was twice mistaken for a virile Rock Hudson— both times while passing mirrors . . . A few of the changes in appearance provoked curious reactions. Rev. JACK WEIMER aroused more hostility for having forsaken his crewcut than for having doffed his clerical blacks in favor of a moderately mod blue suit and semi-splashy tie. The critics seemed to feel JACK had denied his Teutonic heritage . . . Another Rev. KIRK WALSH, S.J., drew concerned comment about his seemingly flushed face. It proved to be symptomatic of nothing more than winters spent on the ski slopes of Colorado. Alas, Kirk is surrendering that chaplaincy to move to Boston, where slaloming is thought to be a Muslim ritual gesture . . . For those who arrived too late or too sane for golf the first event on the schedule was a class cocktail party and dinner in a private dining room in the Hogan Center. Three drinks into the evening we were herded onto the outside steps for a formal portrait. Everybody smiled. Perhaps because the bartender had bought off the cook, dinner was served late and swiftly. When the bar itself closed down (because drought-stricken) much of the party moved to the

Hanselman hospitality suite. RAY MURPHY, the silveriest head in the crowd, apparently couldn't trust Rhode Island to behave for more than six hours without him; he headed home before the bouncer knew he was there . . . And JACK KEENAN induced ED LEE and AL MONGILLO to tour Worcester after-dark. Ed later lamented the error of their ways, calling it the worst prudential judgment since he bought five tons of lawn fertilizer from Billy Sol Estes. Al merely groaned . . . But between two and three dozen guys wedged into the two-chair sitting room on Hanselman II and poured their souls into a medley of once-favorite songs. JERRY GOOD led and misled the singing, which he choreographed with Irish jigs. To keep his Ford dealing from pressing on his brain Jerry has taken up marathon running. There were times when we weren't at all certain the therapy was working. Four stragglers from '59 were admitted to our company and they nearly ruined the evening: they knew the words. BILL TULLY upheld the honor of '54 by getting through all the perverse verses of Waltzing Matilda. His triumph led to rumors that he was planning to migrate to Australia. LOU DOLAN, villainously mustached, put an end to the evening when he weakened the inner walls with a massively resonant rendition of "My Cup Runneth Over." DICK FEELY's wife carried the soprano part, but Dick was beyond caring . . . Saturday, the second of three superlative spring days, began whenever the body had paid Friday's fine. For KEVIN ROCHE, Boston Latin's Mr. Chips, mid-morning meant farewells. With four kids at home he may have timed his stay to coincide with the natural cycle of disasters. At that he outlasted BOB MAIETTA, who departed just as many of us were arriving. The incident made even Dial users insecure . . . JACK RUTHER-FORD breakfasted on a submarine sandwich, one he reportedly buried when his senior food service expired with unsold inventory. Jack entertained for two hours with tales of his commercial successes and his academic tribulations. A bearded hombre in planter's hat and shades punctuated the conversation and punctured the conversationalist with barbed remarks. His name tag said BILL KELLEY, but more likely he was the exiled dictator of a banana republic . . . Among the other bristly brethren was JIM BRINE, whose bwana

khaki costume suggested that he had been trying out for the re-make
of King Solomon's Mines. The owner of a sinister goatee was either
Lucifer himself, Mitch Miller, JOHN ROONEY, or none of the
above. J. CARTER McKAIG carries a lipful of brush, with some
distinction. But how else could he look, living on Honesty Way,
Bethesda, MD? A full set of chin whiskers adorned the face of
ART MURPHY, who flew in from Hollywood to cover the event
for Variety, the Sporting News of show biz: HILL STILL THRILL.
(Without an atlas or almanac it's impossible to award the prize
for having come the farthest. Is Murph's California farther than
BOB DALURY's Venezuela or BRONCO CHATANI's Jamaica?)
JACK REHM, another guy with facial fur, also doubled as journalist
over the weekend. He did a feature article on Campion for Better
Homes & Gardens, though he's moved up from that magazine to
broader lines of publishing . . . Of the fifty-odd—in some instances,
Ripleyesque—'54ers who made the scene it seemed an embarrassing
majority was made up of lawyers. Only three of our doctors interrupted their daily circuit of house calls to detour to Worcester. BILL
McVAY, a Pittsburgh eye-man, traded away weekends for the rest of
the summer to get free for the Reunion, and JOHN SUMMA, a
Connecticut heart-healer, primed his phone with a recorded message
recommending an article in Reader's Digest to confirm a diagnosis
of cardiac infarction. It's not necessarily significant, but both Bill
and John have liberated their scalps. The third doctor, BILL KANE,
will be vilified in a later paragraph . . . But the lawyers were every-
where. ED LEE and MATT BOYLAN stood aloof from the rest;
they're crime-fighting types. Ed is a U.S. Attorney in Boston, and
Matt is the head of the Criminal Justice Dept. for the state of New
Jersey. The squire of Groton, Mass., JIM CULLEN, finds great
satisfaction in small-town practice. It leaves him time for his four
kids and their baseball teams . . . With offices at One Wall Street,
JACK O'GRADY obviously preys on a non-rural clientele, to the
great relief of us farm folk . . . (Egregious Oversight: Momentarily
blinded by the thought of McVay's and Summa's pates, I forgot a
fourth physician. 'Thin' TOM MAGOVERN, whose claim to that
adjective rests more and more on comparison with 'Fat Tom,' is an

ob-gyn doctor in Washington, D.C. Tom wouldn't say how he persuaded his patients to hold off delivery over the weekend.) . . . Back to the sordid solicitors. Two of our three Albany lawyers came down for the occasion. If I have the facts right, FRANK LASCH is involved in a beautiful story. If I have them wrong I am involved in an embarrassing faux pas. Frank married BOB LUDDY's widow, Mary Ellen, and added two kids to the seven young Luddys, the oldest of whom attends HC. The other Albanian, FRANK MUL-DERRY has eight kids, ages 18 to 8, but he hastens to point out that two are twins. That's supposed to assure everyone that he's not a sex maniac. HARRY HILL supplied that last comment. Harry, a lawyer who's trying to go straight in the world of business, has lost his curls, his cherubic countenance, and his innocence, though he clings to honor by managing a girl's softball team. Whatever admiralty law may be, that's what HOWIE McCORMACK practices. Howie was second runner-up in the snowy roof sweepstakes. JACK COLLINS, who introduced Howie to his wife, made an effort to apologize to both sides. In his Easy Rider glasses Jack's face has the same lines as the '57 Plymouth. Jack is so vain about his sequoia size calves he refused to shed his tennis shorts for the Saturday night banquet. So he was banished to the class of '29's table . . . Two of the four padres on the Reunion roster made it only to the Saturday afternoon picnic. Fr. JOE ASH and Fr. JOHN FOLEY ducked out between June weddings to join the throng. Joe, on the Worcester marriage court, also does parish work in lovely W. John, stationed in Boston, boasted a 70 lb. weight loss; he's now a delicate 240 . . . The busiest man at the picnic was RON PERRY, who took groups of Old Purples on tours of the field house. The inspection required some imagination, since the structure so far consists of a dozen orange stakes on the football practice field. But it will be real enough in 18 months, without, sad to say, a swimming pool. (Fr. Hart's lobbying couldn't quite get it done.) . . . CHICK MURPHY, smiling as though he had played his whole career without a helmet, covered the picnic grounds in loping strides. He keeps his hand in by serving as assistant coach for Mel Massucco's WPI football team . . . A late arrival, DICK GUTHRIE, stirred some excitement among his friends and long-suffering creditors. Quite a few guys left the shade of the picnic canopies to seek him out, though no one lost his head and set out without his beer . . . AL MONGILLO put me under strict orders to say only bad things about GEORGE JACOB, but how can you say anything bad about someone who owns a brewery and a beer distributorship? Besides, George deserves to be quoted on the advice he gave his wife when he invited her to accompany him: "You are going to see a lot of 42-year-old men acting like college boys, and that's because the thing they have in common is four years they had together 20 years ago." She came anyway . . . The one-of-a-kind job category award went to JAY SHAPLEY, who seemed content in his work, no doubt because it gives him immunity to insurance salesmen. Jay's a test-pilot for the FAA . . . JIM FOLEY should have been included among those who could still be brought to justice by a wanted poster using his Patcher picture . . . The Saturday afternoon Mass, a liturgical turkey and homiletic horror show, took us up to the open-air cocktail party and the alumni banquet. The food was strictly Saturday night at Kimball: relish tray, cantaloupe, tossed salad, cream of chicken soup, roast beef, baked potato with sour cream, stillborn carrots, asparagi, ice cream pie with chocolate sauce, and coffee. MATT BOYLAN's son Nick, HC '86, dined with his dad and complained that he had been promised beans and franks . . . JACK O'GRADY, confusing the assembly with the Mad Hatter's Tea Party, rose to his feet between courses to cast his delegation's votes for Gus Zernial, 36½, and Calvin Coolidge, 14½. A handful of us waited out the awards ceremony to hear Fr. Brooks' address, and although he spoke as a member of the 25th Reunion class he committed the college to an education emphasizing a morality of earned rewards, a lifestyle of simplicity, and a concern for the active reform of social and political institutions. It was worth sweating through . . . At the banquet GARABED DEGERMAJIAN single-handedly put down a bread-throwing riot. It was a deed reminiscent of the young Matt Dillon . . . After the final kudos had been bestowed the scene shifted to the dance and piano bar in Hogan. The smoothest operator at the dance was CHARLIE MILLARD, who glided from one big bread man to the next, deftly putting the arm on recruits for the President's Council . . . At precisely one o'clock in the morning both the visually functioning patrons of the piano bar were steered to a window overlooking the outdoor basketball court, where they were asked to witness to history that LARRY McGRATH failed to show up for his insomnia shoot-out with BILL KANE. Bill stood at the free throw line and thrice challenged Larry to come out panting. The one-on-none went ahead without him—in charade, since there was no basketball. In fairness to Larry it must be said that he bought new sneakers for the match. He must have succumbed to sanity somewhere between noon and midnight . . . From eviction time at Hogan till four-thirty the dauntless carousers carried on at two party sites. HOWIE McCORMACK's room hosted a trivia tournament matching teams from '54 and '59. In this newsletter we won; in Jim Healey's '59 notes, they nailed us to the wall. (One of the wives humiliated us all. Who the hell was number 34 for the '47 Dodgers? Hint: he was cute.) . . . Sunday morning came too early, and even so most of the crowd had dispersed. The few who stayed on to hear Fr. JACK WEIMER's sermon were left to wonder why he hadn't been scheduled for Saturday afternoon . . . LARRY EAGAN and his wife had the cafeteria to themselves at eleven o'clock. That was just as well, since Larry's breakfast needed three tables to accommodate it. Maybe he sprinted to Springfield and back before breakfast . . . PHIL BREEN and JIM SHEA must be puzzled over their exclusion from the account of Friday evening's happenings. The truth is that they both alienated me by introducing themselves as guys who didn't know me during my time at HC and their tone seemed to say they were glad of it . . . ROBERT X. PERRY must be wondering what he has to do to receive even dishonorable mention. He sent in a green slip with his vitals sometime before the Reunion. My problem was that I didn't know whether to list him under Lawyers—involved 'professionally, not personally' in Watergate—or under skin-domed-but-not-flint . . . If JOHN SPILLANE isn't a lawyer he shouldn't wear so wide a smile. Who else has reason to smirk? John came up the Hill from Worcester for Friday's dinner. He still has a sideline peddling his cousin Mickey's dirty books . . . TED EDWIN

WEDEMEYER rendezvoused with MATT BOYLAN on his way in from Milwaukee. Matt did the decent thing. He let Ted travel without handcuffs.

Outright apologies to the guys I missed altogether. My reportorial skills were unequal to the scope of the events. In a follow-up edition I'd like to publish observations from other vantage points, stories of other incidents, parties, lunacies, and corrections and additions to this record. Apologies, too, to the valiant and invariably lovely wives, who have gone unnamed because of the demands of space. They contributed immeasurably to the good times.

In behalf of the class let me express wholehearted, unanimous thanks to Pat McCarthy and the Alumni Office for their unfailing hospitality in what must have been frenzied circumstances. As always, Fr. Hart deserves the longest hoiah for making each of us feel that the college is planning to erect a monument to honor our splendid deeds.

At the risk of running into extra innings I want to drop in words of thanks to everyone who made me feel a part of things, especially those who bought me beers. Further thanks to the guys who lifted me, whether in or out, up or down. Over the objections of their husbands I send my love to Pat and Mimi, my alluring dinner dates. Jack Rutherford, Indy winner and gentleman, chauffeured us out from Boston and back again—a thankworthy kindness. And there was Bill Kane, whose caring and caring-for gave friendship a new depth of meaning. From dawn Friday to dusk Sunday Bill took total responsibility for my needs. In his unassuming way he was a beautiful parable on the values we think of as uniquely belonging to Holy Cross. I know your admiration counterpoints my gratitude.

Enough for now. Take the necessary steps to set aside time for the 25th Reunion in '79. We will be older then but, hopefully, no wiser.

Succinctly,
Will

A small assembly of '54 classmates arrived at a consensus that Will was a unique marvel; an in-the-flesh miracle, a cheerful conqueror of a seemingly hopeless disability. On another level it was also obvious that he was better educated and more intelligent than the rest of us despite our accumulated experiences of the past twenty-three years. All of what his paralysis had deprived him of was so unfair.

"Just call me doc."

—*Will Jenks*

CHAPTER NINE

Lifelong Learning: An Honorary Doctorate

THE INEQUITY THAT WILL JENKS HAD NO DEGREE WHILE WE OF LESSER learning and intellect had accumulated various degrees was too great to ignore. An ad hoc group agreed to petition the College to award Will a Bachelor of Arts degree, given his homespun and self-directed education. I was chosen to address this issue based on my acquaintance with academic routines.

I sent off a confidential letter to Father Brooks inquiring about the College's view of a belated bachelor's degree for Will. He promptly responded with both pleasant and disappointing news. Will did not qualify for a bac-calaureate degree since he had "not completed a prescribed curriculum as required by the college's charter from the state." However, according to Father, "he would be a most worthy candidate for an honorary doctorate degree from Holy Cross." His letter continued extolling Will's virtues, stating "His life certainly embodies the Christian values for which Holy Cross stands, and it radiates a degree of faith and hope that is a source of strength to everyone of us. I, for one, would be extremely happy to join you in submitting Will's name to the Nominating Committee of the Board of Trustees as a candidate for an honorary degree at next June's Commencement."

A quick note from Fr. Brooks dated September 30, 1974 updated the Honorary Degree proposal and process. He wrote, "The reaction has been extremely positive, and would seem to indicate that I will not encounter substantive opposition anywhere along the line . . . For a starter, you might just mark your calendar for Friday, 23 May—Commencement."

Donald P. Moriarty, '52, a New York City financier, and chair of the college trustees, and Charles E. F. Millard, '54, also a trustee, were two likely "yes" votes, according to Fr. Brooks. The trustees' Honorary Degrees Committee would send their recommendations to the full board of trustees in December 1974. A later update from Fr. Brooks said, "Will Jenks' dossier has already been fully prepared for submission to the Trustees Nominating Committee. I will see to it personally that the case is made for Will."

In mid-December, Fr. Brooks called with great news and asked me to hand deliver the college's invitation to Will. The invitation arrived with a note from Father, stating in part, "thanks a million for your nomination of Will—I'm sure that you'll be interested in knowing that Charlie Millard also submitted Will's name. It's a tremendously meaningful selection, and one that will be enthusiastically received by Will's many Holy Cross friends. Formal announcement of the honorary degree recipients' names will be made public in early May." Also included was a blind copy of Father's letter to Will.

Dear Will,

It is my pleasure to inform you that the Board of Trustees of the College of the Holy Cross has voted to offer you an honorary degree at the May 1975 Commencement.

I need not here detail the reasons for this decision. Suffice to note that your saintly patience and constancy over the years, your intellectual growth and dedication to work, and your profound love of life and people more than merit what Holy Cross can offer you.

I am quite gratified at this action of the Board, for I consider an honorary degree an educational effort on the part of the institution: an endeavor to single out that kind of moral, intellectual, and social achievement which affirms our own best aspirations. In proffering this honor, we proclaim our own educational goals and would feel honored by your acceptance.

Commencement is scheduled for the morning of Friday, 23 May 1975. It is my sincere hope that you will find it desirable and convenient to accept.

On Saturday, December 21, Betty, our children, and I visited Will. While the children had met Will before, they were beguiled again by seeing how he typed the letters or drew the pictures that he had sent them. They were entranced by how he would move the 3½ x 6 card from a stack onto the top of the typewriter and then position it so he could peck out the letters one at a time with his mouth-held clothespin or wand. He could type 16–17 words per minute with fewer errors than most two-handed amateur typists.

Besides extending Christmas greetings to Will, his mother, brother and nephews, I was there to deliver Father's invitation. It was, I believe, the most special Christmas present that Holy Cross could ever give to Will, and it did affirm in an extraordinarily singular fashion Father Brooks' vision for Holy Cross.

"Will was completely and utterly flabbergasted and very much taken, mentally and emotionally, by the distinction bestowed upon him," I wrote Fr. Brooks. I said he voiced some uncertainty that he deserved this honor and was not a little reluctant to accept it. I was surprised by his response, but it was a trait that I came to learn was deeply ingrained in his character, a modesty about himself which was genuine and which I later felt derived from Will's fundamentally spiritual view of his life. This humility and his life view would surface again over the coming years in other matters, large and small. Simply put, he was a holy man, and his hesitancy to accept praise or honors originated in his humility, which manifested itself in many of his letters. He requested I allow him the weekend to deliberate on the matter.

When I spoke with Will the following Monday, he had had additional reflection which allowed him to understand and appreciate more fully the kind motives of the trustees, and there was no further discussion of whether he would accept the honorary degree. On the day after Christmas, I concluded my letter to Father Brooks by extending "my personal thanks because you have honored a friend of mine, and also my thanks as an alumnus of Holy Cross College because you selected a man who can symbolically represent the goals and aims of the school."

24 Dec 1974

Dear Bill,

Last night I said it badly, no doubt because I hadn't finished thinking it through. Now I have a better grasp on the meaning of the event, thanks largely to your thoughts on the school's motives. At another level, though, I came to understanding by reflecting on our friendship. Over the years you have expressed sacramentally—to be felt—the very truth Holy Cross wants to express symbolically—to be thought on. It is no more absurd for a college of HC's stature to confer an honorary degree on a man without power, reputation, accomplishment, or influence than it is for an eminent bone-doctor to keep alive a friendship with a dead-beat, dead-weight, dead-end deadhead. You do great things; at best, I do small. Your world is global and significant; mine is provincial and ordinary. But you accept the differences and remain a friend—how good a friend you showed last June. You may recall that I was concerned about the focus of our classmates' wonder. They tended to admire my spirit rather than your caritas. The greater mystery is not how I manage to smile but why you bother to bother. That same mystery underlies the inexplicable distinction Holy Cross has chosen to bestow on me. My one anxiety is that it will provoke the wrong questions: Who is he? What has he done? Rather than Why would a Catholic college do such a thing? (It just came to me that Fr. Brooks might have asked you to bring the news precisely because he sensed the analogy.) . . . You have been important to the event and to my understanding . . .

Will

On Thursday, May 22, 1975, Will, Ella, and his brothers, John and Jim, and I flew into Logan Airport, and then motored to a Worcester motel. The next morning we drove to Fitton Field, the football stadium, where commencement exercises were to take place. The weather was good but warm—sunny with few clouds, a light, humid breeze, and mid-morning temperatures about 88 degrees and rising. A major story in Thursday's *Worcester Evening Gazette* led off with the grim assessment that the depressed economy, a tight market for jobs and the high cost of living would send many from college processionals to unemployment lines, as the new graduates faced "the bleakest year for employment since the graduating classes of the Depression."

The valedictorian, Mr. David Griesing, '75, a history major awarded two academic excellence medals, also sounded somber as he spoke of alienation, narcissism, and a generation without heroes or a sense of community: "Who are your heroes? . . . John and Bobby Kennedy are dead, most of the radical prophets of the 1960's have faded from the newspaper and there is no one on the Red Sox or the *Times* Best Seller list or, I suspect, on Mount St. James who is an embodiment of the heroic." The college newspaper *Crossroads* later reported that Griesing stated "a stable identity in a pluralistic society depends on a feeling of inner solidarity with a community which one believes transcends in time and space all the many groups and roles to which one belongs. The nation, the Church and the College have not met that definition of Community." He concluded, "these have been angry words," but cautioned his listeners not to take them as "vindictive ones" . . . "Because I have loved the individuals who make up Holy Cross, I hope for something better for them." Minutes after graduate Griesing completed his address, "something better" was awaiting the audience.

Reverend John E. Brooks, S.J., president of the College, called out "William Henry Peter Jenks." Friend and classmate, Charles E.F. Millard, wheeled Will forward to the front and center of the commencement stage.

Garbed in the ceremonial black robe, Fr. Brooks' voice reached the audience of 4,000 as he read the citation:

When a college bears the name of the Holy Cross, it must judge the achievements of its sons and daughters by a standard that not everyone will understand. The meaning of the Cross is that the God of Truth and the God of Suffering Love are one and the same. It was in terms of suffering servanthood that Jesus defined His own life's mission and, whatever its human forms, the cross is still the surest mark of all who travel His path.

"Will" Jenks—twenty-five years ago, you settled into Campion House with your classmates ready to do battle with the mathematics curriculum. After one brief year, your stay on the Hill was cut short by polio and you were left lifeless in four limbs. Your battle was not to be with books and examinations but with life itself, and you made the decision then to disregard the handicap and commit yourself to an involvement in human affairs that few able-bodied Holy Cross graduates can match.

You have been tutor, newspaper writer, manager of the family farm, basketball coach, salesman, artist with a pen clenched tightly in your teeth, leader of the parish council, revered alumni secretary for the Class of '54, and ever the genial dispenser of wit and wisdom from your own front porch. Somehow you managed to transform life's worst shadows into light, reminding us all that usefulness is not the only equivalent of worth. What a reminder goes there for the pragmatists amongst us!

Holy Cross has never ceased to be a part of your life: You have never ceased to enrich us here with the example of your prodigious energy, born of suffering. Today Holy Cross is proud to recognize in you those qualities of heart and mind it most desires in its graduates, and it is honored to confer upon you the degree, Doctor of Humane Letters.

It was impossible for Father to hide his emotions. By now, the audience was intently curious to hear what this man in a wheelchair had achieved, endured, or deserved. Hearing this message of honor and esteem, the audience reaction passed from a rational understanding to an emotional display. Eyes moistened, throats tightened, and handkerchiefs dabbed stray salty tears of appreciation and admiration. Father Brooks, now standing behind Will, positioned the purple and white cowl over Will's head and onto his shoulders, then came around in front of him and placed the Doctor of Humane Letters diploma under Will's hand. It was only then that the hushed audience recognized the meaning of "lifeless in all four limbs." He then placed his right hand on Will's head in blessing; both trying to mask smiles and tears. As Charlie Millard wheeled Will back to his original spot on the stage, Donald P. Moriarty, '52, Chair of the Trustees, congratulated Will and Worcester's bishop, Rev. Bernard J. Flanagan, '28, rose from his seat, approached Will, blessed him and laid a hand on his shoulder.

By now the audience comprehended the full meaning of the moment and began applauding. The applause grew, and graduates began standing. Shortly, everyone was on their feet but one; the one man who could not stand nor clap. But Will Jenks smiled broadly giving a nod of thanks.

Parties unknown in the Alumni Office prepared a lead-in to Will's autobiography and sent out the "underground Class Letter" over Charlie and my names, as we announced the proud happenings of the day.

AN UNDERGROUND CLASS LETTER
TO THE MEMBERS OF THE CLASS OF 1954

May 23 was a purple letter day for our class. Our Class Secretary, Will Jenks, received an honorary degree from the Cross. On a steaming hot Friday in Worcester, Holy Cross rightfully recognized one of its own—and very much one of our own.

Will was awarded a Doctorate of Humane Letters (obviously the powers that be have never read those treasures of trivia he dispatches all too infrequently). Immediately after commencement, as Will was sitting with friends, there was the flicker of a tear in his eyes as he smilingly said, "Just call me doc." It is impossible to recapture the emotion of the moment.

Will was accompanied by his mother, brothers, and Bill Kane, M.D. He brought luster and grace to an otherwise typical Commencement and was fittingly saluted with a standing ovation by all assembled. When the citation had been read, C.E.F.M. had the privilege of steering Will's chair to the podium. Among the cheering crowd were our classmates, Fr. John Foley, Frank Larkin and Hank Lemire. If there were others whom we missed, our apologies.

When asked by the College to submit his biography for the Public Relations Department, Will responded with the attached . . . a Jenks classic. So now our class has—as one of many telegrams received described it—the first dropout in history to receive a full pardon.

If any of us need a special prod to contribute to this year's Alumni Fund, this provides it. We suggest you think seriously about sending your gift—as we have done—in Will's honor. You can honor him this way—just as he honors us. What a great way for the class to add its thanks to his efforts for and dedication to it.

Sincerely,
Bill Kane & Charlie Millard

THE STORY

William Henry Jenks—'Will' to his Holy Cross classmates, 'Jinks' to earlier schoolmates, and 354-24-5303 to government computers—was born in Chicago, Illinois, on March 18, 1932, to Ellen Cronin Jenks and Orra Mack Jenks, both of whom were teachers in the Chicago public school system. His rival siblings numbered two. Older brother John is presently Director of Sales and Marketing for three lines of Bell & Howell business equipment. Younger brother James is a teacher and head basketball coach at Cardinal Ritter High school in Indianapolis.

Having survived five years of fratricidal strife, young Jenks successfully completed the kindergarten course of study at Budlong School. From there he advanced to Queen of Angels School, where he mastered the basic learning skills and contracted every childhood disease known to pediatrics. He also became a choir boy and an acolyte. In 1943 the family moved to Park Ridge, Illinois, a northwest suburb of Chicago, and the gawky lad transferred to St. Paul of the Cross School. At age twelve he joined the Boy Scouts and eventually rose to the rank of second-class scout. He retired after one year of honorable service.

His high school years were spent at Fenwick H.S., an all-male institution conducted by the Dominican Fathers. Jenks was active on the school newspaper and inactive on the varsity basketball team, which in his senior year won the Chicago city championship, small thanks to his contribution. A teammate on that squad was Tom Carstens, HC '55.

From the age of twelve Jenks was gainfully employed at various summer jobs: caddying, a condition of servitude presumably outlawed by the Thirteenth Amendment; opening mail for a 25¢-and-a-label promotion; stacking sections of catalogues for a printing house; and fixing postage to cartons of sporting goods. On the family farm he gained invaluable experience as a milker of cows, a doer of chores, and a hefter of bales.

As a winner of an NROTC scholarship, the eighteen-year-old made Holy Cross his first choice. In September, 1950, he climbed Mt. St. James, made his way to 'roomy, home-like' Campion Hall, and settled in with his seven roommates to butt heads with the A.B. Math curriculum. During his one year career Jenks participated in debating, intramurals, sodality, and the Outing Club, a prestigious if not exclusive organization whose functions—a fall picnic and a winter film series—he faithfully attended. Among his Campion companions he is faintly remembered as captain of the winless basketball team and as a fanatic for dental hygiene.

The summer after his freshman year at Holy Cross Midshipman 4/c Jenks was assigned to the USS Shannon, DM 25, for an eight-week cruise that took him to Copenhagen, Lisbon, and exotic Guantanamo Bay, Cuba. While in Portugal he visited the shrine at Fatima, where with any foresight he would have put a miracle in layaway for later use.

On returning to civilian life Jenks joined his family in a change-of-address. His father's retirement from teaching occasioned the move to a quaint rural home near Dana, Indiana, and even nearer the Jenks Family Farm. On August 27, 1951, two weeks after he had become a Hoosier, the previously lucky fellow ran afoul of a polio germ that left him lifeless in four limbs. A year in hospitals gave him two rehabilitated skills—operating an electric typewriter with a stick clenched between his teeth and turning pages by the same method.

Returning home, where his mother would take on the daily burden of his total care, he began to fashion a life-style, even before he was aware of the word. In 1953 new possibilities opened up when with his parents he moved to the city—Dana, Indiana, a town of 750. Over the next few years he became involved in community life, tutoring irremediable readers and mathematicians, writing features for the local newspaper, and dispensing wisdom from his front porch. In 1970 he was slated to run for the town board, but the election was called off for lack of interest. Two years earlier, when Father Lawrence Moran established a parish council for St. Joseph-

Immaculate Conception parish, Jenks had won the last seat by the flip of a coin. During the five years he served on the council the parish built a new church, and it was his honor to serve as president of that body at the time of the building's formal dedication.

After 22 years in Indiana the country gentleman and his mother moved to Mundelein, Illinois, where they made their abode with John Jenks and his sons. A second radical change took place in November, 1974, when, thanks to an electronic marvel created by Northwestern University Rehabilitation Engineering Group, Jenks found work as a part-time phone salesman for a polyethylene film company.

Holy Cross never stopped being a part of Will Jenks' life. For 18 years after polio had cut short his stay on the Hill he received a letter at least every other day from Father Patrick J. Cummings, S.J., professor, confessor, mentor, and friend. That perduring devotion ended only with Father Cummings' death in 1969. Over the years Father Francis J. Hart, S.J., long-time student counselor and repository of the college's soul, has written letters and sent countless packets of clippings about campus doings and soybean futures.

By default the Class of '54 allowed Jenks to seize the post of class secretary, which gives him license to publish calumnious class-letters three times a year. In June, 1974, he experienced the previous highpoint of his life as a Crusader when, under the care of classmate and friend, Dr. Bill Kane, he attended the twentieth reunion of his class. It is his proudest boast that he never bought a drink.

by Will Jenks

Will underestimated the range and might of Wes Christenson's pen from the public relations office; his press releases led to hundreds of news clippings. The Chicago Tribune editorially praised Will and quoted him, speaking of Father Cummings: "When my letters would be rash or filled with self-pity . . . he would challenge me usually with tact but always with charity . . . He offered counsel, encouragement, caution, or 'whatever it took to keep the banners flying.'" The editorial ended by congratulating Dr. Jenks. "You may have given just the right medicine to a lot of people you'll never see."

In addition to congratulating Will for his faith, courage, and example, the Worcester Free Press also editorialized, "And, especially, congratulations to Holy Cross College for honoring one of their own, even if his time on the Hill was brief. It was a shining moment in a long and illustrious history of the Cross." Indeed it was.

"What I have learned, what I continue to learn daily is that there is only one way to put Humpty-Dumpty together again: Let yourself be loved."

Excerpt from the 6/16/79 Address to the
General Alumni Association by Will Jenks

CHAPTER TEN

Let Yourself Be Loved

"TAKE THE NECESSARY STEPS TO SET ASIDE TIME FOR THE 25TH REUNION in '79. We will be older then but hopefully, no wiser" was the way Will concluded his 1974 Reunion Rundown classletter.

Because of his enthusiasm, willingness, and perhaps even a need to be involved with the activities of the class, Will accepted an assignment on the reunion communications committee in anticipation of the 1979 reunion. But, during the preliminary preparations, Will sensed that he was being groomed for a larger role in the reunion, especially in one communication when he was compared to Joe Califano, '52, and Joe Kerwin, '53, both of whom had been chosen to deliver a 25th Reunion address to the General Alumni Association on behalf of their classes. Will feared he might be slated for the same task. He wrote Fr. Moran [28 Jan. 1979], "If honcho-hood involves public utterance I may gargle with Diet Pepsi until my vocal cords sag . . ."

When he received the suspected but undesired assignment from Barry McDonough, Will turned him down with a definitive "No."

Why such reluctance to speak in public? A combination of factors really. Will's diminished lung capacity made his voice much softer and slightly hoarser than would be expected for a man under 50 years of age. Also, Will read his presentations from a wheelchair and he knew he couldn't gesticulate with arms or body language; he felt this was an enormous disadvantage. Seated, the pages of his speech would be turned by someone else. There was also his experience with Fr. Moran's efforts to ready him to go on the radio where he was embarrassed by the tape recorder, which revealed his halting,

99

hesitant selection of the words he sought and punctuated, he said, with "uh's" and "duh's." He was overly critical of his rhetorical experiences. He had been active in debate club as a freshman, and in class his verbal presentations and responses to questions were direct, well enunciated and persuasive, elsewise he wouldn't have made the Dean's List both semesters. He had no stutter, lisp, or any other speech anomaly, and he was a good social conversationalist. But now Will felt awkward speaking in public, especially after a speech he called mediocre that he delivered in 1973 when he left the Dana parish. He pleaded concern for the honor of the class and for the ears of the audience.

Nevertheless, "against instinct, experience, and wish," he accepted the task when "Bill Kane—more with love than logic—convinced me to be '54's man . . . Had it been left to me, I would have simply gone and come home, with only private conversations and public celebrations to tax my resources . . ." [11 March 1979 and 21 June 1979, Walter and Florence Collins]

Will wrote Father Moran [2 March 1979] that he had changed his mind from NO to MAYBE to YES. He continued, "I have a theme in mind, the subject we discussed so fruitfully at the Pie Palace: My secret has been that I've let myself be loved." As Will noted, "this will be something of a halftime talk, not in the Rockne sense but in the geriatric sense; at some distant reunion the entire remnant of '54 will be in wheelchairs. I can prepare them for the humiliation." A progress note for Fr. Moran was dated 18 May 1979. "Just finished the second draft of my message to the masses. Except for a few rough spots and one or two dead spaces it's not bad. I even brought Jesus into it. Best of all, its fifteen minutes' worth, so I don't have to stall. I can already taste that post-peroration beer . . ." Doesn't that read like someone warming to a task?

Following Charlie Millard's introduction and while Will was wheeled to the table where the microphone and his speech sat, the conversational hum rose in volume. When the audience saw Father Brooks, sitting to Will's left, clearly readying himself to turn the pages for Will, the hum diminished. The speaker was seated in full view as the dais was raised a couple of feet above the floor. More than twelve hundred alumni and wives grew silent as Will launched into his talk, known by those who heard it, and later those who read it, as "The Speech."

Thank you, Charlie (Millard), for that warm, occasionally scalding introduction. I knew Charlie was saving me for something truly treacherous when he steered me down Campion Hill and only pretended to let go. If you are asking yourself why Will Jenks was chosen to speak for the unspeakable Class of '54, you are not alone in your indignation. I had to overcome intense moral scruples to take on this job. A wise and holy man once told me my vocation is simply to *be*, not to *do*. And since then I have religiously avoided doing anything, anywhere. But this must be doing because being doesn't make you sweat.

The blame for this miscasting belongs chiefly to Bill Kane. It was Bill who persuaded me I have something to say. He persuaded me not with compelling logic but with the dark hint that the next ambassador from '54 would be Mike Cooney. As it happened, it was Bill Kane who gave me the main idea for this homily. He noted that at some distant reunion the remnant of '54 would probably all be in wheelchairs and would look to me for guidance. I do know something about the ethics and etiquette of wheelchairmanship. The subject, though, won't become urgently relevant until sometime in the twenty-first century, and I have a previous engagement for that time. I'm going to be a stand-by contestant on "The Dating Game." So, with your permission—or without it—I'll deposit my thoughts in your memory banks now, for withdrawal later.

Let me begin by asking your forgiveness. I intend to depart from tradition and make no attempt to present my wisdom as an affirmation of the ratio studiorum. That has been the inviolate tradition at these banquets. Last year, Joe Kerwin, space crusader, spoke on "The Ratio Studiorum, an Anchor in Times of Weightlessness." The year before, Joe Califano, the Savonarola of cigarettes, addressed the multitudes on "The Ratio Studiorum, Ultimate Weapon in the Shoot-out with the Marlboro Man." And five years ago, Fr. Brooks stood in this very spot and posed the question: "Can the ratio studiorum survive on a campus inundated by 1800 stereos?"

I beg leave to organize my thoughts around another axis. As you know, I wasn't in school long enough to earn my ratio studiorum license. In fact, I wasn't here long enough to earn Fr. Bean's grudging permission to practice rhetoric in public—which brings us back to wondering why I'm speaking for '54.

If my life is not an affirmation of that venerable academic principle, it is, I think, an affirmation of another side of the Holy Cross experience, of values imparted over more than four years to such distinctly off-campus places as Dana, Indiana, and Mundelein, Illinois. I may have had time only to chew the crust of Jesuit learning, but I've had better than half a lifetime to drink from the cup of Christian caring, drawn from the sacramental casks of the Holy Cross community. It would be useful to turn your eyes away from my scintillating smile and toward a source of its light. This smile is not so much an emanation of the Holy Cross spirit as it is a creation, a gift of that spirit, made present in the love of Holy Cross men and women. Celebrated graduates like Joe Kerwin and Joe Califano make the world aware—and us proud—of the College's intellectual and moral influences in their lives. Will Jenks makes a more select audience aware—and most of us proud—of Holy Cross' kindness to the least of the brethren and its rejoicing in the small triumphs of the heart. I ask you to consider what Holy Cross has done for one of you.

How else could I begin but with the prodigious charity, the epic befriending of Fr. Pat Cummings? Reduced to stark numbers, his love was carried across the miles in more than 3,300 letters, over one million words. The Holy Cross letterhead on each of those letters could have been read as a label, describing both content and context, and it could have been read as an imprimatur, the Jesuit community's blessing on those one million words and on our friendship. That blessing was made explicit in the rector's approval of Fr. Pat's four trips to Dana—approval granted despite the rector's deep-seated dread that he was sending a fellow Jesuit to an Isaac Jogues Martyrdom at the hand of Indiana Indians. It was the spirit of Holy Cross that sustained our friendship for 18 years. Through all that time, Fr. Pat made Holy Cross a part of my present, and gave me a sense of belonging. He was mentor, friend, and grace to me. He was a man of God and of Holy Cross.

Father Pat was not my only link to the Holy Cross community. In the early years there were letters from Fr. Luke O'Connor, Doc McBrien, Commander Harmon, and Fr. Donaghy. Later, when I began writing class letters, the Alumni Office seized me in its sweaty embrace. I could drop names like Jim Healy, George Shea, Pat McCarthy, Jim Keenan, or Fr. George O'Brien, but those names mean something only to the members of their immediate families. At the very top of the organization chart—Fr. Miller, Fr. Brooks, Barbara Green—Holy Cross has been no less open-hearted, no less loving. What other college has leaders who care about the cares of an unmoneyed, unfamous, unpowerful ungraduate?

Then there is Fr. Hart. It would trigger a riot if I were to claim more than my fair share of that dear man's inexhaustible love. So I will say only that he has clipped and mailed every word ever to reach print about Holy Cross—its everyday doings and its historic deeds. He has written letters, penned notes, scribbled comments in the margin, and amended greeting cards. And every word has been alive with humor, concern, compassion, and blessing. Here, too, the seal of Holy Cross has been affixed to Father's good works. In support of his postal apostolate, a Harvard-sized endowment has been poured into the stamp drawer at the post office. But if the choice were confronted head-on—endowment or endearment—there is no question that Holy Cross would choose Fr. Hart and the wealth he is over a fat portfolio.

Holy Cross, of course, is more than those who serve it here on the hill. It is everyone who feels the pull of the bond, whether on the day of the miracle victory over Boston College, on the day a son or daughter begins a new generation of Holy Cross life, on the day of reunion with one Crusader over a hurried lunch or with the Silver Anniversary Class over a stately banquet, or on the day a postcard from the Alumni Office tells us we are one fewer and immeasurably less.

For most of us, Holy Cross is our classmates and friends. And from the first, these men of '54 tugged at the bond and made it fast. There were cards, letters, mementos, and, at that first Christmas, a huge wad of money, extorted from the Sophomore corridors. Reluctant donors will be pleased to know, somewhat tardily, that the money was spent on our first TV. So instead of pouring over the ghostly metaphysical notions of Aristotle, Aquinas, and Suarez, I was peering at the shadowy electronic images of Alistair Cooke, Lenny Bernstein, and Uncle Bob Hardy.

Contact with the class was never broken. In fact, the editors of the '54 Patcher gave me a full page, right between the men who had been called to the seminary and one man who had been called to eternity. The accompanying panegyric stated—prophetically, it now seems—that I would always be a part of the class, in spirit. Jack Leviness, editor-in-chief of the Classletter, asked me to give a first-hand account of life as a Hoosier hayseed. Jack was so edified by my work that he signed me on as a cub reporter. In time I lived out the American dream and climbed to the top of the masthead. It hardly matters that the masthead has no bottom. The bond was not maintained by mail alone. Along the way there were intrepid travelers, not at all daunted by the parochial belief that the Wabash is a mythical river. Almost before the iron lung clanged shut, Jack Weimer appeared, breathing reassurance through a gauze mask. Jack repeated the journey after his ordination and again on a junket to St. Louis for some unremembered high purpose. Jim Hessman trekked west at Easter two of the first three years. He came, of course, to bring cheer to a forlorn friend, but he also took cheer from those tours of rural America, out where the groceries begin. Jim hitch-hiked, and so did Tom Hutchinson, who made it from Worcester to Dana with a single waggle of his magic thumb. Bill Harrison and Don Kapp borrowed a car and ventured forth from Brooklyn and the Bronx, along mile after mile of streets without houses or double parking.

Another Brooklyn boy, Bill Kane, tumbled off the running board of a passing creamery truck and confessed he was no less surprised to find himself in Dana than I was, since he had set out for Far Rockaway. Fifteen years later, Bill returned in style, aboard a hijacked crop duster. Since I moved to the Chicago area the local chapter of '54 has included me in all Alumni activities—novenas, tea dances, minor logic specimens. Members of that brave fraternity can be identified by their silver trusses, proudly inscribed, "I lifted Will Jenks." It's true, of course, that many people *not* of Holy Cross have played a large part in my life, but, except for my family and the mystical body, none of those loves caught me up in a sense of belonging. Holy Cross has been uniquely unforgetting. It's worth noting, I think, that not one girl from Becker Junior College hitchhiked out to see me. And that, compacted to fit time and tolerance, and minus one ecstatic happening, at the 1975 commencement, has been my Holy Cross experience, my Holy Cross education. Education, because it has taught me something.

That something is the wheelchair wisdom I promised when this interminable ramble began. What I have learned, what I continue to learn daily is that there is only one way to put Humpty-Dumpty together again: Let yourself be loved. Now, "Let yourself be loved" may not sound terribly profound. But it must be heavy, because it took me all these years to figure it out. And the truth is we were taught just the opposite. We were to do the loving and never mind being loved, which assumes an invulnerability foreign even to the planet Krypton.

A crippling disease is just one of fate's ways of undercutting muscular love. The able-bodied can be brought to the truth through hurts that never show. I think it's likely I am not the most seriously wounded among us, only the most conspicuously bandaged. Sooner or later every one of us will be made to feel flawed, inadequate, powerless. And there's no defense against it. Believe me, the humiliation is devastating. To lose control of the situation is unmanly, un-American, unforgivable. Fear of losing control may be the motive for the frantic banking of wealth and power during the middle years, so that, when erosion sets in, others may be commanded, not asked, to make up what is lacking. The alternative is to let yourself be loved. Not pitied, indulged, or pampered, but loved. It is sometimes a matter of asking others, even those we have no claim on, to carry part of the load, to make room in their plans for our needs. It is sometimes a matter of *not* asking, but of waiting and trusting others to sense our wants, it is always a matter of expecting to be loved. Jesus asks us to become like little children, because little children expect to be loved. For them, life is surprise and delight. For us, life can again become surprise and delight, if we let ourselves be loved.

And the time to begin is now, because asking for help, for understanding, in small things will prepare us for the day when we must ask for help and understanding in larger things. More than that, it will put us in touch with the truth about ourselves and about every other human being: We are precarious, we are mortal, but we are loved.

I know why I was asked to speak for '54, to give voice to the love we have for Holy Cross, the thanks we owe her. I am each of us at some near or far time, drawing life and strength and hope from this place, this bond, this faith, this love, this Holy Cross. . . .

The audience became silent within moments of Will's beginning, and remained so for the following seventeen minutes. Will had done it and in an inimitable fashion—with humor, self-effacement, love, wisdom and drama. He received a deservedly prolonged, standing ovation, but most impressively he had overcome his fear of public speaking.

In his post-speech letter to cousin Walter, Will described his pre-speech thoughts and writing, and then recapped the weekend. "So I set to work, and after three drafts and countless revisions—right up to the day before we left—the speech was ready, packaged in a genuine vinyl photo album I had bought for my Doctorhood scrapbook and never used. The Pope's Christmas message doesn't look as elegant as my script. Like the seasoned professional, I tested the microphones and speakers an hour before the meal began, then dined lightly on cantaloupe and rolls and butter. But I'm getting ahead of myself. From time to time during the carpentering months Bill Kane called to reassure me everyone would be for me, for my success or at least survival. On the plane trip to Boston and at every chance thereafter, he told me the speech would knock the roof off the place, though he hadn't read it. After the Friday night dinner/dance I came to believe him—and you, too, Walter. Man after man, couple after couple, came up to say how much they enjoyed my class letters. It eventually struck me that these same people would be out front Saturday night, one-fourth of the assembled faithful. So I relaxed.

"The introduction, twice as long as the speech, was made by Charlie Millard, classmate, and friend, whose ghostwriter was I. He relied on old class letters and autobiography and a letter I had written Father Brooks, the President, when I accepted the honorary degree. Some of the stuff I had forgotten, and it sounded pretty good. My turn came shortly after the Silver Anniversary gift was announced: $244,300 from fewer than 300 '54 men—some more than others. Catching everyone on a high didn't hurt. I had hoped, expected to have tapes to send a few cousins and friends, but an unpressed record button and an unvigilant recorder lost the event for posterity . . . It was a thrill, not so much for the applause but for the realization that I could write and speak words that would reach over a thousand people.

"The weekend itself will not be repeated this side of Paradise. Except for a sneak cancellation of our 10:30 flight on American, made up by a no up-charge switch to 9:45 TWA, and a delayed and generally screwed-up flight home, things went as though dreamed. Our dorm—young John's dorm—had a hospitality suite, where the Class congregated after arriving, golfing, or tennising. A videotape of events of twenty-five years ago—the NCAA baseball and NIT basketball championships, a respectable football season, the junior prom and the senior ball, homecomings, and all kinds of hi-jinks. The half-hour immersion in our common history disposed everyone to the joys ahead. Friday night's dinner/dance began with a cocktail party, a good news/bad news affair. The good news was shrimp; the bad news, oysters. The dinner, buffet-style, was built around prime rib and swordfish steak. Then came the music and dancing. Through a painful undersight, we had a table in the trombone section of the band. Conversation was possible only during breaks, and unlike the bands of yesteryear, these guys played on and on, with hardly a three-bar rest. Saturday opened with breakfast and a class meeting with a briefing on the state of the college, academically, financially, athletically. The AD, another classmate, boasted that we have recruited a world-class shot putter, female, who may double in football, if her schedule allows. Then, to the top of The Hill for the Alumni Picnic. I missed a half hour of the frolic because a reporter for a local paper wanted an interview. It wasn't enough that he asked questions whose answers were available in the PR file, but he distorted my answers all out of recognition. My paralysis is the result of an accident while in service; Bill Kane was a one-time hockey star and, later, hockey coach at HC. To crown the disaster, he had me pose for a photograph with my eyes rolled to an upper corner. I looked demented or retarded or both. After the picnic there was a memorial Mass for our 25 known dead. A canopy in the quadrangle was the site of the pre-banquet cocktail party. The traditional stampede into the dining hall had to be backed up and started over for the Class photograph. Following the banquet most of us moved up The Hill to the piano bar, presided over by a '52 man who knows every song in the Irish hymnal, including some he had to solo. As soon as the singing died, I died, too, though my two-thirty bedtime deprived me of another three hours' fun. Breakfast led to time to spare, we paid a call on the USS Constitution, "Old Ironsides." What a glorious sight to this long-ago midshipman! The final act of the drama was played out at Logan and O'Hare, and I suppose I should count it a mercy that we were neither hijacked nor incinerated, since we were flying American. We got home safe and semi-sound, and time will heal."

As official class correspondent, he followed up in typical Jenks style with a class letter for both those who did and did not attend. He began with more than a page of praise and thanks for the workers on the Arrangements Committee and the "squeeze squad." He then launched into his memories of the affair.

∞

What follows is one man's recollection of the Reunion. The FBI, KGB, and Black Jack McCarthy together couldn't have kept everyone under surveillance. So I must ask, entreat, implore eyewitnesses to come forward with testimony of friends seen and mischief perpetrated. These affidavits will be published in Reunion Revisited (Part II). Your reminiscences are urgently requested.

For now, R25 from this point of view: the whole story could be told in the exuberant embrace PAUL OTIS inflicted on PETE SANDERSON after a dawg's age apart. The hollering and thumping might have been mistaken for assault-to-do-bodily-harm. That took place in the hospitality suite of Mulledy, a room devoted to study in more sober times—or so my Mulledy-ite nephew avers. For the ungolfing and tennisless the hospitality suite was the beginning of tentative recognitions and raucous greetings. PAUL MAY went past without giving the Campion high-sign, frost-bitten fingers curled in salute to Scotty, but LARRY SCHELL broke away from the Northern Ohio group—ART FITZGERALD, FARRELL GALLAGHER, JIM SCARCELLA—to show me a picture of six midshipmen and their dates for the 1950 Naval Ball. Larry married his date, and so did HERB OTTO (not that night, though). The Ohioans were drawn up in defensive formation against attack by holders of Cleveland municipal bonds. JACK LAVEY, improbable Arky, put a quick end to the Longest Hair competition. There was

a 23-way tie for Shortest Hair. Returning tennis players murmured
hard sayings against host, AL BLOCK, who had aced his way
past their overmatched racquets. AL MONGILLO kept looking
over his shoulder, not for a messenger from Don Corleone but for
JACK KEENAN; Al didn't want to repeat his folly of five years ago,
when Jack abducted him for a night-on-the-town. With age comes
wisdom—or at least discretion. As the crowd swelled and bulged
out into the hall LARRY EAGAN squeezed by and warned that if I
couldn't say something thin about him I shouldn't say anything at
all. (   ). So much for Larry. Everyone's second
stop in the hospitality suite was the TV, to watch Mike Cooney's
video history of our days on the Hill. The production used both
still and moving pictures, and those that moved showed young men
flaunting agility, energy, strength, and other impertinences of youth.
Somehow, though, we forgave them.

Friday's dinner/dance began with a voluptuous cocktail party,
held on the slopes of opposing mounds of shrimp and oysters. Wary
gourmands refused to try the oysters because they flunked the ART
GILLIS test. Even with Art's incorrigible Quincy brogue "June" has
no sound faintly resembling "R." THE FEEGEL, casually attired
in whiskers and polka dot shirt, having just come from an Ernest
Hemingway lookalike contest (JACK HUGHES' calumny), held a
barside seminar on the proper ingredients for a best-seller: sex, violence, depravity, gore, and a kitten named Tiglath Pileser. Feeg's *The
Open Convertible* has four out of the five. TONY BENISON, official starter at the golf outing, tried to organize foursomes to go down
the buffet tables. JIM HESSMAN was allowed to play through as a
sixsome, with one plate for himself and one plate for each of those
five chairs he tilted in days of old. The sumptuous offerings included
one concession to nostalgia, swordfish steak; otherwise the chef was
passionately disloyal to Kimball tradition. Fr. MIKE MATARAZZO
felt at home in the winey environment. He worked Skid Row apostolate in Flint, Mich., for years. Mike's smile is his halo. At our table
BOB BOARDMAN refused to pass the salt to anyone who couldn't
name the state flower of Vermont, and BOB KANE told that his
youngest brother, the seventh son of a seventh son, was turned away

by Holy Cross and went instead to BC, which may account for the curse that was lifted only two years ago. TOM NUSS had a fascinating story that explained why his town, San Dimas, was named for the Good Thief. Regrettably, the band struck up its music and blew the details out the other ear. Tom is Judge in those parts, and he has yet to come across a latter-day Dismas. With the opening blast from the band, conversation became a crash course in lip-reading. But it's a near certainty that JOHN IRWIN admitted to steady employment with New England Bell since graduation. He asked me to notify the culprits that NE Bell hasn't closed the file on the Great Pay-Phone Swindle. Nuclear engineer JIM ALLEN has taken to the woods on weekends and vacations to avoid Jane Fonda's frenzied questioning about his tunnel-to-China project. JOHN PHELAN was one of many reunioners who had hopped from graduation to graduation, at every level of schooling, before landing at last on the Hill. John told of EARL LAVERY's fantastic success as football coach at Fairfield Prep—several state championships and an unrivaled won-lost record over the past 20 years.

BOB PERRY and another old Washington hand traded tales of CREEPs they had known. Then Bob confided his "X." had been passed on to another generation because his daughter had taken Xavier for a confirmation name, not, as the surprised bishop supposed, in honor of the Jesuit missionary but in honor of her dad. Over the blare of trumpets playing "Cherry Pink and Apple-Blossom White" RAY CHARETTE seemed to say that he used these Classletters to motivate his two sons to write clean, spare prose. (Positive or negative reinforcement?) In any low-suds soap opera MORT BUCKLEY's early departure would have been prompted by emergency surgery on Bert Parks. But no, the unglamorous truth is that Mort had to chaperone his daughter's junior-high prom. A real-life investigative reporter, ART MURPHY of Variety, asked when the Classletter would offer coverage of knavery, chicanery, barratry, simony and sloth. It pleased me to quote from RALPH PUGLIANO's latest green slip: " 'Out of the depths etc . . .' Since I last penned you, dear Will, I have gone the route of all "good" entrepreneurs one more time. Went broke again in April 1978. However, several lawsuits, a lost home, and one grand jury indictment later I struck once more. Now selling franchises for Realty World." HUGH FRENCH, erstwhile first-sacker, confessed to frequenting Fenway, where he is on a first-name basis with Frank Lynn, Dick Burleson, and Calvin Fisk. Hugh is expanding his insurance agency to several outlying towns and is looking for aggressive young persons to join him. A few hardy parties outlasted the band, but for the most part the revelers went to bed at a prudent hour. One unnamed night rider forgot his room number and wandered the corridors, knocking at vaguely familiar doors. In time someone took him in.

For fitness fanatics like MIKE KUHN and HARRY HILL, Saturday began with an invigorating trot around the campus. For the rest of us it began sensibly, with a 5000 calorie breakfast. That was followed by a Class meeting, status reports on the college from faculty member PAUL MC MASTER, administrator Fr. GEORGE O'BRIEN, and directors of athletics and recreation, RON and TOGO. During a question-and-answer session JIM DALY, speaking out of a Chicagoan's pragmatism, asked Ron why HC didn't go after a couple of gorillas to enhance its sports program. NEIL MURPHY, professor of law at Pittsburgh, recounted that school's costly quest for a national championship. As soon as the present and the future had been thoroughly discussed, the past came alive in the Perry & Palazzi Show. A shill in the crowd asked Ron if Togo had ever passed the ball to him, and that set off a bantering argument about both occasions. Nobody wanted it to end, but the schedule called for adjournment to the top of the Hill for the all-classes picnic. There were rumors of a challenge volleyball match with '59, but the absence of paramedics suggested that sanity had won the day.

The afternoon was meant for growing corn, not for throwing Frisbees. Of course, POKARDAS CHATANI retained his cool and his charm through the height of Fahrenheit. One wife, who shall remain nameless out of respect for HOWIE (not Sen. NOLAN, who, with FRANK LASCH, had gone back to Albany for the day to shepherd legislation through the Assembly)—anyhow, this weirdo wife flitted from table to table, brandishing a compound-fractured tennis racket and asking if anyone would be offended at her wearing a shower curtain to the banquet. The heat was so oppressive a few people gave her serious replies.

The long descent from playing fields to the Jesuit chapel allowed a passage from pandemonium to quiet, as we came together for the Memorial Mass, at which the entire class, living and dead, present and absent, became one again. The liturgy was concelebrated by Fathers JACK WEIMER, JOHN FOLEY, JOE ASHE, MIKE MATA-RAZZO, ROBERT (GEORGE) MORHOUS, GEORGE O'BRIEN and Father Hart, who for that sublime hour belonged to us.

Fr. ROBERT gave the homily which even Readers' Digest would be too sensitive to condense. But with reverent trepidation, I'll try. The homily grew out of the Scriptural passage that ends, "Seek first the Kingdom of God and His holiness, and all the rest shall be added to you besides." Fr. Robert said that when he entered the Trappists more than a quarter century ago he KNEW what the Kingdom of God was. Didn't we all? Now, after years of praying and studying the Word of God, his certainty has given way to question-ing, to SEEKing, to waiting for the Kingdom of God to emerge, and to serving it in whatever form God sees fit to bring it about. That seeking, waiting, serving gives his life profound freedom and unimaginable excitement (as his face and voice evidenced). (Father, forgive me, for I know not what I undo.) Fr. Jack Weimer, principal celebrant, picked up on that theme and invited all of us to let the Reign of God happen in our hearts as we responded to Jesus' offer in the Eucharist. At the Sign of Peace, love was at high tide.

Saturday evening was launched with a canopied cocktail party on the Kimball quadrangle. At Holy Cross even the cocktail con-versation is different. Fr. JOE ASH was telling a group of us that the responsibility for educating coming generations of Catholics in their faith will have to be borne by Catholic college graduates. PHIL BREEN, who may be one of Fr. Joe's parishioners, hid behind Fr. JOHN FOLEY. The call to Kimball had to be recalled, for a class portrait on the center steps. BILL KELLY'S cinemascope camera and cameraperson caught the same scene, with sound, much of which will need editing by Rosemary Wood. The meal sped through soup and salad, accompanied by CHARLIE MILLARD's chanting of the Reunion classes' gifts—8 of 10 in record amounts. With the steak came the suspenseful announcement of 54's contribution. Then Charlie read unsparingly from old Classletters by way of introduction of the speecher, the very author of these chronicles. The hall was hot, but the talk was quick, and nobody mutinied. John Kershaw '60, president of the GAA, presented the In Hoc Signo awards to three devoted alumni, and Father Brooks expressed the school's gratitude for the unprecedented generosity on the part of the Reunion classes. And with the "Ite, missa est" the crowd evacuated the building through every portal. (The hasty exodus allowed PAUL DUPUIS to make Fr. Brooks the magnanimous offer of an additional gift to the College-the 1200 untouched strawberry shortcakes.)

After a resuscitating interlude in the evening air the Purple people sauntered to the Hogan for the dance or the piano bar. The piano player, Bud Moynihan—'52, knew every song from "The Wild Colonial Boy" to "If You Think I'm Sexy." Or he could fake it. Even here '54 led the way. Whenever the choristers lost contact with the lyrics JIM MORAN or BILL TULLY summoned them back to orthodoxy. JIM soloed through opening lines so obscure that George Burns could only have hummed them. DAN GORMAN had to be shoved into the spotlight to do "Danny Boy," though JACK HUGHES insists he has a mini-cassette of the Perry Como version implanted in his sinus. It is alleged that some merriment outlasted the piano bar, but others will have to attest to that. Sunday's breakfast signaled the dispersal. There were warm goodbyes past noon, and then it was done.

Further recollections and impressions will have to await Part II, when they will be discreetly intermingled with your own musing and memories. Permit me parting personal thanks to everyone who lent a hand to pushing me, lifting me, putting me to bed, rescuing me therefrom, or feeding me. If I were to revise my speech to include the Holy Cross kindnesses of Reunion it would double in length. But I will mention only two mercy-workers by name, BILL and Betty KANE. The unnamed are not unvalued. Bill and Betty are named because their early promise to take me and take care of me made the Reunion a sure happening, a fond awaiting through the long winter. And their careful ministering to my bodily needs made the weekend carefree and comfortable. It is just such love that marks the difference between Holy Cross Reunion and anniversary parties elsewhere.

Next time it's your turn. Don't disappoint your readers.

Euphorically, Will

• All of the parenthetical observations were the work of W.H.P.J.

"Suffering—even the smallest annoyance, disappointment, worry—is not something to fear or flee. It is the meeting place with God, where He gives each of us a glimpse of the plenty we can draw from when it's time to move beyond things as they were to a new creation. When we have come to trust His love we will be freer, calmer, braver—ready, if not really eager, for the next encounter with the Cross and the Resurrection."

Will Jenks' testimony at the Ignatian Mass, 10/24/80

CHAPTER ELEVEN

The Visit

THE ADMIRING AND DELIGHTFUL RESPONSES OF THE FACULTY, STUDENTS and alumni to Will's three Holy Cross visits prompted me to realize that, in fact, the number who had had any contact with him were woefully few; he needed more exposure to the college family. How could more students benefit from Will and his example? Essentially, no contemporary students had even seen him other than the 1975 grads. Although his 1979 Silver Anniversary address to the reunion alumni had been printed and distributed, how could his impact encompass the entire student body?

Pondering this, on March 5, 1980, I wrote Father Brooks with the idea that since others are now becoming aware of the tremendous resource which Holy Cross had in Will Jenks, that it would be most worthwhile if we could get Will up to Holy Cross. It was a shame that he was sequestered in Mundelein when his ability to uplift and motivate people could be used for a few days on campus. Will could participate in some classes and the non-programmed learning sessions.

Travel logistics and care would be easy. Some sturdy young men with a modicum of common sense and attention to Will's instructions could readily minister to all his needs. Based on my own experience, it would be an honor to be a selected volunteer. Will was agreeable to my idea provided the visit remain informal.

Within a week Father Brooks responded enthusiastically to both Will and me mentioning that a schedule for next semester's visit was in progress. Will told Father not to feel obliged to create "some extraneous event to save my ego. I went along with the open-ended proposal because I didn't want to interfere with God's strange ways."

Fr. Brooks advised the College community of Will's impending visit for the week of September 21. "Will's interest in and love for the College knows no bounds and I am convinced that the entire Holy Cross community can only be enriched by his brief stay among us. His wit and wisdom will both charm us and inspire us," Father assured all.

The daily schedule was organized to suit Will's preferences, which included his attending classes "at all levels, in disciplines new and old to Holy Cross. Unstructured meetings with student leaders, junior faculty members, the chaplains, off-campus students, a librarian, a corridor maid, and a player to be named later would give me a variety of perspectives on the school," he wrote Father. "The play of chance will fill the interstices."

Will planned to audit more than a dozen classes, and was invited to speak to the President's Council Saturday morning. Father Harman, John Jenks, '81, and some other students met Will Sunday, September 21 at Logan airport, arriving on campus in time for dinner.

A high typing table and an electric typewriter were obtained, as was a hydraulic lift to facilitate his bed-wheelchair transfers. An infirmary room with a hospital-height bed was chosen for its easy access and the proximity of an adjacent room where someone would sleep within earshot, allowing Will to sleep more soundly.

The Mass of St. Ignatius of Loyola was offered in celebration of Will's visit at the Loyola Chapel for the Jesuit Community on Wednesday, September 24 with the theme "Turn to God with your whole heart and soul!" Following the two readings and gospel, Will spoke of his own experience with suffering and the Way of the Cross:

"In the long-ago age of forbidding Catholicism—in both senses of the word forbidding—we came to understand suffering in terms of the Stations of the Cross and the Sorrowful Mysteries of the Rosary. The scourge, the crown of thorns, the nails, the heavy beams seared into our young minds the frightening truth that suffering is pain, physical, violent pain. And nobody bothered to take me beyond the symbols to the meaning. You can imagine how excited we were to answer Jesus' invitation—no, command—to 'take up your cross and follow me.' There was a line from the fifth station—Simon of Cyrene carries the Cross—when we were made to say, "I do not reject the Cross as Simon did; I accept it; I embrace it; I accept the tribulations Thou has destined for me until Death." Mental reservation (the moral equivalent of crossed fingers) had its most creative moments at that fifth station.

"It was out of that ignorance that I had to find strength to face my personal introduction to Jesus' Cross," Will continued. "For the first year there was pain enough to wear out a platoon of scourge-swingers. But when the torture relented the real suffering began. Loneliness, emptiness, frustration—and all the other anguishes a Kafka hero endures—were mine. I would explain that polio did not thwart some high ambition. I had nothing in mind for my life—only a vague, possibly groundless expectation of doing something and being rewarded for it, both immediately and in the hereafter.

"I won't take you along my own Way of the Cross, partly because it doesn't divide neatly into episodes. What I want to tell you is about the Fifteenth Station—the Resurrection. That is the whole truth of the Cross. Father Brooks once wrote to me, 'I see the Resurrected Christ in you.' If that had been meant as a compliment it would have been blasphemous, to say nothing of embarrassing. But his meaning was theological, giving expression to his faith in God's obsession with making something out of nothing, not just at the Beginning, not just at Easter, but again and again in all our lives, whenever what seemed to be real and right and constant falls apart.

"The Resurrection God worked in me took longer than three days. He turned over the work of bringing me back to life, of creating anew, to the people who made up my world—my family, my friends and neighbors, and, in a special way, Holy Cross. It took time for me to recognize God's presence in their loves, to understand that the miracle I had prayed for was happening in ways far more 'miraculous' than I had hoped. I wanted to find a quick return to the road I had been traveling before polio took me on a detour. Instead,

I was shown a way through—not out of—suffering. My guide through purgatory was Father Pat Cummings, who had been my teacher and confessor here at Holy Cross. Over 18 years he counseled me—always patiently, tactfully, wisely—in 3300 letters. It would put limits on God's love and power to suggest that He could not have found a better way to restore me to wholeness. But I count that friendship the best of God's mercies.

"There is more to the story of my miracle, my Resurrection—and much of it has to do with Holy Cross, but I am a devout believer in brevity. So I will end with this thought: Suffering—even the smallest annoyance, disappointment, worry—is not something to fear or flee. It is the meeting place with God, where He gives each of us a glimpse of the plenty we can draw from when it's time to move beyond things as they were to a new creation. When we have come to trust His love we will be freer, calmer, braver—ready, if not really eager, for the next encounter with the Cross and the Resurrection."

After Mass and dinner, the Friends of Loyola, made up of the Society of Jesus at the College of the Holy Cross presented Will with their IGNATIAN Award. It proclaimed "that even a sickness which radically alters the course of one's life can become not only sanctifying, but also an effective means of apostolic ministry to others—to the glory of God."

Friday night Will attended the black-tie dinner of the President's Council wearing a colorfully elegant formal plaid dinner jacket. At the dais sat Rev. John E. Brooks, S.J., '49, John J. Cummings, Jr., '44, President's Council Chairman, Charles E. F. Millard, '54, Board of Trustees Chairman, and Edward Bennett Williams, '41, keynote speaker for the dinner. Charlie couldn't resist the chance to needle Will's choice of apparel by sending me a note asking if I could identify my odd tablemate "in the plaid." When I showed Will the note, as Charlie knew I would, Will broke into a huge grin which promised Charlie to expect retaliation in Will's next class letter. One of our other tablemates was Jack Rehm, '54. Saturday morning Will participated in the Council Symposium, by noon we were off for the game at Cambridge, and that evening we flew back to Mundelein.

Back home, Will penned a composition about his week, which he promptly sent to Fr. Brooks to do with as he saw fit, accompanied by warm appreciation for the wonderful stay at Holy Cross. Fr. Brooks distributed it to each student and graduate "to inform, encourage, and enlist support for the College of Holy Cross."

28 Sept. 1980

Dear Father Brooks,

First, thanks; then apologies . . . It was not hyperbole to call my week at Holy Cross the best week of my life. The climate is invigorating, even rejuvenating. The people, whether behind mahogany desks or work carts or on either end of the pedagogical log, seem moved by a single purpose—to make Holy Cross a place of joy in learning and living. It was my enviable luck to have tasted that joy, though I am one born out of due time. You have my fullest thanks and my pledge of repayment through lifelong work for Holy Cross, beginning—already begun—with a written recollection/reflection . . . The only wart on the face of the week was my having let you down at Saturday's symposium. I'm not sure how or if I could have done it better. The Q/A format served Thomas Aquinas well, but I suspect he had more time to organize his A's. It is indicative of nothing—but curious—that women seemed to like my performance, perhaps because thinking aloud is a feminine mode of thought. However that may be, I hope to atone for my failing with the work underway. I hope to serve Holy Cross in my small way as creatively as you do in your great way . . .

Yours in Jesus, who is there on the Hill, Will

WHAT I DID WHILE WAITING
FOR THE HARVARD GAME

William H.P. Jenks, '54

For most alumni of most colleges, returning to campus has no purpose beyond the sweet reverie of homecomings and reunions, or the bittersweet chore of delivering a son or daughter and stereo. Occasionally there is a chance meeting with a revered professor who can attest that Immutable Truth has withstood the seismic shocks of *Pink Floyd, Animal House,* and *The Scarsdale Diet.* Otherwise, what is known about the life of the college is a matter of observation— buildings come or gone, hair long or short—and faith supported by a patchwork of rumor, statistics, PR, and football scores. And for most alumni of most colleges, that is enough.

But for an alumnus of Holy Cross, there is a different longing to return. The past 20 years have brought such profound changes in the College that there is a curiosity, even an anxiety, about its inner workings, its soul. Those who came to love Holy Cross in a different age have questions. Is the Jesuit cemetery the final resting place of our Holy Cross? Has the elimination of the Discipline Office encouraged rampant hedonism? What has become of the honored phrase, "a Holy Cross man," now that half the students are women? In mid-September it fell my happy lot to return to the Hill for a week, to see things from within, to find answers to my questions. I was there not as visiting lecturer, not as professional evaluator, but as guest and student. As *student,* I attended classes, a piano concert, and the HC-Harvard football game; ate at Kimball twice (the second time, out of sheer bravado, to please a lady); visited the Pub, the post office, the bookstore, and the library; lolled about the beautiful, sun-soaked campus; and participated in three Masses. As *guest,* I was invited to a liturgy and reception given by the Friends of Loyola and a dinner given by my nephew, John Jenks, '81. Out of both perspectives I think I experienced Holy Cross as it is for those who live it.

And what did the week reveal? I found that the mosaic of faith, statistics, PR, and rumor only begins to suggest the vibrant reality. Holy Cross pulses with health, strength, vitality. There is a palpable energy in its learning and living—not just the extravagant energy of the young but the controlled energy of those with purpose. And the purpose, at every level, on every side, is the making of a future pleasing to God, worthy of man. That purpose is anchored by the Jesuit presence at the heart of things, holding fast against the shifting tides of opinion, fashion, impulse.

Because Holy Cross is first of all a place of learning, its most important work goes forward in the classrooms and laboratories, where students are brought up against new ideas, new questions about themselves and their world, in the enduring tradition of the Liberal Arts. In at least twelve of those classrooms (those I invaded) the quality of instruction is excellent. Teaching is in the hands of men and women who know and love both their subjects and their students, so there is elation as well as pain in having the mind stretched in three dimensions.

New ideas, new questions; self, world. Let a few impressions suggest the experience.

In a class on **Modern Drama** a tingle of excitement accompanied the spiraling journey through Strindberg's *Dream Play* to the author's unsettling refusal of resolution. On the way, Professor Whall took us along Strindberg's detour into Eastern mysticism, which underlies the circular movement of the strange work.

Corporate Finance, which promised to be even more mystifying, was in fact brought to unalloyed clarity by Professor J. D. O'Connell, who initiated the corporate financiers into the working of "operational leverage" and "financial leverage." His blackboard calculations ran three decimal places ahead of an electronic abacus.

Father Paris, whose course **Law & Medical Ethics** is attempted at risk to ego, poses questions of public policy, then cross-examines both sides to uncover buried assumptions and presumptions. The exercise readies tomorrow's leaders for the positions of power and influence they will undoubtedly occupy—humbly, if Father Paris' thrusts are remembered.

A different but equally valuable inquiry into preconceptions takes place in the seminar **Women/Their Stages**, where young women are encouraged to examine, without bitterness toward God or men, the conditioning that seems to define their choices. Neither motherhood-times-eight nor the loneliness of the Oval Office is excluded out-of-hand. Professor Hunt actively discourages only choosing without thinking-through. Her feminism—and so the other women's—is honest, good-humored, feminine. Even enemies like *Vogue* magazine excite no fevered resentment.

At a seminar on **Father, Son and Spirit** a select handful of students encounter the eminent Dutch theologian, Fr. Piet Schoonenberg, S.J.—not through a book darkly, but face-to-face. His gentle, unassuming manner reduces the threshold of awe and emboldens the young theologizers to think hard thoughts.

Each of the teachers I observed, whether relating the self to its history, detailing the development of infants, throwing light into the deep mines Heidegger dug, or luring freshmen away from reliance on the *Thesaurus* to carefully crafted writing, filled the classroom with the power and light of the mind. They nobly serve Holy Cross in its chief reason for being.

For their part, the students are aware and proud of their intellectual environment. After each class my "one-time classmates" invariably asked me if I had been impressed by the professor. I never had to equivocate. The students are also proud of the campus, with its twice-prized landscaping and its powerful bronze Rodin sculptures; proud of the reborn library, (a subtle architectural invention, balanced between piety to the past and duty to the future), proud of belonging to Holy Cross.

They have cause to be proud. Every fall the profile of the incoming freshman class gives rise to the suspicion that the perverse scheme for breeding a new stock of supersmart kids actually went into effect two decades ago and the entire herd found its way to Holy Cross. The truth falls short of that surmise, though not by much. Holy Cross students are bright, serious, mature—relatively mature, anyway. The first night of my visit several hundred chanting warriors staged a midnight waterfight. But even those soggy combatants are numbered among an elite destined to lead in their professions, their communities, their country, their Church. And though they realize their Holy Cross education confers immense advantage, they are not prematurely infatuated with their almost-certain success. More amazingly, though many come from homes on the right side of Enough, most of them betray no sense of "entitlement"—Robert Coles' word for the arrogant expectations of kids born rich.

The young people I met were friendly, in the unchanging tradition of the campus, and helpful against the unyielding challenge of the terrain. No one recruited to be my chair-bearer up and down stairs, or to be a member of the Campion Hill twenty-mule team turned me down. Beyond good deeds were the courage and kindness of the eight young men who readied me for the day and undid me for the night. They offered a telling answer to a questioner who once taxed Father Brooks with myopia for stressing qualities of mind over qualities of heart in admitting persons to Holy Cross. The two ways of being are not mutually exclusive. Both Ignatius of Loyola and Francis of Assisi would embrace these eight students—and more, I believe.

The substance of 1980 values could be seen in the choices made against the pull of ease. Students I met at a party, a reception, a bull session excused themselves early in favor of unfinished assignments, but those who had come forward to escort me never missed a rendezvous, never begrudged me a whim that took us off course or off schedule, never begged off or bugged out. In six days I was in the company of perhaps two hundred Holy Cross students who are more than bright, serious, and mature; they are generous in giving and serving; they are loving.

That giving and serving aptly reflect the way the Faith is lived on the Hill. No more is there compulsory observance; no more, directed devotion. Instead, the Christian community joins in prayer and work, in planning and celebration: morning prayer groups, campus ministry, summer apostolates in Appalachia, one-to-one friendships with children of troubled homes, and an everyday work of mercy that feeds Worcester's hungry transients with leftovers from campus kitchens. In casual conversations several students told me their closed-retreat had been the high point of their Holy Cross experience. And other exercitants agreed. ("Exercitants" is impossible Father LaBran's impossible word for veterans of the *Spiritual Exercises of St. Ignatius.*) Even if these young Catholics are only a saving remnant, they will bring great gifts of caring to the Church's service to men and women.

Because 30 years have passed since my student days I was welcomed as though I were a visitor from a small planet in a distant galaxy. What was life like back then? Has Holy Cross changed? Does it seem different with women on the campus? A sudden seminar on "The Olden Days," convened just outside the Post Office, studied a relic owned by Jim Brock, the former postmaster. It was a de-merit chart: 5 demerits for gambling, 3 for watching. Some casuist must have pondered a month before weighing out the guilt. The crime-and-punishment tablets undercut my tales of floggings and defenestrations, but the contrast between then and now made the now-people glad of their timing.

And yes, I averred, women do make a difference, an incalculable difference, a watershed difference. To suggest the effect succinctly, it is now possible for men and women to be friends, coworkers, accomplices, leaders or followers—and nothing more. Who would go back to the old ways?

Now that I have returned from the mountain I am reluctant to pose as the messenger of truth about Holy Cross, though I do think my peculiar circumstances—complete dependence on others for routine wants of living—allowed me to draw closer to the true spirit of the College, a spirit no pep rally could generate. I went loving the Holy Cross I had believed in; I came away loving the Holy Cross I have known. That is my license for speaking my thoughts.

Holy Cross has created a rich seedbed for growth. It has undergone vast changes to prepare its students for the world as it is and will be, but it has held fast to the conviction that a Liberal Arts education and Catholic bearings will serve the future's deepest needs. It is sending forth men and women to do the work of justice and mercy that will shape the life of the next century, whether in creation of a more human society or in opposition to a less human one.

What is at issue is the future of Holy Cross itself. Will it hold and expand its gains in attracting superior faculty and students, or will it bleed away its vitality as it stands defenseless against inflation, demographics, and other impersonal enemies of the private college? In large part, that future rests with those of us who care about Holy Cross, with our response to the $20 million **CAMPAIGN FOR HOLY CROSS**. The purposes of the **CAMPAIGN** are set forth elsewhere. It is enough to say they were defined by the leaders and counselors who have brought Holy Cross to its present stature. Their judgments ought to be taken seriously. But more than Father Brooks' prestige is at stake. Holy Cross, the best Holy Cross, awaits our Yes or No.

It must be Yes.

Will

"I feel obliged to burst the bubble reputation because, to tell the truth, I find nothing remarkable about the everyday Will Jenks."

Will Jenks 1989 reunion speech

CHAPTER TWELVE

The Chair's Parting Thoughts

AN ANONYMOUS HOLY CROSS GRADUATE, IN RESPONSE TO A CHALLENGE grant from the National Endowment for the Humanities, bequeathed a gift of over $1 million to endow The William H. P. Jenks Chair in English Literature in June 1988. Father Brooks called me with the news asking that I speak with Will. He suspected Will might not endorse the honor and hoped I could melt his resistance, persuading him to do so.

From my experience winning Will over to delivering the main address at the General Alumni Association Banquet in 1979 and earlier to his receiving the honorary degree in 1975, I understood that this mission might be more challenging. I called Will, set up a dinner date, and told him that Betty and my daughter Kathleen, would join us. He chose The Fig Leaf Restaurant and I secured dinner reservations along with an advanced request. Betty, Kath and I drove up to Mundelein to pick up Will on the appointed evening.

Once seated at our table, our waiter arrived with an ice bucket and champagne as I had requested; Will gave me a quizzical look but didn't seem too suspicious. I offered a toast to Will Jenks, Doctor of Humane Letters, and he relaxed as the three of us drank to him. Betty then gave him a chance to taste the bubbly from his own flute.

After some conversation, I refreshed the glasses and announced that I had something else to discuss: An anonymous friend of Holy Cross had requested a Chair in English Literature be established in honor of William H. P. Jenks, and the friend had donated over a million dollars to do so. If I was reading Will's facial expressions correctly, he was first startled and then showed chagrin and disappointment; his first sentence being that he couldn't allow such an honor to be paid him when there were others from the college who were far more deserving. I agreed that might be true, but that wasn't the point. The point was that the donor had his or her own reasons for choosing him. Will felt such an honor would be an embarrassment for him since he didn't believe himself worthy and it might be an embarrassment for the college. I reminded him that the college could look after itself, and that it had said, in effect, when they gave him his honorary degree that it judged "the achievements of its sons and daughters by a standard that not everyone will understand." Holy Cross heard a different drummer and, apparently, it was same one that the donor heard.

Pressing a bit, I also reminded Will that I once heard a wise and experienced voice tell his listeners what he had learned from his life, which was: "Let yourself be loved." I urged Will to follow his own advice.

He agreed to consider it, he wanted the weekend to pray for direction. Satisfied, the topic was dropped for the evening. The food and the conversation were both plentiful, and the agape made for a long-remembered evening.

The following Monday Will agreed to the donor's request but with two stipulations: if the donor wished he or she could change his or her mind, and that if the college wished to change its decision it also could. The following day I called Father Brooks informing him of Will's decision.

Shortly after, the student newspaper, the *Crusader,* announced the donation; later the news magazine for alumni/ae, parents of students and friends of the college, *Crossroads,* quoted Will's reaction, "It's an honor out of all proportion, but isn't every honor?" Will also sent a letter to the donor via Father Brooks.

Dear Mr. Anonymous and Mrs. Anonymous (if so):

The thanks I pass through the veil of anonymity are large with joy for Holy Cross and with awe at your generosity. Since you obviously love the school as much as I do, you will understand my joy.

Every good that befalls our college gives reason for rejoicing. If you are embarrassed by my awe you will understand why I offer no thanks for myself. It is awkward to be the medium of such inconceivable bounty, whether honorer or honoree. Has anyone ever expressed compassion for the poor lout in the parable of the seating arrangement, the fellow who was told, "Friend, go up high"? Imagine his chagrin at being singled out for celebrity.

But Bill Kane, who delivered the tidings, reminded me of a small truth distilled out of 28 years of arduous sitting and 17 minutes of agonizing oratory: "Let yourself be loved." And if there has been any life taught to accept the unmerited, immeasurable, unimaginable, it is mine.

So, let it happen, and I will trust future generations to recognize the fathomless humility of your giving, in naming the Chair not for yourself or your family, not even for a sainted teacher or counselor, but for a person with no claim on your affection. I ask only one recompense. When it comes your time, let yourself be loved, in whatever God pleases.

Gratefully,
Will, '54

The class members of 1954 openly speculated about "the largest single benefaction the college has ever received from a living alumnus," according to the *Crossroads* article. We best knew Will and the speculation logically centered upon our own class—and they probably had the most motivation to honor Will. While few or none of us could learn the innermost thoughts or the private money matters of our classmates, there were the "usual suspects."

It wasn't until later when reviewing my paper trail by and about Will that I noticed his honorary degree citation from 1975 was on behalf of William Henry Peter Jenks, which was slight overkill I thought. Peter was the confirmation name he took, but he rarely, if ever, used it nor did it come into use even as an additional initial until many, many years later. I noticed that the publicity and documents related to the upcoming endowed Chair in English Literature was to be called The William H.P. Jenks Chair. This didn't seem like Will to choose that title.

The cover of his speech at the 1979 Alumni Banquet, and most, but not all, of his class letters referred to him as William H. Jenks, rather than William H. P. Jenks, yet the donor wanted the chair to be named for William H. P. Jenks. That seemed odd!

Curious, I reviewed other documents pertaining to Will's life to see how he was referred to. The first example of him being referred to as William Henry Peter Jenks was the letter advising him of his selection for the honorary degree, signed by John E. Brooks, S.J., President, and Joseph R. Fahy, S.J., Dean, on the Board of Trustees of the College of the Holy Cross stationery. The letterhead listed only Donald P. Moriarty, Chairman, Charles E. F. Millard, Vice-Chairman, and W. Barbara Green, Secretary.

A scrapbook created during the summer of 1975 by Wes Christenson, contained many of the hundreds of news clippings collected relative to Will's degree, and it too was designated as belonging to William Henry Peter Jenks, yet none of the clippings referred to William H. P. Jenks; all of them referred to William Jenks.

The 1989 *Crossroads* article specifically notes the gift is to endow The William H. P. Jenks Chair in English Literature. Then sometime later Charlie Millard wrote me on his stationery embossed with a simple "Charles E. F. Millard," and I wondered if he wasn't the one who started the "William H. P. Jenks" ball rolling when he brought Will's nomination before the Trustees' Honorary Degrees Committee. The use of two middle initials is fairly uncommon and more so for someone to adopt the style at forty-three years of age, especially one whose humility was acknowledged by all who knew him. One other alternative is that Will had little or nothing to do with adding his confirmation name to the 1975 degree citation, but that it was Charlie's doing, adding another touch of exclusivity to Will's honorary degree. Besides, there was no way that Will could deny that he was William Henry Peter Jenks.

As Will reveled in word and letter games and puzzles, I strongly suspect he saw who was behind the 1975 name-game, and in my opinion, as soon as Will heard the name of the new chair in 1988, he knew the name of the anonymous donor but kept his silence. To the best of my recollection, Will and I never discussed the possible donor, but in other discussions I had with classmates one name that came up frequently was Charles E. F. Millard.

Charles E. F. Millard, born in 1933, came to Holy Cross from Regis, an all-scholarship Jesuit high school on Manhattan's upper East Side. After serving in the Army, he rose to senior management positions at the advertising agencies, William Esty and Benton and Bowles, Inc. He joined the Coca-Cola Bottling Co. of New York as president in 1967 and was elected CEO in 1968 and chairman in 1970. Under his leadership the company grew in sales from $60 million to $500 million; it was taken private in 1981 and sold in 1986 to the Coca-Cola Company by Millard and the management team. He was also chairman of other businesses as well as director of a number of financial and manufacturing corporations. He served as trustee and chairman of the board of trustees at Holy Cross, the New York Urban League and the Archbishop's Committee of the Laity (Newark, N.J.) and as trustee of a number of other colleges and secondary schools.

In 1998 Holy Cross conferred on him an honorary Doctor of Humane Letters degree. He and his wife, Marylou, having raised eight grown children, divided their time between Florida and Connecticut, until Charlie's death on October 20, 2003.

Charlie and Will in some of life's categories were almost at opposite ends of the spectra, but in other areas they were very similar. Briefly, Charlie had been a "rainmaker" while Will could only pray for rain; Charlie moved in the halls of power and Will lacked the power to move at all; Charlie thrived in New York City, a city of 7,500,000 and Will in Dana, a town of 750. However, both demonstrated extraordinary intelligence, benevolence, ambition, stoic endurance, quiet generosity, devotion to their college, willingness to let themselves love and be loved, and a bedrock faith in their Lord and Savior.

In the late 1990's, Charlie developed a painful musculoskeletal problem, which led him to consult me by phone for whatever input I could offer him. Though we had not been close during college nor afterwards, he and I, after that initial call, subsequently talked every few months or so. He shared with me his views as I shared with him my views—on "onions and kings and all sorts of things."

When he learned of my decision to begin work on Will's biography, he wrote of his desire to help in any of a number of ways. He also sent me a copy of a letter that he was sending to his friends with a copy of Will's speech from June 19, 1979. He explained that he (CEFM) was doing so "with triune motives: a) it is a great speech; b) it is almost custom-fitted and even more relevant to many of us now than it was then; and, c) you may find it personally helpful . . . or you may know someone who will." He wrote that he "had the honor of: a) getting to know Will fairly well in our later years; b) sponsoring him for an honorary degree; c) introducing him on the occasion of this speech (our twenty-fifth reunion); and, d) participating in the establishment of the Will Jenks Chair in English Literature." The last section convinced me that consciously or not, Charlie had tipped his hand to allow even an inexpert bridge player to follow the truism, "One peek is worth a couple of finesses," but I wanted to certify my suspicion.

On September 24, 2001, I called Charlie with some questions with regard to Will and him. I was finding Will to be even more extraordinary in many ways than my earlier estimate, but because much of his correspondence had been destroyed or lost, there remained some persistent questions. After introducing the topic of the Jenks Chair to give Charlie some warning and time to focus on how he was going to react to my line of questions, I reminded him that Will had told each of us to "Let yourself be loved." Charlie replied that he had modified Will's counsel for his own use by adding a final phrase, "to death." That would be his canon: "Let yourself be loved to death." His physicians had recently told him that he had a potentially very troublesome vascular problem and again he was not a candidate for open surgery due to his coexisting medical diagnosis. Sensing that he knew where I was leading, I was pleased he asked what was on my mind. And so I asked if he knew who the donor was. His response was "We did it," acknowledging that he and Marylou had been the benefactors honoring Will. I was pleased that he also felt it was time for the "veil of anonymity" to be lifted. He also admitted that he thought Will knew who was responsible for the Jenks Chair. When I later asked him if he had been instrumental in ensuring that the 1975 degree citation read: William Henry Peter Jenks, his immediate response was: "I have never trusted anyone with four names!"

∞

In anticipation of our upcoming 1989 reunion, Will sent out what appeared to be a standard class letter with only the subtlest hints for the discerning reader about a completely different topic. I certainly didn't pick up on the underlying message during my first reading.

35TH REUNION

June 9, 10, 11, 1989

Reunion Minus Less and Less

Venerable Sirs—

Again we are called home by the mother of our manhood. Anyone who has never returned to these in-gatherings can seize something of the feeling by recalling the first time adult children surrounded the table for a family celebration. Rivalry gives way to love; anger yields to understanding; belonging bonds each to each, without rank or distinction. There's a hymn, from the Far Right of the congregation, that exults, "Oh blissful morning! Oh, glad reunion!," in anticipation of the Really Long Weekend. Even the theologically sophisticated will attest that those three days every five years aptly foreshadow that Glad Reunion. Incentive enough? Then we'll meet bye and bye. (This paragraph fulfills my promise to BARRY, who asked me to echo PAUL DUPUIS' invitation. It was not that it could be said better; it was just that it should be said again.)

Gleaned from questionnaires: BRONC CHATANI was awarded the Prime Minister's medal for his work with Jamaica's poor . . . If there really is a chapter of the Friendly Sons of St. Patrick in Westchester, FRED MARTIN is its president . . . CLEM DELISO hits the boards like Tommy 'Chrysostum' Heinsohn—Board of Mass. Association of the Blind, Multibank, Mercy Hospital, Bank of Western Mass . . . "Call me, Colonel" PAUL OTIS writes 'home' in the Permanent Vacation Address box. Why not? Who would leave San Diego . . . On the other coast JOHN FEEGEL complains, "What vacation?" Which allows alternate readings: the promise of another book or an index of the prosperity of the Law Office of Same . . . Though BOB DORTON may not be known by name among serious observers of the American scene, he is widely respected by Left, Right, and Center for his work. He's news editor of The Wall Street Journal . . . Need a promotion? See DAN GORMAN, whose The Promotion Group, Inc was voted agency of the year in 1986 and 1987. Dan also held office in the Council of Sales Promotion Agencies . . . Our oldest class member, Col. JIM MURRAY, is retired from the USAF and living in Orlando, FL . . . Nowhere does PAT BERRIGAN note continued diversion as a goalie. Maybe someone told him hockey is not a carry-over sport . . . PAT PALUMBO somehow worked it out so that two of his four Purple children will Reunite in the 4 and 9 years. By then with three tuitions two years in a row and two tuitions for three years, the combinations and permutations must be endless . . . How about Kauai for a vacation address? That's JOE DEVANE's getaway . . . MARK FOLEY circled Special Achievements and boasted, "Five kids out of the house." More like a miracle, Mark . . . For sheer class nothing can rival AL BLOCK's 'President, Longwood Cricket Club.' Unless that's the insect, not the game . . . Tempus fugits ad velocitatem lucis. (Which goes a long way toward explaining why the Chair in Classics remains unnamed.) JIM and Ginny ALLEN's late arrival is already eight . . . GARRY DEGERMAJIAN prefers the salutation, Mister Degermajian, the Principal.' None of that egalitarian nonsense for him . . . The champion commute belongs to PAUL NICHOLAS, who gives his home city as Manhasset and his workplace as the University of San'a, Yemen . . . Grafted to PARK SMITH's q'naire was a page from *Home Fashion* magazine, which had named PBS one of its People of the Year . . . "because two little words, Park Smith, convey a fashion statement everyone can understand." If you wondered who loosed the flurry of dhurries on an unsuspecting world, wonder no longer . . .

Greenies again. JERRY O'TOOLE used his to chortle at the misery the weather inflicted on the game last 8 Oct. His Special Achievement is an 8 handicap, hewn to size by regular visits to the country club in Summerville, SC. A twelve-year expatriate, Jerry works as a facilities engineer for the USN. (Maybe 'faculties.' I compressed the word to 'fcltis,' then forgot the vowels.) As his contribution to the ecumenical movement, he has sent a son to the Southern Baptist Theological Seminary.

In other business news, TOM O'LEARY, Pres and CEO of Burlington Resources, made the NY Times when his fiefdom came

under buyout / takeover / siege pressures, which he had managed
to resist. The details defy retelling by someone who never mastered
the complexity of mortgaging Park Place to put a hotel on Marvin
Gardens. For Tom it has been lonelier still at the top since he lost his
brave wife, Barbara, to a remorseless cancer.

Fate has dealt a hard blow to CHARLES GEBRON. His twenty-
seven-year-old son, Matthew, was killed in an auto crash. Matt was a
cabinetmaker, unmarried. A memorial fund has been established in
his name.

One further comment on the Chairing of the Unworthy by the
Unknown: I am quoted as saying, "It's an honor all out of proportion, but then, isn't every honor?" That aphorism is true only of
the honors that have befallen me. I can think of many instances
where an award or recognition has been earned and even cases where
the honor took on added lustre from the association. I will go to
my grave thankful but perplexed—bewildered by the incongruity
between this oatmeal life and its cordon bleu repute. (Holy Cross
is not the only Fantasyland with a Will Jenks House of Illusions. In
Dana, patrons at the town tavern still insist I have bequeathed my
brain to science.)

If you have studied the reports of each year's Alumni Fund campaign, you may have noticed that percentage of participation
increases as the years-since-graduation increase. For the most part
that phenomenon can be attributed to the disappearance of the
previous generation. When parents, teachers, mentors have gone beyond the reach of gratitude—word, gift, or visit—only the enduring
institutions remain, and of these Holy Cross seems most vital, most
important, most deserving. We are entering the watershed years,
the last decade of middle-age, at the peak of earning power, at or
near the end of financial responsibility for younger and older family
members, on the brink of the long decline of our numbers. What
better time than our Reunion year to acknowledge the lasting value
of our Holy Cross education? To sweeten the gift, someone of great
heart and large pockets has promised to match every new dollar up

to $100,000. The moment is ripe with responsibility. Let's pluck it and bring or send it home to Alma Mater.

Notably,
Will

- Will introduces "alternate readings" to refer to John Feegel's complaint, "What vacation?" in the second paragraph of the pre-reunion letter; I now sense Will is dropping another clue to *his* use of "alternate readings" in the first paragraph, namely, "The Far Right" where the righteous and saved souls will congregate in their eternal "glad reunion," and the "Really Long Weekend," when "we'll meet bye and by." By the end of the year he will take his leave of this vale, and he didn't want to leave without at least something of a leave-taking, even if it was camouflaged on first sight, and only later to be perceived for what it was.
- Writing "Tempus fugits ad velocitatem lucis," Will depreciates his skill in Latin purposely; "Time flies at the speed of light" but "fugits" should be "fugit," and Will knows it but the incorrect spelling opens the door to the following parenthetical remark about the "Chair in Classics."]

At the 1989 Reunion, Will gave a speech without cajoling or arm twisting. He had conquered his fear of public speaking, and more than that he wanted to tell his classmates what was on his mind; he wanted to "burst the bubble reputation because, to tell the truth, I find nothing remarkable about the everyday Will Jenks." The entire text follows:

This time I came prepared for two possible introductions—sardonic or sentimental—I would call Paul's tone sardonic. [Paul F. Dupuis, '54, had introduced Will.] And nothing could have pleased me more. It makes me feel part of things to suffer the zings and arrows of outrageous Dupuis. I like to think my affability suggests that irreverence, in good taste, is welcome. In fact, that's the very tone I'll take in developing my theme, the demythologizing of Will Jenks and its meaning for mankind.

I feel obliged to burst the bubble reputation because, to tell the truth, I find nothing remarkable about the everyday Will Jenks. Over the years so many fictions have sprung up about me that I keep looking over my shoulder to see who people are staring at. In a recent class letter I told of the reigning myth at the Dana Tavern, the one that says I'm going to leave my brain to science. I have no idea how that started. I do know that Frankie, the bartender, used me as his personal almanac to settle arguments.

One time I had to relocate the Yalu River, which some of the boys had moved down to the border between North and South Korea. Another time, to my shame, I bluffed my way through a question I still don't understand, something about the length of a day on the moon. How I jumped from the reference shelf to the pickling jar is beyond reckoning. Then there was the rumor that I wrote children's books.

The nearest truth is that I wrote with a childish scrawl when last I practiced penmanship. More likely, it came of my habit of entertaining young porch-visitors with ghost stories. The few I invented are better left in the oral tradition, out of reach of child psychologists. Another fiction came straight from that usually reliable source, the women's john at Walgreens. A friend overhead two cleaning women discussing that 'nice old man in the wheelchair who smiles at all the ladies.' They convinced each other that the geezer is a member of the Walgreen Family.

Otherwise why would he be allowed to roam the corridors of world headquarters? Believe me, I've done nothing to discourage that misconception. In fact, I'm working on ways to channel it through middle management. Probably the most embarrassing misreading of my fate is the idea that I endure excruciating pain. I have been told, by people in real pain of their own, that they have drawn courage from my example. What was I supposed to say? That after the first few years polio ceased to give me the slightest twinge? Or nothing, to keep another's courage intact? I've played it both ways.

Almost as blushable is the notion that I "Deserve" the good things that have befallen me. I remember the first time the word was misused. I had returned from a week-long tour of California, and a neighbor comments, "I'm glad for you. You deserved a vacation." This, from a man who worked as a hired hand, at modest wages and without vacation, to a man who spent two hours a day tutoring. Nobody this side of the lottery winners is further from deserving his good luck—in family, friends, gifts—both heavensent and man-made—and certainly, in his life's course. What you see before you is an ordinary man who has been extraordinarily blessed and heralded way out of keeping with his deeds.

By way of contrast, let us now praise famous men—two of our own, famous only among our ranks and here only after their deaths. They will stand in place of all the others whose good works have surfaced in obituaries, at wakes, in belated awards, distant recollections, and chance conversations. Their common principle is the Ignatian determination to take arms against a sea of troubles, and by oppos-ing, end them. Consider John Rogers. It came to light to most of us on reading The Posthumous Tribute from his hometown paper that he had worked so long and so hard to improve the lot of the re-tarded in the state of Maine. He was not content simply to lobby the legislature for state support of schools for those lifelong children; he devoted his days and years to assuring the quality of those schools.

Or consider Tony Turo, who was praised for his service to the least of our brethren in a eulogy offered as consolation to his mourning family. If Father George O'Brien hadn't tracked down his obitu-ary, how many of us would have known he had been an exemplary Christian? . . . Their lives—and those like theirs—raise a greater question. There is an incongruity between quietly heroic lives, honored by the few, and the brief heroics of one-time life-savers, celebrated by newspapers and networks from coast to coast. Why does a nation rejoice over the rescue of a single child trapped in a well and then turn a blind eye to the shame of millions of children left unrescued in the ghettos and backwaters of this country and the world?

The fault lies with our imaginations and those who inform them. There is an equivalence and a difference between the moment of peril and the long-term pathology, and there must be someone to illuminate both for those who would bring relief. If we can begin to understand lives that embody a complete drama—the problem, the working-thru, the resolution—we may find clues to the working-thru of the larger problems. Perhaps it's to avoid involvement that people seem intent on supplying a miraculous medal to my drama. Somewhere between the problem I obviously carry in my body and the resolution to be read on my face there must be a mysterious infusion of strength to account for my unlikely outcome.

That would seem to send the larger problems back to God. I can't pretend that the test I have been sent has been beyond human resources or that it took a personal Pentecost to see me thru to the joy my smile discloses. On the other hand, I'm not too sure how it did happen. I do know my worst days were times of self-pity, what Thomas Aquinas called "despondent sadness," and the best days were times of grateful acceptance and glad giving of love. There has been nothing superhuman at work within me, nothing secret about my success. If anyone would examine my life in a glimpse, let him listen to my thanks, let him heed the whole context of life in the names I thank—many of them Holy Cross names—Cummings, Hart, Brooks, Miller, Kane, Weimer, O'Grady, Rollins, Hill, Millard, Robinson, McGrath, McDonough—and on and on. In those names I have found my strength and God's grace. And that has been enough.

Will's last Class Letter arrived in the midst of the 1989 football season proclaiming:

After the fall from the ranks of the unbeaten
Fasten your seatbelt!
This will be a full-throttle, straightahead run, without digression. Otherwise we may find ourselves overrun by a miniature sled and eight tiny reindeer. Besides, if we are to be fueled by memories of Reunion we had better tank up before evaporation robs us of thrust. So, let's launch this missive before the metaphor outweighs its lifting power.

At the risk of being redundant I invite us to recelebrate '54's record-breaking 35th Reunion gift, already given its first Hoiahs in BARRY MCDONOUGH's letter and in the CROSSROADS.

Our $350,000-plus effort won kudos for Chair BARRY, co-gift-leaders JACK REHM and CHARLIE MILLARD, and secretary WILL JENKS. The honors belong equally to the faithful agents and all our check-writers. The Alumni Office presented small Revere bowls to members of the Gang of Four, but there should have been 150 more, one for each '54 man. Until equity reigns, words will have to do. A hoiah a piece, then.

At the Reunion I used a minute of my mike time to ask the literate brethren to supply accounts of the three days for this edition of the Classletter. The response was not-quite-whelming. JOE CORRY came through with a photo album and a two-page reminiscence, and HENRY NIETSCHMAN offered several group shots of the occasion and a paragraph of eye-witness testimony. JOE GUM-MERSBACH came through with a note.

Gad, hoist by my own petard! I lied earlier when I said that this edition would be straightahead, full-throttle. I had already hammered the greenslips down to papyrus replicas, which I had planned to slip into place as soon as the true beginning had been fabricated. But the Muse Fickle awayed with the dangerous copies and left a laughing blackhole in its space. So now, much later, having prayed to be delivered out of nothingness, I accept the answer to my prayers and observe the radical sequence of events: let the first be the first, and let Poland be Poland. (They're coming to get me for sure after that inburst.)

Writing in an equally one-dimensional squiggle, KEV ROCHE sighs, "Nest to us alone, at last! Two married, two engaged, one very eligible." Jo has switched careers from nursing to social work. The school teacher's leisurely summers allow such indulgences as a 1987 sailing rendezvous with roommates DAN GORMAN and LARRY McGRATH. That same year Kev had a Fulbright to the U.K., plus travel from Belfast to Cairo and Majorca to Turkey. Summer '89 found him at Harvard as an NEH fellow in lyric poetry. You Donne us proud, Kev.

Father ROBERT (George) MORHAUS, OCSO thanks Barry for the Class directory—as do we all—and asks to retract his business phone number. Ma Bell's feelings will be hurt, but that marketing strategy should make his cheeses all the more covetable.

Ms. Leslie Ann Mines tipped over the bushel basket her boss hides his light under, to alert us that the Home Tex Design Awards for 1989 have been announced and—guess what!—her boss was one of six honorees. Hint: he's that 'flurry of dhurries' man.

Answer to Mystery Tex Design awardee: PARK B. SMITH. Gotcha!

Out of the past come the thundering words of the great mate, HEAVEY. JERRY-of-which writes again. And he claims he's now VP for Corporate Communications, The One Bancorp, a $2.5 billion asset bank holding company in Portland, ME. He's remarried to Janet Jarman Heavey and seeking reconciliation with JIM HESS-MAN, BERNIE 'DIZ' MORIN, Col. OTIS, and myself, erstwhile co-Campionite.

How's this for an alibi (as you no doubt remember, that's Latin for 'elsewhere' and Sicilian for 'haha, haha')? BRUCE HOEFFEL says he was in Russia Reunion weekend. He's Director, Hum Resrc, for 3M, in St. Paul.

Too often, word of a classmate's death is just that—a word, 'died'—and the crude limning of a life in the few short lines of a family census. Unless Father GEORGE O'BRIEN chances on fuller obituary or a fellow '54man comes forth with a eulogy, we are left to shirk every duty but generic prayer. To remedy that pathology, we should consider some strategy to counter the slide into indifference. I have a proposal, which you are free to reject, revise, or replace. It's this: each of us should write a reflection on his own life and entrust a copy to a healthy friend or, perhaps, the Alumni Office, with instructions to publish in the Classletter when it is beyond updating. (How's that for euphemism?) That way we are assured a favorable review and a final glimpse of the whole man. Any other suggestion will be offered for consideration. Please give thought to the problem. It is an embarrassment to our history and an impediment to our spirit.

Almost too painful to relate, CHARLIE GEBRON's consecutive greenslips, the first, recounting the establishment of the Gebron Family Scholarship Fund, honoring the memory of his parents and his three sons, and the second, passing along news of his wife Marilyn's death in September. She was a great Christian, who could always smile, despite the loss of three sons." Your prayers are requested.

My own recollection of Reunion '89 bounced out my van window when we hit a Chuck Hole in Rochester. That was his name, honest to Ollie.

Yours for Primal Chaos,
Will

"We can facilitate a very rapid discharge home . . . Psychologically, this is very important for the patient."

Dr. Michael Greenberg

CHAPTER THIRTEEN

Bumps in the Road

"THE ONLY THING BILL EVER COMPLAINED OF WAS HOW NICE IT WOULD be to have a shower," recalls Madelyn Bussing Hendrix. "When they moved to Mundelein, their house had a big shower. They would wheel him into it, leave the shower door open, and turn on the water. He thought it was wonderful."

The 1973 move to Mundelein required new physicians to oversee Will's medical treatment and care, especially since Will developed pneumonia in September of '73 requiring a brief hospitalization. Will first became a patient of internist Dr. Michael Greenberg, who treated him for upper respiratory tract infections and/or urinary tract infections, both related to his paralysis due to the polio. Because Will's rib cage musculature and diaphragm were partially paralyzed, he couldn't expand his lungs normally, nor could he cough as strongly causing greater susceptibility to respiratory tract infections. Aside from his history of bilateral kidney stones, which led to the removal of his right kidney in 1969, his inability to bear down with his abdominal wall musculature to help complete urinary bladder emptying led to chronic residual urine remaining in the bladder, a factor also disposing to infections. These two problems would persist over the remainder of Will's life and represented potentially significant threats to his health and well-being.

Dr. Robert C. Munson, Jr., also an internist, joined Dr. Greenberg on the staff at Condell Memorial Medical Center, Libertyville, in 1978, and the two shared caring for Will's and his mother's medical problems.

In 1979, Will's Walgreen Company pre-employment physical indicated he was "found to be in relatively good health" with a normal electrocardiogram and a normal set of blood values.

Around Thanksgiving 1981, Will felt like he had an acute flu attack with fatigue, chills and fever. The fatigue increased in early December and by mid-December he developed severe right-sided flank pain, worsened by motion of his torso. There was no history of a back injury, yet Will described the ache as deep, not superficial. A white cell count was elevated but other lab tests including chemistries were normal, so Will tried to ignore the pain for two more weeks until he returned to Dr. Munson on December 30 for a scheduled appointment.

At that visit, he "appeared toxically ill," with severe right flank pain "over the scar of his previous nephrectomy site." His white cell count was now definitely elevated, his hemoglobin was in the anemic range and he had a temp of 100 degrees. He was immediately admitted to Condell Memorial Hospital, and placed on antibiotics for suspicion of an intra-abdominal abscess, perhaps at the site where his right kidney had earlier caused him so much trouble. Multiple imaging studies were performed without a conclusive diagnosis; recurrent pain and fever spikes caused his inpatient stay to extend until January 14, 1982, when he was discharged with the diagnosis of chronic gallbladder inflammation, a paravertebral intramuscular abscess at the previous nephrectomy site, and recurrent urinary tract infection.

At various times in Will's hospital charts, Dr. Munson reports that the patient was "very anxious to go home" and "very eager to go home." It is a testament to Will's stoicism that he ignored his increasing fatigability [due to anemia] for over a month and worsening flank pain for over two weeks [due to the abscess and the inflamed gallbladder] until he was ready to appear in a doctor's office, "toxically ill." When he showed even marginal improvement, he wanted to leave the hospital.

While he was indeed eager to return home, there was also the matter of his job. His "office" was in his bedroom and most of his Walgreen work performed there in addition to the twice-weekly visits to the Walgreen information center for conferences. Will did not want a protracted absence from his work to jeopardize his employment, his sense of accomplishment in returning to compensated work, and his release from the dissatisfaction of earlier having had obligations of only his own choosing; in his view, Walgreens had paid him a high compliment by hiring him, and he would repay them with his loyalty and attention to their needs. His work area allowed him a greater degree of independence than a hospital room—the independence to type letters, to read with his page-turning rubber-tipped wands, to make and receive phone calls, and to continue computer programming for Walgreens. Aside from welcomed medical and nursing staff interruptions, the two-plus weeks' hospitalization would have been a boring interlude, with the added worry that his job status might be at risk.

In late November of 1983, it was Will's left knee which began to bother him and had done so again without any recognized injury. The knee region became reddened, swollen, warm and tender. He was seen at the Greenberg/Munson office where the knee was aspirated and the joint fluid sent for culture that might indicate possible infection of the knee joint. Hospitalization was recommended and Will called me for the name of an orthopaedic surgeon who could direct his in-hospital care, preferably in a hospital near Mundelein. Since I was not on staff at any hospital in his area, I recommended Dr. Gregg M. Moga, a well-regarded orthopaedist, who practiced in Lake Forest, IL, and was on staff at that city's hospital. He also happened to be the older brother of Dr. Jerome J. Moga, from the class of '54, who also practiced orthopaedics in Westchester County, just north of New York City. Dr. Moga admitted Will to Lake Forest Hospital on November 23 and ordered a standard work-up including a peripheral blood count which showed an increased number of white cells, a finding which supported the diagnosis of a potentially inflamed, or even infected, joint. Will's infection could have evolved from bacteria in the blood stream from a recent calf wound or it could have come from his recurrent urinary tract infection, which was detected by the appearance of white cells seen on urinalysis.

With the subsidence of fluid within the knee, and continued improvement in his appetite and sense of well being, the antibiotics were switched from intravenous to oral and Will was discharged home on December 8, to continue oral antibiotics for another three weeks and to use a stabilizing knee brace as needed for comfort. Dr. Moga prescribed daily Betadine cleansing of the sore on the calf to help keep it clear of bacteria. Will's knee continued to mend at home and Dr. Moga later wrote to say symptoms had thoroughly disappeared.

In late January 1985, Dr. Greenberg admitted Will to Condell for left leg deep venous thrombosis [DVT]. Pain had developed four or five days earlier, and John observed that the left ankle was red but not swollen a day later. The pain increased and Will's morning helper felt a "cord" in the back of the thigh; the same night he couldn't sleep for the pain and finally Will called Dr. Greenberg and asked if he would make a house call, which he did. Dr. Greenberg couldn't be certain of a DVT but was sufficiently suspicious to bring him by ambulance to Condell where a venogram was performed when radio-opaque dye was injected into the venous system to see if a normal flow existed. Since it was blocked, Will was admitted to the hospital and treated with heparin, an anticoagulant to reduce the likelihood of a pulmonary embolus, which is a fragment breaking off the main clot in the leg and being capable of moving to the lung, which can be lethal. Here again the quadriplegia bore a causal relationship; Will's legs, while he was sitting most of the day, were always in a dependent position and Will's atrophied and paralyzed muscles could not "milk" the veins, which is the normal way the blood from the feet and calves is moved back up to the heart, assisted by venous valves which prevent the blood from flowing backward down the legs. Given the factors that increased Will's risk of DVT, Dr. Greenberg dictated in his initial admission note, "It amazes me that the patient has not had a DVT in the past." His treatment plan included intravenous infusion of the heparin for 7 to 10 days, checking the coagulability of the blood so that it was within a desired range, pain medications, elevation and heat for symptomatic relief, followed by the initiation of an oral anticoagulant, coumadin, so that "we can facilitate a very rapid discharge home, where the patient is obviously more comfortable . . . Psychologically, this would be very important for the patient." Dr. Greenberg thoroughly understood how valued the Walgreen employment was to Will's psyche; he noted the degenerative joint disease "as recognized in his spine, knees and ankles on previous films." Will was allowed home on an oral anticoagulant regimen on February 3, 1985, with a non-steroidal anti-inflammatory medication for his arthritis and an antibiotic for his continuing urinary tract infection. Four days later Dr. Munson was called because of a very dark, almost black, bowel movement, and on a house-call he diagnosed Will with gastrointestinal tract bleeding, advising him to return to the hospital, however Will refused. That day his hemoglobin was 9.8 grams—down from his normal of 11 or 12. The anti-inflammatory medicine, which might have caused gastric lining irritation, was discontinued and instead he was prescribed an analgesic that would not cause gastrointestinal bleeding nor exaggerate coumadin's anticoagulant effect. He was also started on medications formulated to diminish gastrointestinal irritation and to neutralize his gastric acid.

Will seemed to stabilize over the next few days while at home, but on February 10th his morning aide, Ann Gerstenbrand, found him very pale with an increased pulse rate. Dr. Greenberg had him brought to the E.R. and once there he was found to be very pale, with a pulse of 120 and a rapid respiratory rate. His anticoagulant regimen had led to the gastrointestinal bleed, which in turn, had led to a severe anemia with a hemoglobin of only 3.9 grams requiring a number of whole blood transfusions; antidotes to the coumadin were begun, and Will was admitted to the intensive care unit. His cardiac exam and EKG were within normal limits aside from the rapid rate. Dr. Greenberg obtained consults from Dr. B. Miller, a surgeon, and Dr. E. Kirch, a specialist in gastroenterology. Despite the still-present risk for a pulmonary embolus, the active bleeding had to be considered the prime problem and the anticoagulant regimen was discontinued. On February 12, 1985, Dr. Kirch performed an upper gastrointestinal endoscopy to visualize the esophagus, stomach and duodenum, finding no obvious source of bleeding. Thirty-six hours later, after replacing the lost blood, Will showed some signs of congestive heart failure, which quickly responded to oxygen and a diuretic; however, it did signal that his ability to manage the physiological alterations in a number of his organ systems was diminished. The multiple equibrium points which are constantly being watched by the body's monitoring systems were not as readily stabilized in Will as would have normally been the case, absent the proximate and remote consequences of his polio paralysis. With no evidence of active bleeding, upon discharge February 13, 1985, Will restarted a low dose anticoagulant program with coumadin.

He avoided hospitalization and enjoyed relatively good health from 1985–1988, for which he was very grateful.

"I had discussed not ventilating him in case of failure and Mr. Jenks said 'no heroics and that he had lived a full life.'"

Dr. Robert C. Munson, Jr.

CHAPTER FOURTEEN

Another Reunion

WITH THE START OF 1989, ON MONDAY, JANUARY 23 WILL WOULD END what he described as "a four-year stretch of doctorlessness when I meet my MD in his parking lot for a quick physical. There's nothing grievously wrong with me, just a bunch of annoying problems—fitful sleep or unappeased drowsiness, morning hoarseness and sinus congestion, swollen ankles, internal hemorrhoids. All or none of those complaints may be associated with Post-polio Syndrome, a mysterious affliction that seems to strike people who have lived 35 or 40 years with residual effects of polio. In some cases, victims have had to return to a respirator. Most of all, I need to be reassured that the wheels aren't coming off the wagon." [Fr. L.J. Moran, 21 Jan. 1989]

Will "nailed" the diagnosis and it is certain that his symptom complex, which had only been recently named, had attracted more than a little of his attention, especially after the death of his morning aide, Willard Tonyan, also a polio survivor, nine years earlier, as the result of cardio-pulmonary failure.

Two months later Dr. Munson saw Will in his office when mild congestive heart failure developed. This indicated the heart was becoming incapable for a variety of reasons of preventing edema fluid from accumulating either in the peripheral tissues or the lungs. Dr. Munson treated him with a digitalis preparation that strengthened the cardiac contractility and a diuretic that helped rid the body of excessive fluid. Will improved rapidly and markedly.

Shortly thereafter, Will took delivery of a customized van. According to John, Will had been obviously hesitant to purchase the van, dilly-dallying over whether he needed it or not. John now believes that Will's reluctance reflected his doubt that he would get much use out of it. He had been getting

147

sleepy at odd times, and the congestive failure was similar to what Willard experienced before he passed away. Will may have suspected a similar course was beginning for himself—an unspoken concern or premonition.

With the new van's improved transport, John and Will decided to drive the one thousand miles to Worcester for Holy Cross' 35th reunion and then visit Saugus, MA, the site of the first American iron works which was built by Joseph Jenks, Sr., 1603–1683, the family's progenitor, and to visit Pawtucket, founded by his son, Joseph, Jr.

At the reunion, many classmates noticed that Will had lost some of his vitality; he was less energetic in his conversation and less assured in his recall. I was his roommate again for the weekend, and it was apparent to me that he was having increased difficulty in his routine activities—such as giving me directions and instructions during his morning grooming and nighttime preparations. Many concerned classmates asked me about Will, and I did my best to deflect the questions. I pointed out that Will had made the trip out from Mundelein in the new van, with John, and that meant sitting in his wheelchair for 1000 miles, a trip that would have fatigued any of us. While I was not privy to all of Will's medical background, I was a partner in some of his care, and felt it inappropriate to discuss his medical status with our classmates.

Following the reunion, Will and John did their sightseeing and returned to Mundelein the second week of June.

On Sunday, June 18, 1989, Will called Dr. Munson complaining of a sensation of heart "palpitations." An EKG showed a heart block [a disruption of the electrical signal system within the walls of the heart] and a pulse rate down in the 60's; his digitalis medication dose was reduced and a follow-up EKG was back to normal. A couple of days later John drove Will down to the Dana farm for a few days' visit. Just before the planned return to Mundelein, John left Will with some friends in Dana, and drove to Montezuma, ten miles east of Dana to meet Jim, only to learn that Jim couldn't meet up with him. Returning, John found Will sleeping, which he was doing more and more. During the previous winter, for example, Will had fallen asleep occasionally during meals and even during a basketball game—two activities which usually kept his interest at a peak.

John relates that when he saw Will sleeping, he gently nudged the wheelchair without waking him. John finally roused Will by shaking him softly and telling him, apparently now awake, that Jim couldn't get away. John lifted Will via the power-ramp, and positioned him in the back of the van in his braced-to-the floor wheelchair. As they headed out the driveway, Will asked where Jim was. This question, in the face of John just having told Will that Jim was not coming, alarmed John because it signaled to him that Will's somnolence and attention deficit were worsening. John, as well, had in the back of his mind a story of a neighbor who had traveled by car to Tennessee with his wife. The man had been afflicted with some type of breathing difficulty. On the return trip he began to experience a recurrence of his troubled breathing; his wife wanted to stop at a hospital but her husband said he'd rather get home. John concludes the anecdote by noting "He didn't make it." That lesson weighed heavily on John, and because he faced a three-hour trip to Mundelein, he decided to first have Will checked out at the hospital in Clinton. The emergency room physician, according to John, examined Will, performed some routine tests, and concluded that he was able to tolerate the remainder of the trip home. Nevertheless, Will's doctor was notified and plans made for Will to be seen at Condell Memorial Hospital upon his return.

John tells that Will promptly fell asleep once he was in the van and slept the entire way home. Their first stop was the Condell emergency room where Dr. Munson examined Will. He admitted him to Condell on June 25 because of "change in mental state, cause undetermined; rule out sepsis." In his initial note, he recorded that the hospital at Clinton had found Will's vital signs stable and a complete blood count normal despite his somewhat lethargic appearance. Upon admission to Condell, his temperature was "quite low"; his blood pressure was stable and his pulse ran between 60 and 70. A culture showed a urinary tract infection. Both a chest film and computerized tomogram of his brain were normal. Will started antibiotics, leading to a marked improvement and discharged home, alert and oriented two days later. The discharge diagnoses were urinary tract infection, chronic atrial fibrillation [the upper and lower chambers of the heart were not working synchronously due to a block of the atrioventricular conduction system] and the chronic quadriplegia due to polio.

Will called Dr. Munson on July 15 complaining of a low-grade temp and "internal shaking symptoms." He was seen in the ER where blood cultures were drawn and lab data were considered unremarkable, but his symptoms continued and reports from his family noted that he was continually lethargic and falling asleep. On July 27, Will told Dr. Munson that his limbs were swollen. Will's blood pressure was 170/70, pulse was slow at 54 and regular, "but he had total body anasarca [generalized edema] with pitting edema to the thigh and upper arm level." Dr. Munson's initial impression was protein deficiency and anemia of undetermined etiology and a possible electrolyte dysfunction. He started Will on diuretics and admitted him. Dr. T. Engel, a cardiologist, saw Will and recorded his temperature at 94 degrees; noting Will "cannot take much of a deep breath." His impression was that Will had mild congestive heart failure, a probable cardiomyopathy [intrinsic weakening of the heart muscle] and an occasional heart block [the spread of the heart's electrical impulse is slow or disrupted in a part of its normal pathway]. He also suspected that Will might not have adhered to a good fluid and salt restriction program "and because of the presence of only one kidney and probable damage to the cardiac muscle he became fluid overloaded." He felt Will was "doing remarkably well" considering 38 years of quadriplegia. "I am surprised he hasn't had more respiratory or cardiac problems in the past." Pulmonary function test studies conducted showed severe restrictive lung disease. The total amount of air he could move after a maximum inspiratory effort followed by a forced expiration was only 24% of the predicted normal for a male of his age, height and weight. It was as if he were only breathing with one-half of one lung. Other results confirmed the restrictive nature of pulmonary problem, meaning that Will's lungs were essentially normal, but he couldn't move his chest wall and diaphragm with sufficient strength to move enough air in and out of the lungs to allow the blood to pick up oxygen and discard carbon dioxide in an effective fashion. The "bellows" action of his chest was restricted, as it had been since the onset of polio in August 1951. His intercostal muscles were designed to contract and cause the rib cage to expand, allowing "new" air to enter the lungs and then to relax, allowing the "old" air to move out of the lungs. They had been markedly weakened by the polio paralysis. Although there was no definitive proof found in 1951, it is probable that the diaphragm, a muscle which works in unison with the intercostals, was also weakened by the polio requiring the iron lung, until Will regained some strength in his muscles of respiration, allowing him to be weaned from it during the four to eight months right after the onset of the disease.

Dr. S. Agijar, a surgeon, was called in to insert a cardiac pacemaker with Dr. Engel. Dr. M.F. Gonzales, a physiatrist, was also consulted because Will had mentioned some difficulty with his head and neck movements and some pain from the neck into the shoulders suggesting degenerative discogenic or arthritic changes in the cervical spine. That would not have been surprising considering all the neck motions Will had performed typing his letters, creating his computer programs, and drawing his pictures and cartoons, and turning the countless pages of books and magazines plus factoring in 37 years of clenching a clothespin for typing or an eraser-tipped rod clenched to turn the pages. By August 7, Will was ready for discharge as the pacemaker rectified the severe slowness of his cardiac rate, as well as the intermittent heart block, both of which had led to the congestive heart failure. His temperature had improved to about 97 degrees "for the first time in six months." It appeared that the sleepiness had also improved in the hospital.

The somnolence, however, returned and worsened over the subsequent months so that he was brought to the ER in mid-December to be tested for CO_2 narcosis. At that point, his arterial CO_2 level was 76, about twice normal. Simply put, Will's respiratory function wasn't capable of getting rid of the carbon dioxide [CO_2] from the venous blood returning from his peripheral tissues and organs. He was admitted on December 15, 1989, "to see if there is anything we can do to improve his severe restrictive hypercapnia." ["Restrictive" meant the thoracic cage was not being enlarged with each breath sufficiently to allow an adequate amount of air to move into the lungs, and "hypercapnia" meant elevated CO_2 in the arterial blood]. Dr. Munson stated "his shortness of breath seems to be just related to exertion." By that he meant breathing was an exertion for Will. The fact that his lungs were clear meant that so far they themselves weren't responsible for the high levels of carbon dioxide, just that Will's respiratory muscles weren't moving enough air in and out of the lungs. However, if the lung tissue was to be compromised in any way—with pneumonia, fluid accumulation due to congestive failure or a collapse of a portion of the lung—then that would compound the problem. His lungs were "clear, anterior and posterior, with decreased breath sounds throughout, except when he forces himself to breathe using mostly his accessory muscles of his neck." His chest film on admission showed some enlargement of the heart, indicating weakening of the heart muscle; the failing heart also could lead to a backup of fluid in the lung tissue.

Dr. Barr, a pulmonary disease consultant, also reported on December 15, that Will was using the strap muscles of his neck while "at rest." This was another ominous prognostic sign as it indicated that Will was calling on all the breathing power that he could muster even though it would be costly in terms of fatigue and the accessory muscles of respiration would be an undependable source of assistance once exhaustion felled them. They were not muscles created for constant contraction and relaxation, typically 16 times a minute, day in-day out, as were the primary muscles of respiration. The accessory muscles would fail—sooner or later. Dr. Barr advised intubation by putting a breathing tube into the windpipe and positive pressure ventilation if an emergency arose.

By this point in 1989, unfortunately, Will was into the fourth stage of poliomyelitis known as post-polio syndrome. This referred to another stage of muscle weakening which developed many years after the initial attack. There is no definite explanation for why this recurrence of muscle weakness develops.

A CO_2 level of 76 could typically cause, as in Will's case, intellectual alterations involving personality changes with confusion and somnolence. Will was edging toward end-stage respiratory failure because of the dysfunction of his muscles of respiration. If he exerted maximum effort for a short time or if mechanical ventilation of his lungs were utilized, the CO_2 would return toward a normal level and the somnolence and confusion would clear. Regrettably, Will couldn't maintain prolonged maximum respiratory effort without exhausting himself, but he was able to achieve periods of lucidity which allowed him to sort out what lay ahead and to discern his choices, which weren't many.

During this hospitalization, various attempts at improving Will's respiratory efforts were made including a cuirass, named after a piece of medieval body armor extending down to the waist and consisting of a breast plate and a back plate fastened together. The medical variety fit snugly over the upper torso. Heavy balloons would inflate and deflate in the space between the plates and the patient's thoracic cage, theoretically causing air to move out of and into Will's lungs. It was a miniature iron lung, but not nearly as efficient compared to the iron lung, though some minor improvements were noted in Will's repeat arterial blood gas studies.

Will and his medical staff clearly understood the problem. Dr. M. Gonzales, the physiatrist, phrased it most succinctly: "At the present time the goals . . . are to stabilize his ventilatory status and make some plan for continuing ventilation assistance at home, compatible with keeping him employed. The loss of respiratory function . . . appears to be restrictive lung disease . . . strongly suggestive of post-polio muscular atrophy. His use of the ventilator should also be coordinated . . . to permit him to maintain the maximum level of independence for the gentleman who has, up to this point, compensated extremely well for a quite severe level of physical impairment."

On December 18, Dr. Barr recorded "Patient still experiencing daytime somnolence despite 24 hour/day cuirass ventilator use." The cuirass could move almost three times as much air in and out of Will's lungs as he could by himself, but the arterial blood gases didn't improve proportionately. This failure to improve also suggested intrinsic deterioration of the lungs themselves by virtue of either pneumonia or clumping and consolidation of the lung tissues—in effect, diminishing the surface area available for gaseous exchange with the blood coursing through the alveoli—the fundamental unit in the lung's structure. This was another sign of more trouble for Will.

The following day, Dr. Schneider, an associate with Dr. Barr, reported Will's CO_2 is "likely not going to improve much more with the cuirass ventilator." His arterial O_2 saturation level had fallen to 57 from a normal value close to 100, and the chest film showed the consolidation of portions of the left lung. He had an associated low-grade temperature, which was anticipated in view of that finding.

One day later, Dr. Barr wrote what was essentially the medical staff's opinion consensus. "We have hard choices to make. First, it is unlikely that the cuirass ventilator will be sufficient to maintain this patient. It is unlikely that any other negative pressure apparatus will help. There is question as to the efficacy of a rocking bed or a pneumobelt, but again, the chances for success are low. If positive pressure ventilation with air or an oxygen-enhanced air mixture being pumped directly into the lungs is employed, this patient will lose speech which is a <u>major</u> loss for one who is already quadriplegic." [Dr. Barr himself underlined "major."] He suggested that they determine by x-ray if the diaphragm was paralyzed or not, try the rocking bed empirically, consider phrenic nerve [the nerve to the diaphragm] pacing, which he thought might not be possible after "30 years of disuse," some physical therapy for the left lung consolidation, and finally a "frank discussion with patient and family as to the possibility of tracheostomy and positive pressure support."

Dr. Munson reported that on the evening of the 20th he had a long discussion "with family about all of plans, options and problems. They seem to understand the mechanics and physiology involved."

The rocking bed utilized the organs of the abdominal cavity moved by gravity to assist diaphragmatic motion. The supine patient's bed would tip through a total excursion of about 60 to 75 degrees—across the horizontal—about 16 times a minute—head up, head down, head up, head down—incessantly trying to add a few percent more to the inspired and expired air volumes. It's a somewhat uncomfortable and unpleasant sensation with the patient having to keep orienting himself in a space while conversing or watching a TV; while being washed or treated in some other fashion by the nursing staff, the bed motion was halted.

On the morning of the 21st, Will was in the rocking bed and afebrile; vital signs were normal and lungs clear via stethoscope, and arterial blood gases and labs being checked. The same day, it was reported, Will felt better and he tolerated going to X-ray on a gurney without difficulty while he was off the rocking bed. A fluoroscopy done with Will lying in a supine position showed little active motion either on the right or left sides of the diaphragm. These various chest imaging studies also depicted the deterioration of pulmonary appearance between late July, when the lung fields were "grossly normal," and late December when there were the characteristic signs of pulmonary consolidation or pneumonia, either of which would have signaled a still bleaker prognosis.

Aides Ann Gerstenbrand and Claudia Greenlee both visited Bill on Thursday afternoon, the 21st. Ann recalls Bill telling her "there's only a few minutes in the ballgame." Looking tired and paler, he said his good-byes to both women. However, according to Madelyn Bussing Hendrix, Bill gave no indication of the seriousness of the situation when the two spoke by phone. "He called me himself," she says, "And I told him I was coming to see him. 'Oh no, I'll be out,' he told me, which of course, he knew wasn't true. He absolutely gave me the impression that he was not as ill as he really was although he said he had PPS. He didn't want me to come because 'there were too many people here anyway.' I called Fr. Moran and he and Bill also spoke on the phone, but Father never went there either. Bill never talked about his health concerns toward the end nor that he had a 'do not resuscitate' order. I know I didn't talk to him very long, but then I didn't think it was the last time I was going to talk to him. He joked and said he didn't bring his typewriter with him so he had to call me. He didn't want to tell me anything, but he did want to be in contact with me, I guess. His voice didn't sound that bad and I had not one inkling he was so close to death. "

A film taken on Friday showed worsening of the enlargement of the heart, engorged pulmonary vessels and evidence of edema fluid in the lungs themselves with areas of pneumonia. The normal functioning of the heart and lungs was now severely compromised by the changes occasioned by the post-polio syndrome affecting his breathing and the cardiac deterioration affecting his circulation.

On the 22nd, the arterial blood gases weren't "much different than with cuirass." Dr. Schneider didn't "feel he is going to have much more improvement in ventilation with this rocking bed ventilation adjunct." He did mention the possibility of using a "negative pressure body suit which would be akin to the old iron lung."

That same morning Dr. Munson wrote that the "problem of long-term commitment to mechanical ventilation is frightening." The rocking bed had not provided any change in Will's arterial oxygen or carbon dioxide levels—they were still in the dangerous range. He summed up, "overall. . . . progress poor." He also indicated that at 8:45 A.M., December 22, he had a "long discussion with patient; he is adamantly against tracheostomy and ventilator, will try any other means of ventilation."

Early Friday afternoon, I talked with Will from Minneapolis, where I was now in practice. He asked me to explore treatment options, which may have been available at Chicago's Northwestern Memorial Hospital and its affiliates, which I agreed to do. One condition which Will insisted upon, however, was that I "not let them do a tracheostomy," the opening into the windpipe which would have been part of a long-term positive pressure ventilation system, if he was to go down to Chicago. I reassured him that I would respect his wishes. He just wanted to make sure there wasn't something some other doctors or medical facility could do to help. It was clear he wanted help, but not at the cost of a tracheostomy or of returning to the "iron lung."

From college ethics lessons, we had been taught that patients did not have to submit to "heroic treatments"; in the ensuing decades there had been a rising tide that further emphasized the patient's autonomy, given a clear mind with maintenance of their emotional and intellectual faculties. I had no qualms responding to Will's request despite its dreadful and sad implications. I recognized that for some patients a tracheostomy would not be considered "heroic treatment" if a different set of circumstances—such as an overall positive prognostic assessment for survival, or a treatable disease process—were in place. Such conditions were not in place for Will, and I tacitly agreed a tracheostomy would be heroic treatment for him. Patients with tracheotomies may be able to talk if the trake tube doesn't completely occlude the upper windpipe and if the patient can remove the mechanical respirator tube and put a finger over the external opening of the trake; expired air could then move between the vocal cords and the voice, perhaps modified or softened, could turn into speech. Will's problem was that once intubated he couldn't independently remove his respirator tube and cover the trake tube with a finger; nor could he rely on sipping and puffing to manage the electronic "black box" on his desk, which Dr. Childress and his team had fashioned for him, nor could he sip and puff to steer his electric wheelchair with a permanent trake in place. Afterall, where could he go if he were hooked up to a respirator the size of an ordinary washing machine? At a minimum, Will would lose the ability to speak and to move about in his electric wheelchair—he would, in a sense, be "locked in" by the trake—able to absorb information but unable to transmit it.

I strongly suspect Will perceived his condition as one of inexorable deterioration based on what had transpired since the beginning of the year. As it was, he couldn't count on being able to think clearly for any protracted time without sinking into a carbon dioxide-induced lethargy, followed by a profound sleep. It had started last winter, worsened over the summer and now he was hospitalized with the problem. His medical team was trying everything but getting nowhere. In essence, Will was saying "Now they're talking about putting me back in the "lung" or doing a tracheostomy. I know about the former and seen the latter. No thank you, very much! Not for me!" Will was reflective, thoughtful, logical and realistic, and over the last few months he saw what was in store for him.

Earlier in his polio battle, he had faced death—and had traveled through the stages described by Elisabeth Kubler-Ross, M.D., in her monograph. She wrote of the initial stages of denial and isolation; what could be more isolating than to be put in an iron lung and certainly, no nineteen-year-old soon-to-be a college sophomore could accept the prospect of death, rather he would deny such a possible outcome. Anger would follow; to paraphrase his thinking "the damned unfairness of this scourge being dumped on me when I had such wonderful opportunities in front of me." His brother, John, tells that Will actively engaged in bargaining, the third stage in the process, while initially hospitalized, praying "Please get me better, Lord and I will devote my life to you and your work." The realization of the permanence of the paralysis and the loss of any hope for a physical recovery led Will into his "slough of despond"—the fourth stage, namely depression, from which he credits Father Pat Cummings for rescuing him, only to arrive at the last stage. Acceptance.

Acceptance enabled him to be the person he became. He accepted his fate, which left him poor, but he also accepted God's love and the love of his family, friends and neighbors, which made him rich. "I accept what God gave me, what He gives me and what He will give me." In his view, the cost-benefit analysis of a trake or the lung was unfavorable, especially given his mood of acceptance. This wasn't new for him. He had lived a life of acceptance for the latter two-thirds of his life, and he could accept God's invitation to what Will had written of as "That Glad Reunion" of "The Really Long Weekend," in his next-to-last classletter. The undesirable consequences of a tracheostomy for Will were looking exorbitant as he saw them, and as I saw them myself. I knew Will hoped that I would understand without his having to list reasons for his decision during that phone call on December 22. When I acceded to his stipulation of "no trake," he knew I understood and agreed with him. I was satisfied he was mentally clear and had considered the alternatives.

Having concluded our phone conversation, I immediately contacted physicians from Northwestern Memorial Hospital [NMH] in pulmonary medicine, anesthesiology and emergency medicine. They separately listened to Will's clinical findings but beyond what was going on at Condell, each saw no "magic means" to solve the situation. No avenue of help seemed open. Will's medical background, his present status, and his stipulations were presented to physicians whom I deemed skilled in end-stage respiratory failure. Here were three separate and independent assessments that little else could be done under the circumstances. I thanked them for their time and consideration.

Meanwhile, Will told Dr. Munson after his first telephone call with me that he was hoping to go to Northwestern Memorial Hospital and that brother Jim, who had flown up from Indianapolis, was making tentative arrangements for the ambulance down to Chicago. When I phoned Will back and told him I had found no volunteer to accept him in transfer, given the clinical situation, his position on a trake and the care he was receiving at Condell, he apparently told one of the nurses to cancel the ambulance.

John was upset when he learned that the ambulance transfer that he and Jim had requested and expected, based on Will's earlier conversation with them, hadn't been effected. He says that a nurse came up to him and with a nod of her head in Will's direction said, in effect, "It looks like there has been a change in plans." Looking at Will, John later recalls seeing a sort of self-satisfied smile on his face. In spite of Will's physical status, his intellectual status was still sharp and well enough to state his choices. I recognized that also during his two phone conversations with me on Friday, as had Dr. Munson earlier in the day when he had the "long discussion" with Will, who ruled out a tracheostomy. It is clear that Dr. Munson accepted that Will was intellectually capable of such a weighty decision or he would not have written "No Code Blue" into the hospital order sheet. He also wrote: "Brother [John] claimed he [Will] wanted to try PEEP [Positive End Expiratory Pressure—a type of mechanical ventilation] at Northwestern. I had discussed *not* ventilating him in case of failure and Mr. Jenks [Will] said 'no heroics and that he had lived a full life.'"

Later that afternoon, Will became sleepy, and shortly thereafter began convulsing, shaking his head and neck. He had two more seizures despite anticonvulsant meds and between the first and second and between the second and third, he "seemed to clear" and recognize Dr. Munson. Will's hyperventilating on his own didn't clear his mind adequately after the third seizure, and Dr. Munson wanted to rule out an intracranial cerebrovascular accident [a stroke] that could also cause the seizures. Therefore the decision was made to ventilate Will on a short-term basis by means of an endotracheal tube [one that passes through the patient's mouth and then into the trachea/windpipe] and a mechanical positive pressure respirator. It is not a tracheostomy but a temporary method to ventilate the patient. Will was moved to the Intensive Care Unit [ICU], and given additional anti-seizure medications to forestall any additional seizures. A cranial computerized tomogram of the brain was performed that evening and read negative for any signs of a "stroke," meaning the cause of the seizures was the end-stage respiratory failure and the arterial blood gas abnormalities—low oxygen and high carbon dioxide.

At this point, still late on the 22nd, Dr. Munson met with Jim and John "individually trying to make them realize this heroic attempt was not justified by William's own wishes." It turned out that Dr. Munson had overridden his own order written earlier that day. He did so in the forlorn hope that the convulsions were due to a stroke and not due to the derangement's in Will's arterial blood gases. This was a brave and momentous move by Munson, for now the medical/ethical question was not one of not initiating therapy but of discontinuing therapy that had already been started.

Meanwhile, about 5:30 P.M., John phoned me that Will had had a seizure and was on a ventilator; I told him I would come as fast as possible. It is hard to believe on the Friday evening of a long Christmas weekend I managed to get a seat on a Minneapolis to O'Hare flight and, mercifully, to obtain a car.

I arrived at Condell Memorial Hospital about midnight and was directed to the ICU where I introduced myself to the nurse-in-charge. When John told Dr. Munson I was coming, he noted in Will's chart that "Dr. Kane may review chart," and the nurse provided me with it. Will was asleep due to his therapeutic sedation; his vital signs were stable since he was being mechanically respired via the endotracheal tube. An intravenous line was in place and above his head various monitors flashed their EKG tracings as well as readouts of other data. Review of the chart indicated that Dr. Munson had written "No Code Blue" on 12/22/89 before the seizures began. This meant no resuscitation was to be undertaken in case of a cardiopulmonary arrest. It was a direct response to Will's insistence that "no heroic measures" be taken. Will had told both Dr. Munson and me what he would not accept, and both of us saw Will as competent, and accepted his autonomy and, ultimately, his decision.

The fact that Will had a convulsion rather than a cardiopulmonary arrest may be considered a very fine distinction, but there was the remote possibility that the seizure was due to a cerebrovascular accident or stroke, and as Dr. Munson had ordered "No Code Blue," he could countermand it. Additionally, an endotracheal intubation was not, obviously in Dr. Munson's view, and I would concur readily, "heroic treatment" in the face of the seizure. My conversations with Dr. Munson, then and more recently, led me to conclude he would not have performed a tracheostomy for a cardiopulmonary arrest. Neither would I. Both Dr. Munson and I agree that Will was specific on that issue, and we independently had accepted his decision on medical and ethical grounds.

After sleeping at John's home, I arrived at the hospital early Saturday morning and introduced myself to Dr. Munson. He knew who I was from John's earlier message, but I had the impression Dr. Munson was uncertain about my role. I explained I was there for Will and would not derail any arrangements that Will and he had made. I had already read earlier his Friday note that Will didn't want a tracheostomy, which is exactly what Will had also told me on Friday, and I knew of the "No Code Blue" order, which was the medical consequence of Will's decision for "no heroics."

Will was still asleep due to the dilantin, valium and phenobarbital of the previous day and I had no exchange with him, even a one-way conversation, as he showed no sign of awakening; his color was good and his monitor studies were in normal ranges. Dr. Munson, John, Jim and I had a brief conference; afterwards I was left with the feeling that, short of a tracheostomy, John and Jim wanted all the stops pulled out. I ached for the brothers in their waning hope that Will would "make it and come home," but I also empathized with Dr. Munson who saw the worsening prognosis, and who had the additional responsibility of accepting Will's restrictions.

Dr. Schneider visited that day and noted that Will had no spontaneous ventilatory effort. He wrote, "It will be difficult if not possible to wean pt [patient] from ventilation quickly, i.e., within two weeks."

Will's brothers and I went back to John's place where we had a prolonged conversation about the situation. I asked if Will had discussed his wish for "no heroics" with them and they responded negatively, obviously hurt that Will hadn't done so. I countered that it was my impression Will wanted to spare his brothers any hurt or distress and that Will had reached a point of hoping that the end of his life would not be complicated or heroically prolonged. They accepted that but wished he had been more explicit in expressing his end-of-life preferences.

When John told me that morning, and has since repeated, how Will had smiled at him on Friday afternoon when the ambulance trip to Northwestern Memorial Hospital had been cancelled, I said that proved my point that

Will didn't want to prolong the process, knowing that no one, under the circumstances, could offer much that was different or better.

That same Saturday, there was another anecdote related by John from the previous day's events; this involved a visit by Ann Gerstenbrand, then Will's morning aide and a dear friend of his who, as she was leaving, leaned over to kiss Will on the cheek. Will reportedly turned his head and face away from her, apparently not willing to accept a final kiss. John, Jim and I knew Will would not have knowingly hurt such a friend unless, in this case, his own tears and loss of composure might cause even more pain for his friend; it further reinforced my sense of the determination of Will's wishes.

Later, on Saturday, December 23, at about 4:30 P.M., Dr. Munson noted that a discussion was held "with brother—he now seems to understand Bill's wishes more realistically and is aware of his last wishes not to be on the ventilator." Dr. Munson also wrote that Will was "awake and alert now and understands whole process to attempt to wean him off ventilator . . . But success very unlikely. Then nature will take its course if all parties agree." A grim but likely prospect.

Sunday, December 24, at 7:30 A.M., I went to Will's room alone and found him awake, alert and smiling, but still intubated and being respired mechanically. I asked how he was and he nodded that he was well. His lips were red and cheeks were rosy; his eyes were bright and clear. After some small talk, I inquired if he wanted the tube removed and he nodded "yes." I asked him if he understood the possible consequences of this and he didn't hesitate to nod again. I had always, as long as I can remember, and still do, start my prayers with an Act of Contrition—and I will never forget stumbling through it as I held his hand. I recovered to say an Our Father and Hail Mary. When I finished, Will's eyes were still bright and smiling. Mine were not.

Dr. Munson appeared in the hallway and I went out to him to tell him Will wanted the tube out. As he entered Will's room, I told both of them I would bring John and Jim who were in the waiting room down the hall. In a few minutes, the three of us entered.

Dr. Munson and I left the room as the brothers visited, and Dr. Munson asked if I wanted to be present as he weaned Will from the ventilator and removed the tube. I said yes, if it was all right with Will and him. It was the least I could do to affirm, by my presence, Will's decision and the act by Dr.

Munson to remove the endotracheal tube keeping Will alive. Will had said "no heroics," but what I witnessed that Sunday morning met my definition of "heroic" behavior by both of them. As he had lived his life, so Will would die his death—teaching, accepting, giving example, loving and letting himself be loved. Jim and John understandably did not want to be there for the tube removal as we all were uncertain as to how events would transpire.

Before beginning the weaning process, Dr. Munson completed his chart note: "Family and friends now understand William's wishes of no heroics and I plan to wean off ventilator and see if he can function on his own. Assessment: Chronic Respiratory Failure Due to Polio. Plan: Comfort. No Code Blue." Dr. Munson, a respiratory therapist, and I were with Will. Dr. Munson explained to him how the ventilator would first be programmed in such a way that Will's own inspiratory effort would trigger a supplementary assist from the machine. Then a brief delay would allow Will to stabilize at that stage; then the machine would be programmed to help Will less, step by step, until Will was breathing on his own through the tube and the machine was turned completely off. Then the endotracheal tube would be detached from the machine; Will would be independently breathing through the tube without distress or difficulty. Then Dr. Munson gave him instructions for the last step; he would deflate the cuff of the tube, which provided an airtight seal inside the trachea, and finally remove the tube.

The index fingers' nails pressed into the pads of my thumbs in nervous anticipation as Dr. Munson slid the tube out, accompanied by a short cough from Will. The therapist used a plastic suction tube to clean out some oral secretions and Will coughed again. Dr. Munson asked how he felt and in a voice somewhat more raspy than usual he said, "Okay!" Dr. Munson, the therapist, and I exchanged glances signifying "So far, so good," and looked back at Will who seemed comfortable and satisfied, with the beginnings of a smile showing on his face. The process had taken less than half an hour. I went down to the cafeteria and told John and Jim that Will was alert, talking and contented. They relaxed visibly and the three of us went back to his room.

About 9 A.M. Dr. Munson noted "Good enough minute volume, voice OK, no signs of seizure activity." Three hours later he charted "BP 106/49, Resp 28, Pulse 70, temp 98.0. Nasogastric suction [to rid the stomach of any excess secretions] working. Breathing room air. Lungs relatively clear. Wakes easily." At the same time, he wrote on the order sheet "If bed needed may move to private room." This meant that Will could leave the ICU if an ICU bed was needed for another patient.

The brothers and I visited for a while with Will, and then Jim and I, in turn, kissed him and caressed his head and face. Jim and I together drove to O'Hare—he to fly to Indianapolis and I to Minneapolis. We were, for the moment, satisfied with the morning's events, but resigned to the inexorable and the inevitable.

Just after midnight, at 12:44 A.M., on Christmas morn, Will, who had become more hypoxemic [insufficient oxygen in the arterial blood] during the evening with increasing pulmonary congestion and decreasing urine output, was discovered with no signs of respiratory effort. His vital signs revealed he had succumbed to chronic restrictive respiratory failure, for which the polio attack of 38 years earlier was ultimately responsible. His journey home was now complete.

"The time is here for me to leave this life. I have done my best in the race, I have run the full distance, I have kept the Faith and now the prize of victory is waiting for me, the crown of righteousness which the Lord, the righteous Judge, will give on that Day."

2 Timothy

CHAPTER FIFTEEN

The Prize of Victory

WILL'S DEATH, BECAUSE OF HIS LIFE, WAS A CAUSE FOR GENUINE celebration by his family and friends. He left his message which, was so simple and meaningful that it could not be forgotten: "Let yourself be loved." Will lived and died in that confident belief, and we loved him for it and the example he set for others. We celebrated our good fortune in knowing a man such as he.

Since 1989 I have frequently relived Will's final 48 hours of life. The memories are more firmly etched than any other single event or comparable period in my life. Nothing could compare with the gut-twisting moment that Sunday morning when Will let me know of his decision. It still is a haunting reminiscence of his courage and acceptance of a lethal truth.

Will struck me as the holiest person I have personally known. It wasn't an overly pious or doctrinaire religiosity, but a brawny, intellectually muscular dedication and application of the admonitions of the Sermon on the Mount. He absorbed the fullest meanings of the Beatitudes into his life, his spirit, and his writings; they were demonstrations of his acceptance of the Way, the Truth and the Life.

Will's visitation was held Wednesday evening at McMurrough's Chapel in Libertyville, IL, and crowded with relatives, friends, neighbors, schoolmates, and Walgreen coworkers and executives, including President and CEO Daniel Jorndt. Each visitor had a special memory of Will, a personally magic moment to be shared with a listener.

The concelebrated Mass December 28, was led by Will's cousin and great friend from their earliest childhood days, Rev. Charles E. Cronin, at St. Mary's Church, Freemont Center, IL. The college was represented by Rev. John E. Brooks, S.J., Rev. Francis X. Miller, S.J., and Rev. George L. O'Brien, a diocesan priest of Worcester who left for the seminary after three years with the class of 1954, and who was assigned to the Development Office of Holy Cross. Rev. John C. Weimer joined Father Cronin on the altar.

Father Cronin's homily was rich with memories of Will. He said it was "in many ways the easiest homily I've ever had to offer, but in another way it's the most difficult." There was an abundance of material due to the quality of Will's life, but it was difficult "trying to express suitably the qualities of mind, heart and soul that made Will's life a sermon."

He advised us that we did not come to face the death of Will Jenks but to celebrate a life of Faith, never arguing with his fate but accepting God's role for himself, and at the end knowing that his Lord would receive him. Father Cronin told the congregation that the three Jenks boys and the two Cronin boys, Dominic and he, lived at the same address and naturally played together. He said John and Will, who were respectively four and three years older than he, were his childhood heroes which said something about his own deprived childhood. He supported his opinion that Bill was an aggressive basketball player by remembering that he once fouled out of a high school game in six minutes.

After the polio, he said there was a different Will; a Will who, paralyzed from the neck down, buoyed up those who came to console him—and who left richer on leaving than when they'd come to visit. Father Cronin saw Will as an example of St. Paul's observation that "God purposely chose the weak in order to put the powerful to shame." Through the thirty-eight years of his quadriplegia, he inspired all whom he met—his neighbors, the high schoolers he tutored, his former classmates and faculty of the schools he had attended, his coworkers at the Walgreen Company and on St. Joseph's Church Parish Council in Rockville, Indiana and even those he never met—through his writings, interviews and the speeches that were later printed and circulated.

Father Cronin spoke of Will's vetoing the suggestion that he have a tracheostomy, refusing to be an object of pity or a specimen, and even if the alternative was death, he simply said . . . "So be it." Father likened Will's

"So be it" to Jesus' "It is consummated. I have done the Father's will—soon I will be free." He concluded with a quote from 2 Timothy: "The time is here for me to leave this life. I have done my best in the race, I have run the full distance, I have kept the Faith and now the prize of victory is waiting for me, the crown of righteousness which the Lord, the righteous Judge, will give on that Day."

John Jenks offered me the opportunity to eulogize Will after Communion. My theme was also a celebratory appreciation for Will's life as was my acknowledgement of the loving labors of his heroic parents, his brothers and nephews, and his morning helpers. I spoke to the victorious aspects of his life, victories in conquering the human tendency to bemoan one's fate, in separating his body from his psyche, in conquering his absence from a formal higher education yet becoming the most learned of the class of 1954, his extraordinary skill at turning a phrase, "It's likely I am not the most seriously wounded among us, only the most conspicuously bandaged," and his axiom, "Let yourself be loved." I reviewed fragmented memories of his remarkable life—from his freshman year at college with *The Hound of Heaven*, which we learned was not a dog-story or just a simple allegory. During his rebirth, he found that it contained a valued truth and that he was the wood that had to be charred before the message of *The Hound of Heaven* could be drawn for the benefit of others.

For me, Will Jenks was iconic. I was enthralled by him and his spirit from my first visit the summer of 1953 to his last day, Christmas Eve 1989. He was a model of sanity as he cast aside the infirmities of his limbs and became immune to their distress; he rejected the notion that without useful arms and legs he could only be a lesser person. His message overcame the stillness of those bones and joints, concentrating instead on his intellect and will, and what he could teach others.

At the end, there was his forewarning of a not-too-distant death and his insistence on affirming God's will in whatever way it was manifest. A few lines from a college song—"You'll know when battle's done, You'll know when victory's won!"—led into my final exhortation, "Let us therefore celebrate! Gaudeamus igitur!"

After Mass Will was brought to Dana, his hometown, for a reviewal that evening and Mass on Friday morning at the Church of St. Joseph in

Rockville, celebrated by Fr. Moran, and attended by his family, many friends and neighbors, chief among them Madelyn and her children. He was then buried in the Bono Cemetery, near the farm, adjacent to his parents and grandparents.

Ms. Barbara Green, secretary to Father Brooks, wrote of Will, "No one could express himself the way Will did. He was and always will be an unparalleled Holy Cross legend. We were so fortunate and blessed to have known him as our friend—the best there was! His magnificent smile lit up the world! . . . Will was truly one of God's Chosen sons, who suffered his Cross gallantly and honorably and was ready to shed his pain and restrictions and finally share in the full glory of Heaven with God and his Blessed Mother, and his parents and friends who were waiting to welcome him. Ave atque vale, dear Will!"

In the January 7, 1990 parish bulletin of St. Peter's Church where he was the pastor, Father Cronin told his parishioners about Will's death and his philosophy of life and love. He told how Will reacted to the suggestion of heroic treatment and his decisive refusal to accept that course of action, despite being told what the alternative was. Again, according to Father Cronin, Will adamantly responded, "So be it." Will, I surmise, believed that Father Cronin could deal with the stressful rationale of his choices and that Father Charlie would have accepted his judgment, considering both the moral and medical considerations.

Since 1989, there has been much more discussion about end-of-life issues, and today, for example, each healthcare facility in this country which receives government funds must provide "Living Wills" or similar legal instruments, which allow mentally competent patients to spell out in detail their preferences for the kind of medical care and treatment they desire under a variety of end-of-life circumstances.

"The story of Bill Jenks' life is a testimony to humanity and love," wrote Dr. Dudley Childress. "It's a Christmas story because, to some extent, it is the story of a gift from one man to another. Father Pat Cummings gave Bill the gift of life and helped him become so rich in spirit that he was able to render severe disability inconsequential in the total scheme of things. Father Cummings helped Bill dwarf disability. Father Cummings did this by taking time to write Bill thousands of letters—one every other day, for 18 consecutive years—from the time of Bill's bout with polio until his own (Cummings) death. It is a truly magnificent story and giving of oneself. Everyone who knew Bill Jenks also, in some sense, knew Father Cummings. The experience makes us realize what one man can do for another and how this can have such a positive influence on society in general.

"Bill was born in Chicago, but lived for a time in Dana, Indiana—Ernie Pyle's home town—and he considered Dana his home town. At the time he became involved with our laboratory he lived in Mundelein, Illinois with his brother. He was one of the early users of new technical equipment developed by our laboratory (breath-operated wheelchair, environmental controller, etc.) We came in contact with Bill because of Dr. William Kane, formerly chairman of the Department of Orthopaedic Surgery at Northwestern University, who requested we see if we could be of assistance to Bill. Dr. Kane had been one of Bill's associates at Holy Cross—he too was under the Bill Jenks spell.

"For the past ten years or so Bill has worked effectively and with much diligence as a computer programmer for Walgreens. It's too bad the current technological equipment—also the improved social environment for disabled people—was not available to Bill when he first became disabled, because I believe it would have enabled him to become a great teacher and writer. Society would then have been able to receive the full benefit of his great intellect. This is why rehabilitation technology is so important for disabled persons, and for society. Make no mistake, the person rehabilitates himself, with assistance of others—in Bill's case Father Cummings—but technology can play an important supportive and enabling role. As Horowitz's piano technician said, 'Horowitz created the tone—I just gave him the best instrument.' Bill created the life, we just helped give him the technology (the instruments) through which the beautiful music of his life could be played," Childress' essay concluded.

Liz Helt and the Book Club sent the Holy Cross Department of English an "inscribed copy of the Oxford Classical Dictionary . . . Bill's love of his Latin and his grounding in many of the Classics in translation make this gift seem an appropriate memorial from us to you," requesting that it stay in the departmental library, if possible. She explained the inscription was William Cory's translation of Callimachus' lament for his friend Heraclitus of Caria.

The poem became more famous because of the lovely translation than it might have been otherwise:

They told me, Heraclitus, they told me you were dead.
They brought me bitter news to bear and bitter tears to shed.
I wept as I sat remembering how often you and I
Had tired the sun with talking and sent him down the sky.
And now that thou art lying, my dear old Carian guest,
A handful of gray ashes, long, long ago at rest,
Still are thy gentle voices, the nightingales awake,
For Death, he taketh all away, but them he cannot take.

Because many of Will's friends from '54 could not attend his funeral on the short notice between Christmas and New Year's, they organized a Memorial Mass on campus for Saturday, April 7, 1990. Three or four dozen attended and Father Jack Weimer was chosen homilist.

Father Jack chose his opening passage from *My Name Is Asher Lev* by Chaim Potok, in which a father explains to his six-year-old son after they both spotted a dead bird, that "Everything that lives must die." "Why?" "That's the way the ribbona shel olom [The Creator] made his world, Asher." "Why?" "So life would be precious, Asher. Something that is yours forever is never precious."

Jack said his train ride to Indiana in 1951 to see Will in the iron lung was long, lonely and scary. Shocked by Will's complete immobility he, in his own telling, blurted out "At least you can read," which he ranked as one of the "most fatuous remarks in the annals of Holy Cross" and as well "a mind-boggling understatement." Jack encouraged Will to write professionally but Will answered: "I don't know anything. Well, perhaps I do. I have come to realize that you do not know what it means to be a human being until you have been totally humiliated."

Father Weimer submitted that we had known a man of passion, gentle-ness, wisdom and wit who set out to demythologize his own persona and who was kind, loving and a delight to be with. "He was nicer and less the fraud than any man I ever met or looked at in a mirror, and he too could consume the entire combustible universe in a small room. Bill lives, we believe, and his words and his presence demand that we do more than bask in nostalgia. Neither we nor the world we live in can do without the spirit of Bill Jenks, our classmate, our friend, our teacher," he said.

The May–June, 1990, issue of the corporate magazine, *Walgreen World* took note of Will's death in a full page article by Laurie L. Meyer, Manager of Corporate Communications. She wrote "The halls where he wheeled will never be the same. For nine years his intelligence, compassion and wit left their mark on Walgreen people in Deerfield's Systems Development and Mount Prospect's Retail Systems." Gary Pradarelli told of hiring Bill as an entry-level programmer. "Initially I was worried, wondering if Bill would pull his own weight. The worry was pointless. We were ready to give him some breaks, but I don't remember ever doing so . . . Bill was a unique character, full of humor and a great practical jokester. And *talented*—he could write better with his mouth than I can with my hand . . . It is our turn to celebrate the fate that allowed many at Walgreen's to love and be loved by an extraordinary man named Bill Jenks."

On November 1, 1993, Joseph Cardinal Bernardin, Archbishop of Chicago, and himself a recipient of an Honorary Doctor of Laws degree at the Holy Cross 1983 commencement, was the homilist at the college's Sesquicentennial Mass. He confessed to having studied and researched diligently in preparation for the day and wished to "focus on two people, who, I think, exemplify something special about this school." The first was Father John E. Brooks of the Society of Jesus, President of Holy Cross. Of all the presidents of the college, he had been the most durable, having served for 23 years; he had had the ability to combine the spiritual depth of a man of prayer with the wise insight of a scholar and the decisiveness, courage and judgment of a skilled administrator.

The second person of whom the Cardinal spoke was Will Jenks; he said that Will, after only one year at Holy Cross, somehow had learned how to make sense out of a tragedy. He characterized him as a "remarkable Christian gentleman" who loved movies and books and conversations and good arguments . . . And he never pitied himself and woe to anyone who ever dared to pity him! . . ."Like Father Brooks and so many other graduates of Holy Cross throughout the years, Will Jenks was a Renaissance man, a deeply spiritual person, a man of joyful spirit and profound faith . . . And we see the face of

God in outstanding people like Father Brooks and Will Jenks and Bishop Fenwick and countless others who have been a part of Holy Cross for the past 150 years." High praise indeed, from a beloved Prince of the Church, to be mentioned in the same breath with the founder of the college and the man who would lead it for 24 years. The Cardinal had brought three legends of the college together in one sentence.

Will was given the grace to prepare for the end we all face, and both he and, later, the Cardinal were to teach us that there were lessons of dying to be learned, to let go, to accept, to face "death with dignity."

In 1994, at our 40th Reunion, the Class leaders invited me to share some recollections of Will after we attended Mass in a room dedicated to him in the Hogan Student Center. Near the room's doorway was a collection of photos and memorabilia of him including a copy of "The Speech," given in 1979. I told my listeners who had just concluded Mass by singing the Prayer of St. Francis that I had no foreknowledge that that hymn would be chosen by our class Reunion Committee, but that it would be the major theme of my remarks, since Will had lived and died according to that supplication.

I began by thanking the class for the Holy Cross chair, given to Betty and me "in grateful appreciation" for our efforts with Will. I thought it was anomalous for us to be honored for having enjoyed so deeply the experience of his love and vitality, to have him share his insights and viewpoints with us and to entertain our family with his visits, letters, cartoons, jokes, and laughs. It was marvelous to be with him, and an honor to help when needed.

I called him the sanest, saintliest and sagest man I ever knew—he would have sighed at such a string of alliterations—but I gave my basis for each of the three qualities. I praised the Honorary Degrees Committee of the Board of Trustees for the honor which fit Will so aptly and precisely. He was a doctor—Latin for teacher—of humane letters and I asked if anyone ever delayed reading one of his letters, with his phrases, polished by him and loved by us, and the messages full of witty ideas and lofty ideals. I lingered on his phrase, "Let yourself be loved," that simple, profound and exquisite admonition we will always associate with Will.

Will's life taught us much and so should his death. He justifiably refused heroic therapies offered to him because such intervention would have destroyed three essential talents of Will Jenks—his ability to talk, to type and to retain the independent mobility of his chair. He preferred neither to prolong his dying nor to make it a distressing process for either himself or his loved ones.

After retelling the events of his last days, I read the final lines of the Prayer of St. Francis.

> For it is in giving—that we receive,
> It is in pardoning—that we are pardoned,
> It is in dying—that we are born to eternal life.

He challenged us.
"Let yourself be loved."
By your God!
By your neighbor!
By yourself!
So be it, my friend.

Appendices: Genealogy

WILLIAM HENRY HARRISON **JENKS** (1843–1898)

+SUSAN **TURNER** JENKS (1846–1929)

:   ELSIE **JENKS** MILLER (1877–1959)

:   +MORT **MILLER** (1876–1968)

:   •   JESSIE LOUISE **MILLER** (1912–1965)

:   •   +RAYMOND **GOSNELL**

:   ROYAL E **JENKS** (1881–1963)

:   RAYAL TURNER **JENKS** (1881–1883)

:   ORA AMY **JENKS** COLLINS (1885–1919)

:   +ALVA GLENWOOD **COLLINS** (1881–1940)

:   •   WALTER W **COLLINS** (1911–dec.)

:   •   +VIRGINIA **SMITH** COLLINS (1910–1970)

:   •   •   ERNEST KENDLE **COLLINS**

:   •   +FLORENCE WOOD **BURCHFIELD** COLLINS

:   •   HELEN M **COLLINS** SHAFFER (1914–dec.)

:   •   +CLAUDE **SHAFFER** (1905–2000)

:   ORRA MACK **JENKS** (1885–1966)

:   +ELLA **CRONIN** JENKS (1901–1979)

:   •   JOHN MACK **JENKS** (1931–dec.)

:   •   +CAROLYN **PAPLEY** JENKS (1936–dec.)

:   •   •   WILLIAM PETER **JENKS** (1957–dec.)

:   •   •   +HOLLY **CADDEN** JENKS (1958–dec.)

:   •   •   •   JAYMIE MARIE **JENKS** (1987–dec.)

:   •   •   •   WILLIAM JAYSON **JENKS** (1989–dec.)

:   •   •   JOHN CRONIN **JENKS** (1959–dec.)

:   •   •   CHARLES DOMINIC **JENKS** (1964–dec.)

:   •   •   +MARIA **THOMAS** JENKS (1964–dec.)

:   •   •   •   JOHN RICHARD **JENKS** (1992–dec.)

:   •   •   •   MARY KATHERINE **JENKS** (1994–dec.)

:   •   WILLIAM HENRY**JENKS** (1932–1989)

:   •   JAMES EDWARD **JENKS** (1934–dec.)

:   •   +CAROL **WELSH** JENKS (1936–dec.)

:   •   •   KAREN **JENKS** (1964–dec.)

:   •   •   NANCY **JENKS** (1972–dec.)

WILL'S MATERNAL GENEALOGY

CATHERINE **CONWAY** CRONIN (1869–1932)

+PETER **CRONIN** (1863–1934)

:   ELLA **CRONIN** JENKS (1901–1979)

:   +ORRA MACK **JENKS** (1885–1966)

:   •   JOHN MACK **JENKS** (1931–dec.)

:   •   +CAROLYN **PAPLEY** JENKS (1936–1995)

:   •   •   WILLIAM PETER **JENKS** (1957–dec.)

:   •   •   +HOLLY **CADDEN** JENKS (1958–dec.)

:   •   •   •   JAYMIE MARIE **JENKS** (1987–dec.)

:   •   •   •   WILLIAM JAYSON **JENKS** (1989–dec.)

:   •   •   JOHN CRONIN **JENKS** (1959–dec.)

:   •   •   CHARLES DOMINIC **JENKS** (1964–dec.)

:   •   •   +MARIA **THOMAS** JENKS (1964–dec.)

:   •   •   •   JOHN RICHARD **JENKS** (1992–dec.)

:   •   •   •   MARY KATHERINE **JENKS** (1994–dec.)

:   •   WILLIAM HENRY**JENKS** (1932–1989)

:   •   JAMES EDWARD **JENKS** (1934–dec.)

:   •   +CAROL **WELSH** JENKS (1936–dec.)

:   •   •   KAREN **JENKS** (1964–dec.)

:   •   •   NANCY **JENKS** (1973–dec.)

: JOHN FRANCIS **CRONIN** (1904–1913)

: DOMINIC CONWAY **CRONIN** (1906–1953)

: +MARION **BOERSTE** CRONIN (1907–1993)

: . DOMINIC CONWAY **CRONIN, JR** (1934–dec.)

: . +MARY **BIRREN** CRONIN (1939–dec.)

: . . MICHAEL EDWARD **CRONIN** (1971–dec.)

: . . MARTHA ELIZABETH **CRONIN** (1977–dec.)

: . CHARLES EDWARD **CRONIN** (1935–1996)

: . CATHERINE MARIE "SUE" **CRONIN** CROSS (1938–dec.)

: . +MICHAEL LEE **CROSS** (1937–dec.)

: . . TERRI ANN **CROSS** HARRIS (1961–dec.)

: . . SUSAN **CROSS** ZIMMERMANN (1962–dec.)

: . . MARK CONWAY **CROSS** (1963–dec.)

: . . SCOTT ALAN **CROSS** (1966–dec.)

: . PATRICIA ANN **CRONIN** (1941–dec.)

: . MARY LOU **CRONIN** MURPHY (1946–dec.)

: . +JAMES ANDREW **MURPHY** (1941–dec.)

: . . ERIN MARIE **MURPHY** MCVEY (1970–dec.)

: . . KRISTA JEAN **MURPHY** FIFIELD (1971–dec.

: . JUDITH ANN **CRONIN** KRUGMAN (1948–dec.)

: . +MURRAY **KRUGMAN** (1949–dec.)

: . . MOLLY ANN **KRUGMAN** (1983–dec.)

: . . BRYAN **KRUGMAN** (1985–dec.)

: . MARION **CRONIN** CORRIGAN (1951–dec.)

: . +MICHAEL CHRISTOPHER **CORRIGAN** (1949–dec.)

: . . COLLEEN MARIE **CORRIGAN** (1979–dec.)

: . . MICHAEL CHRISTOPHER **CORRIGAN**, **JR** (1982–dec.)

: . . RYAN PATRICK **CORRIGAN** (1986–dec.)

: MARGARET **CRONIN** (1909–1974)

The five boys were down on the Dana farm during the summer of 1941. From left to right: William H. Jenks, 9, James E. Jenks, 7, Dominic C. Cronin, Jr., 6, Charles E. Cronin, 5, and John M. Jenks, 10.

Ora Mack Jenks and Ella Cronin Jenks attended a 1960 wedding reception.

William H. Jenks, circa 1949–1950.

Jack O'Grady and Will were classmates during their freshman year, 1950–51.

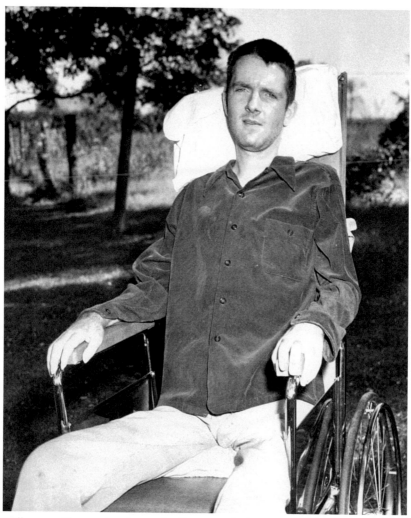

Will returned home, six miles south of Dana, in the late summer of 1952, after nearly a year in hospitals and a half year in an iron lung.

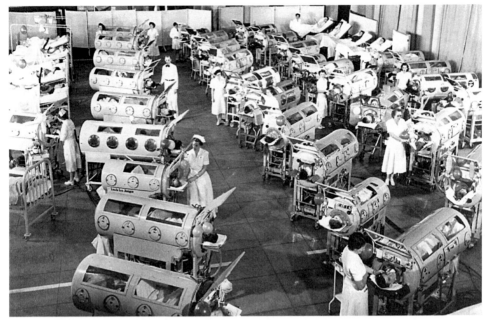

The polio epidemic of 1952 caused an influx of pulmonary patients needing iron lungs and rocking beds at the Rancho los Amigos facility of Los Angeles County. *Courtesy of the March of Dimes.*

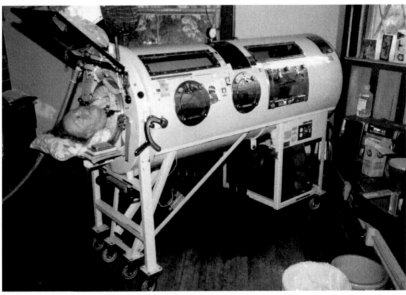

A close-up of an iron lung. Marilyn Rogers has lived either in an iron lung or with a respirator since 1949. *Photo by Charles E. Cudd, 2003.*

Rev. Patrick J. Cummings, S.J.

Rev. Francis J. Hart, S.J.

Rev. John E. Brooks, S.J.
Photo by Gabriel A. Cooney.

*Photos on this page courtesy of the
College of the Holy Cross Archives.*

The Three Musketeers: D'Artagnan (Bill), Athos (Fr. Moran), and Porthos (Madelyn).

Madelyn Bussing Hendrix.

Rev. Lawrence J. Moran.

John M. Jenks.

John's three sons: (left) William P., (top) John C., and (right) Charles D. Jenks.

James E. Jenks and family, Carol, Nancy, and Karen.

Will enjoyed one of the author's comic observations at the 1974 reunion.

Will and Joe Corry visited the Jesuit cemetery and stopped at Fr. Cummings' gravesite in June, 1974.

On Saturday, December 21, 1974, Will received Fr. Brooks' letter inviting him to receive an honorary degree as his mother watched proudly.

Dinand Library. *Courtesy of Tom Parsons, College of the Holy Cross Graphic Arts Department.*

May 23, 1975, Will is blessed by Fr. Brooks and applauded by Charles E. F. Millard, after receiving his degree. *Photo by Michael J. Novia. Courtesy of the College of the Holy Cross Archives and of Thomas J. Carstens, '55.*

At Fitton Field, the new Doctor of Humane Letters was with his escort, left to right: Bill Kane, Fr. John Brooks, John Jenks, Ella Jenks and Jim Jenks. *Photo by Michael J. Novia. Courtesy of the College of the Holy Cross Archives.*

Will at his desk in Mundelein in the mid-1970s; note the clothes pin on the typewriter and the "sip and puff" straw (attached to the extension arm) which orchestrated the environmental control system, i.e., lights, phone, radio, etc.

Professor Dudley S. Childress, of the Northwestern University Rehabilitation Engineering Program, innovator of the "sip and puff" control system.

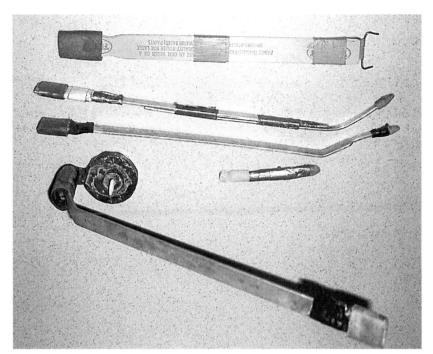

The tools of Will's trade included eraser-tipped wands and a clothes pin; felt-tipped pens enabled him to sign his notes and draw his cartoons.

The Three Musketeers, *a là* Mt. Rushmore.

```
                                        25 dec 1980
       All-out Adventist -
            This must be a Christmas card, since it's
       being written on Christmas Day, in lieu of
       Mass. The wind-chill stands at -33, ideal
   weather for pneumonia for me or a heart-attack for John,
   lugging me up St. Mary's double-run of stairs... I can't
   recall feeling so futile as I've felt the past week.
   As Christmas moved closer and closer it seemed things
   were more and more out of control. Gluttony and Sloth
   took command of my will. I ate every cookie within
   50 light years of the Great Black Hole in my face. And
   at night, after supper, I simply sat before the type-
   writer, as though faithful vigil would be rewarded by
   spontaneous Selectricity. This is perhaps the eighth or
   ninth card I've written since I finished my past-due
   Classletter. It would be easy to claim fatigue, but the
```

```
   truth is that dejection begets a weariness of escape.
   I suppose it's not feasible to maintain as many friend-
   ships in my new life as a workingman as it was in my
   long leisure. I begin to appreciate your angst whenever
   you feel there is too much world and not enough you,
   though for you the sense of inadequacy must be more pro-
   found, because caring-for is your vocation. I finally
   worked my way through, relying on prayer... Father Brooks
   sent me a book of short pieces by fellow Jesuit, Francis
   Sweeney. To write with such clarity and simplicity I'd
   have to rework something for a month. In a litany on
   Boston he wrote, "Boston,is Jack Kennedy saying, 'I'm
   glad to be back where words are pronounced as they are
   spelled'." During Viet Nam he ended a piece on his
   passion for singing national anthems with, "Oh, my
   country, I cannot sing your anthem now". .. Must haste.
   Our guests are arriving...        D.
```

The front and back of a card (reduced by 24%) to Fr. Moran. See in letters section on
p. 383.

27 jun 1985

Dear Betty,
        Bill told me several weeks ago that
you had 'picked up a little something' for me
at The Antipodes. I guessed a boomerang. If
I had put my Jesuit-quickened wits to work on the mystery
I would have roamed the vast terrain of the subjunctive
and never stumbled upon so luxurious a something. Except for the extravagance the sheepskin seems exactly
right: you are a nurse - still, always - as well as my
friend, and you know that a sheepskin is the surest
protection against pressure sores. What better gift
for Will? How did you intuit that I've grown concerned
about skin breakdowns? Ever since I saw a TV segment
on post-polio syndrome I promote every tingle to gangrene
and every rash to an ischemic ulcer. So now, thanks
- goodly thanks - to you I am spared one of those worries

... Saturday John and I will travel to Dana for a four-
day revisit. (If Brideshead, why not Dana?) The chief
reason for the trip is a farewell party for my friend
Father Moran, who has been transferred to Terre Haute
after 18 years in our parish. We'll see other lifelong
friends, including one woman we've bade a final goodbye
three or four times. In September she'll be 92. My
idea of fun... Love to everyone, first of all to yourself.
                                        Will

Add-on: A note from Bill told that you and he celebrated
25 years of married life last week. Your five children,
now grown-up, are the richest trophy of your love and
struggle. Blessings on you both for that good work.

The front and back of a card (reduced by 24%) to Betty Kane. See in letters section on
p. 464. The cards are the design of The Printery House, Conception Abbey, Conception, Missouri.

I love you, Mom.

♂Bill

More than a Hallmark.

Where's the elephant ENT man?

Oremus = Latin, "Let us pray."

The Letters of Will Jenks

CONTENTS

The Cousins

Letters from Bill Jenks

to

*Sister Teresa of Christ the King, OCD
(Patricia Ann Cronin)*

Mary Lou Cronin Murphy

Walter Collins

In letters to members of his family, Will usually signed his name "Bill." That is the name he was known by before he entered Holy Cross College.

∞

Sister Teresa of Christ the King, OCD (Patricia Ann Cronin)

Selections Written 26 November 1962—1 March 1976

Patricia Ann Cronin, the fourth of Dominic and Marion Cronin's children, was born in Chicago March 2, 1941. After her sophomore year at St. Mary of the Woods College near Terre Haute, Indiana, she entered the Order of the Carmelites Discalced in 1961 at Mount Carmel Monastery in Des Plaines, Illinois, where she remains in 2003.

∞

26 Nov 1962

Dear Sister Theresa of Christ the King,

You have to admire my versatility. I have never spelled the name Teresea the same way twice. If someday I should mistakenly stumble into the proper method, please don't notify me of my good luck. I'd like to keep my streak alive.

It just occurred to me that I really don't know whether Advent begins on the First Sunday of Advent or on the Monday following the Last Sunday After Pentecost. Ordinarily I am not concerned about the niceties of the liturgical calendar, but since this letter must reach you before Reverend Mother hangs the Advent wreath over the monastery mail slot I find myself wishing that I had a more reliable authority than the Farmers' Almanac to reassure me. It could be of course that I am wrong in thinking that the Carmelites live incommunicado during the pre-Christmas season. Perhaps instead you turn on the radio to hear mindless disc jockeys celebrating, a month in advance, the birthday of their Savior with such soulful anthems as "I Saw Mommy Kissing Santa Claus, Cha-cha-cha." That would be penance enough for the most ardent ascetic.

I waited until now to write this billet doux because I wanted to include a report on the Thanksgiving weekend. We had not seen the Jenks boys since early August, and so I had run out of Billy-and-Johnny stories—the chief in-gredients of my letters. Now my stock is replenished. The boys, their parents, and their great-aunt left us with a wealth of memories, many of them pleasant. (The others? Well, blame them on the human predicament.) The family was not at full strength for this year's turkey test. Jim and Carol enjoyed an excused absence. Jim used his four-and-a-half day holiday to chauffeur Uncle Roy to Florida. Carol was invited to ride along, but she declined the offer, pleading an aversion to air travel, the only means of getting home. Aunt Mimi was a part-time guest. She took the train back to Chicago on Friday in order to be available for a wedding on Saturday.

John's little red wagon pulled into our driveway at ten-thirty on Wednesday night, a full three hours after Grandma had given its passengers up for dead. Billy was hardly inside the door when he began spilling his brain of all the things he had learned at school. His narration was made more amusing by Johnny's grave nods of concurrence. Billy was especially eloquent in praising his teacher's virtues, notably her good looks. Carolyn, who views the admired Miss Ohls as a potential rival for the affection of all three of her men, interrupted this account to record that the Queen of the Kindergarten is in fact a dish-water blonde farm girl. At first glance the quality of Billy's education seemed irreproachable, but later, after he had exhibited a cardboard turkey made in art class and had printed his Christian name for me, I decided that the Skokie schools are less than miracle factories. The turkey looked like a cross between an ostrich and a hippopotamus. Or, to condemn it more cruelly, it looked like something the artist's Uncle Bill might have done at age fifteen. The attempt at spelling was curious. On the score sheet of our tic-tac-toe match—at which game he cheats unashamedly, drawing crooked lines to connect his three marks—Billy scratched "M-A-I-L-L-I-W," his name backwards. Let Dr. Spock figure that out.

Friday night John took the boys and me to the Dana Theater to see *Big Red*, a typical Disney story about a boy and his dog. During the scene in which Big Red fought with a mountain lion Johnny, who could generally be counted on to side against any dog in any quarrel, was transported from reality by the whole spectacle. He flinched at every flick of the cat's paw and he jumped at every parry of the dog's teeth. Ironically, he almost cried when a real dog came up to greet him after the show. When we got home he told Grandma, solemnly, "You should see it, Grandma."

Sunday, after Mass, John was supposed to switch me from my small traveling chair to my large lounging chair, but, predictably he made himself unavailable. So I asked Billy to do the preliminary chores. He put the straps in the right place, hooked them to the hydraulic lifter, and then, after recruiting Grandma's aid, cranked me up, helped let me down, removed the straps, and pushed me out into the living room. (Before Mass, as we waited for someone to lend John a hand in unloading me, Billy remarked, "I think I could help you, Daddy." He must have been serious because when I asked him if he would rather take the bottom or the shoulders he said that he thought he'd better take the shoulders because they're easier to handle.)

Well, worthy woman, I have undoubtedly overstayed my welcome, so I will bid you a speedy farewell and depart forthwith. I depend upon your prayers. You may rely on mine. Yours in Christ, Bill

∞

20 Feb 1963

Dear Sister Teresa of Christ the King,

I may not have known the starting date for Advent, but I do know that Lent begins on Ash Wednesday, next Wednesday according to our St. Joseph calendar. . . . Since Reverend Mother is obliged to clamp a padlock on the mailbox at the outset of the penitential season I am hurrying to beat the deadline with this Mardi Gras missive. . . .

Through the courtesy of the St. Joseph Aspirin Co. I have become aware not only that next Wednesday is Ash Wednesday but that a week from Saturday is your birthday. Because March 2 lies within the purple boundaries I suspect that all greetings will have to be delivered before Lent begins. So, in anticipation of that glad day, I offer a gift of prayers—prayers of thanks to a generous God, who gave the world a woman whose beauty easily calls to mind the beauty revealed in that Singular Woman; and prayers of entreaty to a loving God, who will beckon that woman to come still closer to the Fire of His Love. (How accommodating poverty is. The only gift I can give is the only gift you can receive.) To your Sisters in Christ and St. Theresa your birthday is probably not so important as the anniversary of your enrollment in the order, but to your cousins in Peter Cronin March 2 is the day for celebration. And logic seems to be on the side of your flesh-and-blood kinfolk. After all, your being born made all of the ensuing choices possible. I supposed as Christians we ought to observe one another's Baptismal day. It was then that each of us was truly born. But however pagan the sentiment, I wish you joy on your birthday, May your twenty-third year abound in blessings.

If I am to account for my actions during the past three months I will serve accuracy best by recalling what is closest to mind. Only last week my status erratically altered. I gave up my wholly carefree way of life to take on the crushing responsibility of tutoring. You may remember that I have had a uniformly disastrous career as mentor of befogged intellects. After my last failure I resolved never again to light a lamp in an impenetrable darkness. But because in this case I was asked merely to help a momentarily bewildered lad and not, as in the other instances, to work a miracle that would undo the mistakes of a short lifetime, I took the job. The scholar under my care is an earnest (His name, fittingly enough, is Ernest. That fact would have been important to Oscar Wilde.) farm boy of fourteen years and two hundred pounds. The field of interest is algebra, in which, as at least three once-agonized teachers will testify, I am hardly adept. The very first meeting found me hopelessly confusing a problem by ignoring the inviolable rules governing the changing of plus and minus signs. In time I may learn; in the meantime I can only teach.

Except for infrequent outings—basketball games, movies, and, once, a small party—I have huddled close to the hearth on these cold winter days. During the Christmas holidays I spent half a week with Jim and Carol. The details of this excursion won't be recited here, since they are of interest only to the District Attorney's office and to my mom, the upholders of righteousness in my immediate environment. Otherwise I have given my waking hours to ordinary pursuits, chiefly reading.

Your elder brother supplied me with my current object of study, the recently published final volume of the New Testament series—the first thirteen volumes of which he also furnished me. (Volume is perhaps inaccurate. The booklets average 100 pages each.) This last number explains *The Apocalypse*, no doubt the least understood book of the Bible. The commentary is at once lucid and reassuring. It completely eliminates all of the sensational interpretations of the text and instead reveals the work as a Semitic-phrased statement of supernatural reality. . . . Yours in Christ, Bill

• "Your elder brother" refers to Rev. Dominic C. Cronin, Jr.

∽

12 June 1963

Dear Sister Teresa,

Since Easter I've been putting off almost all my correspondence, perhaps in the unconscious hope that science might make a break-through in ESP communication. The prospect of sending messages along thought-waves is especially attractive to lazy letter-writers, among whom I hold a rank of distinction. But the approach of the anniversary of your taking the habit has moved me from the couch of indolence to the work-bench of activity. Besides, it is no longer seasonable to excuse my negligence with the immortal words of Jim Rivera: "I had a tough Lent." (Jim, you may recall, was a notoriously weak hitter who once wandered around the outfield in a Sox uniform. He gave birth to his prize utterance late one spring as he tried to explain his .037 batting average. Personally, I suspect that Gandhi could have done better after one of his famous hunger strikes.) . . .

I have had second-hand assurances that you are in fact happy in your vocation. Your distinguished brother—that would have to be Father Dom, since cigar-smokers are patently undistinguished—was in Dana Monday. He appeared in the role of chauffeur to Aunt Mimi, who is spending the first few weeks of her convalescence with us. (You will be pleased to know that through God's grace and the doctor's skill, our beloved aunt has been restored to good health and high spirits. She was persuaded to seek a quiet environment in which to regain her strength completely. Can you imagine a more tranquil place than Dana for that therapy?) . . . God love you, cousin. Bill

• The "cigar-smoker" referred to is Rev. Charles E. Cronin, Sister Teresa's other brother.

∞

4 Sept 1963

Dear Sister Teresa,

Whatever the calendar may say, summer is over. Since it is over I suppose I must end my vacation from letter-writing and resume my vocation of annoying tolerant relatives and friends. (There is no truth to the rumor that the Holy Father intends to give my epistolary victims formal recognition as outstanding members of the Apostolate of Suffering. I'm sure the Little Flower would have accepted the burden with resignation.)

For the Dana Jenkses this summer was the quietest in many years. . . . As you know, Mimi was with us for two weeks, and she was delivered and collected by your brothers. Jim boarded here for six weeks while he worked on a farm. Carol joined him for one of those weeks, the one that Billy and Johnny spent with Grandma. The boys used their time profitably learning a vice—gluttony. Johnny put away enough ice cream to burst a whale, and he was scarcely less awesome with spaghetti. Billy's lust for bananas would have thrilled a militant evolutionist. It seemed suspiciously simian. After a momentary respite the season's wild finale got under way. Four of your immediate kin—Father Charlie, Lou, Judy, and Marion—thundered into our midst just in time for the Dana Fall Festival. As you might imagine, they were overwhelmed by the splendor of the event. They were especially delighted with the free bar-b-q, which Marion unaccountably accused of containing buffalo meat. The stage show, the band concert, and the street dance won varying degrees of approval. Most of the attractions on the midway earned a piece of Cronin money, but one booth, housing the most obvious con game in the history of petty larceny, prospered mightily at Marion's expense. For an investment of fifteen cents the patron is entitled to pick up a floating plastic duck with a number on the bottom. The number indicated the shelf on which the prize was stored. Marion hauled ducks out of the water as though she meant to save them all from drowning. For her efforts she was an incredible assortment of junk—a tin heart on a tin chain, a Japanese gymnast toy, a miniature kewpee doll, a little brown jug, and innumerable unidentified gizmoes, the total value of which could not have exceeded twenty-five cents. I should add that Judy was not immune to the pitchman's propaganda. Lou, who now knows the need for thrift, passed that temptation by in favor of the cotton candy stand. All of the Cronins tried their hand at the basketball throw and, without exception, suffered injury to their reputations. The Big Fellow, as Father Charlie styles himself, did redeem himself somewhat at the baseball throw: twice he dropped a man off his perch by hitting a small target. He also distinguished himself at the pie counter. . . .

Since time, the tide, and the ten o'clock news wait for no man I must say a hasty goodbye. During the inevitable search for an envelope I will have just time enough to beg a few prayers from you and your Sisters. My need is great. God love you, Sister. Yours in Christ, Bill

• Mary Lou was born in 1946, Judith in 1948 and Marion, the seventh and last child of Dominic and Marion Cronin, was born in 1951.

∽

24 Nov 1964

Dear Sister Teresa,

Just like clockwork. I happen to know the starting time of Advent because our diocesan paper long ago began the count-down to V-day, the date for the introduction of the vernacular in the Liturgy. . . .

The reference to V-day brings to mind your remarks about the retreat—partial, for the nonce—from Latin in the Church's worship. Did I detect a note of premature nostalgia for the music that is to be scuttled? Shame, Sister. If there is to be aggiornamento, as our beloved Pope John wished, the non-essential accretions to the liturgy must be removed, and new, relevant settings must be created. Perhaps you and your Sisters could experiment with suitable musical forms for the English prayers. (With your permission I will include this paragraph in my forthcoming book, "The Collected Sermons of a Loudmouthed Layman.") . . .

In my last letter I probably mentioned the invitation I received from the local Methodist minister. He invited me to a low-level ecumenical encounter with the youth group from his church. I accepted gladly, and when the designated evening arrived I presented myself for questioning by the youngsters. In a way the session was disappointing. None of the queries were silly or 'loaded,' and so I had no opportunity to flash a witty answer. The only inquiry that brought a smile was "Are Jesuits Catholics." My instinctive reply was "There are two schools of thought on that question." For the most part, though, the problems posed reflected intelligence, sincerity, and charity. After the cross-examination all of us stayed on for a round of cider and doughnuts. The whole experience was encouraging. I doubt that it could have happened five years ago. It might not have happened now if Rev. Crough were not a man of courage and conviction. How humbling it is to meet a deeply committed Christian who honestly seeks to close the scandalous separation between the Churches that profess Christ as their Redeemer . . .

Well, Sister, I must wave goodbye quickly if this missive is to be posted today. When your prayers are not aimed at eschatological goals, please pull a bead for your unworthy cousin. In turn I will ask that you will enjoy a spiritually profitable Advent season. God love you. Yours in Christ, Bill

• To "pull a bead" means to say a "Hail Mary" on one's rosary beads for the intention of the supplicant, in this instance, Will.

∞

16 Mar 1966

Dear Sister Teresa,

. . . . It will be a bleak carnival season for you if this is the last word from the outside world before Lent begins. But I can't break the habit. When the deadline looms, the typewriter beckons. (Tonight's news report told that to-morrow the Vatican will announce new Lenten regulations. I doubt, though, that the revision will affect your mail service.)

Last night, during a costly phone conversation with my mom, Aunt Mimi disclosed that she and several other Cronins visited you on Sunday. They probably gave you all of the news from Dana, meager as it is. On the off chance that they omitted something I will recount the events of the past two months in the succinct style of *Readers' Digest*. If you were told that I am completely recovered from my kidney excision you have been listening to the right people. After six weeks of unpleasantness, caused as much by the anti-biotics as by the infection, I began to feel stronger and steadier. I regained my appetite and then got back all of the weight I had lost—a dubious benefit. Now I feel better than I had felt for several years. Things are not so heartening for my father. A month ago he suffered three consecutive seizures—brought on, it is thought, by lack of blood to the brain—and since then he has been bedfast. The attacks did no perceptible physical damage, but they left Pa in an even more confused mental state. At times he seems fairly lucid, and at other times he seems almost beyond reach. My already heavily burdened mother now has to care for two invalids. So far she has found the strength to do double-duty. Obviously, all three of us need your prayers. Have a holy Lent and a joyous Easter. And say a prayer or two for Cousin Will

• This is a rare letter to a family member in which "Will" is the name he closes with.

∾

19 Sept 1966

Dear Sister Teresa,

Earlier this morning I bade farewell to three wayfaring Cronins, the two Woodsies and their mother. They had spent the night here after having dumped their worldly goods at school, and today they returned to the campus to resume their avid pursuit of wisdom. Judy professed to be sick of this season's hicks even before she has met them. Lou, faced with a social boycott at Rose, expressed the hope that one or two hicks would wander her way. . . .

You and your Sisters have our thanks . . . for your earnest prayers urging Heaven to receive the soul of my father. It is the only expression of love left to us. We were easily reconciled to my father's death, since his last years, and especially the last eighteen months, held nothing of human value for him. His eyes had dimmed; his mind had clouded over; and even his tongue had found a grave. Our mourning was for the death he endured in life . . .

Over Labor Day weekend Mom and I left Dana to fend for itself and took up our abode with Jim and Carol and Karen. The purpose of the trek was to give Mom a change of scene and a change of pace. In that aim we succeeded admirably. Mom was able to shop at the countless shopping centers without worrying about disaster befalling the world in her absence. She bought nothing, of course, but that in itself is some measure of the pleasure she found. I, too, went to the big city, less for rest and relaxation than for fun and excitement. And where do you suppose I spend my first evening away from home? In a Dana-like town thirty-five miles north of Indianapolis. Jim had to scout an up-coming football opponent, and so I accompanied him and assisted in that chore. . . .

There will be prayers from here—and from there as well, I know. Stay close to Him and remind Him of your needy cousin, Bill

• "Rose" is the abbreviated name for the Rose-Hulman Institute of Technology, mainly male in enrollment, on the eastern edge of Terre Haute.

∞

22 Feb 1968

Dear Sister Teresa,

The big news from this quarter concerns my election to the Rockville-Montezuma parish council. Our new pastor, Father Moran, decided to introduce democracy into the awesome deliberations of the Church Militant, micro-congregation division, and so he proposed an eight-member board to be selected by the combined membership of both churches . . . As it happened, I tied with another man for eighth spot and won the seat through the toss of a coin. But last Sunday, when we had our first meeting, I didn't allow my tainted status to get in the way of participation. Every time the discussion lagged I jumped in with some profound thought. Luckily, we didn't draft any impeachment procedures by which I could have been drummed out of the company . . .

The second coming-together was occasioned by the archbishop's scheduled appearance for Confirmation. . . . Archbishop Biskup, the recently appointed coadjutor, greeted us cordially, without fuss, and assured us he was acquainted with the folkways of country people, having served in Iowa before coming to Indiana. Whether or not he was prepared for the typically Hoosier conversation that accompanied dinner and time and again derailed the serious discussion that followed the meal I couldn't tell, but it took some firm steering to get us through the reefs of anecdotes, reminiscences, and non sequiturs which imperiled the archbishop's purpose. The diners dispersed to various Confirmation-day duties, and I was left alone with our visitor. He used the next fifteen minutes to outline his theological views, which seem to be conservative rather than liberal. Since he didn't solicit my opinions on the great issues I merely listened. My silence saved him the trouble of conducting an ex tempore heresy trial. Our interview ended when my colleagues fetched me to the church, where the archbishop celebrated the liturgy and administered Confirmation . . . May Easter dawn with the glory of the risen Christ. In Him, Cousin Bill

• Dana is fourteen miles west of Rockville, the site of Saint Joseph Church. Midway between these two towns is Montezuma, the site of the Church of the Immaculate Conception. Both churches were the pastoral responsibility of Rev. Lawrence J. Moran.

∞

[Undated. Circa Christmas 1972]

Dear Sister Teresa,

A week ago we entertained a priest and three Franciscan nuns. . . . Father Moran brought the sisters here to meet a 'charismatic layman,' as I once facetiously described myself. For more than two hours we discussed the role of the nun in the modern world. At one point one of the sisters asked, perhaps in panic, "How many laymen think the way you do?" I could count only two *Commonweal* editors and myself. If you hear of a three-woman coup at next summer's Franciscan convention you'll know the seed took root . . . In Christ, Bill

∞

20 June 1973

Dear Sister Teresa,

The family grapevine—or the jungle drums—probably alerted you to the transplant operation your country cousin is about to undergo. By this time tomorrow I will have forsaken my Hoosier citizenship for the inferior status of Illinoisan. ("Ich bin ein Mundeleiner.") It would not have been my choice to transfer allegiances, but the sacrifice is being made in a good cause. The boys seem to be pleased with the arrangement, no doubt because it offers them an escape from the previous tension. I think it will work out. (But can I charge them for tutoring?) . . . A week ago Sunday some of the people of the parish threw a going-away party for us. . . . Father and Madelyn had lured me to Rockville with a hint of an afternoon of three-sided laughter. . . . The Jenks boys and their dad, Aunt Mimi and Mom, all the Bussings—including Gert, visiting from Savannah, Ga.—and a few dozen more friends had cake and tea, sang cruller songs, and listened to impromptu speeches celebrating the accomplishments of the past five years. It was touching and moving. . . . Say a prayer that all goes well . . . Bill

- "Previous tension" refers to the state of affairs as John and Carolyn Jenks's marriage was breaking apart.

∞

5 Oct 1973

Dear Sister Teresa,

After fifteen weeks as a city person I've almost lost my country instincts. I no longer smile and nod at everyone I see; three threatened arrests for invasion of privacy cured me of unpremeditated friendliness. And when I hear a siren I don't bother to trace the sound to see if the fire truck is heading south. In no time I'll be as oblivious to people and things as the next hard-shelled urban dweller. . . . More out of desperation than out of apostolic zeal I volunteered for CCD work in our new parish, and last Wednesday I sat in on my first orientation meeting. From the program presented for our scrutiny I would say the missionaries to the heathens took fewer pains to avoid offending primitive beliefs than we are expected to take to spare the sensibilities of Catholic teen-agers. Curious, no? . . . You might say a prayer for good weather for the Rockville bridge festival. It's cruller time. Bill

- The Jenks ancestral family home was located south of the town of Dana, hence the concern if a fire truck was heading in that direction when Bill lived in Dana.
- "Cruller time" refers to St. Joseph parish's effort to raise money by selling crullers during the autumnal weekend festival when the covered bridges of Parke County are visited by thousands from across the Midwest and even more distant regions. The festival has since grown so that it extends over two weekends.

∞

Summer 1974

Dear Pat,

In grief we are family . . . What is there to say in the face of the mystery of evil? How can a merciful God allow a good and gentle woman like Mimi to suffer a literal hell on earth? Answers come hard, if at all. But yesterday, at Charlie's urging, I searched the Bible for possible readings for the Mass, and I found several passages that gave my mind ease. (It just occurred to me that Charlie put me on that task precisely to help in the calming.) Psalm 143 (Jrslm), which your brother—again with motive—asked me to look over, tells of the torment Mimi must have felt and of the prayer she must have prayed. Then in Romans 9, 14–21, I found Paul's theology of good and evil, which can be understood in the context of Mimi's inner struggle. Even the self-loathing eventually worked God's mercy and freed her forever. Now she lives in the midst of love, where her only enemy can no longer reach her. And with time our memories will be not of her days in death but of her years of life, when she loved all of us more than we deserved. It may be that we are given grief to throw us back on our first and last resource, faith. There is nothing else to hold things together when reason cannot. It's not as though you don't already know these things; it's just at times like this there is no other way of saying it. Since prayer is your life I needn't ask you to pray for all of us. We will have much to live through. Love, Bill

• Margaret (Mimi) Cronin was the younger sister of Ella Cronin Jenks. She, too, was a Chicago public school teacher but was burdened with manic-depression (bipolar disorder) which worsened in her later years. She had moved temporarily to John's home from the Lake Shore Drive apartment she shared with Dora Smith, also a teacher, for many years. She took her own life four days before a scheduled hospital admission.
• "Jrslm" refers to the Jerusalem version of the Bible.

∞

1 Mar 1976

Dear Sister Teresa,

. . . . Tomorrow is more than Mardi Gras. It's your birthday. I'd tease you about your age, but I realize you live more in eternity than in time, so the taunts would misfire. What is to be remembered—and celebrated—is the life that entered the world on a long ago March 2. It began predictably enough and moved through all the phases on schedule. Then suddenly it seemed suffused with radiance. God had chosen you and you had said yes unreservedly. Therein lies the 'super-' dimension of supernatural. It at least prods the rest of us to examine the depth of our commitment. Happy Birthday, serene sister . . . Bill

∞

Mary Lou Cronin Murphy

Selections Written 14 August 1963–12 July 1989

Mary Lou Cronin, younger sibling of Sister Teresa (Patricia Ann), was born July 15, 1946. She began writing her first cousin while in high school. Though he was only fourteen years older than she, Will became for her, as she explains it, something like a combined uncle-father, since her father had died when she was seven years old. The available correspondence begins in the summer before her senior year in high school.

∞

45793 B.C.

Urgu urgu,

Klurp hurnt url. Murb purpur urdvu. Grsknuk.

Ides Mar 44 B.C.

Ave, soror,

Hodie erat mala die. Caesar occisus est. Scribebo.

23 Ocktober 1531

Dere cousine,

Hast hearde ye layteste rumore? Hys moste royale majestie, gude King Henrye, hath ben discurvrd wantonen withe ye wenche yclept Anne Boleyn. Fie on it.

4 July 1776

Fond friend:

A most impudent incident occurred this afternoon. A group of rowdies gathered in a nearby basement and composed an unintelligible insult to our gracious protector, King George. They arrogantly pledged "their lives, their fortunes, and their sacred honor" to overthrowing the crown. They have neither fortune nor honor at present, and they will not have life for long.

14 Aug 1963

Dear Lou,

As you can see, you are not the only one who writes a letter on the installment plan. I began this one some time ago and tried to pick up the thread on more than one occasion. I seem to have suffered several momentary interruptions.

Your latest billet-doux, despite its compound fractures, was unutterably precious—not because of your scintillating wit and enthralling charm but because of Judy Koch's magnanimous gesture in inscribing that tender sentiment on the envelope. I value that message so highly that I have pinned it to the inside of my undershirt, right next to my autographed picture of Roy Roger's wonder-dog, Bullet. It hangs in a place that is equidistant from my heart and from my prized tattoo, the one that reads, "Keep Cool With Coolidge." If Katie O'Connor were to scribble an intimate greeting on a Popsicle wrapper I would assign that treasure a place of honor. I might even wad it up and stuff it in the hidden compartment of my Captain Midnight Secret Squadron ring. (Don't laugh. I had to drink fifty gallons of Ovaltine to earn membership. And not even vodka can help Ovaltine.)

From your account of your love life I would infer that Carolyn is right. You are attractive to older men. With that thought in mind I have presumed to fix you up for the Friday night dance at the Fall Festival. I'm sure you'll find this young man endlessly fascinating. Perhaps he'll tell you about the plans for his next birthday party. At his last birthday celebration the fire department was called in to put out the candles. There were ninety-nine of them. If he already has a date he will certainly be available next year.

I haven't strayed off the premises in two weeks (and then I took leave to get a haircut) so obviously I have nothing to tell. I suppose I could tell about Billy and Johnny's stay here, but why should I be a stool pigeon? I will save my best thoughts until we meet. Au revoir, chere. (Pleonastic?) Yours in Smokey the Bear, Nero

• "Pleonastic" means an example of redundancy, i.e., ". . . until we meet. Au revoir, . . ."

∞

3 Dec 1963

Dear Perfect Catholic Mother,

I understand that the Woods has anticipated your matriculation by install-ing a new curriculum that will lead to a B.M.C. degree. With this diploma, cer-tifying competence in such maternal arts as nose-blowing and bottom-wiping, a young lady will be able to name her own terms in dealing with prospective partners. It would seem, though, that the school administration is not wholly confident that B.M.C. graduates will automatically attract superior mates. To preclude disappointment in the event of the program's failure, the dean is con-sidering offering girls enrolled in the course a four-year supply of bust cream.

As you no doubt know, the dispersed Jenkses and Aunt Mimi were here for the Thanksgiving weekend. The four-day affair was memorable for the constant gorging, the incessant talking, and the inescapable overflowing of the john . . . The best quotes of the weekend belonged to Johnny, who once proudly announced, "I almost picked up the kitty," and who admitted to his Aunt Carol, "I was a little bad in Church." Obviously Johnny is going to explain himself with lightly shaded nuances . . .

Well, prom princess, I will let you return to your contemplation of your finger nails. Never forget what Confucius said, "He who . . . " Hmm. I seem to have forgotten myself. A lady, though, should never forget herself. Yours for less poise And more boys, Prudence Playfair

• "B.M.C." is perhaps an abbreviation for the Latin "Baccalaureatus Maternitatis Cath-olicae," i.e., Bachelor of Catholic Motherhood.
• Carol is Jim Jenks's wife.

∞

13 May 1964—Freedom minus nine

. . . . Everyone here was pleased and excited by the announcement of little Charlie's debut. A few trouble-makers had been praying for a girl, but they have promised not to demand a recount. We are still hovering over the phone in anticipation of news from Indianapolis. Predictably, Carol is taking her time with the project. She had better deliver the goods before Memorial Day, else the racket from the nearby Speedway may exert a disastrous pre-natal influence on the child. Imagine a kid conditioned to expect speeds of 155 mph on her first cruise in a perambulator. (You may have noticed that I've conceded this contest to your team. I figure that Jim exhausted his luck when he won that $2000 last fall.)

If I were a hat-wearer I would have to be shopping for a size nine fedora to accommodate my slightly swollen head. One day this week Mom got a letter from the president of my class at Holy Cross. He asked her if it would be possible for me to attend the tenth reunion in Worcester next month. The class would pay my expenses. In the event that I would be unable to make the trek he proposed an alternative gesture: the class would give me $100 to buy some coveted item. In a postscript he suggested a conference-style phone conversation, by which I could talk to everyone at the reunion. At my request Mom declined the first two offers and accepted the third. So now I will have to re-learn the words of the school song, which we will no doubt render harmoniously at some stage of the program. I should note that His Excellency, the President, was eager to dip into the shallow class till not merely because he was a close friend and intended roommate of mine but because he wanted to show the class' lingering loyalty to the last of the brethren. He may have meant to repay me, rather handsomely, for my work on the seven or eight begging letters I have written for the Alumni Fund, which the Assistant Secretary for Alumni Activities has said are the finest of their kind. (The compliment loses some its savor when I recall that the Ass't Sec. is also a classmate.) . . . Yours for Bermudas, H. Toulouse-Lautrec

- "Charlie" is Charles Dominic Jenks, the third son of John and Carolyn Jenks, named for his two Cronin cousins.
- "Class president" refers to John J. O'Grady, III, '54, an attorney in New York, N.Y.
- Assistant Secretary for Alumni Activities is Rev. George L. O'Brien, '54, a diocesan priest of Worcester, Massachusetts, assigned to Holy Cross at the time of this letter.

18 Nov 1964

Dear Lulubell,

In all honesty, I am disappointed that you cannot spend the weekend here. If the matter were put to a vote I would opt for you instead of Mahlie. Don't be flattered. I would opt for Mao Tse Tung instead of Mahlie. You must have heard of her. She is one of my mother's 'girlfriends': still a friend if no longer a girl. Mahlie has baffled the medical world by going for twenty years without inhaling. I suppose she's afraid to give anyone an opening to interrupt her monologue. This filibuster offers information, usually ominous, about anyone Mahlie has ever known and anyone she has come to know second-or-third-hand. A typical stream-of-unconsciousness babble begins with one of her sons, finds its disaster-strewn way to the second cousin, once removed of an unidentified filling station attendant, and returns, seemingly through the pages of the phone book, to one of her sons. The boys, as you may know, are in 'show biz,' which isn't very 'bizzy' for them at the moment. We probably will get the inside story on nepotism as practiced on Broadway. Actually, Mahlie is a good soul, and she can laugh at herself. Her husband has a vast fund of knowledge about everything, and so part of the time should be tolerable. . . . Bust wishes, M.T.A. Kupp

∞

28 Mar 1965

Ma chere jeune femme,

As you know, a week ago the Jenks tribe convened its annual Bill's-birthday-and-basketball meeting. All of the General's progeny were on hand—all save John, who was embroiled in a platonic triangle at a nearby nunnery. (You will be relieved to learn that John survived the experience in good style, perhaps even in good spirits. He was audibly enthusiastic about *The Sound Of Music* and especially its female lead.) The babies, Charles and Karen, did no irreparable mischief, except to those who hadn't read the newspapers before the confetti kids shredded them. Billy and Johnny did what damage they could to my typewriter. (The FCC should prohibit the commercial that shows college students hammering on a Remington—with a real sledge hammer. It gives imaginative urchins wicked notions.) Otherwise they behave rather civilly. The boys persuaded Grandma to take them to town for the Saturday night 'action,' the weekly auction of unmovable merchandise for locally distributed ducats of 'play money,' as Billy called it. Billy surveyed the stuff to be auctioned and immediately conceived a great lust for a nifty flashlight. Sad to say, a more prosperous ducat-holder quickly left Grandma in the dust. But Billy was determined to come away with something, and so he urged Grandma on with, "Go, go, go" until she outbid the opposition for a plastic sprinkling bottle. Predictably, Johnny hardly arrived on the scene when he expressed the desire to go home. Grandma collared him and warned, "Young man, if you don't sit still I'll spank you in front of the whole town." Billy turned his gaze on the sparse crowd and asked, incredulously, "Is this the whole town, Grandma?" . . . Polobius [?Polonius]

• The "General" was Will's dad Mack Jenks, who served in World War I and taught American history and also military science to the Junior Reserve Officers Training Corps at Chicago's Austin High School.

∞

9 May 1965

Dear Ribs,

As you know, I spent twenty hours last weekend in the company of various of our clansmen, who had come together to observe the First Holy Communion of St. William of Lincolnshire. Jim and I were the Hoosier delegates to the affair, Carol and Karen having fallen victim to divers afflictions. We set out at six o'clock Friday evening and arrived at John's house shortly after ten. (No speed record, but an enjoyable trip.). . . . Not long after we dropped anchor your most holy brother, Rev. C.E. Cronin, sauntered in to kill a few hours and two coffee cakes. He had decided to pay his respects on Communion Eve because he was to perform a marriage the next day and so would not have time to join the regular festivities. . . . The five-way filibuster closed down at one o'clock, and we were snug in our sacks by one-thirty. Five hours later I was roused from a coma by the First Communicant himself, who obviously was too excited to sleep. (It no doubt reflects unfavorably on my sanctity that I was fully prepared to snore through an entire litany of "Uncle Bill, do you know what.") Billy and I talked theology, baseball, farm, and school until the slackers heeded reveille—a good forty-five minutes later. The ensuing chaos can't be recounted. It is enough to say that the Palm Sunday tornadoes were mere zephyrs by comparison. In the end Carolyn refused to wait for John and Jim and me. She hauled Billy to church long before the scheduled starting time; we three stragglers made it just in time to wait half an hour for the procession to begin. Guess who led the troops onto the field? That peerless leader of men, Billy Jenks. By a remarkable coincidence Billy was the shortest guy in the class. The Mass followed the script until Communion time, when a handsome young priest grabbed a ciborium and intercepted the pastor before he could give the Host to our hero. Needless to say, the surprise starter was Rev. C.E. Cronin, who had come to the church to be on the altar for the great occasion. Rev. D.C. Cronin also occupied a prominent place in the sanctuary. After the service we collected several stray passengers and joined the caravan to John's house. There in the midst of monumental confusion Billy welcomed his guests—fifteen of them—and took inventory of his presents. (Are you a member of the generation that got a rosary and a Jansenist prayer book for First Communion? The new breed gets balls and bats, books and games, toys and money.) Your family was there in force. Judy wasn't terribly alert; she had been flitting about until three-thirty that morning, Tulip-Trotting, I believe. Little Marion took Charlie Jr. in hand and then fed me when the smorgasbord was thrown open. (Carolyn was in her glory. She had enough food to feed the Chinese Peoples' Republic for a decade: ham, meatloaf, black and green olives, little tomatoes, baked beans, potato salad, jello salad, a First Communion cake, cookies, and mints.) . . . Before we had anything to eat John popped the cork on a few bottles of champagne. Judy poured the stuff down my gullet with her left hand and down her own with her right hand. It took but a few swigs to get things swinging and people swaying. When the crowd began to disperse Jim and I prepared to take our leave, but we had a stop to make before we pointed the prow for Dana. Your mom had interceded with Reverend Mother at the Carmelite Monastery to get us an interview with Pat, and so we headed for that establishment first. Jim and John (John had come along to assist with the loading and unloading.) reconnoitered the place and the two of them dragged me over a shaky plywood boardwalk to the entrance. There we gave the password (Luther to the stake!) and were admitted. Not long after we started our business Pat and another nun, a delightful woman who knows when to talk and when to listen, appeared in the grill-room and opened a ninety minute conversation that would have been no more lively if the scene had been a cocktail bar. We exchanged all of the jokes we knew and all of the family gossip, and we left reluctantly, prodded by the suspicion that we were keeping the sisters from their supper. (They insisted all the while that the only thing we were keeping them from was work, which they would heroically do without for our sakes.) Pat seemed a trifle embarrassed by your measles. She feels that you are too young for a second childhood and too old for a first. I assured her that you are studying feverishly, and she accepted that hyperbolic testimony without flinching. She is either very innocent or very tactful . . . The trip home was neither swift nor hazardous. (Deo gratias.)

I may have more data stuffed into the corners of my memory, but I'll leave it there for another time. Adieu, fond gras. Sparkle Plenty

- "The five-way filibuster" consisted of Father Charlie Cronin, Will and Jim Jenks at the home of John and Carolyn Jenks in Lincolnshire, Illinois. Rev. D. C. Cronin is Father Dominic Conway Cronin, Jr., Father Charlie's older brother, also a parish priest in the Chicago Archdiocese.

∞

9 Aug 1965

Dear Jezebel,

Don't let those bush-league Inquisitors force you to recant your belief that blondes, even partial blondes, have more fun. The question, after all, is aesthetic, not moral, and so the opinions of non-oglers are hardly binding under pain of sin. In this age of wide-spread toplessness, bottomlessness, and inbetweenlessness the average dirty old man (if I may be allowed to speak for my peer group) no longer considers streaked, tipped, or tinted hair the distinctive badge of the trollop. There would be considerable risk in approaching a Clairol girl with an unprefaced "Voulez vous . . . ?" For my part, I think every cosmetic experiment you've made has shown good taste and good sense. So when the votes are counted—if the issue is to be decided democratically—add my proxy to your side. . . . Well, liebling, there isn't much else at hand, so I will bid you a fervent adieu. Please assure your sisters that their time will come, possibly before the close of the decade. Virtuously, Getcha Hansov

∞

5 Feb 1966

Dear Lou,

You made no mention of the reception your pierced ears got from the Inquisition. I expected Dom to trade you to a tribe of Gypsies for an off-key tambourine. My objection to holey lobes is neither moral nor aesthetic; it's merely practical: someone, especially a child, might grab your earring and pull. The thought raises goose pimples all over my yellow streak. Good luck, Miss Van Gogh.

By the way, I should thank you for the Candy Cane gum. I should, but I won't. The darn stuff tastes good, all right, but it lures me into the vicious habit of over-chewing, which gives me a headache and innocent by-standers an ear ache. (The most painful part of adjusting to life at home after four weeks in the hospital was grinding down food that has some resilience to it. The fare at the hospital was flabby and feeble, and it offered no resistance to my teeth. When I finally flexed my chewing muscles by pitting them against a steak, an apple, or a raw carrot I had cramps on the side of my head. It hurt for a week, but I carried on in spite of the pain. What courage.) Lubriciously, Sal A. Schuss

• "Four weeks in the hospital" was occasioned by removal of the right kidney because of stones and frequent infections, due in part to the nephrostomy tube which had been put into place back in 1952 to help drain the kidney. Dr. Humphrey was the surgeon.

∞

22 Feb 1967

Miss Mod-bod—

Whadda ya mean, whose side am I on? If I must declare myself, I'm irrevocably on your side in important things, like love, cosmetic effects, and ceramics. It's only in my estimation of Lou Cronin that I'm obliged to serve as the loyal opposition. This has nothing to do with Tom; it has to do with your wrongheaded notion that this is a now-or-never situation. If you valued yourself at all you'd have confidence that you can wait till it pleases you to consider a lifetime commitment. For you there will be unending chances for happiness. So don't fret.

You behold a man whose life has been emptied of meaning, whose world has come tumbling down on top of him. My connection with the existential situation has been severed. The man who gave me his old *Playboys* has let his subscription lapse. The cruel news took me by surprise. In fact, it took 5000 ccs of adrenalin to revive me. As a Valentine prank I wrote a waggish verse to my pornographer's daughter, the fair damsel who usually delivers the goods. The jingle confessed: "It's not for your laughter or not for your smile/ Or not for your charm that I miss you/ It must be instead your ineffable style/ When you hand over *Playboy's* last issue." With that subtle hint I hoped to snare the overdue February and perhaps the still-warm March editions. Instead I got a phone message informing me of the calamity. I wonder if Sargent Shriver has a program to take care of that kind of deprivation. Cousin Wilkins

∞

10 April 1967

Dear Lou,

Congratulations on several counts. The summer job at Fields sounds like a dream come true. I just hope you don't get dish-pan hands. If you work in Fields' tea room, maybe you could find out how those fancy places make their own potato chips. . . . Kudos, too, for your firm attitude towards the rustic romeo. You may make a man of him yet. Most women wait until they've snared a man to set him straight, and by that time they've lost their bargaining power. (Crudely put but apt.) I hate to admit it, but most guys are pathetically childish when it comes to dealing with women. They want a toy, a mommy, an ornament, and everything except person-and-partner. Hell, a jeep isn't that versatile.

There's not much to tell about life in Dana. We did have a surprise visit from Jim and Karen last Friday. That kid could win the heart of Jack the Ripper. She has the sweetest disposition in girldom. When Mom was feeding me she promised to help feed me when she gets big. I'm sure her intentions were genuine, but I somehow doubt that she will ever have time during a meal for anything except eating. She stokes food into her mouth as though she were fueling a hummingbird metabolism. On the way out to Grandma's Jim stopped at a drive-in restaurant and got two hot dogs and a milk shake for his buddy. Less than an hour later she ate lunch with us—two glasses of milk, two thick slices of peppered sausage, and three rolls with butter and jelly. By four-thirty she was tying on a bib and taking her seat at the table to indicate that she was ready for supper. Supper wasn't served until an hour later, by which time our omnivorous friend was chewing on the woodwork for nutriment. After watching her go through an Everest of spaghetti I would be willing to bet that she'll be eating out of laundry tubs by the time she's five. Unlike the rest of us, Karen isn't penalized for her gluttony. She hasn't gained a pound in six months. How unequal are Heaven's gifts. See you sometime? Willful

∞

4 Oct 1967

Luckless Lou –

Jim and his ladies were here last night and today, the Feast of St. Francis and the first day of World Series play. Karen surpassed herself for sheer charm. (Pedantic aside: Camus defines charm as a way of getting the answer Yes without having been quite clear about the question.) She snowed her poor old uncle with her flutter-eyes attention. Almost before she had finished her greeting speech she was tossing water down my gullet. An intuition (cousin to Judy's voice?) had told her that I was thirsty. When she climbed up on my lap she scrupulously avoided sitting on "Charlie's leg," the one her sparring partner had occupied at the Fall Festival. I didn't realize at the time

that, like Spain and Portugal, they had divided the world between them. . . .
Down with inhibitions, E. Mann Cipation

∞

13 Jan 1968

Dear Lou,

. . . . The Christmas holidays—holidays from what?—held both delight
and disappointment. We didn't get to Indianapolis for the annual New Year's
bash because the wind delivered murderous snow and cold to Indiana just
as we were preparing to set out. Otherwise, though, the interlude was pleasant. Dan and Liz Helt and an army of their friends marched in and out at
all hours. Among the people they brought over were two English exchange
students Dan had met on the boat-trip back from Europe. They were dis-
armingly witty and no more patronizing than, say, John Lennon. For their
amusement I let them read the *Chicago Tribune,* especially the editorial page.
Liz read aloud the Character Clue, the funniest thing on the comics page, and
informed us that people who write fast are 'go-getters,' ambitious, etc. Then
she asked one of the guys, Julian, if he is a fast writer. He replied, off-hand-
edly, "No, but I mean to become one." Get this: the visitors were traveling
around the Midwest in Thornton Wilder's car. Julian is his godson. We got
the car's autograph by inking a tire and rolling it over a piece of butcher
paper. Cousinly love, Bill

∞

5 Feb 1968

Dear Lou,

Before I forget it I want to make certain that you have no intention of re-
peating last year's extravagant birthday joke. Eight bucks out of J. Paul Getty's
pocket might not rasp my conscience, but ten per cent of that amount taken
from your puny piggy bank would sandpaper my soul long past eternity. It's
not that I haven't enjoyed the subscription. The monthly moment of make-
believe delivers me from the dreary wholesomeness of Dana. Besides, there's

really nothing like sounding out one's honest attitudes by giving the Puritan super-ego a vacation and letting the Id have its day. (I've discovered the depravity is neither as close to the surface as retreat-masters have hinted nor as remote as the Prophet Hefner would have us believe.) Anyhow, I thank you for that past folly and urge you to save the rest of your money.

Karen was here twice last week—once for Gram's birthday and once for my dentist appointment (Feasts of equal rank). Both times her parents accompanied her. As an impartial uncle I have to say that she's the cutest little kid in the immediate cosmos. We had coached her all afternoon—while Gram was at bridge club—not to give away what the birthday present was. She took her solemn oath that she would never betray the secret. Mom was half-way through the unwrapping ritual when Karen yelled, "it's a surprise; it's a toaster." Wednesday evening, before they had set out for home, Carolyn called, and so we let Karen talk to her pal Charlie. She came away from the phone percolating with excitement. I asked her what Charlie had said. With uncontrolled mirth, as though Bob Newhart or Bill Cosby had just done a new ten-minute routine for her, Karen exploded, "He said 'Hi.'" Friday night, when the Jinxes returned to 'the yidda vilwig of Dana,' Karen wore a red sweater with a black-and-red 'R' on it. "That's for Witter, daddy's school. I'm a cheer-weader." She then went through an elaborate drill which ended in a stance something like parade rest. "That's how we stand for the song"—the Star-spangled Banner. Jim told that during one of his games Carol sent Karen down to the bench to ask if she could sit with her boyfriend, Father Cleary (the principal). Just as she approached her father one of his players did something stupid, and he let go with, "Oh, shit." At that Karen turned around and went back to her seat, where her mother asked, "What did Daddy say?" Yep, she quoted him word for word. Yours for the Maxi look, Y.I. Strain

• A year earlier, Lou and some of her friends at the Woods had chipped in to buy Will a year's subscription to *Playboy*.

❧

1 April 1968

Dear Lou,

How about Lyndon's deft side-stepping? I couldn't have been more surprised if he had announced plans to divorce Ladybird on grounds of incur-
able nausea. This morning everyone's assigning motives to the decision, few
of them charitable. I think he simply recognized—a trifle late—that he has
come to symbolize the threat toward their own interests that most Americans
experience only viscerally. He has become, probably with some justice, the
scapegoat on whom people can project their secret guilts and anxieties. So
the question remains: Who will the voters turn to—or on? It must be great
to be a Kennedy and have history detour to stop at your doorstep. I'm still
for Gene . . . Father Moran continues to foul up my reading routine. He
sent me two paperbacks dealing with parish councils, one theoretical and
one practical. Then he hit me with a copy of the bishops' 70 page pastoral
letter, The Church In Our Day. I'd like to know whose day. It's for damn-sure
I know whose church. The bishops,' and don't you forget it, peon. Gad, it
was disgraceful. Their excellencies clutched at their prerogatives like two-
year-olds fearing the loss of their toys. If I had known that a bishop speaks
with the voice of God to his people I would have listened more attentively
to the divine utterances when I had dinner with our walking hot-line. The
whole thing will be filed under 'Forget It,' along with several of Paul's silly
encyclicals . . . Did you hear about the movie Twiggy and LBJ have signed
to make? Boney and Clod . . . Bill

• After Eugene McCarthy decisively won the New Hampshire Democratic primary
  with over fifty percent of the vote, President Lyndon Baines Johnson announced that
  he would not run for the presidency again. Robert Kennedy then joined in the race
  until assassinated in Los Angeles. Hubert H. Humphrey won the nomination at the
  tumultuous Democratic Convention in riot-torn Chicago; McCarthy stood aside after
  his loss, failing to endorse Humphrey until he did so, weakly, ten days before the election. Richard Nixon won.

∞

13 May 1968

Dear Lou,

The end of your odyssey. Gad, I'm so chopped up I can hardly keep from swallowing my cud of morning-glory seeds. It's strange how quickly the time passes for other people. I find it hard to believe you've been at the Woods long enough to get unpacked. Viewed from the inside, your incarceration may have seemed more than momentary, but such are the charms of hell . . . Your thrice-great triumphs, boldly proclaimed in the TH *Star*, made us mighty proud. Mom has told everyone who happens by, including an Electrolux salesman and two Jehovah's Witnesses—all of whom were duly thrilled. I was a bit disappointed, though, that you didn't win the Priscilla Prissly Prize for having the cleanest shoestrings on campus (saddle-shoes division.) In all honesty, I think it's great that you earned recognition for competence in your field, especially since the Penn State grant in effect ratifies the judgment of the department. Even more important, you managed to take your specialty with seriousness but not with ultimate seriousness. That's why you've emerged from this experience with personal depth as well as professional breadth. It's useless to speculate on the relative good or harm attending the Woods produced in you; it's enough to know that you have escaped with Self intact and skill enhanced. For that alone you deserve high honors . . . Last Friday Clinton H.S. had its prom, possibly the most subdued event of its kind in the country. Susan Summerville, the girl who lived across the alley from our previous residence, attended the dance on an ambulance cart. Her doctors decided that the outing could hardly reduce her chances, since the cancer attacking her spine is inoperable and inexorable. Since last fall, when a sore on her hand was identified as a rare type of malignancy, Susan has fought a losing fight against the Big C. Even so, she wanted to go to her senior prom, and the local undertaker agreed to transport her from the hospital to the Clinton gym. I understand that she had a good time and the kids carried off the whole thing with grace and dignity. In the eternal scheme of things the gentle sham may count for nothing, but it's good to know that one dying girl was not left for dead by her friends . . . Bill

• "TH" refers to Terre Haute.

13 June 1968

Dear Lou,

It didn't take a Jeremiah to predict that the weekend would turn out badly for you. Only in Doris Day movies do old wounds heal, and that's only because the guy ritually mutilates himself before taking vows of Perpetual Adoration and Abstinence. The trouble with your version is that Tom wanted to play the Doris Day role. Your experience simply confirms a belief I've been developing ever since I read Kierkegaard's *Fear And Trembling*. Soren-baby maintains that human relationships ought to be moral rather than aesthetic, which translates roughly as 'self-revealing rather than self-concealing.' Of course, that fails to take into account the social necessity of playing it less than straight until mutual confidence has jelled. But the great American hallucination has lovers amputating limbs and organs that get in the way of bliss. If you think about it, it's actually more savage than the ancient Chinese practice of binding a little girl's feet to make them attractive. My gripe about this kind of dishonesty applies more to social and interpersonal attitudes than to sexual postures—I-Thou more than He-She. Middle-class values emphasize empty exchanges, gracious hypocrisy, and pretty wit almost to the exclusion of honest give-and-take. Cocktail party decorum has become the ruling spirit of public and private dialogue. Even worse, opinions on serious questions are so shallow and subjective that it's impossible to answer them without looking like a pedant and a bore . . . Genuine, adult love expects and accepts some disparity between the beloved's ideal and real self. And for his/her part, the beloved is not afraid to live with his/her own flaws and foibles, in the expectation of forgiveness, tolerance, and support. The soul, too, has its small bust and big bottom, but love draws it all into its embrace. So don't shy away from being yourself. THE man will want you just as you are . . . Anyhow, love and other indecent suggestions, Bill

∞

1 July 1968

Dear Lou,

So what else is new? . . . Good grief, woman, you sent me into cardiac arrest with your untrumpeted disclosure of the Murphy merger. I thought you were ridiculing the man-woman thing in general when you said "but to avoid a big build-up, etc." Three paragraphs later I was sure it wasn't sustained satire, and so I had to start all over and read it straight. If it were anyone but you I'd recommend instant commitment. Four dates and already you're picking out his-and-hers tomb stones. Even *Time* magazine can't handle events that develop that quickly. But everything I know about you and everything you told about Jim persuade me that the whole bewildering episode is authentic. His age, his Peace Corps work, his concern for people, and most of all his incomparable taste in women—all underscore the reliability of your judgment. It is altogether possible for two mature people to create an interworld (good word, no? Shared but not exclusive) through an intuition of a common commitment to life, even in a single encounter. Still, it's the mark of a mature person to discover the extent of mutuality through experience, both in response to each other and in response to the world. Time and honesty are all you need now . . . It hardly needs saying that I'm happy for you. No one deserves more to be loved. And if Murphy loves you with gentle strength you will become still more lovable . . . Of course, it had to happen sooner or later. And I would have said better later than sooner. But in your case, nuts to formulae. You're ready . . . My prayers encompass the whole of your life and love. Joy and peace . . . Bill

∞

11 July 1968

Dear Lou,

Twenty-two and still unwed. No wonder you loathe the barrenness of white. I want you to know that this Murphy business wrecked the filigree sentiment I had laboriously wrought for your birthday. So you'll have to make do with an honest banality. The truth is, of course, that you have always been, in embryo, the woman who has suddenly come alive through the divine breath of love. In this time of self-discovery you will come to know the Lou all of us recognized long ago. The experience can only give you joy. My prayers echo your hopes for happiness and fulfillment. Happy Birthday, valued virgin. . . . Bill

∞

30 Jul 1968

Dear Lou,

You know, my belief in you must run deeper than even I suspected. I read your letters with their matter-of-fact observations on Murphy and marriage, and it never occurs to me that with any one else at the center of this madness I would reject the whole adventure as a case of post-Woodsian decompression, a kind of sexual 'bends.' But damned if I don't think you know what you're about. Glad to hear that the first reunion didn't disillusion you. Somehow absence lends itself to distortion of the other's good and bad points, and in time that can replace the person you loved with a subjective image, compared to which the real guy seems an imposter. Continue to keep the thing going as an existential project; stay open to the shifting situation. (Sounds like your daily horoscope.) The idea of living in Penn. for at least a year after you're married appears to be so eminently sensible that there must a huge flaw in it. Nothing really falls together quite so tidily. It was good to learn that my sagacious (as opposed to salacious) advice at 'dating around' proved to be redundant. Even the sex-obsessed guys can give you a better perspective on the world, a sort of post-graduate amplification on my letters . . . How about our beloved pope and his quaint encyclical? His has to be the finest mind of the sixteenth century. I can't imagine what he was out to prove, unless it was that one man, strategically placed (like at the top), can drive a wedge into a mountain and with one blow sever the summit from the base. Good luck to him and the two thousand bishops with their new sect . . . Yours for flesh, Hy Protein

• The encyclical is *Humanae Vitae* by Paul VI.

∞

12 Jan 1969

Dear Lou,

Back in business after a month of writing Christmas notes and thank you notes. That gets to be an industry here from mid-December to mid-January. Take it from an abused receiver, it truly is more blessed to give than to receive, if only because the giver doesn't have to pound out a thank you note . . . After reviewing my verdict on your Jim I've changed my mind: you don't deserve him. Why don't you do the decent thing and introduce him to Judy Koch? He's everything you claimed, and I suspect he likes you somewhat. Play your cards right and he might even ask you to the spring dance. Jim's experiences in Africa seemed to have prepared him for the cultural shock of Dana. He barely winced when we explained our folk ways. Admirable aplomb. . . . Unspeakable shame has besmirched the Jenks escutcheon. We have had our first drop-out since great-uncle Elijah gave up on a correspondence course in mule-breeding. Little Charlie defiantly announced that he would have no more of nursery school; he is tired of people reading at him. I suppose now he'll hang out at the corner with that gang of good-for-nothing loafers and beatniks. Next thing he'll be sniffing paste . . . Bill

∞

17 Feb 1969

Love-lost Lou—

. . . Two weeks ago Madelyn Saxton, youngest of the Bussing girls, took on the chore of hauling me to an adult education meeting at the parish hall (sometime garage) in Rockville. Father Moran showed the film *Parable* and then set up discussion groups to fight it out like Christians. It was a fascinating experience on several levels. Most of the men proved to be blind to metaphor: the clown couldn't have been Christ; Christ had a beard and frowned a lot. The women were more perceptive, but they let orthodoxy get in the way of the film's intention. I, of course, plumbed the depths of its symbolism and articulated its meaning in an inspired disquisition, which the assembled heretics chose to ignore. Anathema sint . . . Warning to J. Murphy: Last night I talked with a guy who married a Home Ec

person. His jowls hid his collar. Those parsnip casseroles are murder. . . .
Write when those monogamous spasms pass . . . With more love than you
deserve, Your Constant Cousin.

∞

22 April 1969

Lou—

I think I'd be within my rights to sue Jim for alienation of affections. It's
always these convent-coddled girls who surrender their whole being—body
excluded, of course—to the first tall, dark, sincere man who makes them feel
like a woman. (Thus spake Jealousy.) When the thrill is gone and Jim no
longer feigns interest in the ingredients of a kumquat casserole, remember
kindly old cousin Wilfred and repent. And then just try to coax a letter out
of me . . . Last Saturday Madelyn Saxton (Trudy's sister) hauled me over to
Rockville where she and I and Father Moran diddled around with a tape-
recorder. Father has some kind of obsession about putting me on the radio,
and so he tried to acquaint me with my shortcomings as a disembodied
voice. Gad, it was shattering. I 'ah' as though there were a tongue depressor
stapled to my uvula. For variety I substitute 'you know' and eternities of
dead air. Worst of all, though, is my laugh, which has an authentically idiot
hollowness. A tard's laugh. It's the written word for me . . . Love and other
misrepresentations, Bill

∞

21 May 1969

Dear Lou,

Your old suitor, Bus Tate, arrived home from Viet Nam ten days ago. He's
as jumpy as a virgin in the Cook County lock-up. Apparently one doesn't
begin to feel the pressure until it's removed. Last Friday Bus brought over two
six-packs and we guzzled away the evening. At eleven o'clock Liz Helt and a
man-friend popped in, bringing a bottle of cheap red wine and a guitar with
them. So the four of us shared our resources and sang peace-and-freedom

songs until one o'clock. Fortunately, Bus was amiably disposed, and there were no hawk-dove confrontations . . . Bill

∞

11 July 1969

Dear Lou,

Your last birthday as a maiden. How poignant. I'll let Jim tell you how good it is that there is a you. I don't trust my memory to call up all the things I once found lovely in you. With a year of love those charms have undoubtedly been transformed into a new, deeper beauty. The years to come can only create the Lou that God intended; love will be the shaper. My prayers would have it so . . . Sorry I didn't make it to your graduation. (Not really, of course. I went to a graduation once.) Did you win the Betty Crocker Homemaker of Tomorrow award? Now that you've learned how to cook for 250-2500 do you intend to feed Jim left-over stew every day for 125 straight days? I never quite understood what privileges accrue to a certified dietician. Salary can't be that much better. You have to be a janitor in a public institution to make more than $1.65 an hour. Even so, congratulations on seeing the thing through in the face of a strong temptation to do otherwise . . . Bus Tate is rumored to have taken leave of his senses and re-enlisted for three more. The town bugler will have to start practicing Taps again . . . Happy Birthday, Beautiful. Bill

∞

21 Sept 1969

Dear Lou and Friend,

Assuming, of course, that you still count him a friend . . . You seem to have fallen into the domestic routine with no thought for the indignity of it all. After a few months at 'Prez' you may be ready to join the Equal Rights for Women movement, whose aims no one has bothered to make clear. I think they want babies to drop from vending machines—pre-weaned, pre-housebroken, pre-disciplined, and pre-cocious. Something like Sodality . . . Yea, verily, we had a great time at your wedding. I've petitioned Rome to declare your marriage invalid so we can enjoy an instant replay. The best part about it was that the two of you seemed to be having more fun than anyone. I hope the photographer caught Jim's smile when his bride first came into view. All the promises that followed were mere formality; that smile was pledge enough . . . Bill

∞

4 June 1970

Dear Lou, Jim, and Mini-Murph,

I'm not proud. I'll accept laundry lists, doodle sheets, streetcar transfers, or case studies—anything that will save face with the post office . . . I'm for pregnancy or obesity or whatever it takes to get a Cronin out of training bras. Judy reported that the little mother has already exceeded the allowable weight gain for the whole nine months. Too bad for you, junior . . . If time and prudence permit, try to get to Dana sometime soon. In any case, take care of yourselves and little William Henry. (If it was a good enough name for a President of the United States it should be good enough for my first cousin, once-removed.) Love, Bill

∞

8 Sept 1970

Dear Lou and Jim,

There is rejoicing in my heart for the two of you—no, the three of you—and for the world. A child born of love brings joy and hope to those who believe. She bears the promise of new goodness, new love. I can think of no blessing to ask for her. She has been fully provided for in her luck in parents. Enjoy your gift to each other as you enjoy each other . . . It was good to see you, if only for an afternoon, when you made that side-trip to Dana. At least now I can nod wholeheartedly when someone in the family remarks on the love you have for each other. If you weren't aware of it, the Murphys—J&L—have been the topic of much happy gossip. It was even worth the indoctrination course in Renaultism to have a chance to see you again . . . The four little Jenkses—the boys and Karen—spent a week with us in early August. It was pure bliss for Karen. She had a chance to get to know her cousins and especially Charlie, who is 'so funny.' (He is.) All four of them trekked to town a dozen times a day, mostly to tank up on root beer floats and vanilla floats. The boys bought their father a pipe, in the hope that he'd kick the habit—Charlie's phrase. At last report he was still smoking it. Karen bought her mother and her nana beautiful rings at Thomas' Corner Store—for 10 cents each. Luckily, the guys who heisted Zsa Zsa's baubles decided against making two hits in one month. Most of the daylight hours were devoted to an open-ended baseball game in our yard; all the kids n the neighborhood brought their lungs to the fray. Make a joyful noise unto the Lord. Good fun . . . Peace and love to the three of you . . . Cousin Bill

∞

14 Dec 1970

Dear Lou and Jim and Erin,

If Erin had been watching Sesame Street regularly she may want to read this on her own . . . The channels of communication between here and there take some curious turns, and so I'm not sure how reliable my information is. The story that reached here has you transplanted to a town 70 miles from Pittsburgh by the first of the year. And Jim is said to have a job working with retarded children. It will be interesting to learn the original version. Wherever you go, whatever you do, God's blessing go with the three of you. Your happiness is important to me; it reassures me that there are people loving enough to create a community of joy that says Yes to life.. Christ's peace by with the Murphys at Christmas and in the New Year. Love, Bill

∞

12 July 1971

Dear Lou,

So long as conscience isn't blind to signals from the calendar there is hope for the revival of ardor. As your birthday comes into sight I am reminded of the joy it gave me to watch an impertinent young lass grow into a soft and lovable woman. It was all the more delightful because I knew it would happen, even to the appearance of the man who would discover the hidden beauty at the center of you. And now with motherhood you are complete. If there is more happiness to be had you will be open to it. So my prayers for you are to thank, not to ask. Happy Birthday, old girl . . . Jim, who's celebrating the acquisition of his M.S. by abstaining from servile work this summer, has brought his ladies to Dana two or three times, but they've come and gone as though the devil were a step behind. Karen continues to hold her old uncle in thrall. She talks almost without stopping, and yet what she has to say is entertaining: "Don't worry if your teeth fall out, because you can buy new ones in the store; Nan Welsh did." "If Aunt Julia—who is a real Italian, from Italia—spoke only Italian and I spoke only English, we'd have to stop and explain what we were saying to each other." . . . Dan is cramming for his bar exam. So far he is jobless, having turned down four or five good offers. Liz is ten hours short of finishing her course work for a PhD . . . Best to Jim. Love to Erin. Same to you. Bill

∞

20 Feb 1972

Dear Lou and Jim,

I have no news to match yours. Or at least I haven't been notified of any offense against God and Zero Population Growth. You hardly need my blessings on your now-doubled family to complete your joy, but you have them nonetheless. May an angel stand between the Murphy four and harm, especially in the guise of a rutabaga casserole . . . Since my last note—at Christmas?—my status has undergone a notable change. I'm half again as rich as I was then. Cousin Walter, from the magnanimous side of my family, deeded his one-eighth share of the farm to me. The gift was all the more remarkable in view of his second wife's consent to the consignment. If corn prices improved I may leap over the poverty line . . . You've probably heard that Mimi is back in the hospital. She was on a high for the Christmas holidays, and when that ran out she slid into a depression that requires hospital treatment. I've taken it upon myself to write her doctor to suggest continued treatment on an out-patient basis after he guides her out of this low. In the past he has left her on her own when she's had almost no perspective on her problem. She still doesn't understand that a high is just as unhealthy as a low. If you have a free minute, drop her a note. She lives for and through the Cronins and Jenkses . . . Dan Helt has returned to Dana to practice law and, after June 14, to make a home for himself and his bride. She's a senior at UMich, from Boston and, incredibly, not at all upset about settling in Dana . . . May the girls' diapers be drought-stricken for at least an hour . . . Fondly, Bill

∞

11 July 1973

Dear Lou,

. . . . As the return address indicates, the Dana Jenkses have been uprooted and transplanted. Our home for the indeterminate future is this ranch-style house in the middle of nowhere. John's craving for the wide open spaces and my peculiar needs conspired to bring us to T40 Osage Rd, in a clump of thirty houses two miles south of Mundelein. The former owner built the place 16 years ago and allowed his Norse heritage to influence his judgment. The living room, my room, John's bedroom, the kitchen, and the family are walled—in part or in whole—with wood. The FR reverberates with Viking overtones. Everything is wood except the north wall, solid stone, with fireplace and two narrow, translucent windows. The size, 26″ x 16′, awes tourists. If it were in Dana it would inspire no objections . . . Until last Friday I had spoken to no one over eight who didn't acknowledge some degree of kinship. Then Liz Helt Gavin (The 'Gavin' tacked on May 19 in a woodsy wedding in Turkey Run; he's a young lawyer.) drove out from Hyde Park to spend the afternoon with me. Since then a string of visitors, some of them adults, has passed through. Maybe I can cancel that order for a Trappist cowl . . . Bill

∞

11 July 1975

Dear Lou,

Having recently been made into a symbol (not always rightly read), I have begun to look at others for their sign-value. You translate easily. Your life is a triumph over conditioning. Like most girls of that unlucky hybrid strain, the middle-class/strict Catholic cross, you were indoctrinated to live by received rather than acquired wisdom, to choose prudently rather than dare recklessly, to exchange shrewdly rather than give freely. Risking has made you singularly Lou. If your future needs a prayer it would be for the courage to throw off today's contingent truths when experience shows them to be out of joint. Blessings on your days, whole woman . . . For the most part the Great Event is behind me, though I still receive occasional clippings from remote if not obscure newspapers and letters from van Winklean classmates. The HC publicity man reported that the pinnacle of fame was reached with the story's appearance in *The Times*—of London. The day itself went gloriously. The procession, to the inevitable strains of P&C, took us to a canopied stage in the center of the football stadium. After inconsequential matters like the awarding of diplomas and the delivery of a weltschmerzian valedictory were disposed of, the five honorary degrees were conferred. I was second, alphabetically; Fr. Brooks, the president, called me to center-stage and then read the citation, a necessarily lop-sided account of things. With the purple, white, and black hood over my shoulders and the diploma under my hand I became henceforth and forevermore or for 24,000 miles, whichever comes sooner, Doctor of Humane Letters. (As in those apostolic epistles I wrote to you during your days in the nunnery). Later there was a lavish party under a tent-top on the baseball field. Security forces weeded out dissenters. Only people with kind words were allowed in the August Presence. For $1.00 plus postage and handling ($24.95) I'll send you a pictorial scrapbook compiled by HC and mailed to selected alumni . . . The boys and John are on vacation through the Deep South. After a quick tour of the French Quarter Johnny dubbed the place 'wall-to-wall Cheetah II.' (ChII is a local industry—a nude dance palace.) Otherwise their summers are going swiftly. . . . Congratulations on your Black Belt in the marital arts . . . Bill

∞

16 July 1979

Dear Lou,

. . . In all truth, the thing I find most attractive in you is your unashamed craving for life just where it's lived, in your body. You are present—fully, unmistakably present—in whatever here-and-now takes hold of you. You feel, push, grab, stroke, scratch, squeeze, punch, shake, pat, and prod it, as it deserves. Your heart holds no fear, and your face, no lies. You are Lou and beautiful. Happy Birthday, foxy lady . . . The large happening in my recent past was the 25th Reunion at Holy Cross. Bill Kane and his wife Betty took care of me over the weekend. About 250 of the 350 known classmates showed up for one or all of the events. Our class gave a record $250,000 Silver Anniversary gift. We also supplied the speaker for the Saturday night all-class banquet. He was super. He was me. . . . Bill

∞

22 Mar 1982

Dear Jim, Mary Lou, Erin, and Krista,

I'm keeping the kite. I like the kite. I believe in the kite. Honest to Ben Franklin. I really, truly do. So you can take the receipt and wipe your glasses with it. . . . Rainbowed thanks for the differentest gift ever, anywhere. It pleases me that you knew I'd like it . . . Longer thanks for making the long trek to Mundelein for the party. It added hugely to the surprise and the delight. . . . Thanks, Jim, for letting Mary Lou stay on to keep us up past bed-time. The best laughs were saved for last . . . I studied the Nutritionist's Guide To Paradise, with its qualitative blasphemies against all the delectables America holds dear, and I discovered that a small DQ can be slipped past my gallbladder without offending the Natural Law. Tears stained the page where it was revealed that a Whopper would likely be fatal. Au revoir, Whopper. And Big Mac. And Kentucky Fried Colonel. Those Truths shall be graven on my heart . . . Love to all. Bill

• "DQ" refers to Dairy Queen.

∞

12 July 1989

Dear Lou,

.... You should serve as The Feminist Ideal, strong, assertive, glad to be a woman men find attractive, not at all put off by maleness. If the first of the sisters to go public had been less shrill, they would have been more readily accepted. If they had been more Lou-like, they would have been recognized as champions of a worthy cause. As it is, you will have to make Woman believable. May you carry it off smilingly. Happy Birthday, best of kind . . . About three months ago we took delivery on a new van, a super deluxe mini-bus with hydraulic lift , twin a/c, and eye-high windows. Then five weeks ago John and I vanned our way east to Allentown, PA, and Worcester, MA, to tour the plant he built and the College I attended. My destination was a 35th Reunion, for which I had been invited to unload a few remarks. That went well and early, so I was free to enjoy the rest of the weekend. On the way home we stopped to see Niagara Falls, a first-time thrill for me. Three weeks ago we had an abbreviated stay in Dana, cut short by a near-coma that brought me back to Condell Hospital with a 91.5° temperature. Sulfa drug and blankets gave me quick remedy, and since then I've been hearty and happy . . . Love, Bill

• This is the last of the ninety-nine saved letters and cards Will Jenks wrote to Lou.

∞

Walter Collins

Selections Written 2 March 1966–31 August 1989

Walter's mother, Ora Amy Jenks Collins, was the twin of Will's father, Mack Jenks. Ora died of influenza in 1919, leaving her children Walter, eight, and Helen, four, to be raised by their father's sister, also named Ora, and her husband Ernest Cooper.

∞

2 Mar 1966

Dear Walter, Virginia, and The Big Fellow,

Sometime in the long ago I shuddered through a minor film classic, *The Return Of Fu Man Chu*. Now it seems to me that if a sinister old misanthrope like Fu can return to polite society with impunity, a lovable young Boy Scout like me should be able to return to the company of his kinfolk without arousing hostility. So I have returned. (A nice succinct statement, that. Perhaps someday it will find its way into *Bartlett's Familiar Quotations*, minus the extraneous 'So.' Naturally, it will be credited to someone famous. Us nobodies never get credit for nuthin.)

You will be pleased to know that my father's condition is markedly improved. He is as lucid and well-oriented as he has been in the past six months, but he remains a total care. Mom feeds and bathes him and tries to keep pace with his uncontrolled bowel activity. And of course she tends to all my needs, too. Hers is a full-time, round-the-clock job that leaves little time for those household cleaning chores that a woman considers sacred rituals. To a mere man, afflicted as he is with rational faculties, this needless stalking of such domestic enemies as dust, fingerprints, cobwebs, and smudges offends common sense; but not so with a woman. It's for that reason that I must be so ungracious as to ask you to postpone your intended visit with us at least until we can hold our parley on the front porch, which is relatively neutral territory. I know you have no thought of creating work for my mother, but I'm afraid that she would react instinctively to the situation and would try to rid the place of every mote of dust. Her legs just couldn't take that extra punishment. I'm sure you understand.

Two weeks ago I observed my formal emancipation from convalescence by spending a weekend with Jim and Carol. During the forty-eight hour liberty I staged sit-ins at a basketball game (which the Coach's team lost), a respectable pub, a Slovenian wedding and reception, and a beery party for the Scecina H.S. coaching staff (where our side won every game that was re-played). It was grand, truly grand. Until soon, adieu. Best to all. The market mis-analyst, Cousin Will

• "Someone famous" was General Douglas MacArthur, remembered for announcing "I have returned" as he landed at Leyte in the Philippines on October 20, 1944, during World War II. "

• The Big Fellow" was Ernest Kendle Collins, son of Walter and Virginia Collins.
• Will's "convalescence" refers to his recuperation from the removal of his right kidney; the nephrectomy was performed by Dr. Humphrey at Union Hospital in Terre Haute, Indiana. In addition, he needed to recover from a subsequent infection and his toxic reaction to the antibiotics used to treat it. For the rest of his life Will would make do with only his left kidney, which had also been damaged by stones in 1952.

∞

18 Nov 1968

Dear Walter, Virginia, and Herr Hefty,

Herb Aikman finished picking our corn last Wednesday, 17 Nov. Our half of the crop was 8982 bu. That figures out to 107 bu. per acre. In mid-August, when contract prices had dropped to 84 cents, I would have crumpled up and died at the mere hint of 107 bu. corn. By mid-November, when reports of 80 and 90 bu. corn had become commonplace, I was relieved at Herb's news. Apparently, the more-than-abundant rainfall hereabouts was not so beneficial as we had believed. That and the relentless heat and humidity seem to have taken their toll, not just in Indiana but well into the big corn counties of Illinois. The 23 cent jump in prices indicates the disappointment was wide-spread. On our ground, the performance virtually reversed the yields of previous years. That new field back in the woods made over 100; the 10 acres east of the barnlot, which have been pampered and limed for 20 years, yielded 80—almost 60 per acre less than in previous years; the 25 acres north of the house, an 80 bu. mystery the past two seasons, came up to 120-plus. The 120 ac west of the road did well overall, but several low spots contributed very few ears. Is a puzzlement. Moisture was surprisingly low; it averaged under 19%. Under the circumstances, it seemed wiser to take the dock than to run it through a drier. With almost 9000 bu. in storage and with prices rising we may show a decent profit this year. Expenses were down; fertilizer, especially nitrogen, was cheaper. Then, too, we made over $400 on the ten acres put to beans. (Clay ground that had done poorly in corn; we planted beans just to be able to sow wheat-with-clover. The 35 bu. beans were a pleasant bonus.) Pray for $1.20 corn.

Three weeks ago, Mom and I spent a long weekend with Jim, Carol, and Karen. Ostensibly the purpose of the sojourn was to see Jim's freshman football team in action, but the unspoken motive was to give us rural folks a taste of city living. Mom fulfilled every pilgrim's dream; she toured three or four shopping centers, one of them a new enclosed mall structure. I did get to the game, actually, and I watched the two teams divide things evenly. During the first half the enemy forces, larger by fifteen pounds per man, controlled the ball and their own destiny, but timely tackles and well-spaced breaks kept the score down to 6–0 at halftime. The second half saw a complete reversal of fortunes. Ritter (the good guys) discovered its passing game and moved 80 yds in four plays to even the score. The rest of the afternoon was spent in going goalward only to be thwarted by interceptions and the final gun. A respectable showing for Gideon and his band of fifteen valiant men. Karen delighted us with every kind of diversion. Her big thing now is Sunday School, where she learns everything about Jeslus (sic) except how to pronounce his name. On the Sunday we were there, she came home with the story of Jeslus and the time he was asleep on the boat. It started to rain and storm, and so Jeslus' friends woke him up and they all yelled 'Help, help.' Then they went home and locked their door. Maybe the people who worked on the new translation of the Bible ought to be investigated.

I'll try to be more conscientious and less cornscientious about keeping in touch. If the little Jenkses supply me with more tales, I'll try to preserve them for early delivery. Best to the others. Farmiliarly, Cousin Bill

• Herb Aikman, and later his son, Michael, worked the Jenks farm, being compensated with the standard 50/50 split of the net profits after expenses were deducted. The Aikman and Jenks families are related through (William) Henry Harrison Jenks (1843–1898) and Marietta Jenks Aikman (1849–1916), who were children of John Jenks (1803–1885). It is clear that Bill had a firm grasp of the micro-economics of farming.

∞

3 June 1969

Dear Walter,

. . . . To begin with, the corn is in and up. Herb finished planting May 16, a week later than last year. The ground had been plowed in mid-March, but untimely rains in early May delayed things. . . . A month ago the County Assessor sent out the new Tax assessments. As seemed to be the case with most nearby farms, our assessment was almost doubled. I suspect the jump can be attributed to the county's desire to create a favorable tax climate for industry. Eli Lilly is building an antibiotic plant near Summit Grove, on a 600-acre site which includes Uncle Mort's farm. Anyhow, I was given the opportunity to protest the increase, first in writing and then in person. Fortunately, I had a strong argument in the disparity between their figure on acres under cultivation (200) and the actual figure (180). I also complained about the appraisal of the improvements, noting that the house rent barely paid for maintenance and that the farm buildings were economically barren. Yesterday I appeared before the review board and discovered that the land had been measured from aerial photographs. Quite by chance I had brought along ASCS photo-soil-maps, and so I was able to make my point. The board will notify me of its decision in 10 days, at which time I can appeal to the state review board. Should be interesting . . . We have a new arrangement on privilege rent. Herb will give us 10 days of clean-up fix-up for use of the pasture, and Wrights will pay us $25 a month for the house. That'll give us $200 a year more . . . I wince when I hear current corn prices. The elevator is still operating, if shakily . . . Best to Virginia and Hercules . . . Cornsanguineously, Bill

• "Hercules" is Ernest Kendle Collins, son of Walter and Virginia, previously referred to as "The Big Fellow." Bill is detailing the financial aspects of the Jenks farm for Walter, who lives in Missouri. Walter Collins and his sister Helen Collins Shaffer each own one-eighth of the farm through the bequest of their grandmother Susan Jenks. The owners share any annual profits from the farm. Bill is managing the property because he lives in Dana and is therefore better able to consult with Herb Aikman on their choices for planting.

∞

22 Jan 1970

Dear Walter,

As my face must have told you, it was a genuine joy to be able to visit with you in a more relaxed situation than we usually encounter. A one-to-one conversation seems to allow casual exploration of personalities. If we had had more time, we might have discovered areas of disagreement on large issues; that would have made the day even more enjoyable. For one thing, I would have found a way to tell you that I am not quite the hearty hero you admired.

Believe me, I have had profound depressions and moments of bitterness, especially when I became absorbed in the possibilities I have lost. If for the most part I seem cheerful, it is because a few people have loved me enough to let me develop the possibilities that remain. It's probably true that I'm the most intellectual of the Jenkses, at least in terms of depths probed, but then no one else in the family has had eighteen years of leisure time in which to sound new bottoms. And I can tell you in all truth that my circuitous quest has taken me back to the simple truths we are taught as children: love God, love neighbor. Getting inside those truths is the work of a lifetime, of course. So I am happy, not through my own doing, and I do understand that it isn't important that a man should make his mark in the world. But living from day to day can be just as discouraging to me as it is to the next man . . . I might add that I wouldn't trade my suffering for yours. It's incomparably harder to accept the destruction of someone we love than it is to adjust to loss of physical capacity in one's own body. You bear grief manfully, with quiet dignity. The praise you showered on me belongs more fittingly to you. You have my prayers for continued courage . . . Even if we never take you up on your thoughtful offer to take care of me so that my mother can have a vacation, we are grateful for the suggestion. Everyone else simply assumes my mother is indestructible . . . Thanks for the phone calls. They made me feel like part of the Chiefs' triumph . . . Hope Virginia has shaken the bug . . . Bill

• "The destruction of someone we love" probably refers to Virginia since she isn't part of the letter's salutation as was the case in earlier communications. However, the statement of concern, "Hope Virginia has shaken the bug," seems too mild to refer to a problem that could cause her "destruction." Perhaps she was suffering from a less serious infectious disease in addition to a more lethal condition.

∞

4 April 1970

Dear Walter,

You have my heartfelt sympathy for your loss in the death of Virginia. I know that no words of consolation can fill the void at the center of your heart, but I hope this will reassure you that your grief is shared, simply because it is yours . . . In time, you will find that the love you had for Virginia will be the surest comfort in her absence. She will be present to you in a continuing love, more intimate than mere memory. She will live as part of you . . . You and Ken will have my prayers for strength and courage and for acceptance of God's inexplicable will. My mother adds her sympathy and the promise of prayers. Sincerely, Bill

• Virginia Collins died April 3, 1970.

∞

27 April 1970

Dear Walter,

I was glad to hear that Ken stayed on after the funeral. If he would give himself a chance to know his father better, he might discover that serenity affords its own kind of satisfaction, a quiet joy that doesn't instantly give way to emptiness. As you have said, there's much good in him . . . We seem to have hit a snag in the plan to give my mother a vacation. The good but bewildering woman announced that she doesn't want a vacation since she has nowhere to go and, typically, nothing to wear when she gets there. I think I'll be able to persuade her to try a three or four day sojourn in Chicago while you're here. . . . We can negotiate the details between now and then . . . My best to everyone . . . Bill

∞

11 Aug 1970

Dear Walter,

. . . . After a lifetime of a little more than nodding acquaintance, it was good to have time to get to know you. Both my mother and I were amazed by the discernible Jenksness of your personality. The quickness of your step, the precision of your grammar, the catholicity of your interests put us in mind of Uncle Roy, and the mildness of manner—a gentleness coexisting with a strong sense of discipline—reminded us of my father. Of course, you are more than those traits, but we were delighted to find something familiar in the center as well as on the surface . . . My best to the kinfolk . . . I'm not unmindful of the magnanimity of your intended bequest of the farm: I'm too numb to say thanks. Bill

∞

5 Jan 1972

Dear Walter and Florence,

My mind is no closer to finding words for the thanks I owe than it was two weeks ago, but at least it can give shape to good wishes on your first anniversary. Perhaps I could do no better than to wish you new luxuries to replace the hardly extravagant ones you gave up with your share of the farm—things like an undiminishing zest for life, unflagging vitality, and unlimited years to enjoy each other. If Heaven will do as much to make your life worry-free as you have done for my mother and me, you will live all your days in serenity. There is no need to wish you the best of all blessings; you already have that in your love for each other. Happy Anniversary, kind cousins . . . Money may not buy happiness, but its availability certainly affords a sense of well-being. Your gift has changed the whole tone of our daily concerns. We no longer mourn the inevitable departure of dollars in the envelopes and pockets of licensed extortionists. (At times it seems that way, anyhow.) So far we have not learned to spend more; we've simply learned to spend with less anxiety—a not inconsiderable boon. Thanks for that, as well as for a catalogue of other kindnesses . . . Fondly, Bill

• Walter married Florence W. Burchfield in January of 1971. In December of 1971, Walter gave his one-eighth share of the farm to Will.

∞

20 Sept 1972

Dear Walter and Florence,

You have grounds for complaining that I 'discriminated against' you in accepting John's invitation to fly to California after having refused yours to

fly to Lee's Summit. But I plead extenuating circumstances: two years ago
I was reluctant to try anything out of the ordinary, mostly because I could
imagine ten thousand inconceivable calamities, any one of which would
hurt, hinder, or humiliate. In all honesty, the boat trip on the Wabash went
a long way toward exorcising my cowardice. I foresaw disaster there, too, but
I didn't want to spoil everyone else's fun—especially Karen's. When I found
out that reality's obstacles are not nearly as formidable as imagination's, I
relaxed and enjoyed myself. With that reassuring experience behind me, I
managed to overcome my timidity about flying—not so much about flying
as about boarding the plane. So I'm doubly indebted to you for the trip to
Never-neverland . . . The corn refuses to dry out. If the humidity doesn't
drop we may have to make whiskey . . . Best to the others. Good luck to the
KC Chiefs . . . Bill

• "Exorcising my cowardice" is not a melodramatic representation of Will's fears; he
harbored sensible and well-grounded apprehensions about his physical status. He had
just one remaining kidney which was susceptible to urinary tract infections; he had
only twenty-five percent of expected lung capacity, essentially leaving him with no
pulmonary reserve; the bones of his skeleton were osteoporotic and thus imminently
breakable. He was aware of these conditions and, rightfully, they concerned him. While
Will did not allow his paralysis to stifle his determination to be as active as possible in
sedentary roles—typing, tutoring, talking—he was hesitant to put himself in situations
where he couldn't accurately gauge the likelihood of danger. His fears of water and
heights were reasonable given his complete dependence on others for mobility in or out
of an emergency situation. He thanks Walter and Florence for facilitating the "boat trip
on the Wabash" which helped him conquer his fear of being carried up steep boarding
ramp steps onto a plane in the care and hands of strangers. Being unafraid to fly opened
the door to Will's later travels to Hawaii, Acapulco and other distant destinations.

∞

27 Mar 1973

Dear Walter and Florence,

. . . . There's unhappy news in the family, and I don't know an easy way
to reveal it. Carolyn has divorced John. Her reasons are her own, though her
most vocal complaint has been that John is more devoted to Bell&Howell
than he is to his family. That might have been true a year ago, but since the

threat of divorce jarred him loose from his single-minded service to B&H, John has come to know the boys as individuals. We're hopeful, without compelling evidence, that a period of glorious, onerous freedom will prod Carolyn to consider a reconciliation. In the meantime Bill and Johnny will live with their father, after school's out and the house is sold. Mom and I have been invited to make our home with—and make a home for—John and the two older boys. We will probably attempt it on a trial basis and leave this house intact . . . Sorry I had to hit you with that thunderbolt. Further developments as they occur . . . Best. Bill

∞

19 Jan 1977

Dear Walter,

With the rest of the country I've wondered what Jimmy Carter is really like, and the clueless wonderscape made me uneasy. Then, two weeks ago, TV news cameras caught him just after he had decided to cut loose of the family business. The obvious sadness in his face as he spoke of the hard work he had put in and now would be putting behind him made me realize that he has a great deal in common with you. Both of you owned and operated a farm-related business in a small town, where your customers know you personally, not merely commercially. Both of you invested money and muscle in the building up of the business. And both of you prospered as the American Dream promised. There is nothing to indicate that Jimmy ever gave a large portion of his wealth to a rediscovered cousin, but otherwise I took great comfort from the parallel. I think we've had enough of leaders whose adult experience has been limited to the military and national politics. Those virtues we consider peculiarly American belong [in] the Carter-Collins background, lives lived in the belief that people are decent, work is satisfying, and every day is good. If what I saw in Jimmy Carter is what I've seen in you the country will be safe and strong . . . No doubt your marriage has enlivened your blood for this Second Spring. Equal happiness to both of you . . . Love, Bill

∞

28 Aug 1977

Dear Walter and Florence,

Today was Johnny's first day at Holy Cross. Friday morning, long before the neighborhood rooster rolled out of the sack, John, Johnny, Charlie, and Carolyn (yep!) launched the 900 mile trek to Worcester. The front wheels merely caressed the pavement, because the trunk contained the worldly goods of the young collegian, an inventory envied by Sears-Roebuck. We just had a phone call from Carolyn, who reported on the day's events, designed to entertain and edify the parents. (How different from 27 years ago, when Mom drove me to the train station and bade me goodbye at the ticket window.) Johnny's room is the farthest room in the farthest dorm on campus, but the geography is so intimate he's really not far from anywhere. The 25 buildings are laid out on five levels on the side of a hill. On a map everything looks snug; from the bottom it looks unattainable. (The football stadium lies 80 steps lower than the dining hall, normally the foothills of Mt. St. James, but there are only five home games.) . . . Bill.

∞

19 Jan 1980

Dear Walter,

For me the memorable event of the past month was *The Elephant Man*, a play fresh from Broadway, where it won the Toni award. My cousin Sue and her husband Mike took me downtown to a matinee. The experience was aptly called 'luminous' by one critic. The Elephant Man was an Englishman born in the second half of the nineteenth century, a poor wretch visited with grotesque growths of bone and flesh. He was saved from the life of a sideshow freak by a doctor at the London Hospital. . . . As I watched the story unfold, I saw intimations of my own rehabilitation—less physical than psychological—under the loving tutelage of so many friends, who refused to let me sink into pathetic isolation. I count the two of you among my remakers. Apart from the gift that renews itself and frees me from dependency, there have been the visits here and there. I trace the beginnings of courage to try the unconventional to the river cruise. When I learned that only timidity kept me from tasting excitement, I was launched on the high seas of adventure . . . By my reckoning you just celebrated your ninth anniversary. In a world where almost nothing seems to be going right, at least with the Big Issues, it's good to be reminded that somewhere love is making things happen as they should. May your tenth year be happier still . . . Love, Bill

∞

12 April 1980

Dear Walter and Florence,

Computering has taken over my days, nights, and now weekends. I just finished filling out the weekly worksheet and job report. . . . I can't recall doing anything away from the terminal for the past six months . . . I had a solar-plexus surprise last month. My friend Bill O'Malley, priest, teacher, writer, actor, sent me a copy of his latest book, three stories about five Jesuits who have been killed by terrorists, government Gestapo, and right-wing vigilantes. When the package arrived, I looked on the inside cover for a scribbled greeting. There was none. Later, as I flipped through the title pages, I found a message with an understood-verb, which I understood only after I glanced up at the dedication. The book is dedicated to Bill Jenks and Judy O'Malley. I doubt that life holds greater thrills . . . Love, Bill

• The dedication of Rev. William J. O'Malley, S.J.'s book, *The Voice of Blood: Five Christian Martyrs of Our Time,* reads "For Bill Jenks and for Judy O'Malley who have made me understand what being truly human means." In a letter to me dated March 23, 2003, Father O'Malley said that Judy is his "cousin who has had cerebral palsy now for 55 years."

∞

9 Dec 1980

Dear Walter and Florence,

. . . . To answer your long-ago question, the van is driven by anyone the State of Illinois and I find qualified. So far the Northwestern Magic Works has devised no huff'n'puff steering system for a vehicle, and even if the wizards did, I don't think I'd trust myself on the highway. One sneeze could blow me into eternity. I have managed to recruit chauffeurs whenever I've had somewhere to go—Walgreens, chiefly. The chair lift requires no engineering skills, and the latest of three tie-down devices clamps the chair in place without strain. Shortly after I took possession of The Tan Van, Bill and Holly drove me to Indianapolis for a wedding. The day was October at its best, and the windows I had had installed in the front of the camper top gave me tingling glimpses of autumn's glories. The heavy-duty springs and shocks and my new inflated cushion made the 450-mi round trip easy on my underpinnings. My first car, and, typical of the American male, I'm enthralled with it . . . The fold-over pamphlet tells something of my week as a born-again sophomore. It was an exhilarating time, almost fair compensation for the work of recounting it. Young John, a senior at the college, invited 60 of his closest friends to a dinner he prepared, with the help of a friend and a deli. Never one to be caught short, John bought seven hams and had three-and-a-half left over. I was proudest of him for his decision to give the leftover ham to Mustard Seed, the work-of-mercy to the homeless and hungry. The hours in class awakened brain cells that had slumbered half again as long as Rip van Winkle, though in the last class on the first day—a summery day—I found my mind drifting toward Nod. One of the young men who took care of me in the morning is the son of my would-have-been roommate for my second year. Other sons and daughters of classmates approached or yelled greetings across the campus. . . . Friday night of My Week, the President's Council met for its annual dinner. I fall a few bucks short of membership, but I crashed the affair, wearing a borrowed dinner jacket and clip-on bow tie. The jacket, a 'festive' plaid, in the opinion of its owner, Bill Kane, who wore a somber black model, was one of two bold departures from Proper Attire. We had hardly sat down when Bill got a note from the head table; "who is the fag in the plaid jacket?" The smile on the face of a high-powered classmate—and the tone of the gibe identified the author. Alas, I had no piercing retort. Age dulls the wit. Or maybe the blame belongs to computering . . . Implicit in my account of vanmanship was the unending thanks I feel toward the two of you for the gift that literally made the venture possible. In my heart the van wears a giant ribbon and a large tag, "From Walter and Florence, with Love." Inadequate thanks for still another freedom. Love, Bill

• "My would-have-been roommate" was John J. O'Grady III, '54. His son is Glennon J. O'Grady, M.D., '81, later a physician in Massachusetts. The "fold-over pamphlet" is Will's report of his visit to the College, presented on p. 119.

∞

12 Dec 1981

Dear Walter and Florence,

At this time of year, I always look back to the day when the two of you gave me that unthinkable gift, your share of the farm. Over the years, it has made the difference between worry and carefree living, between tagging along and doing my share. Now, suddenly, I have a good job at a good salary, enough to support my van and attendant vices, and it occurred to me that inflation could be squeezing your holdings. I have a suggestion: as long as I have a job and continue to live with John, I could send you a tax-free gift of $2000 a year. It wouldn't be much, but if it would help I'd be proud to return the kindness. Please think about it. Glad Christmas, good winter, full days . . . Love, Bill

∞

23 Jan 1983

Dear Walter,

Seventy-two measures depth as well as length, though there is no gauge ready to hand. Inner growth goes on so long as the heart renews itself through love. You have had a second season, a springtime in autumn, to add new layers of goodness to a life already thick with good. All of us who love you echo your own gratitude for that blessing, and we wish you more years' deepening. Happy Birthday, cousin and friend . . . Come this way when you can. Till then, glad days. Love, Bill

∞

24 Mar 1985

Dear Walter,

As I recall, I quit in mid-wish to give full attention to a phlebitis that had hospitalized me. A week of immobility and blood-thinners supposedly left me fit for a return to duty, but I returned home to a week of lethargy and inner gloom. By the following Sunday I was virtually albino, with a pulse rate of 120. A dizzying trip to the emergency room gave the doctors and nurses a chance to stabilize me, then move me on to ICU for reblooding—8 units of whole blood and 6 of thawed plasma. A bad mix of medicines had drained my system of red blood cells, below the danger line. The quick fix pulled me back to health and happiness almost instantly. This time I left the hospital and didn't look back. I've been fine since, having discontinued one of the offending medicines. Exciting, isn't it? . . . Shortly after I came back I read a news story in the Tribune with the heading, "ROTARIANS PLEDGE ERADICATION OF POLIO WORLDWIDE." Naturally, I thought of the Rotarian I admire most, and it gave me great pride to think that you are working toward that noble goal. Several years ago I was approached by a nun whose order runs hospitals for Colombian children afflicted with polio. The unvaccinated muchachos live in villages beyond the reach of government health services, so they are vulnerable to the virus. What a happy day it will be when those sisters can close their hospital or convert it to the next pressing need. God bless Rotary International . . . I watch the weather map and think of you enjoying summer. No envy; just joy for two warm people. Love, Bill

∞

12 Dec 1985

Dear Walter and Florence,

Several weeks ago, I attended the wedding of a young woman I tutored in algebra 9 years ago. We became friends, and during the painful adolescent years I listened and let her talk through her unhappiness. As I was about the leave the reception, she came over to tell me my love had been important to her. My heart still wears the smile. And that moment convinced me I should do the same this Christmas. Apart from the inconceivable generosity of that gift, you have made me feel welcome in your home, in your lives. Even more, you make me feel my life is not at all pitiable and in fact is almost admirable. Thank you for that. Love, Bill

• The "young woman" was Julie Torossy.

∞

24 May 1986

Dear Walter and Florence,

About a month ago, I went to the 40th reunion of—ready?—my eighth grade class. To public school products the event seems redundant, but to anyone who went to Catholic grade school, the idea makes good sense. The 36 members of the St. Paul of the Cross Class of 1946 went to at least 6 different high schools, and some were never seen after the ceremonies of June 12, 1946. As you discovered with your 40th high school reunion, the preliminary man/womanhunt was nearly as much fun as the gathering. Of the 36, two were known dead, and one—a fellow who lived in Park Ridge just the one year—was undiscoverable. Otherwise, we tracked down people as far away as Germany, as remote as backwoods Maine and downtown Idaho. The most enterprising member of the committee is the daughter of the Catholic undertaker, and she called the area cemetery to find out who takes care of the grave of Joe Busch's mother. Through that round-about tactic, she found Joe, now an architect in Warren, Ohio. Twenty-three classmates reunited at the SPotC church on a Saturday evening in April. . . . People came from as far away as San Francisco, Boston, D.C., and Dallas and from as near as Park Ridge itself. Several had seven kids; one had had three wives. Two guys had had bypasses; one poor devil was in a wheelchair. (Luck handed me a straight line for the evening's loudest laugh. Our m.c. suggested each of us should stand and tell something about him/herself. I led off and delivered the obvious punchline, "Bob, if I stand up, this place will be a shrine tomorrow.") A nun who taught us in seventh grade was able to join us. She took a good measure of genial ribbing. At 75, she remains remarkably lively and alert. The class clown, untamed after all these years, asked Sister if she feels at all remorseful for having rapped his now arthritic knuckles with a ruler almost daily during seventh grade. She came back with an apology for all the raps he didn't deserve. We parted near midnight, euphoric, vowing to repeat the experience in ten years. Whether or not that happens, we at least had this memorable reminiscence . . . My cousin Charlie, Uncle Dom's second son, had his twenty-fifth anniversary of his ordination this month. John and I took a day off and went down to the cathedral for a Mass and reception. The cardinal said a few words, then stayed around to shake everyone's hand. He and I are both honorary doctors from Holy Cross, but I couldn't think of anything doctoral to say to him. (I have since suggested to Father Brooks, the President of HC, that doctorate types should be given a password to acquaint one another with our common bond. What if I should meet Joe DiMaggio, Doctor of Fine Arts '82, and can only say I like Mr. Coffee's work?) Then last weekend Charlie had a party for 1250 intimate friends at his parish. We met a woman who had baby-sat for us 45 years ago. She still remembers seeing my dad in his army uniform . . . Best love to you both . . . Bill

- "SPotC" is St. Paul of the Cross.
- The babysitter would have seen Mack Jenks in his uniform in conjunction with his role as supervisor of Junior ROTC activities at Austin High School.

∞

17 Jan 1987

Dear Walter,

Ordinarily, your birthday would bring a smile to my soul, pleased at the thought that you embody the virtues and values we like to think of as the American character—generous in heart and mind, moderate in needs and wants, whole-hearted at work and play. But as your latest letter noted, the Walter Collins way has become less and less the American Way. The reigning lifestyle among people under 40 overthrows self-restraint, labeled, conveniently, 'a side-effect of the Depression.' And sadder still, they enjoy life less in their obsessive getting and spending. Unless the things and experiences that enrich their days are advertised in snobbish catalogues they are considered worthless. Singing in a choir? Discussing fiction? Looking at slides of

Holland/no, Italy/no, Austria? That sort of thing carries no price tag and therefore holds no attraction. That whole syndrome of neurotic excess traces back to some change in the process of growing up. My guess is that this generation was the first to reach adulthood without having faced hardship, and so its members haven't discovered the resources available within themselves and their near ones. Strange, that your difficulties and disappointments have given you a sense of what matters, of where life is lived. The contrast between yuppie frenzy and your calm tells me that misfortune, borne with faith and courage, can become good fortune as it teaches trust in God and the self He has given. Happy Birthday, a stalwart cousin. May you have many more years of good life . . . Love to Florence, Bill

∞

24 Jan 1989

Dear Walter,

. . . . Early in my celebration of the life I am proud to call cousin you questioned my first-sight portrait of the whole man. The years have done nothing to change the features of the Walter held in memory. Like the sketch underlying every great painting, that immediate image carries the truth only highlighted by further refinement. And it is no dime-store paint-by-the-numbers technique that makes me say, again, that you are the embodiment of what we think of as peculiarly American virtues—decency, generosity, modesty, good humor, idealism, sharper focus. It deserves tribute not just because it is increasingly rare but because it is admirable in its own right. So, with my Happy Birthday, you have my thanks for living out the belief too many of us honor only in others . . . In recent weeks and months, I've played host to various vague symptoms that, taken together, overflowed my anxiety level. So I took desperate measures and saw my doctor, for the first time in four years. The preliminary diagnosis—to be weighed against test results, is congestive heart failure. There's no call for alarm. My dad lived 15 years after he was visited with the same affliction. The latest medicines and long-avoided dietary discipline will return me to full health and strength in a month or so. I tell you this, not to upset you but to keep you from hearing it after Rumor has magnified it to Black Death. (I just heard from the doctor, who pronounced the results of my tests normal and went on to say my problem is minor, treatable by medicine and diet.) . . . Love, Bill

• The "various vague symptoms" were fatigue and sleepiness.

∞

31 Aug 1989

Dear Walter and Florence,

When last I wrote, cousins, life was simple and food was tastier. Much has happened to change things. After a merry pilgrimage to Holy Cross in June, John and I agreed that the new van would easily repay our investment, so we began plotting stretch weekends and mini-weeks of travel to places like Dana and K.C. The first such holiday ended abruptly when John became alarmed at my dozing off in mid-conversation, even with an attractive young woman. He drove me to the Clinton Hospital for an OK to return to these parts forthwith. We drove directly to Condell Hospital for a two-day stay. That resolved little, but a later ten-day hospitalization left me equipped with a pacemaker, which keeps a 70-stroke beat going, even during impromptu naps. I've been working full time for the past three weeks, and we are making plans for a jaunt to Ann Arbor in mid-Sept, for the Michigan-Notre Dame game. Further good times are tentatively set for Oct, a week of which is allocated to KC and the young Jenks people . . . Bill

• "Left me equipped with a pacemaker, which keeps a 70-stroke beat going, even during impromptu naps," indicates that Bill realizes the pacemaker will not cure his "impromptu naps."

∞

The Three Musketeers

∞

Letters from Will Jenks

to

Madelyn Bussing Saxton

Rev. Lawrence J. Moran

Over time, Will Jenks, Madelyn Saxton and Father Moran became close friends. Recognizing that their support for each other illustrated the credo of the Three Musketeers, "one for all, all for one," Will assigned each of them a Musketeer name. Father Moran became Athos, Madelyn was Porthos and Will called himself D'Artagnan. In his letters to these friends, Will often used only the first initials of their assigned names to refer to the trio members.

∞

Madelyn Bussing Saxton

Selections Written 25 March 1969–February 1973

Madelyn Bussing was born April 11, 1938, and grew up in Dana, Indiana. She attended the parochial grade school in nearby Saint Bernice, but completed her secondary education at the public high school in Dana, graduating as valedictorian in 1956. After a test run in nursing school, she chose to turn to secretarial work at the county offices in Newport, Indiana. Her marriage to Ron Saxton brought forth a son, Ron, Jr., in 1959, and twin daughters, Christy and Tracy, three years later. Although she tried to avoid it, the marriage failed and ended in divorce. Many years later, when her children were grown, Madelyn sought and received an annulment. Her subsequent marriage to Max Hendrix, now in its twentieth year, was blessed and celebrated by Father Moran.

On Thursday, December 21, 1989, the day before his final seizure, Will spoke to Madelyn by telephone to dissuade her from driving to Libertyville, Illinois, to visit him in the hospital. He camouflaged the seriousness of his condition and told her he'd be out of the hospital soon.

∞

25 Mar 1969

Ghost-reader for our Leader –

    I use the term 'effete' to describe myself simply because I've discovered that intellectual attainment—or in my case, ambition—doesn't answer the deepest human need. I think it's far more important to come into one's self, to live one's own life fully, than to know all manner of things. If you'll forgive the presumption, I would like to be as wholly me as you are wholly you. I'm only 37 years late in getting started . . . Your unapologetic ambivalence toward the blessings of motherhood struck me as admirably wholesome. I sometimes wonder, perhaps uncharitably, if some women don't immerse themselves in full-time maternity in order to avoid the responsibility of assuming the role of an adult. In the long run those very mothers find they can't communicate with their grown children. So they go to novenas and play bingo. Sacrifice, si; immolation, no . . . Bill

∞

27 Mar 1969

Dear Madelyn,

I begin to understand a source of your strength—an almost reckless faith, a kind of wild abandonment to God's love. Because your life informs your words with truth and because I sense intimations of that truth in my own life—no more than the hope of faith—I read your letter with greater surrender-of-mind than I would have allowed a work of a spiritual master. (I've come to the conclusion that books tell a person only what he's learned already. Letters, from an "I" to a "Thou," disclose what can be believed, risked.) To be quite frank, if I had read your letter even six months ago I would have been repelled by it, probably on the pretentious grounds that such God-talk represented an "abdication of human dignity"—or some equally pompous nonsense. Of course, I supported my 'human dignity' at the cost of splendid misery, but I was a 'free-man,' free to suffer nobly my meaningless fate. I almost bought the whole Existentialist package. What happened? It's impossible to say. Maybe, like the prodigal son, I ran out of coin and decided to come home. I know you had something to do with my return, but I can't estimate how much. And as you would be the first to point out, that was merely another instance of God bouncing grace off one of His mirrors. Anyhow what all this is leading up to is an affirmation of your insight that suffering is intolerable so long as a person insists he has some unaccountable sovereignty over body and soul and so long as he says that the game can't be played without complete equipment . . . Do you remember the joke about the guy with the trained mule? He hit him over the head with the two-by-four because 'first I have to get his attention.' Well, that's the way I see my predicament. Everyone has to learn, usually through some kind of suffering, some inescapable limitation of selfhood—self-defined selfhood— that Conscience, in its silence, calls him back to God-given and therefore unmanipulable individual being. I tried it every way but the right way. I wanted to be almost anyone but myself. (Another mystery: why don't others run away from someone who is running away from himself?) It just doesn't work. So now I pray for the courage to take on this life to face the sorrows and embrace the sufferings, and to do whatever I'm called to do. I won't lie to you. Sometimes it seems too much and sometimes I'm not sure that there's anything to hold onto. But it's this way or despair . . . Flannery O'Connor wrote a book *The Violent Bear It Away*. The title is taken from a passage in the gospels—Matthew? The idea, I think, is that faith is not something to be picked up timidly, gingerly. Your Psalm-stern prayer—God, let me either straighten things out or give me the grace to accept them—echoes with such holy violence. You are to be envied that grace . . . The quote from Gibran requires prolonged thought, but on the face of it I would say that it would be difficult perhaps impossible, for anyone to learn to love if there were no physical or spiritual deprivation to summon him out of himself. We might never discover what our lives are for if there were no one to give them to. Of course, changing the 'given' of a situation changes its structure. It's pointless to speculate (Can this be me saying harsh things about idle speculation?) on how man would be if his world were different. Heidegger says "Good night and good luck." . . . Your friend in need, Bill

∾

Below is the text of Madelyn's response to Will's correspondence of March 27, 1969. This, the only surviving letter written by Madelyn to Will, was preserved because Madelyn kept a carbon copy.

29 Mar 1969

Dear Bill,

    Congratulations, you ruined my entire evening. I couldn't get your letter out of my mind. Does any human really know another or does any person really know himself?

    I can't help but believe that to have real faith you first have to lose it. I'm thinking of people like ourselves, who were born into faith; being raised with the image of God 'forced' on us. I think this is good in a sense, because we know the

basic rules; but the time comes when we all need to feel freedom. Once we have declared our freedom, we eventually realize that we have not in ourselves all the freedom we need. Our freedom never conquers God.

You said my letter would have repelled you six months ago; it would have done the same to me around seven years ago. I went through a long period, (nearly two years) of my 'imaginary freedom'—it was hell and I was independent enough to mistake it for 'life.' I didn't become disillusioned with the Church per se, but with God. I led such a hypocritical life, keeping up a 'front' for the family and going to church with the same emotions I would have going to the grocery store. I refused to believe that there was a God or that he could do anything for me. One day I was totally exhausted. I fell across the bed and thought if I can only stay there forever. I found myself saying, "Dear God, please let me die." I was shocked—not because I wanted to die, but because I had called to God. For the next few months I tossed God around in my confused mind. Some graces are difficult to accept! I think the climax came when Dad died. I just couldn't let him die for the sake of dying. When we lose one blessing another is often, most unexpectedly, given in its place. Anyway, I like to think of myself as a 'convert.' I have chosen my 'way of life' not because it has been drilled into me, but because I, as a mature person, found it to be the only way.

I cannot help but believe that your misfortune which has defeated you in life is the very power that raises your soul to the throne of God. Illness, accepted, has all the spiritual value of voluntary penance. I think one is given strength to bear what happens, but not the 101 different things that might happen. God's grace is sufficient for this day, this minute, but not for the future or remembrances of the past.

May God continue to support you—that He has done so is apparent from the fact that you are not embittered. I, too, will pray for your courage.

I'll end with a quote . . . "Nothing gives us greater happiness than to become what we must be, thinking, feeling, and saying what we are."

Madelyn
CC: Father Moran

∞

30 Mar 1969

Dear Madelyn,

I should have known—or guessed. The reason you are so surely on the Way and ahead of me is that you lost and then found the Way much earlier. I couldn't understand how a hot-house faith could survive and flourish in the hostile climate of reality. It would seem that the root system was ruthlessly cut back before the transplanting. I don't know if that agonizing experience is an indispensable part of the fruit-bearing process, but I don't have the imagination enough to conceive an alternative. Anyhow, (forgive my callousness) I'm glad you went through it, too. Real communication would have been impossible if neither of us knew that the other is underway along the same Way. Like you, I kept my inner condition masked with hypocrisy. Who could I have talked openly with? How could I have sensed that uncomplicated Madelyn had gone through hell before me? I would have been suspicious of anyone who would advertise "Soul-saving Solace—Cheap." I suppose everyone has to go through that ordeal by himself. Only afterward can he speak of it, and then reticently, to someone he recognizes as free in God's thralldom. Thank God that you are such a one; that thought reinforces my hope with borrowed courage . . . The chief obstacle to finding a common basis for the two experiences seems to have been an artificial opposition I had conceived between the moral and the aesthetic, between internalizing and externalizing truth. No doubt in reaction to the overblown claims of art and literature, self-anointed mediators of Goodness, Truth, and Beauty, I've come to attribute all real virtue to the moral, to love and responsibility and acceptance. Starting with that prejudice, I was getting nowhere fast in my quest for the musicness of Madelyn and the Madelyn-ness of music. Then I remembered the key to all problems: when in doubt return to Heidegger. So how about this: the moral and the aesthetic are merely different modes of being/doing. The moral emphasizes the doing and so reveals being; the aesthetic emphasizes the revealing of being and so involves a doing. In their purest form—the doing you and the being music—the revelation is of the one Being Whose doing is our being . . . Just because I pick out this one insight does not mean that I didn't ruminate on all the others: I have never read any thought so devastatingly lucid as your statement that we don't enjoy grace enough for the 101 things that might happen, only enough for the things that do. That is the cornerstone of personal peace and freedom, the perfect articulation of faith. (Please stop dazzling me with these incandescent profundities. I'd rather do it myself, mother. And if I'm granted another 147 years I just may succeed.) Less flippantly, thank you for sharing these precious—because earned through pain—thoughts with me. And thank you for the promise of prayers . . . Bill

∞

6 May 1969

Why grrr, tiger?
The threat posed to our friendship by that slant-eyed superstition has driven me to frenetic assaults on fate. I requested the Foundation for Undeniable, Certified Genius to reduce me to an IQ of 130. (Those 40 points are gladly tossed away.) . . . One more reason a degree is a dubious blessing. (If it seems to you that I have a mental twitch on this point, you're right. Self-persuading?) The whole rationale of American education is to teach people how to serve their fellow man without ever having to think of them as human beings. Do good, but do it professionally . . . You're distressed disaster, Y.A. Monkey

∞

16 May 1969

Dear Madelyn,

To return to your letter. Your elaboration of the idea that loving is giving of self to be loved shed a pure light on both the thought and the thinker. I find it hard to separate the one from the other, and I'm not at all sure I should try to. Real learning should somehow take into account the truth that no thought exists apart from the person thinking, that it is not enough to seize the product of another's gathering, that what is to be taken is the way of encountering. I intend to meditate on your way of moving through, for it yields a rich harvest . . . Bill

∞

22 May 1969

Dear Miss Oddbod,

If my tone gave the impression that I was being intellectually smug about belief in miracles I want to correct that impression. Quite literally, I believe that life and love and grace and creation, which are merely four faces of the same thing, are all the miracles I could wish for. Sometimes I get far enough outside myself to see what a superabundance of grace each of us is given. Look at me: my physical 'death,' which on the face of it should have brought about an equivalent loss of freedom, has in fact compelled me to live more fully and more freely. That's the miracle of having been given more than we can lose or throw away. For a long time I resisted the possibilities that remained on the grounds that "Yes, I still have a family who loves me, friends who are blind to my lack, a mind that savors thoughts, and a civilization that has some compassion for the afflicted, but what if I had been born without family, friends, wit or John T. Myers?" (There, in a sentence, is the great Existentialist fallacy: Sure, life is good, but under the right conditions it could be terrible.) You taught me to exorcise that bogeyman with the words: "we're not given enough grace for the 101 things that might happen; only for the things that do happen." Anyhow I've had my miracle . . . And you have had yours. How else could you explain the appearance of Christendom's foremost original thinker (Sorry, Herr Heidegger. I cannot tell a lie) in this unlikely place, a thousand leagues from downtown Nowhere. It was no more your own doing than mine was my own but at least you let it happen . . . Bill

∞

13 Jun 1969

Dear Madelyn,

. . . You are as nearly capable of loving unconditionally as any human is likely to be, and in a sense that's terrifying to anyone you love . . . It's hard for a person, especially for a man, to accept the truth the genuine love seeks not just what is good and strong and noble in the other but rather the whole, unconcealed self, however weak and foolish. Your love will break through the shield of lies because it is God's love through you . . . God's grace in you is beautiful. Bill

∞

1 Jul 1969

Dear Madelyn,

In what was probably an attempt to reconcile Catholic kids to second-class citizenship the nuns used to teach us that the admonition "What does it profit a man to gain the whole world . . . ?" referred to avarice, to getting rich. I think it means something more than that; it refers to the counterfeit mastery man exercises over the world through knowledge—'scientia.' There is no possible way to juggle all the known facts to discover the one truth that matters: what is man for? Faith alone supplies that answer. At times, of course, it's hard to keep that in mind especially when some especially seductive philosophy catches the fancy . . . I'm just beginning to learn that we really know a person only when we have seen him carry his cross. Even then, of course, we can scarcely sense the depth of suffering; we can merely recognize the reality of suffering and perhaps, like the women of Jerusalem, weep inwardly for grief-burdened innocence. But through its tears the eye glimpses a beauty in the midst of ugliness, a dignity in the midst of humiliation, a peace in the midst of turmoil. Here, surely, is the mystery of resurrection—that those who love God cannot be killed in their ability to love and that instead they live on to love more completely. I wish that I had never had the opportunity to witness this miracle of grace, because it was done at the cost of great pain to a friend. But if it had to be made manifest, I could have asked no more compelling evidence. May you always be a communicator of God's life-giving forgiveness . . . Bill

• "What does it profit a man to gain the whole world if he suffers the loss of his own soul?" Mark 8:36.

∞

[Sometime in mid 1969]

Dear Madelyn,

Your mood is the indicative; mine is the subjunctive; A's is the imperative . . . Bill

∞

"TRULY IT IS MORE BLESSED . . . "

His eyes, smile-lighted,
Find love-illuminated hers,
And his hand, fixed in a fist,
Thrusts heartward his secret.
"A flower, Mommy—for you."
Taken tenderly as an orchid,
The crass, brassy dandelion
Is vased to grace her table.
Pleased with her pleasure,
He flees to the field
That yielded this gold
And gathers other kiss-gifts.
But more is not her need,
Only the giving and its sign.
She wins him back from tears
With a mother's loving hug.

∞

9 Jul 1969

Dear Madelyn,

Because you are my friend I will tell you about my friendship with Father Pat, for no other reason than it should be recalled. On the face of it, I suppose, the relationship looked unpromising at the start. I was young and brash and self-important; Father was old beyond his years and touchy and set in his ways. He was professor and confessor; I was student and sinner. Yet somehow we had made the beginnings of a friendship, perhaps on a father-son basis, even before I left school at the end of freshman year. When I got sick my first thought was to notify him. He responded with a letter and another and another—every day during that year in the hospital and every other day in the next 17 years. More than three thousand letters in all. At first Father was concerned solely with my morale, but as time went on and after I had a way to respond, his letters dealt with all manner of things—Holy Cross, literature, politics, whatever interested me. And always there was a word of counsel and encouragement to support me in the struggle for acceptance of God's will. Over long periods in the middle years, when my thinking had diverged widely from his, I found it hard to mask my impatience with his out-moded views and with his grating insistence that faith would see me through. Then gradually we moved toward a person-person understanding, and I came to realize that the message all those letters bore was nothing more than 'someone cares.' When I learned that I began to find that same message beneath the words and deeds of others. It was that grace that got me underway along the way. And in that light Father's one recurring theme took on meaning. Again and again he repeated, "All that God asks is that you don't quit; the rest is His job." And so it comes down to that—a great slice of a lifetime to teach one dunce one simple truth. God squanders His goodness on the likes of me. The mystery of love makes no sense at all, but God be thanked for it and the fools who know no better than to give their lives to the service of Love. Father Pat, unlikely friend, certain saint. Rest in peace. Bill

Thanks for listening.

• This letter was prompted by the death of Father Cummings on July 7, 1969. See also Will's letter to Father Swords dated July 10, 1969.

∞

Vacation, 1969

Dear Madelyn,

Actually, I've never been west of the Shady Rest, except for a childhood trip to Iowa, to visit maternal kinfolk. . . . The Girls in my Life. Chapter 5. Threesome. The unlikely number three recurred a third time in our protagonist's career on his first honest-to-gosh date. Quite without the knowledge of parents or peers the precocious fifth-grader asked the demure Lorraine Brieske to go to the Saturday matinee as his paid-for guest. Lorraine's charms included a pair of braids long enough—and seemingly strong enough—to dock the Queen Mary. She was also tall and blonde, the Northern European type. The great day arrived and dauntless Bill stood out in front of Lorraine's house and yelled, suavely, "Yo, Brieske, ya ready ta go ta da show?" After the inevitable wait the young lady emerged—with her best friend, Mary DeLorme—and presented an ultimatum: "Mary goes with us or I don't go." Mary came. It was the worst afternoon of the poor lout's life. One of the movies was mushy, and Mary kept asking for another Milk Dud. At one point our hero fashioned a noose out of a braid and tried to throw himself into the next row, but the usher wouldn't allow it. Chivalry alone compelled the six-legged walk home . . . Bill

∞

2 Aug 1969

Dear Madelyn,

I've given sporadic thought to what you said about writing on the change my whole order of values has undergone in the past ten years. My first, tentative conclusions don't look very promising as the stuff of which essays are made. The change (which is important to no one but me and perhaps a few others) was not a natural process, easily traced backward from effect to cause. It had its source in love—a mystery that defies analysis, and I don't know how I could treat the subject in a general, abstract way when it is intensely personal. The reading public seems to be interested in the struggles and confessions of drunks, addicts, whores, and queers and not of Republicans . . . Roughly, this is the history of the reborn Bill Jenks. My adolescence extended almost into my thirties, because I persisted in trying to deceive myself about my weakness and vulnerability and most especially about my particular condition. My dreams of the future were based on the incredible assumption that my predicament would go away, and I resented any reminders that it would not. I devoted all my energies to creating an image of a man in command of the situation. A quick mind and a sharp tongue warded off deflating thrusts. And it was not a duel of egos that finally reduced me to size; it was an invitation to love—not as a super-stud but as a friend. Your sister was the first person to trust me with a whole personality; she let me see the side of self most of us try to mask—the fears and worries and follies. Somehow I understood that this revelation demanded respect, humility, a surrender of self. Which is not to say that I repented overnight. Self-delusion has a thousand guises, and I tried them all. My opinions became the new idol. Liz Helt lovingly made me conscious of the arrogance of my pontifications. So I retreated into the sacred precincts of belief, but as my favorite theologian has said, "No one conquers God." Just at the point when I had conceived a self-sufficient faith (Which had already begun to wreak destruction) I was granted one more revelation, again in the love of a friend. The Truth, lived, is simple, and a lie is complex. Suddenly nothing but love was important—love of God and love of other. And that doesn't translate into words. (As the preceding amply proves.) . . . Life may hold greater joys than being with you, but I don't think I'm ready for them . . . Bill

∞

5 Aug 1969

Dear Madelyn,

Does it bother you that I use words like 'grace,' 'revelation,' and 'holiness' to indicate what passes from you to me in our I-Thou? I realize the danger of misunderstanding—my own misunderstanding, principally, but I can't believe that it's wrong or sacrilegious to attribute to God the best thing that has happened in my life—through the goodness of one of His creatures. In my mind and my heart I make no distinction between you as Madelyn and you as God's action through Madelyn. Our I-Thou has not only a 'between' but a 'beyond.' I think that's why I feel such freedom and yet such restraint in your presence . . . Bill

∞

15 Aug 1969

Dear Madelyn,

How can a reasonably intelligent adult admit that he spent more than ten years of his life trying to ignore the fact that he would never dance again? Accepting one's 'here' and 'now' is difficult under any circumstances; I made it almost impossible. And tracing the course of God's grace requires more acuity that I own. It's enough to say that love within and love without—both God's doing—wouldn't be separated by the wall of Will-fulness . . . Bill

∞

1 Sep 1969

Dear Madelyn,

The muddying of Clean Gene really shook me up, but I wasn't sure why until I gave thought to what you said about 'no more heroes.' A hero is someone we know in his public personality—and even then only partially. We make him a hero by filling in the gaps with belief, by assuming that there is a consistency at all aspects of his life. But belief—and the hero—can be destroyed by the disclosure of facts that don't square with the image. Perhaps those who know McCarthy personally and know his reasons for this seemingly unpardonable act could explain how it is not out of character. A public explanation would be impossible of course. Even if Mrs. McCarthy were a real bitch, with sins of every kind to her credit, it would do no good to blame her for the collapse of the marriage. The hero has to live and die with his image. (Maybe it is asking too much of a man to make him a hero. Who among us would care to be under constant scrutiny?) . . . Bill

• "Clean Gene" refers to Minnesota senator Eugene McCarthy, a popular but unsuccessful contender for the Democratic nomination for president in 1968. Young people working in his campaign embraced the strategy of being "Clean for Gene," which required that they trim unruly hair and dress conservatively. At the time of this letter, Sen. McCarthy, a Catholic, had recently separated from his wife, Abigail Quigley.

∞

3 Sep 1969

Dear Madelyn,

You are right—again. The rise and fall of a hero are the doing of the people. And the process that raises him up and dashes him to the ground is very often a form of idol-worship, almost in the Old Testament sense. People attribute to the hero the virtues and powers they lack and yet feel they need to control their destiny. (How is that different from 'religious' belief that shapes God in the image and likeness of Man?) As you observe, one slip and the angry mob demolishes its handiwork. But answer this: Has anyone besides Jesus ever refused the role of hero? Has anyone ever cried out to those who would adore him, "No, I am only a man like yourselves, and I can do no more than try." For a time Clean Gene protested but at last he succumbed and used the easy way of image-making. The Kennedys—Teddy less than John or Bobby—exploited all the modern means of idol-carving; we will never know whether they raised false hopes. Ironically, their enemies believed more strongly in their power than their followers did.

The regrettable part of the hero-phenomenon is that his truth perishes with him. If the public would accept men merely as spokesmen for a cause, the merit of which is unrelated to the personal conduct of its advocates, we might salvage something of the good they bring to light. I still believe McCarthy's critique of our society was apt and incisive, and none of his personal peccadillos will make me think otherwise. (The same is true of Shannon.) But a spokesman has some responsibility to those who support him. A sudden, unexplained desertion of his position leaves the impression that the cause was perhaps not so important in the first place. (And who is to say that politics—civil or ecclesiastical—has any ultimate importance?) Idol-worshippers deserve their inevitable disillusionment; faithful followers deserve honest answers. If none of us can invest a reasonable trust in a reputedly honorable man we may as well join the inarticulate swarms who riot to express their visceral discontent.

It's probably accurate to call Teddy Kennedy's actions at the time of the accident a "mistake." Faced with confused alternatives, he picked the wrong one. If he has lied, that is something else again. But McCarthy and Shannon were not under the pressure of time and circumstance; they had opportunity to consider the consequences of their decisions. They made their choices and will have to live with themselves. But I think they have forfeited any claim to public consideration. The nation and the church are the poorer for their retirement from the scene—not as heroes but as critics. Where does the fault lie? One kind of blame belongs to us for not assuming responsibility for our lives and for history, and surely another kind attaches to those who knew what was expected of them and allowed us to believe they were equal to those demands. For them, a tragedy; for us, a discouragement. Life's like that, I understand.

You'll have to goad me into further debates to keep my brain from atrophying. Thanks for the scrimmage. You won, of course. Bill

- Rev. James Shannon, auxiliary bishop of Saint Paul, Minnesota, leaves the priesthood and his episcopacy because of the conflict between his conscience and "Humanae Vitae," the encyclical of Pope Paul VI regarding contraception and marriage.
- Teddy Kennedy, U.S. senator (D) from Massachusetts, is involved, at least indirectly, with the death of Mary Jo Kopechne at Chappaquiddick, off Martha's Vineyard.

∞

9 Sep 1969

Dear Madelyn,

The strength which you disclaim—with misplaced modesty—has its source in faith, 'the courage to be' even in the face of unknown peril. It is not the giddy belief that everything will turn out all right but the understanding that whatever happens will be God's will for you. By surrendering control of one's fate to God one somehow comes into full possession of it. Barth says that, but you live it. You have taught me more than all the books I've read. . . . Bill

∞

11 Sep 1969

Dear Madelyn,

Your 130 didn't surprise me. I knew you were dangerously brainy. It's just as well there is no test to fix the Goodness Quotient. Your score would run past infinity. (Does it ever make you wonder why you were given so much? To give it all back, of course—with thanks. But it is a mystery, isn't it?) . . . Bill

• Her "130" likely refers to Madelyn's intelligence quotient (IQ), her score on an intelligence test.

∞

2 Oct 1969

Dear Madelyn,

Since I didn't get an answer to my provocative question about 'the sin against the Holy Spirit' I guess I'll have to be content with my own notion. Which is that the unforgivable sin is to use the truth of faith as a means of self-aggrandizement, as a discipline to marshal spiritual power for one's own ends and not for the will of God. If that is so, it would seem to be a temptation peculiar to the ' strong'—those Barth identifies as having discovered the un-absoluteness of law or church or book. Freedom is the ultimate temptation; its perversion, the ultimate offense . . . I had you to understand about my friendship with Father Pat, but I have no one to tell what your friendship has meant to my life. It is such a rare and beautiful thing to love and be loved for no other reason than the pure joy of it. Only your singular goodness has made our unlikely I-Thou possible. There should be words that sing themselves to celebrate the wonder of you. Someday, perhaps, when my heart can hold no more . . . Bill

∞

6 Oct 1969

Dear Madelyn,

. . . . Will this resolve our disagreement? Those who have been given the ability to love must try to love everyone. But in trying we discover that not everyone is capable of responding to love; some in fact reject it violently. We still owe those people what you call 'justice-love,' but it would be futile, if not presumptuous, to force a personal love on someone incapable of returning it. Personal love needs a return of love. Otherwise the person cannot grow. I think you could say that Jesus loved the Pharisees with 'justice-love.' Yet he had his intimate friends as well. (I still say it's impossible to know why some love and others do not.) . . . Bill

∞

27 Oct 1969

Dear Madelyn,

. . . . That word 'coward' really rattled me. But you're right. It's easy to call a passive submission to fate sanctity, but it's a cop out. I'm guilty of just such Noble Suffering. No more, though. Friday I mailed a letter to an organization that has no idea it needs my talents. I asked for a job writing anything that doesn't require research. If I get turned down I'll take my offer elsewhere—and elsewhere and elsewhere, until I get a paying job. I haven't given up on 'writing' writing, but I want some kind of work that will provide built-in discipline and, most of all, purpose. (Please say nothing of this to *anybody*. I want to do it my way.) . . . Bill

∞

2 Nov 1969

Dear Madelyn,

. . . . You're right, trying is all God asks. Your own trying, in this trying experience, affirms the purity and strength of your faith. I knew from what you told me in the early stage of our correspondence that you had found the truth in struggle and that you would finally assent to whatever fate God assigned. I would have wished you a quicker crucifixion, but that's not a matter for wishing. . . . Your suffering isn't meaningless, and your spirit isn't pleasing only to God. You are a grace to me and no doubt many others. I thank God there is such a powerful sign of His love . . . My sudden, unaccountable ambition, my urge to get a—forgive me Conscience—a job, comes from an attack of restlessness. For the past three or four weeks I've reacted against all the pointless habits that fill my day, especially reading. This may sound arrogant, but I've come to feel I've read everything necessary for my education. In fact, I've come full cycle; I now think life can be understood with a few homely truths—like Love God, Love Thy Neighbor. The rest is all repetition or entertainment, and I don't need any more of either. So I have to find something to do with my time, and I decided it may as well be something socially useful and rewarding (i.e., m-o-n-e-y). I realize a job will not assure my salvation, but it may safeguard my sanity. Besides, I notice that you get satisfaction out of working, and the more demanding, the better. My first prospect hasn't answered, so I've written a second possibility. I'm not quite sure how much to tell about my condition. I don't want to be a token: "This is Birnbaum, our token Jew; this is Gilliam, our token Negro; this is Jenks, our token freak." On the other hand, I have to explain my limitations. Tricky business . . . Bill

∞

9 Nov 1969

Dear Madelyn,

. . . . So far no answer for my second job-hunt. I wonder if a private employment agency would mess with my case. A commission would be a trifling matter if it would buy me escape from this erosive emptiness. (There are three primary modes of being—doing, loving, and suffering. And the greatest of these is doing. It is for everyone else; it must be for me, too. Taking your lumps and smiling sweetly just doesn't get it. I have yet to meet a stranger who asks 'what have you suffered?' or 'who have you loved?' It's always 'what do you do?' I'm going to get an answer. Don't bother to work up a rebuttal. My mind is closed. Besides, anyone who goes full throttle 19 hours a day is in no position to preach pious passivity.) . . . Bill

∞

20 Nov 1969

Dear Madelyn,

Father fed me half my dinner last night. Then Mary Byers took over and finished up. Is there another pastor in Christendom who would neglect his role as host to the archbishop to serve the least of his brethren? I told him in this morning's card that his kindness paralleled the washing of the feet. That will probably embarrass him, but it's true . . . Bill

∞

30 Nov 1969

Dear Madelyn,

. . . . I think I know why you and Father and I are friends. We all see life as comic rather than tragic. Tragedy views the individual and his will struggling against his fate as the highest expression of human good; comedy takes a God's-eye look at man's foolish ambitions and laughs him gently back into obedience. (Sentimentality takes the ego and its whims, tastes, idiosyncrasies as ultimately important.) Anyhow, the three of us, in varying degrees, have learned to get outside ourselves and surrender our pretensions to greatness. If that's not the case then we're all nuts; laughter can be something less than holy, I fear . . . Bill

∞

10 Dec 1969

Dear Madelyn,

Thanks for fishing me out of the Slough of Despond. I'm ashamed of myself for succumbing to imaginary woes and then burdening you with them. God knows you don't need to borrow misery. You are Gibraltar . . . Bill

∞

13 Dec 1969

Dear Madelyn,

. . . . Madelyn, knowing you has been better for me than reading The Lives of the Saints. You showed me the fortitude of a martyr, the wisdom of a doctor, the faith of the confessor, and the selflessness of a virgin. I draw hope from your courage . . . Trust your own judgment in coming to a decision. Whatever you decide will be right . . . Bill

∞

20 Dec 1969

Dear Madelyn,

. . . . I believe you when you say you are thankful for what has happened to you—and not out of pride. That is why you have been able to stand up to the worst fate has dealt you. Some good has come of it. You have given glory to God, whose grace upholds you, and you have given hope to those of us who have witnessed your serene acceptance of the cross. I have learned to have confidence in God's presence from having known your ordeal and victory. For that the only thanks is to live your truth . . . Bill

∞

Christmas 1969

"And the angel of the Lord came upon them,
and the glory of the Lord shone round about them."

Probably not. More likely He was born in quite ordinary obscurity, and His birth was an occasion for joy only to family and friends. But because His life revealed God's meaning in our lives we are right to believe that His Sonship was evident even at the beginning. The mystery of holiness has its own truth, unknowable to mind alone. So let us rejoice that Faith brings us to a stable to worship a baby who is the Christ, the Son of the Most High . . . If the world were mine to give I would not offer it to you as my gift because it would not be enough. Only the immeasurable, the incalculable is worthy of your thanks. Whatever of Peace, Joy, Grace, Love, Goodness, Hope, Courage, Holiness is mine—from God—I give to you. A Blessed Christmas, Madelyn . . . Bill

∞

29 Dec 1969

Dear Madelyn,

A person never knows what he is capable of doing until God asks him or Father Moran recruits her . . . Unless something calamitous happens in the next two days I think it's safe to say that this past year was the best year of my life. I was about to add 'and the worst year of your life,' but I recalled what you wrote about being thankful: Everything is a grace. In that light 1969 may be seen as your best year, too, since you came out of its hell with a deeper faith and a greater capacity to love. And if it means anything to you it was in large part your heroic (no exaggeration) living-out of belief in the face of hopelessness that convinced me of the necessity of unconditional surrender to God's love, even as made present in suffering. Until I saw life-death-and-resurrection in your ordeal I had held out some small space—my 'human dignity'—against God's claim. Now I know that it is that final defeat—God's victory—that brings freedom, wholeness, true dignity. I told a friend that you had taught me more than all the books I've ever read. But it goes deeper than that. What you have done is to give me the key by which to know the truth of all the books I've ever read. Only a person who is himself in the truth can be the source of truth to another. What thanks can I give in return for this greatest of all kindnesses? Perhaps the only acceptable thanks for any gift is to take it up and put it to use. So my thanks will be my life, lived in faith, hope, and love, full of meaning and happiness. And if it pleases God I may someday be a Madelyn to some poor wretch like yesterday's me . . . Bill

∞

1 Jan 1970

Dear Madelyn,

The moon shots did something for us. Men had always thought the moon's brilliance suggested a beauty, a purity totally unlike the mottled, warty face the earth shows to the universe. Now we know that the moon, seen close, has an ugly, abrasive surface, and the earth, seen from afar, gives off the deep blue of a sapphire. I think you look out from the planet Madelyn and admire the radiance of others' moon glow, all the while believing your own life to be without light. If you would glimpse the jewel God sees dazzling back His light, look into the faces of those who love you. Love is an eye outside yourself through which you may behold beauty God entrusts to you. Have no fear of pride. Your unreserved thankfulness will keep the perspective true . . . Bill

∞

12 Jan 1970

Dear Madelyn,

. . . . I intended to argue the 'someone cares' idea, but a seemingly unrelated thought made me see things differently. I suppose every teenager hears parents, teachers, priests—adults in general—telling him that there's more to dating than just making out, and of course he doesn't believe them. But if he dates a girl who laughs off his 'line' and yet doesn't turn him away he will discover for himself that there is a great deal more—like loving a person instead of an object and learning that he is capable of loving. (I learned this from Edie but forgot it and had to learn it all over again.) The point is that it's almost impossible simply to tell someone what's good for him. The truth can only be communicated by those who show concern for bringing out the good, not merely suppressing the evil. That's what real forgiveness does. But I think it only works with a person who recognizes his need for help. No one is so evil as he who thinks himself incapable of evil. . . . By coincidence, one of the subjects Father, Virg, and I discussed was Situation Ethics, which Father sees as ad lib sensuality. V.B. pointed out that the Situationists stress positive morality—thou shalt use property justly—rather than negative strictures—thou shalt not steal. Similar approach . . .

At a higher level God says no only that He may say yes more fully. You are the parable for that revelation. You have told me, wordlessly, "Put no terms on love, make no claims, and I will give you the best of me." How suicidal it would have been to have stopped short of the best. That would have lost me everything, including my soul. Thanks to the caring enough to say no to less-than-Bill and yes to Bill . . . Bill

∞

26 Jan 1970

Dear Madelyn,

. . . . I spoke too soon of peace. Over the weekend war broke out again inside my troubled soul. Fortunately, it was as quick and decisive as the Arab–Israeli war. And the good guys won. What carried the day was a quote from T. Aquinas: "The erotic is an attempt to return to man's original condition." It hit me that the great attraction of 'falling in love' is that it seems to surrender the self to a primordial rhythm where the ego can be abandoned. If that's understood as a parable of our relationship to God then a person must 'fall in love' (too bad the phrase has been cheapened) with God by giving himself over to the rhythm of life-death-resurrection. (The analogy to sexual love, with its 'death' in orgasm, probably explains why the mystics use erotic imagery in their writing.) Whoever is afraid of Death is afraid of Love. Your life convinces me of that truth . . . Bill

∞

15 Feb 1970

Dear Madelyn,

Your Valentine gave me inexpressible joy. It is more than I deserve that you have given me your friendship; it is grace of the purest kind that you would thank me for my friendship and make those words your own. It would be nearer the truth to say that I am at least trying to be and do all those things.

For me the love of a friend for a friend is almost as demanding as the love of creature for Creator—more demanding perhaps, since oafishness doesn't leave any bruises on God. The love of a friend is freely given, with the sole hope that it will be received as good. It requires faith that the giving of love is good in itself. I have only begun to learn what you have to teach, but for the chance to learn you are thanked in my prayers. (I try not to figure out why God let me stumble into your life. Let it be counted one of His more inscrutable mercies.) . . . Thanks for the minutes past leaving time. They are a kindness no clock can measure . . . Bill

∞

RESURREXIT

What do you make of it
—The empty tomb?
They say He lives.
Lifeless for three days,
Alive for all time.
I think it's true.
I think He lives in those
Who do the Father's will:
Who love the ugly
And help the halt
And shoulder their wood
Without wince or whimper.
I think He lives in you.

∞

16 April 1970

Dear Madelyn,

I never heard from Edie for my birthday. A 'season' must extend more than a month on either side of the target date. Or it could be that she wasn't terribly amused by my witticisms on the subject: "Bill's birthday is (A) Feb 2 (B) July 19 (C) Nov 29 (D) None of these." (One by one I alienate the loves of my life.). . . . Sorry about bothering you with my dark moods. The problem is all inside me. I just can't find faith enough to let go of the last vestiges of self-importance, so I'm trying to hide behind a screen of hate and rage. I *know* that my loneliness would vanish if I'd give in, but I can't *believe* it. Pray that God doesn't give up on me and that those who love me don't lose patience with me. . . . Thanks for listening . . . Bill

• Edie Lahrman was Will's most serious girlfriend before polio put an end to their plans for the future. They had known each other since he was sixteen and she was thirteen.

∞

17 April 1970

Dear Madelyn,

I'll spare you a replay of the thinking that liberated me from oppressive self-concern. It's enough to say that for the moment at least I'm content, even happy, to be just what I am. I think I can love others by affirming whatever life I have left to me after fate has done its damnedest. It's even possible to see my situation as a blessing, since it almost imposes a simplicity of life, a bare minimum of wants and needs, and frees me to become whole—perhaps holy. (It's a tribute to the deviousness of the debbil that I can lose sight of that obvious truth.) . . . Bill

∞

27 April 1970

Dear Madelyn,

Sorry if I seemed abrasive last night. I was still coming out of one of those inexplicable rages against everything and everybody, and I wanted to keep at least a million miles between myself and the nearest living thing. Yes, you came in for a severe pummeling. If I were less cowardly I'd direct my anger at God, but I can't put those lightning bolts out of my mind. Nothing in particular brought it on; it seems to be just part of the problem of being me. The one thing that makes it bearable is the thought that love forgives and accepts the dark side of one's soul. . . . There are times when I can almost understand your inarticulateness. Sometimes life acquires such a density of feelings that it seems impossible—and even sacrilegious—to express them in words. The difference between a man and a woman is that a man will attempt it anyhow and either fail miserably or succeed gloriously. Thanks for tolerating my failures . . . Bill

∞

14 May 1970

Dear Madelyn,

It's coming up to the twentieth anniversary of my senior prom. If I could figure out the exact date I'd send Edie a card reminding her how much it cost. (She wore a white eyelet gown with a square neckline and short puffed sleeves—like something Scarlet O'Hara might have worn to The Stars And Bars Ball. The corsage—$3.50—was made up of yellow sweetheart roses. I looked incredibly suave in my rented—$7.50—summer tux. Somewhere I still have one of those prom photographs—$2.50. I recall that I looked remarkably brave for a guy plummeting into bankruptcy.) . . . It really distresses me when we disagree on some matter of belief because I know I'm going to have to think the whole thing through again to find some place for your insight. It's not that you demand total conformity to your thought; it's just that I've learned to mistrust notions that don't square with yours. Which leads me to a retraction of my judgment on the world's state of soul. It's just as you say: I read too many books. And books are written by and about a very small fraction of the world's people. The great majority live out their lives humbly, accepting whatever comes and making sacrifices for those they love . . . I would like to think as you do—instantaneously, concretely, but I can't. I'm a prisoner of the state library—and a mere man besides. Try to think kindly of me despite all that . . . Bill

∞

17 June 1970

Dear Madelyn,

King Richard calls across the years / From the realm of Knights departed / "I yield to Madelyn, damsel brave, / The title Lion-Hearted"/ . . . It seems inconceivable that still more shock and pain would lay in wait for you along the way, but the history of this abominable situation leaves nothing beyond the reach of possibility. Yet that same history gives grounds for confidence that you will find the courage to meet and conquer whatever adversity—or perversity—fate devises. Think of what you've been through. It would be enough to destroy the faith of Joan of Arc, and you have risen from each encounter with evil not only with strength undiminished but with strength greatly increased. You are a miracle of grace, a proof of the power of goodness. Now you are nourished by bitter herbs and roots, but one day you will feed on warm bread and honey . . . I have to confess to an unpardonable surrender to cowardice that, tangentially at least, involved you. I knew that Jack Weimer would call for ad lib petitions during the Prayer of the Faithful, so I readied a 'relevant' one about the young and their impatience with injustice and another about 'those whose love has been rejected.' When the time came I tried the first one and heard my voice quavering pitifully. I knew the emotional content of the second intention would have hung up my adam's apple, so I passed. You are not passed over in my private prayers . . . Love, Bill

∞

29 June 1970

Dear Madelyn,

Tracy's observations about my being a citizen of Dana by chance, not by choice, set me to thinking that if fate hadn't stationed me here we very likely would never have become friends. I won't lie and say that even now I wouldn't trade everything but my soul for the freedom to live an active, as opposed to passive—life, but I can say knowing you has made me more a whole person than I might have been otherwise. From you I have learned patience (with my self), courage (with my cross), humility (in the face of forgiveness), confidence (in the certainty of grace), joy (in the presence of beauty), and, I hope, love (in response to love). I have none of these gifts in great measure, but if it weren't for you—and by Tracy's reasoning, polio—I would be a stranger to the best things life has to offer. I have no time for thoughts of the might-have-been; I have time only for thanks for the life-that-is. God gets first thanks; yours are second only to His . . . Bill

• Tracy is Madelyn's eight-year-old daughter.

∞

20 July 1970

Dear Madelyn,

Now that I think of it, us seventeen-word-a-minute typists are cuter than you twenty-seven-words-a-minute flashes. I just retired from the cartoon-stamp business. Too much sweat for too little satisfaction . . . I've been fighting the empties off AND ON for a week. I can't bring myself to believe this is all I was meant for. I feel like a 1970 Continental up on blocks. (Well, a 1927 Pierce Arrow, anyhow.) . . . Nobody needs what I have to give—which is nothing less than an answer to the world's ills. "Physician, heal thyself." I try to think that God uses a different scoring system, but it doesn't help . . . Bill

∞

10 Aug 1970

Dear Madelyn,

I suppose every kid thinks his father is the greatest man in the world, but it's something else again when the kid-grown-up can remember his father's teachings and acknowledge their wisdom. Among the best blessings of your richly blessed life the love of your father must be counted one of the most fruitful. (I'll never forget my surprise at hearing Ed, then twenty, repeat your father's views on racial justice. They were appallingly, radically Christian. The Church hasn't caught up with his thinking.) . . . If I were permitted to join a kitchen-table commentary on Madelyn I would say, "Madelyn never says thanks; she lives thanks by taking the smallest gift and making it a part of herself and then giving her whole self in return. Madelyn has a way of being and loving all her own. No book in the world could offer a clue to the mystery of her personality, no words could capture, once-for-all, the more-than-this of every revelation. Loving her requires great patience, constant awareness, much humility, but its rewards exceed all measure. Madelyn is Woman, whose heart knows, whose love invites, whose forgiveness restores. Madelyn is Madelyn. God be thanked." . . . Even when these cards say nothing they say something. Ignore the words, which only annoy, and read the meaning, which your eyes easily perceive . . . Bill

∞

21 Sept 1970

Dear Madelyn,

I assume Father told you about the Late Show offering, *The Three Muske-teers*. . . . The truth is that I faintly remembered that D'Artagnan was not one of the original 3 M's, but I couldn't come up with the name Aramis. Besides, I had the uneasy recollection that Aramis was killed in the final reel and that D. was then admitted into the unholy trinity. I didn't want to jinx anyone with that role, although otherwise Father would be ideally suited to Aramis' character, especially his quasi-clerical habit of reading the breviary. (I have the suspicion that Father resigned from the group in the early scenes, when the guys dueled with the Cardinal's men. "Gosh, I didn't know they were atheists.") I stayed with the film until one o'clock, at which time Aramis was still alive. I guess I'll have to invest in a Classic Comics version of the story to see if we have to reassign names. . . . Bill

∞

8 Oct 1970

Dear Madelyn,

. . . . In recent weeks I've had some success in restricting myself to the here and now, in praying your prayer: Just let me get through today. Heaven has to have its own accounting procedures or else my vocation is supposed to be schizophrenia, because inside my motor is still turning over as though I had somewhere to go. (Did you ever think how closely the illusion of independence is tied to the ability to move? There seems to be an unconscious assumption that if things get really bad I can always go somewhere else. When mobility is lost the assumption simply shifts modes. I keep telling myself that things will be better as soon as I find something useful to do—a conceit that keeps me from doing the good the immediate situation requires.) Anyhow, I'm trying to suppress my appetite for Meaning and to satisfy myself with humbler ambitions. I have to shout down cries of 'coward' from the male ego, which considers anything less than global conquest as an abdication of manhood. I think I've hit on a clue to the immeasurability of good. By jet-set standards the joys in my life—a church picnic, two guided tours of Brazil, Ind., a baloney sandwich—wouldn't keep a hermit from dropping a rock on his head to end his misery. Yet those small kindnesses (small only by the world's standards) were unlimited graces to me. So perhaps the same is true of the infinitesimal deeds I'm able to do. It may be that these cards have helped in some small way to keeping you in courage and Father in optimism. Pray that I'm not deceiving myself . . . Bill

∞

25 Oct 1970

Dear Madelyn,

The fall foliage and you remind me of the same awesome truth: Beauty is completely gratuitous. Everything that is could function just as well if it were unexciting to the senses. Beauty summons us to drink deep of life; it tells us God is for us. . . . Why don't you write me a letter—about anything or nothing? Honestly, it involves very little pain. People have been known to do it three or four times a year without adverse side-effects. Try . . . Bill

∞

8 Nov 1970

Dear Madelyn,

. . . . I can understand your reticence about writing and surrendering a letter. If I don't get rid of these cards almost immediately I worry myself into thinking that it would be better to tear them up. The only way I can overcome that hang-up is to have faith in the reader, to believe that love will make up for my shortcomings. Otherwise I'd be walled in by self-doubt . . . I don't save letters, but I remember them, like the one that ended "I am what I am." Beautiful—the thought and the thinker . . . OK. "Like." Bill

∞

11 Jan 1971

Dear Madelyn,

At the insistence of A. I've written a short article about Father Pat. Inadvertently I left out the best piece of writing: "It would be closer to the truth to say that he was square, sometimes irascible, and at least subconsciously intolerant of anything not identifiably Irish." . . . On one of those rare occasions when you let words express your feelings you said that you would not allow yourself to hate because that would rob you of your freedom. By refusing to hate you remained free to love others, to free others for love. You have become a fountainhead of grace for many lives. Perhaps the best thanks would be to do the same . . . Bill

∞

19 Feb 1971

Dear Madelyn,

You're right again, of course.

After mulling over the Father Pat piece I came around to your view. Part of the trouble may stem from habits acquired while writing these cards—not just to the listees but to others as well. Lack of space forces me to economize, to throw away words, phrases, whole sentences that don't move the idea remorselessly along to its point. That's good discipline, but it tends to squeeze the juices out of things. So it's back to relearning the art . . . The untranquilized unhappiness abroad in the land seems to be a symptom of misappropriated love. People love either too much or not enough. For a culture obsessed with fun ours affords little joy; there's no sense to play with life-and-death matters, no laughter at God's strange ways. Your laughter is a hymn celebrating the mystery of the near-and-far of love and freedom. You could lose everything yet lose nothing. You love as if the world were yours and if it were God's . . . Bill

∞

2 Mar 1971

Dear Madelyn,

I have only my own experience to go by, but I have a theory that the body somehow generates a state of euphoria after it has escaped a close scrape with death. The process works below the level of consciousness, it seems. At least I had no idea that my last surgery was a near-miss until you recounted what Dr. Veach said about it. And yet after I got out of the intensive care I was on a high undreamed of among potheads. Could that be the incentive for guys who repeatedly risk life and limb in foolhardy stunts? . . . One reason a woman understands people intuitively is that watching a child grow provides recapitulation of the history of the human race, evolution in miniature so she sees a person as a becoming rather than a being . . . If I could play God with three wishes I would do away with selfishness, not suffering. (Maybe they're the same thing.) And I would make winter two weeks long and let no harm come to children . . . Bill

∞

6 Mar 1971

Dear Madelyn,

It occurred to me during one of my dialogues with the Jerusalem Bible that the cross each of us has to take up is the ordeal of being no more and no less than himself. It's being responsible to God for others, and there are so many ways of dodging that responsibility—all of them seductive—that it takes real courage to make honest decisions. (I don't mind carrying a cross; I just wish they had waited till the end to nail me to it. It's hard traveling uphill with those spikes cutting into the flesh.) . . . Bill

∞

Easter 1971

Dear Madelyn,

For the Christ-follower, the cross-bearer, truth has no more reassuring resonance than the joy at Easter. Only one who has suffered, died to what seemed to be the world, known the hell of nothingness, and returned to life and the capacity for love can believe in the Resurrection. Because you have entered into the mystery with a faithful heart you have experienced the fulfillment of Christ's promise. Christ lives. You live. God be praised . . . Bill

∞

1 Apr 1971

Dear Madelyn,

. . . . I had my first kidney stone attack when I was on my midshipman cruise, and knowing of nothing of either kidney or stone, I imagined I had appendicitis. That terrified me because it roused memories of the two guys we had sent over to a battleship in some kind of basket. They survived the transfer and the surgery, but I was harried by visions of dropping into the drink and spending eternity in the company of an overbearing octopus. When I couldn't stand the pain any longer I dragged my tortured body to sickbay, woke up the corpsman (it was 0300, which translates into 'the dead of night' in lubber lingo.), ignored his unfriendly greetings, learned that it wasn't appendicitis, took two aspirin, and skipped back to my rack, humming "Anchors Aweigh" . . . Bill

∞

9 May 1971

Dear Madelyn,

How does this sound? A man is taught, in the absence of evidence for something, to doubt it; the woman is taught in the absence of evidence against something, to believe it. If love is grounded in belief, a man's love is in a sense more fragile than a woman's because he can't be left alone with his doubts. As you know too well, a woman assumes that love continues unchanged in the spaces between encounters. (Which probably accounts for my thinking that writing on a regular, twice-a-week basis reassures you of my love and relieves you of doubts; and it seems to explain your thinking that I believe in your love imperturbably during prolonged absences. A 'prolonged absence,' according to a man's reckoning is anything more than a week. During the winter, when you were observing a calendar with ten days to the week, I finally learned to keep my doubts suppressed for that long a time. I felt as ascetic as one of the desert saints. But unexplained change, seeming indifference, any kind of uncertainty really gnaw at a guy's vitals and lead to the temptation to reduce his own efforts. I know that is stupid, but I didn't invent the situation.) . . . Bill

∞

11 May 1971

Dear Madelyn,

It gets more complicated. The evidence a man requires to still his doubts is different from the kind a woman needs to kill belief. His evidence has to be in the form of Ideas; and hers, in the form of Feelings. (Heidegger sides with her. He says thinking is a 'taking-to-heart.') Anyhow, leave him alone and the ideas that undergird his love will be subject to doubt and to the devilish meddling of the imagination. At least that's how he experiences love. The truth lies deeper. If there is love it is rooted in 'irrational' faith, the same—though less intense—memory of Feelings she lives by . . . Bill

∞

21 May 1971

Dear Madelyn,

I was applying principles of aesthetics to the understanding of a woman: a woman should be perceived as a work of art, since her being is 'expressive form,' a consciously created personality intended to make her inner reality, her feelings, known intuitively, immediately, without intervention or rational processes. A woman, like an artist, communicates to the heart by developing a technique for using her materials—voice, face, movement—to make known how she relates to persons, things, ideas, life, the world, even feelings themselves. What she says is not the message: the way she says it is. (All of which is hardly news to you but it represents a great breakthrough for the duncy half of humanity.) . . . Using that idea I made the further discovery that there are great women for the same reason there are great artists: originality in sensing the richness of life and devising means of communicating that insight to others. I know that's true because it accounts for your ever-more-fascinating personality and your constantly renewed and enriched beauty. If there is a single word for you it is 'original.' You see with your eyes and not through the murky lens of *McCall's*, "As The World Turns," or Faith Baldwin. And you give expression to your feelings, your inner life, in ways you learned from no one. It's just for that reason you aren't always easy to understand. A man relies on conventions—other men's insights and language—to communicate his matter-of-fact ideas and feelings. So, like Picasso, you have to be patient and wait for the world to catch on . . . Related reflections: you will never grow old and boring; you know how to keep from dying . . . You are simple only in your single-minded commitment to love. Otherwise you are infinitely complex and subtle. It's a struggle and a joy to understand you . . . Bill

∞

29 May 1971

Dear Madelyn,

Why are high heels like stragglers? Because they bring up the rear. (Nothing like starting off on a lofty level.) . . . I suppose I should thank you for prodding me into rewriting the Father Pat piece, but it hurts too much to surrender the last foot of ground where I felt superior to you. Now you have left me with nowhere to keep my pride. But thanks . . . In writing the additional material *Guideposts* requested I had to recount the events that led up to Father's death, which I had purposely avoided doing, even in my card to you. At the time it happened I managed to control my emotions—or repress them, but when I had to put it in words I found myself welling up with tears. I don't think I was merely being sentimental over my own prose; I think it's more likely that, male-like, I experienced nothing until I put things into words. We are a strange race . . . Since communication has become an obsession with me I've listened to what men have to say, too. Invariably it's a lot of gassy nonsense. Guys like Paul Harvey and WHPJ talk in noble generalities which mean absolutely nothing, least of all to them . . . Bill

∞

1 Jun 1971

Dear Madelyn,

You hand me wheat already free of chaff / the winnow breeze, your self-effacing laugh . . . Bill

∞

8 June 1971

Dear Madelyn,

. . . . Sunday afternoon Bennie Strohm stopped by to visit. He worked on the farm when the original three Jenks boys were young—the eighteenth, best of all centuries. We had a special fondness for Bennie, probably because at 4'9" he was the first adult we looked down on, if only in the literal sense. Now 70, Bennie is semi-retired, which means he does odd jobs for a dollar an hour "for some old folks." His reminiscences inflict cramps on my smiling muscles; he recalls the events of his simple life by calculating the money he's spent. In 1933 he went to the World's Fair in Chicago and stayed two nights in a hotel—on the sixth floor, facing north—and the whole excursion, including the ride up and back, cost him $12. Before he left Bennie got out his fiddle and played some old tunes. I tried to play along on my harmonica during "Red River Valley," but my tempo limped badly. Bennie prefaced the playing of "Believe Me If All Those Endearing Young Charms" by saying that he had picked up the tune by listening to the Jenks boys sing it on cold, rainy evenings. (His ear is infallible; he flatted the same notes we did.) For some reason it pleased me immensely that Bennie carried some memory of us all these years. It gave me a feeling of being immortal . . . Sunday I was reading my KJV (Sorry, but I got hungry for the Psalms.) and I happened upon one of the Suffering Servant chapters in Isaiah and it came to me like a flash of light: Jesus was somehow disfigured or deformed. He may have been a hunchback. Long before he faced his final agony he learned God's truth through suffering. Only by colliding with an immovable No to human potentiality does a person discover that nothing, no handicap or limitation, walls off God's grace, which is the ability to love. And he must have borne some outer sign of his suffering, a pre-crucifixion imprint of the nails by which the poor, the sick, the despised immediately recognized him as their brother . . . Bill

• "KJV" stands for King James Version.

∞

10 Jun 1971

Dear Madelyn,

After a night of thought I'm more certain than ever that I'm right about what you find mysterious in A. He identifies completely with the Church. The best metaphor I can think of is that he is in love with the Church the way some women are in love with their husbands: All feeling is invested in the beloved's fate. You could kick A in the shins without provocation and he would merely blink and look puzzled. But if you belittle the Church or the pope you can depend on a vigorous counterattack. Think back to the few times when he has let his anxieties show—like the time he accused Gregory Baum and other radical theologians of seducing priests; his deepest anguish expressed the fear that somehow he would be deprived of his priesthood. Just last Friday he framed a silence that told me he wanted to unburden his mind of a worry. Six priests are leaving. I would guess that every depression, every hurt he suffers can be traced to a wound inflicted on the Church. (Use that hypothesis in trying to understand him and see if it's valid.) . . . A woman can't know what it is to be a man cut off from the world, and a man can't know what it is to be a woman betrayed in love. But we can treat each other lovingly . . . Bill

∞

15 Jun 1971

Dear Madelyn,

On further thought the wheat-and-chaff image seems incomplete. It is in the encounters of friendship that the wheat is freed from its husk. Then love winnows the chaff with breezes of forgiveness . . . Bill

∞

9 Jul 1971

Dear Madelyn,

Remembered smells: before the farm got electricity we toasted bread on a primitive four-sided pyramid that rested on the burner of the kerosene stove. Invariably the bread turned black, and even with zealous scraping, the aroma of charred wheat destroyed whatever taste the shingle retained . . . The point of being a Christian is the belief that whatever you happen to have is enough. Grace will make up the rest. But grace isn't some kind of invisible energy available in a wafer; it's the support of love of the community, the church you experience. That's not the pope's church or even the priests' church but the church of those who love one another and help each other to learn new ways of loving. It's an 'unnatural' community in the sense that it believes that there are ways of loving besides the natural ways—sexual love, parental love, patriotic love, brotherly love, platonic love. Its grace is the opportunity to love and be loved, inclusively. That kind of church isn't conspicuously evident, but it exists, potentially, in the hearts of all who follow Christ. The

Musketeers is such a church in miniature. If we love each other and still others that could be enough. . . . Bill

∽

28 Jul 1971

Dear Madelyn,

Last week I wrote a tardy classletter for my Holy Cross brethren. The contents were predictable, but the form was not. I signed my name to it. That's my first-ever signature—a collector's item . . . Bill

∽

4 Oct 1971

Dear Madelyn,

Last night I woke up and found a sliver of pure moonlight cutting across my shoulders. Somewhere in the unplumbed depths of my soul lurks the memory of our pagan past, because I felt strangely blessed. There is magic to the moon . . . I won't say that I couldn't have written my now-famous article without your help, but I can say that I wouldn't have written it in the right key without your nagging. For a person who is tone-deaf you have a remarkably good ear for feeling. Thanks for teaching me to be me . . . Bill

∽

7 Dec 1971

Dear Madelyn,

Cancel our friendship. I find it too unnerving to expose my thoughts to a mind-reader. You'll never know—or maybe you do—how timely your letter was. I have teetered on the brink of ending it all, card-wise. Perhaps a woman can cross a desert of matter-of-factness without thirsting for approval, but a man needs an oasis every fifty feet. (I'm rather proud of myself for having endured so long without succumbing to soul-fever or despair.) Everything

I've ever written about you has been true, however inadequately expressed. But it's hard to seek new truths when their disclosure seems to make no difference. So thanks more than heart can hold for the kind words. I needed them to go on being me to you . . . Love, Bill

∞

18 Dec 1971

Dear Madelyn,

. . . . Last week I had a letter from an old polio whose physical condition parallels mine but whose personal history has been far less fortunate—indifferent family, few friends, no money. Now things are a bit better; a church group has adopted her. But these same well-meaning ladies have been bullying her into sham cheerfulness by hitting her over the head with the October *Guideposts*. I wrote an apology, intended as much for the ladies as for my sister-in-suffering. It used to bug the hell out of me to have some clod tell me about his cousin Rufus, who 'had the polio a while back, but he just kept lifting weights till he got his strength back and now he's bustin' broncs again.' Rufus, of course, was being held up as a rebuke to my sloth, cowardice, and impiety. Even worse do I resent being compared to anyone with arms and legs. If I had escaped polio I might have become an archbishop or an alcoholic (or both). But never mind 'might-have-been.' I am me, and I absolutely refuse to be matched against another person. Those who don't accept me for what I am and do can go to hell—in the express lanes . . . Bill

∞

23 Feb 1972

Dear P.,

I've been thinking about me and not about you. Father's phone call shamed me into giving thought to what you must be going through— reliving the whole ugly episode and, even more, having to worry about your economic circumstances. None of it is fair, of course, but you are not without strengths. You have a good case and a good lawyer, one who will fight for you and consult with you. You have the sure knowledge that even the most flagrant miscarriage of justice could NOT deprive you of the courage to overcome any hardship. And you have the love of family and friends, not least of whom are your fellow Musketeers . . . So don't let yourself think that what has happened or may happen is somehow a reproach against you, a cause for guilt feelings. Love has power only to invite a return of love; it is powerless against hardness of heart. You loved and so you are blameless. Believe that . . . Love, D. (This reads as though I'm trying to prepare you for the worst. Not so. I'm confident of a victory for truth.)

∞

25 Feb 1972

Sweet Sickie,

Wake up, Sleeping Beauty, it's Prince Charming. (Or how about Peasant Churlish?) Just learned of your misery and so I'm a little behindhand with wishes. As soon as I finish this I'll phone Brother Oral and ask him to sprint to the top of the Prayer Tower and advise the Big Daddy of Us All of your needs. In my own stammering way I'll do the same . . . The psychology of sartorial impact indicates that you mustn't wear a short skirt to court. We want the men to keep their minds on the matter at hand. Just wear your biggest, bluest eyes and things will go your way. There's even an outside chance that the judge will sentence Ronnie to be publicly flogged for flagrant stupidity . . . Has it occurred to you that among the charges to be brought against you at the Last Judgment—a trial that even one of Father's meetings won't prepare you for—there will be full blame for encouraging me to write and, by extension, draw? For my part, I intend to invoke Calley's plea: I was only following orders. (My mother found a letter I wrote from Holy Cross, and I've been saving it to show you how un-deft I was with pen. The writing is almost as embarrassing as the contents, some of which doesn't make any sense, even to me.) Thanks for urging me into broadening my ways of communicating. Now find me some way of making money . . . It may sound strange, but I was relieved to hear you say that at times you feel bitter about your predicament. If you had put all that behind you too easily it would have meant that you were repressing emotions and building a volcano in your soul or that you were incapable of any feeling. I refused to believe that second possibility, but I worried about the first. The important thing, as you have shown, is to taste the gall but then to rinse your mouth with love and savor life's occasional sweetness. You are as beautiful to the heart as you are to the eye . . . Take care of yourself. You mean much to many, me among them . . . Love, D.

• "Calley" is a reference to a U.S. Army officer blamed for atrocities committed in Vietnam.

∞

7 Mar 1972

Dear P.,

In less than twenty-four hours you will be rid of the worry that has plagued your thoughts over the past month, and then you can return to your carefree life as cook, housekeeper, laundress, nurse, referee, teacher, chauffeur, purchasing agent, plumber, water-bearer, full-time omnicompetent courthouse worker, and mother-surrogate, secretary, bookkeeper, memory adviser, spirit-raiser to our dynamic pastor, to say nothing of high-ranking Musketeer and leg-scenery for the council. Even though I'm certain the outcome of the hearing will be favorable, I can understand how the threat of a radical change of circumstance could upset you. It seems unfair that you should have to bear this strain in addition to the suffering of the original betrayal, but you know well enough that life isn't fair. What matters is that you are not without grace—the grace of your own inner strength and of the love that would, more willingly than Simon the Cyrenian, share the weight of your cross. You will emerge from this latest tribulation not only unharmed but enhanced. You are gold that has been purified in the fire. God grant you peace within and without. Love, D.

∞

10 Mar 1972

Dear P.,

. . . . During the council discussion of the youth revolution you mentioned the period of rebellion natural to most adolescents. I think what you said is true, that every young person tries to assert his independence by rejecting the values of his home, school, society. The difference today is that kids have found allies in sometimes thoughtful, sometimes perverse adults who criticize received truth. So it's no longer a matter of conforming or going it alone. There are other, valid options—alternate life-styles and all that—to choose. Return to the old ways is no longer automatic or even, I think, desirable. It would be exciting and terrifying to be young today . . . Though you are conscientiously non-verbal in communicating the content of your secret self your eyes reveal every nuance of feeling. Watching them Wednesday morning was more moving than listening to a Beethoven symphony. So long as I can remember those eyes you will be loved . . . D.

∞

15 Mar 1972

Dear P.,

Revised Rankings: On researching my memory I discovered that I once paid $12.00 for two tickets to *South Pacific* for Edie and me. So, inflation aside, that puts you in first place. (And in those days it was nothing for me to put stamps on my letter—three-centers, as I recall.) . . . Dan and Shea, his intended, have dropped in for a few rounds of bridge during her spring vacation / orientation week in Dana. It amuses me to see Dan cooing blissfully, even when the cards are running against him. It must be nice to be young and in love. For that matter, it must be nice to be young OR in love . . . Sunday the wind delivered the sweet scent of you to my enchanted nostrils, and so still another sense feasted on your presence. In recent months I've become aware of breathing the memory of your perfume, much as my mind's eye sees that joy-awakening face. Though it's incomparably better to be with you it is mercifully impossible to be without you . . . Under the crush of fate you have become a flawless diamond that needs only light to radiate beauty . . . D.

∞

16 Mar 1972

Dear P.,

Thanks for your part in rehabilitating my typewriter. Since I'm beyond repair myself I count it the next best thing to have a vigorous, fully versatile machine, which after all is an extension of my personality, possibly the most indispensable part. . . . I'm eternally—or for as long as the back-spacer works—grateful for your Musketeer work of mercy . . . Yesterday when Dan announced that the multitudes had assembled to console me in my hour of tribulation I was haunted by the thought—the presumption, perhaps—that you and A. had picked last night to renew that hallowed tradition of surprising me with cake and Pepsi (or lemonade) and party games and balloons and readings from Garry Wills' Catholic memoirs. I looked to my mother for some sign of panic over a schedule conflict, because in other years you had forewarned her of your coming. And seeing no maternal grimaces, I accepted the invitation without reservation. I must confess I was moved to decisive action by the consideration that I might set some condition on the Helt bash—a time limit, and then spend the night regretting a bad guess if you hadn't come. Besides, if the truth were known, I hoped to have the best of both worlds, the Christian and the pagan . . . The party was great fun. Liz and Shea concocted the meal; every course was to have been a flaming spectacle—Greek cheese cooked in olive oil and doused with cognac and ignited; chicken breasts browned in olive oil, mixed with sautéed mushrooms and onions, given the cognac treatment, and simmered for thirty minutes (We ate at nine. I had prudently crackered beforehand.). Dessert was to have been cherries jubilee, but Dan had overjubilated already on the gravy and Liz's homemade wine. After dinner we sang Irish songs. Once again it was my lot to be the second-least tuneful singer in the crowd. Dan is to monotones what Caruso was to tenors . . . Heard Andy W. sing Danny Boy this morning. It gave me the shivers . . . Thanks again for taking care of my sickly servant . . . D.

Just got your beautiful St. Paddy's Day book. I'm going to make myself believe you didn't anticipate the postage-due penalty.

• "Andy W." is Andy Williams.

∞

22 Mar 1972

Dear P.,

What is it about the three of us that lets us float in joy when our loves flow together? It's something more than the communion we shared at Booger Chef; more, even, than the singing of MacNamara's band. It must be that each of us knows the others take his heart into their hands reverently, tenderly, and so each is free to be himself. Life offers no sweeter feeling . . . Your birthday note made me envious. How heartening it would be to be a person of few words who is able to use those words movingly. If there is even a tinge of truth in what you said then my life has some meaning, and if I could believe you learned anything of courage from me I would be at least as proud as Arnold Palmer's caddy. Thanks for the kind words . . . I love the love in you . . . D.

∞

25 Mar 1972

Dear P.,

Did it ever strike you that being pretty, bright, and lively can be an impediment to love? A person who grows up with a reflected image of himself as faultless comes under great pressure to appear perfect, since it seems that love will be withheld at the first sign of weakness. Even when such a person becomes intellectually aware of the superficiality of that kind of love and comes to know the kind of love that accepts the whole person it takes a lifetime of inner argument to teach the self not to hate itself for not measuring up to adolescent expectations. (There was an acute case of just such self-hatred in your former friend.) To digress only slightly, I was hurt that you think A. and I judge you as sternly as you judge yourself. I suspect that I know you as well as anybody, and as much as I delight in the beauty of your eyes or the splendor of your contours I love you just as much for being the Madelyn who could freeze flame with a chilling mood. You are loved just as you are, blessedly human and therefore worth loving. Love yourself as tenderly . . . D.

∞

Easter 1972

Dear Madelyn,

In that long-ago Age of Piety we were told that Easter would hold more meaning for those who had kept Lent with unrelenting rigor. Life has since taught us that God sometimes demands infinitely more of us than the temporary shunning of candy, gum, and movies. But the truth of that innocent doctrine translates into the truth of experience. A person who has suffered pain, loss, humiliation, who has died to what seemed to be the whole meaning of his life, and who, though faith, has been given new life out of the abundance of God's grace feels the joy of Easter through every fiber of his being . . . Easter has dawned in your soul. You are radiant with resurrection, for your heart knows that Christ lives. Love, Bill

∞

5 April 1972

Dear P.,

A film critic noted that Charlie Chaplin's silent films were better than his talkies because he believed that words kill the sense of mystery; once a person tells his feelings his audience believes it understands what he means and closes its mind to what can't be spoken. I imagine that's why women seem—to men at least—inarticulate; they know that love demands constant attention to the particular, to the whole person in each unique instance. Men are in a hurry, though, and would rather 'know' once and for all. Thanks for the candy, the cake, and the eggs, for getting me to the church on time, and for being my friend . . . D.

∞

15 June 1972

Dear P.,

A. drove me home. We went the long way, via Thomas cemetery and Chrisman. (How come we never do that?) We discussed his dilemma. I think he's prepared to argue strongly for staying on at least another six months. What seemed to worry him most was that Musketeer feelings might be influencing him to make a selfish decision. I tried to reassure him that his real vulnerability could be the temptation to do the 'unselfish' thing, with too little thought for the weighty practical considerations on 'our'—the parish's—side . . . D.

• Father Moran has heard that he may be transferred to another parish, hence his conflict: whether he should stay at St. Joseph with the Musketeers to finish the new church or move on as directed by the bishop.

∞

30 June 1972

Dear P.,

If all mail-carriers were as lovely as you and all letters as loving as yours, getting mail would become the highest joy man could savor. Thanks for the treasured letter. Nothing could have pleased me more. I was proud of that wretched scribbling because the will to write to you overruled the objections of every irksome muscle in butt and back. And the message it delivered, not in words, got through . . . Tuesday night's impromptu Musketeer meeting reminded me of something I too easily forget: you have lived through the cruelest human experience, the slow death of trust. If you keep your feelings hidden from view it is only because they have been exploited and trod upon. In time, perhaps, you will learn to trust love not blindly but understandingly—and not just the love of a saint but of a mere man as well. I value your letter for the courage it took to overcome acquired suspicion and natural shyness. You are strong in faith, alive in hope, beautiful in love, and indestructible in courage . . . D.

∞

11 July 1972

Dear P.,

It's hard to believe that the sun, serene in golden majesty, is in fact a constant torment of volatile gasses, seething, boiling, erupting in angry bursts of energy. It's harder still to believe that your inner life is not as placid as your beatific face would suggest. But I know that you live with as much hidden turmoil as the sun, that you feel loneliness, anxiety, humiliation, anger, and all the turbulent emotions that rock the heart. I know, for instance that you are woman enough to feel the shame of a worn rug, an ugly chair, a fixtureless ceiling. It is a miracle of courage that you don't allow those and a thousand other deprivations to overwhelm you. It must be that you sense that nothing is lacking where your beauty has its home. The poorest rag, imbued with your being, is more precious than linen, silk, or damask. What governs the sun's life the mind one day may learn; what rules your soul the heart already knows. It is love . . . D.

∞

17 July 1972

Dear P.,

Let sunset palette-play with evening skys / And learn to covet blues of your rich eyes. . . . The birthday dress is so stunning I've just about persuaded myself that A. and I picked it out ourselves and surprised you with it. If it would be possible for us to be prouder of you than we already are, that might come to pass whenever you wear our dress . . . Thanks for Sunday night. Just being with you, luxuriating in the soft climate of your loveliness, would be joy enough for any heart, but to have popcorn too exceeds the promised delights of the Mohammedan heaven. Even more I value your offer to take me, because to make it you had to overcome a reticence to be seen with me unchaperoned. Generosity that requires the sacrifice of some fear or uneasiness, however small, is rarer than emeralds and more beautiful than pearls. In your unpredictability you confirm the belief that at its center your mystery is unimaginable goodness. Woman is gift, and none more than you . . . D.

∞

11 Sept 1972

Dear P.,

. . . . I meant to let you read A's last card. He says he's been depressed quite often the past month. . . . He also said that you and I are the only ones he can talk to, explode in front of. All three of us have borne with each other during times of emptiness, frustration, confusion, turmoil, and if we haven't done anything to make the situation better, at least we haven't done anything, consciously, to make it worse. That's quite a lot in the way of love. It's good to be a Musketeer . . . D.

∞

17 Sept 1972

Dear P.,

This card is the equivalent of a Jewish mother's chicken soup. It's not what you need, but it's all I can do. If it were possible to guard you from all harm you could walk serenely into a dragon's lair, for A. and I would protect you. Life, alas, knows no such fabulous chivalry, and so we must let love bathe and wrap your wounds, whether outer or inner, and remind you that even if pain should hold you captive we would go your ransom . . . The only pleasure I got from the magazine article was seeing your face lighted with joy for my tiny triumph. It wasn't what I wanted; it wasn't what Father Pat deserved. It lacked all feeling, humor, honesty. The article you and A. approved at least had the shading truth requires (though not so candidly written as the card I wrote to you after Father Pat's death. But friends understand where strangers do not.) The Musketeer party was consolation enough. The candlelight flickering in the black pools of your eyes still plays on the mirrors of the mind . . . If I were asked to relate the impact your life has had upon mine I would need a hundred times the space *Guideposts* affords—and a hands-off pledge from the editors. No sketch, no profile could suggest the sense-drowning beauty you bring to the world. Perhaps the cards I've written to you over the past three years would, by their volume and their frequency, intimate that you are forever new, a limitless depth of mystery, a mine whose precious ore is inexhaustible. If everyone could but sip of the wine of your love, history would be as joyous as a Musketeer meeting . . . Take care of yourself, for the sake of those who love you . . . D.

∞

29 Sept 1972

Dear P.,

Three years ago we spent a sunny afternoon on the porch while you pasted cardboard to the back of Covered Bridge mass schedules. You wore an avocado jacket and grey slacks. As you were leaving you asked me to guess how many letters I had written to you. Either my guess or your answer was 65 . . . Last night on the news there was a report on the California drought, and for an instant the screen showed a dusty barn lot with three or four cows outlined against an unpainted barn. That brief scene sent a rush of forgotten feeling through me. I suppose that's why it saddens me to visit the farm, now no more than a boneyard of boyhood memories . . . In his autobiography Yeats, the Irish poet and playwright, says that love sees the other's secret self and mirrors it so that the other may recall who he is in the midst of the thousand daily selves. No doubt you experience your daily self as roman candle or as cold grey ash, but the truth lies in the eyes of those who love you: you are a glowing ember that warms and lights the souls gathered round you. Two mirrors celebrate your beauty, A. and D.

∞

10 Oct 1972

Dear P.,

You are wild strawberries, sweet / Surprise in thicket's midst . . . How insensitive of you to overshadow the sky's proudest blue with your three-blued eyes. The outer ring recalled Lake Tahoe through a tunnel of cloud; the middle, shell of lark's egg; and around the lucent dark, the light-washed air surrounding the sun . . . It grieves me that we were robbed of our party by a villainous flu bug, because you are at your loveliest when warmed by the wine of laughter. But after you left yesterday I was reminded yet again that simply being with you is a joy beyond the contrivance of history's most lavish party-givers. Food, drink, music, atmosphere are nothing compared to the company of a friend, more indisputably when that friend is a beautiful woman. Though we say little and do less, there is a caressing warmth to voice and gaze that art could never imitate. You are party, banquet, ball, festival . . . Just the way you are, eye-prized . . . D.

∞

14 Oct 1972

Dear P.,

. . . . I had forgotten how invigorating an argument can be until we engaged in Wednesday's shouting match. It ventilates the lungs, quickens the pulse, and excites the spleen. Discretion forbids a flat-out argument with A., lest he brood over latent apostasy. Nothing that surfaced really surprised me. I had been aware of your concern for appearances—not as a hypocrite, who wants to seem better than he is, but as a scrupler, who wants to seem no less than he is. For you are a good girl, luckily for the Musketeers, who can tolerate that deficiency since it assures your lifelong membership in our celibate cell. Blessings on your strange ways . . . D.

∞

18 Oct 1972

Dear P.,

Your rain slakes desert's thirst and breeds / A sudden swarm of blue-sweet bloom . . . Abject apologies for an unintended calumny. In times past I have none-too-imaginatively compared your green eyes to emeralds and your blue eyes to sapphires. Yesterday, browsing through Nieman-Marcus' _____mas catalogue (where no hint of the manger-born carpenter intrudes), I came upon a $150,000 emerald ring and a $135,000 sapphire bracelet, neither of which imprisons light so bewitchingly as your eyes. The incomparable difference is life, which celebrates itself, its mystery, through miracles of beauty. No mere thing could pretend to hold life's surprises, still less your gift for making new . . . I'm reading a smile-raising book about the saints by Phyllis McGinley, a woman of gentle, genial wit and good sense—which she demonstrated early by professing an aversion to the Little Flower. Ms. McGinley sets about to rehabilitate some of the poor plaster-of-paris saints, who have been victimized by well-meaning but overpious press agents. Dominic, for example, is said to have admitted that he enjoyed talking to young women rather than old ladies. The single shared virtue of all the wildly dissimilar people is their obsession to give away everything they own. That would seem to strengthen the case for our saintly friend. If you oversee the writing of his life, don't exclude any of his foibles. Human saints are so much less forbidding. . . . The 'bright minutes of joy' you have given flooded memory: your reaching out to touch my new-lengthening hair, your leaning forward excitedly to tell A. and me the vivid recollections of your youth, your uncontrolled laughter when A. asked, seriously, if Patre Pio had indeed levitated, your five performances of our birthday productions, your note promising to be buried in the orange sweatshirt, and—and—and. Thanks for unnumbered rainbow moments . . . D.

- "____mas" is Will's way of indicating that "Christ" was left out of "Christmas" in the catalogue.
- "Our saintly friend" is Father Moran, the third Musketeer.

∞

21 Oct 1972

Dear P.,

I work to turn watery thought / To wine of words for warming the soul. / Not six stone crocks but a rusty cup / My powers browbeat: Be ye grape! / No Cana vintage. Crushed, I rush / To banish cup but brake for new hope: / A cup of water given with love / Is wine of a kind. So drink, fond friend . . . Actually, what Myron Cohen said was rather flattering. He told of seeing "this vision of loveliness, a Gaelic goddess—her face was so beguilingly Irish it almost made me think God isn't Jewish—and I found myself hoping against hope that she was my stewardess, because if she were to ask me, 'Coffee, tea, or me?' I was all ready to say, 'Vell, to tell you da troot, wit coffee un tea I don't schleep so good'" . . . One further 'bright minute of joy.' Even in nightmare solitude I can spark a smile by recalling that quarter portrait of an N-folded girl, bent legs enfolded in her own embrace, beaming face fixed in a world-winning grin that proclaims, "I'm fourteen—and beautiful!" (But nowhere near as beautiful as now.) . . . D.

∞

14 Nov 1972

Dear P.,

There's an intimacy to candlelight / Communion of faces drawn toward flame / Shedding their shadowed mystery to feed / The eyes' breath-need for other eyes . . . It was less the candlelight magic and more the lovelight miracle that made Sunday's eyes glow like an underwater cave walled with phosphorescent jade. As the evening lengthened those eyes lured us deeper and deeper until there was only radiant darkness, where your beauty lives without face or voice, where we saw the living love that is Madelyn. If ever Time should change its mind and strip you of 'those endearing young charms which we gaze on so fondly today' you will still be loved for what you are, a woman of glowing soul . . . Which is not to say that the eye could find no delight along the surface. I'm sure a man attentive only to outer beauty would have let his gaze play over your face and form for as long as the law allows. Even A. seems pleased that one of the Musketeers happens to be the world's most attractive woman . . . For me all of Sunday's conversation about love said less than the occasion itself. Love takes time, time to forget everyday worries, time to create trust, time to admit need, time to celebrate the joy of being together, time to thank. And even afterward there must be time to ponder what was said, savor what was done, but we have to give thought to nurturing that grace. If there is to be Musketeer love there must be Musketeer time . . . In your woman's way you said more without words than either A. or I could express in verse or song. Your heart speaks its own language, sings its own music. With a mere touch you answered every question the doubting mind of man could raise. Thanks for that tenderest of kindnesses . . . Love, D.

∞

7 Dec 1972

Dear P.,

. . . . More and more it seems that we are pool balls that only by chance tick each other on the way to opposite pockets. . . . And your work and worries keep you elsewhere. But there are memories that almost sacramentally replenish the joy of you—the early spring day when walking down the street, you tilted your head, bird-like, to curve a smile around an intervening telephone pole; the evening in church when you turned crimson with stifled laughter at the sight of the cotton in my ear; the summer morning when with impish delight you presented me with three pages of council notes—all in shorthand (ostensibly to make amends for "Tom went out to round up cows. Tom returned.") I'm not sure why it pleases me to have such a strange girl for a friend, but it does. And the certainty that you are still the same person, unconquered by the worst sort of torture, lets me believe that there will be new joys to be remembered. That hope makes the dreary meanwhile tolerable. Thanks for yesterday and tomorrow . . . D.

∞

26 Dec 1972

Dear P.,

This digression from duty is being justified to both my consciences—internal and external—under the rubric 'thank you note.' And it is just that. I come with thanks for a sackful of gifts—the huggable mouse, the toothsome candy, the prized letter, the midnight mercy, and the sight of you. The mouse is the sweetest of those smiley sacramentals that convey your teddy-bear feelings. The candy, better than Godiva, pleases the soul as well as the mouth, since it restores me to a list from which I had been inexplicably dropped for two years. (A. is right: the Kandi Kitchen could be a gold mine.) Have no fear that I will use the letter as footing from which to lunge at you. It would have been enough if you had said only that I am needed. That is the greatest of my needs: to be needed and to know that I am needed. Midnight Mass might have been beautiful if I had been in the care of any fellow Christian, but being with you made it a communion of friendship as well as belief. And however sublime the joy of Christmas, it is stale champagne when tasted after the nectar of your presence. You are joy summer, winter, spring, or fall. Thanks for all but most of all that . . . D.

∞

16 Jan 1973

P.

Tracy's made a convert . . . Sunday night Garry Wills, evoker of the Catholic ghetto, appeared with William F. Buckley, papist patrician, in an hour-long argument over What's Happened To The Catholic Church? A. would have wrestled the TV set to the floor and demanded that Wills recant all his seditious assessments of the papacy, all of which were made temperately, even charitably. The birth control issue, according to Wills' reading of history, simply illustrated the pope's siege mentality: he insists on holding fast to his prerogatives even when it puts him at odds with the whole church (minus one). At one point Buckley chided Wills for generalizing his experience of Catholic schools into a sociological fact: "You make it sound as though you attended every Catholic school." The truth, as demonstrated at the Musketeer reading of Wills' reminiscences, is that we all attended the same school. Someday I'd like to hear Wills' views on self-control, that peculiar moral affliction visited on us by Id-iotic nuns. The control was all repression, no expression. We knew how to be against but not for; it was more important to avoid sin than to learn love. I think we were crippled emotionally by the milieu, especially the 'good' kids . . . Since it seems there won't be any opportunity to talk freely with you until spring arrives I'll have to write what I've meant to tell you for the past few months. There is going to be a divorce in the family; Carolyn is suing John, for reasons best known to her. It's enough to say that the fault rests with both of them. Reconciliation seems to be out of the question, at least until both of them have lived the consequences of their decision. A complication has arisen. The two older boys, given the option to live with either parent, have chosen to go with their father, and so now he faces the problem of setting up a home for them. He has asked my mother and me to consider the possibility of moving in with the three of them. It would kill me to have to leave Dana, and I think it would literally kill gram to keep house for five people. But if it comes down to doing what we can for the boys we'll have to go, though no earlier than June. Sorry I had to break the news to you this way, but the time was never right. Haven't told A. yet . . . D.

∞

TRANSPLANT

Take heart, she said
And gave me
Part of her own,
Large with loving.
And grafted on,
It squeezed life
Into my faint heart
And stirred a pulse.
Health seeped,
Then streamed,
Then surged
Through once-dead flesh.
Alive with joy,
I thought to thank
The donor who gave
More than Shylock's pound
And found her,
Whole-hearted again,
Herself thankful:
The heart is for giving.
I walked away,
Puzzled until
I met a man
Down-and-empty-hearted.
Take heart, I said
And gave him
Part of my own,
Large from having been loved.

∞

Valentine 1973

LITANY OF THE UNTHINKABLE

The day without sun
The night without stars
The sea without wet
The sky without blue
The child without fun
The apes without Tarz
The Church without debt
The world without you

∞

Reverend Lawrence J. Moran

Selections Written 15 January 1972–21 January 1989

The Reverend Lawrence J. Moran was born May 8, 1927, in Indianapolis, and received his elementary education at Our Lady of Lourdes parochial school. He attended Saint Meinrad, a Benedictine academy in southern Indiana, for both high school and college. Called to his priestly vocation, he then entered the Archabbey Seminary of Saint Meinrad. He was ordained on May 3, 1952, as a priest for the archdiocese of Indianapolis. In 1967, after serving as an associate pastor in the archdiocese for twelve years, he was appointed pastor to both the Church of Saint Joseph in Rockville and Immaculate Conception Church in nearby Montezuma, Indiana. At that time he became Will's confessor, friend and admiring fan, warmly urging him to write and speak for wider audiences. After serving these two parishes for eighteen years, he was appointed pastor of Saint Patrick's Church in Terre Haute, where today, fifty-one years after his ordination, Monsignor Moran joyfully continues his blessed work.

∞

15 Jan 1972

A-typical Ataraxian:

I notice your Italian friend has attributed the crisis of faith to a general inability to think (except in scientifically quantitative terms). It surprised me to find myself agreeing with him, but I suspect we would part company over the division of the sheep and the goats. In my goat pen go all the Scholastics with their overconfident epistemology and their Natural Law. I am more and more convinced that one knows the truth of something only when he knows how it is not true. That is the function of experience—to provide the antithesis in the dialectic with ideas, and until a person can establish that yes-and-no mode of reflection on his present he can't begin to make distinctions between contingent form and durable truth in the expressions of other selves. Maybe that's why poetry has greater resonance than philosophy; it confesses the contingency of its form. (I doubt that even you would require a 'concrete example' of "Ode To A Toad.") . . . D

• "Your Italian friend" is Pope Paul VI.

∞

4 Feb 1972

Maginot Mindset –

. . . . I think the heart of our disagreement was less to do with the nature of marriage than with the nature of Christianity. In recent weeks I've been reading Paul's letter to the Galatians, where the argument for the Spirit and against the Law is articulated. In that context, of course, the word 'the Law' refers to the Mosaic Law of the Pentateuch, as developed by rabbinical interpretation. But it seems to me that the truth applies equally to any body of law, to the very concept of law—an externally maintained code of behavior, enforced by the threat of punishment. And that is indeed deadening to the Spirit, which requires faith—an internally maintained set of attitudes, values, manifested in acts of love. The Church should teach those values by preaching the Gospel, by making Christ's love present in its corporate charity, and

by building community. (And by being attentive to us Pentecostals.) . . .
Semper amicus . . . D

∞

18 Feb 1972

Steadfast Faster –

There's a cardinal outside my window. He must be Italian; he asked for
olive oil to pour over the bread crumbs . . . Four years ago today (my today)
the council came into being. Of the original eight I'm the only survivor, at
least on an uninterrupted basis. Obviously it is not always the littlest that
survives. More often it's the marginally fit, whose weakness is his strength.
Looking back on the high drama and low comedy of those years, I'm almost
grateful that you kept flipping that coin until it came out right . . . One of my
Sixty Second Scripture Scannings plunged me into that passage about pluck-
ing out an eye if it offends thee, and for the first time I realized this statement
is not hyperbolic. I would rather be immobile and free than strong-limbed
and fettered by passions. P. may have been grievously wronged, but she is less
to be pitied than her self-absorbed tormentor . . . I wish to enter an objection
to an opinion you voiced at the last council meeting: "women are more pious
than men; they're naturally more religious, more spiritual." 'Pious' I'll give
you, but 'religious and spiritual,' no. All the great God-questers of history
have been men, with the possible exception of St. Theresa and all the minds
seeking transcendent truth have been men. Women tend to be more accepting, more enduring, more obedient to received wisdom, but they shun the
ambiguity where the Eternal Mystery dwells. (Rebuttal?) . . . D.

• Her "self-absorbed tormentor" is Madelyn's dissolute husband.

∞

25 Feb 1972

Not-at-all-cross-Examiner –

In recent weeks I've been trying, with small success, to become aware of how much motion and emotion is self-generated simply to afford myself the sense of well-being that comes out of being—or believing oneself to be—engaged in the world, even through imagination. My low-stimulus situation should make me receptive to quiet, patient prayer, with its reassurance that God bears my life along even though I do nothing. But I can't keep from revving my motor, from persuading myself that I should be doing something, and so I miss the chance to do whatever good reality summons me to. Is it 'human,' cultural, masculine, or personal compulsion? I would be at peace and am not . . . D.

⚭

3 Mar 1972

Pastor Noster, Nunc et Semper –

. . . . Tonight's CBS News retaught me that the view from this ivory tower is sometimes obscured by clouds. Last Saturday CBS covered Muskie's emotional scene in front of the Manchester, N.H., *Union Leader*, a newspaper that had attacked him on a phony local issue and had printed disparaging remarks about his wife. After a show of subdued rage over the first issue Muskie got choked with emotion while trying to defend his wife's good name. The display of feeling was genuine and, I thought, reassuring—evidence of human qualities in an otherwise phlegmatic man. Apparently the voters of New England don't share the opinion. Muskie's popularity has dropped precipitously during the past week. Does the man on the streets see tears as a sign of weakness? It would seem so. (Heidegger never explained that other people might behave insensitively.) . . . Usually at some point during your confessional encouragement you say, "I don't know how you do it." If I do it at all it's because of your monthly reassurance that it's worth doing. The tendency of most people is to assume that every one knows where duty leads and therefore where salvation follows. Maybe my situation is more ambiguous than most, although I doubt it; for me, at any rate, it's important to be told that I'm on course, even though

I have no sure fix on North. Being loved is how I do it. Thanks for keeping me at it . . . D.

• "Pastor Noster, Nunc et Semper" is Latin for "Our Shepherd, Now and Always."

∞

10 Mar 1972

Knight in Shining Serge—

Your idea of keeping the vigil with P. proved to be even more valuable as things turned out. The wait, endured alone, would have been torture. If you noticed P.'s eyes you know that it took all of her incredible strength to turn her gaze outward. It was the Musketeers' finest hour . . . D.

∞

16 Mar 1972

Solicitous Listee –

I feel patently unworthy of this rejuvenated machine, with its bold, forceful strokes. Its efficiency contrasts so painfully with my own ineptness that my writing will seem all form and no content. Even so, I'm grateful to you and P. for lavishing TLC on my most prized possession. As with dogs, so with typewriters: Love me, love my dog. It embarrasses me to think of the cost in time and money that your gift represents. A day at the IBM clinic must be as exorbitant as a day at Mayo's. Thanks for an inspired kindness, not least of all for restoring the back-spacer. (I just covered that last line in reverse in 2.7 seconds—a new world's record, which I dedicate to A. and P., the Andy Granitellis of speed-typing.) I'd make a pledge to back-space diligently but back-slide discreetly . . . Theological Side-effect: Do I lose the merit—quaint word—I had credited myself with for having surrendered my typewriter to P. in the belief that it was to be used in some emergency? I offered up the feeling of abandonment all the while I was without my single link to The Great World Out There. (Or at least I'm assuming that it's out there.). . . . Again, multi-jubilational thanks for restoring my machine to health . . . D.

• It's Will's fortieth birthday and Father and Madelyn, "A." for Athos and "P." for Porthos, have had his typewriter overhauled as a gift.
• Andy Granitelli was a professional race car driver and mechanic.

∞

24 Mar 1972

Skeptical Scavenger –

I've been mulling over Sunday's conversation about the difficulty of forgiving oneself and of believing oneself forgiven by the other. It goes back to fear, fear of being unlovable. We somehow suppose we are loved only for our strengths, and those exercised in behalf of the other. (A very concrete example: Monday P. phoned and asked me to get the plumber across the alley to drive out and fix her electric pump. The best I could do was to get his wife to promise she'd tell him about the problem. Then I tried to report to P. and couldn't reach her until 9:00 P.M. and had to cut it short because my mother was waiting to wash my hair. It took me two days to get over hating myself for not being able to handle the situation with aplomb.) When we are told to love our neighbor as ourself it is assumed that we already love ourself as we love our neighbor. Not necessarily true. We are ashamed of weakness, especially the telltale loss of once-proud strength. I can intellectualize self to acceptance; I just can't live it . . . Pax . . . D.

∞

31 Mar 1972

Fidelissime Amice –

A Garry Willsian Reminiscence of Good Fridays Past: the mournful chanting, the processional cross draped in purple, the priest coped in black, the Mass Pre-Sanctified with no organ and that plaintive wooden clacker, the unveiling, limb by limb, of the black-shrouded cross of veneration. The stripping of the altar, the open tabernacle. Man, whoever conceived that ritual sure knew how to create a mood—stark melancholy. I doubt that the Oberammergau Passion Play is any more successful at persuading its audience that it has been present at the crucifixion and burial. (Does the meditation of the fourteenth station still include the chilling line, "Then they sealed the tomb and all withdrew"?) We can argue the theology of ghetto Catholicism, but no one can question the powerful emotional appeal of the old Holy Week rites. . . . The rhythm of Holy Week, with its upsurge of joy on Easter, is so much a part of your personality that your heart is ready for any test. For someone who loves Christ so totally it becomes a martyrdom of its own kind not to be asked for some heroic proof of that love. And its everydayness is your cross, your Easter will not burst upon you in a flood of light but will seep around you in a rising tide of love and peace. But it will be no less Easter for that. Rejoice: Christ lives in your love . . . D.

∞

7 April 1972

Tither, Tither, Burning Bright

. . . . The intensification of hostilities in Vietnam again makes the evening news surpass the Theatre of the Absurd for sheer irrationality. The killing of other human beings for some cause that ostensibly transcends life itself has to be the most incomprehensible of man's aberrations. In the name of God, History, Nation, Idea, a man will throw himself at the jugular of someone no different from himself in needs, fears, feelings. How do we detach ourselves from what summons our loyalties so we can see both its value and its threat? How do we belong without belonging? . . . This week's *Commonweal* offers an essay on the University as the monastery of the modern era. The writer suggests that an excess of relevance in intellectual life can blind activists to the whole of which their interest is merely a transitory part. He urges contemplation as a salutary corrective. But for some reason the argument irked me, even though I had previously reached the same conclusion. I think he may have put me off by implying that only some people should do all the contemplating. Until everyone contemplates we will have divided hearts and alienation . . . D.

∞

14 April 1972

Bomb-of-the-Month-Man

The sixtieth anniversary of the sinking of the Titanic occasioned all sorts of stories, most of them poignant but at least one of them edifying. Did you know that there was a plaque in the ship's lounge that read: "Not even God could sink this ship"? That must be the world's record for short-lived hubris. The Villain of the piece was not God, of course, but the poor schlep who bugged Him . . . D.

∞

21 April 1972

Layman At Law—

The debate over Law vs. Justice was illuminating for the distinction it raised between dialectic and scholastic thought. One relies on process to reach an ad hoc truth; the other relies on a precisely defined truth to determine the process. That's probably why Anglo-Saxon jurisprudence is based on a constitution of a few constantly conflicting principles and Roman law is based on an elaborate code of specifically applied principles. The first is dynamic; the second, static. I must say my sympathies lie wholly with dialectic, not just in law but in all thought. It recognizes that man has many pasts, that none of them is completely adequate to the future, that the new is created out of reorganized elements of the old. It may allow temporary aberrations, but it holds promise of eventual reformation . . . Quite by coincidence the Know Your Faith page of the *Criterion* last week carried a piece on faith in which the point was made that faith finds security not in the institutions of men—the forms we give things—but in the loving presence of God. I think it requires more faith to cast your lot with a system that is unpredictable because incomplete than to accept the reassuring stability of a foreordained order . . . Thanks for including me in Monday's wait-and-pray squad. We'll never know whether it would have been easier for P. if she had been left alone, but everything in my experience insists that together is better. It must have meant something that we tried. (Maybe someday we will learn that what we did was to distract P. from worrying by requiring her loving tolerance of our fumbling friendship. If our foolishness can serve, God be thanked.) . . . D.

• The *Criterion* is the archdiocesan newspaper.

∞

28 April 1972

Easily Awed Audience—

For a woman love is an ambience; for a man it's an activity. She needs to feel that her wishes engage his thought and guide his action; he has to feel that his deeds are valued. (The greatest impediment to love is lack of imagination, an understanding of the other's unspoken needs.). . . . D.

∞

Anniversary 1972 [5-8-72]

Dear Father,

It wasn't just your mystification in the presence of numbers that destined you for the priesthood. You were foreordained to be ordained. As a deservedly obscure poet once observed, "From moment of quickening He was priest in the depths of his soul." The sacramental rites of 20 years ago merely put your inmost being wholly at the disposal of the church . . . It has been a hallmark of your priesthood that you have great love both for the Church and its teachings and for people and their feelings. You have healed the deepest hurt and have awakened the loftiest joy. Your life has made Christ present to the world. I thank God I have known you as priest and friend. Ad Multos Annos . . . D.

• May 8, 1927, is Father's birthday.
• "The sacramental rites of 20 years ago" refers to his ordination.

∞

19 May 1972

Aggrieved Aggiornamentist—

How Could I Not Be Irish-Catholic?: It just occurred to me that during my six-and-a-half years in Queen of Angels School the rectory was occupied by Frs. Doody, Barrett, Kennedy, Sullivan, McCarthy, Fitzgerald, Conrad, Cummings, and Duffin . . . It will take six months of reading Frank Sheed to bring me down from the high last week's *Criterion* launched me on. It printed the remarks of a bishop—a *BISHOP!*—who urged the revamping of catechetical programs to bring about not just assent but conversion. The comment that set off my ecstasy had to do with the *Baltimore Catechism*, which His Most Excellent Excellency admitted had been written during an ebb-time in theology. Amen to that. It will take us three generations to recover. . . . D.

∞

16 June 1972

Implaque-able Pastor—

New Republic prints a review of Abigail McCarthy's book about life with Gene. Apparently its tone is not at all vindictive. But its point is sobering. A man will ask a woman to be the mother of his children and the maker of his home, and when those intellectually stultifying roles leave her far behind he begins to hold her in contempt. That course isn't inevitable, but it's predictable enough to be a vexing social problem. Is it possible that we have reached a stage of institutional complexity where a man must choose between fatherhood and professional responsibility? Perhaps like the Greek Church, society will have to restrict leadership roles to the celibate—or childless . . . D.

∞

21 July 1972

Fortnight Foreigner—

   In trying to discuss Aunt Mimi's problem with her I made an important 'discovery' about prayer. It may be the most effective human means available for dealing with one's feelings. It should be the instrument for determining which things need changing and which need accepting. I think much of the emotional instability abroad in the land is the result of feeling—sensing the need for useful action—more than the body can translate into deed. The inner turmoil then drives the person into frenetic, and usually meaningless, activity or into partial or total withdrawal of feeling. Prayer gives thought to those feelings and attempts to learn where one's own responsibility ends and God's (actually, that of others beyond communication) begins. Prayer gives perspective and purpose, which are more necessary than the geegaws we think we require . . . Who's the patron saint of heavier-than-air craft? Put in a word for a faint-hearted friend . . . D.

• Will, whose body couldn't tolerate a long cross-country trip in the van, will fly to and from the West Coast to join his brother John and John's three sons for a tour of California.

∞

4 Aug 1972

Tireless if not Tubeless—

   It would be intellectually dishonest of me to develop a theology of Disneyland, condemning the frantic pursuit of distraction in a patently commercial exploitation of people's alienation. The truth is I enjoyed whatever magic Walt worked and I didn't care what base appetite he was appealing to. It certainly wasn't sex; the place is as chaste as a Victorian novel. I suppose escapism is at the root of D'land's appeal, but the flight to other times and other places can't be altogether unhealthy. I'll have to leave the moralizing to less easily seduced observers . . . It was good to go and good to come home, especially when there were friends to share the joy. Thanks for listening . . . D.

∞

25 Aug 1972

Missionary to the Mannikins—

I'll have to consult my attorney to see if the law offers any remedy for the grave injury the Republican convention inflicted on my spirits. It literally depressed me to hear Reagan, Goldwater, Agnew, and Nixon deliver their message that all's right with the world. The values they espouse, the truths they ignore, the smugness they engender are all the more deadly because the self-satisfied want to believe them. It vexes my vitals that I'm not able to answer their distortions—not just because I'm stuck in this backwater but because I haven't really worked at understanding what it is man expects of life and how to communicate that understanding once it is gained. My conscience has been prodded by a book Liz lent me. It has to do with mythology, especially the ubiquitous story of the hero who ventures into the unknown and brings back magic power to conquer a hostile force. The myth symbolizes man's need to go beyond the received definition of 'human nature' and seize creative powers within himself. Invariably the myth places the hero under obligation to share his understanding with others. I'm no Jason or Galahad, but fate has thrown me into a dimension of being not mapped out by Rand McNally, and I should work at trying to discover what it is that gives strength to overcome. It's not enough simply to call it grace and let it go at that. There are choices that put a person in touch with inner sources of God-given strength, and it is the 'how' of those choices that makes the difference. . . . D.

∞

1 Sept 1972

Picky, Picky Picassophobe—

Why I Wasn't Born In Gospel Times: "Now at that time a certain paralytic, borne on a pallet by two friends, caught Jesus' sleeve in his teeth, and holding fast, even though Simon Peter pummeled his nose, he besought Jesus, that He might cure him. Jesus, taking pity on him, said, "What would you have Me do?" And the man said, "Lord, that I may scratch." Whereupon Jesus made a sign unto Andrew, who helped Simon Peter pummel until the sleeve was released . . . It may not be a fair judgment, but it seems to me that vocal proponents of abortion don't want to take responsibility for their own acts or for the acts of others. They want to be free to go their own way, as though their interests constituted an Absolute Good. In time, I think that attitude will be recognized as the source of the spiritual malaise variously called alienation, angst, depersonalization. The search for a sense of belonging will probably spawn as many aberrations, albeit reactionary, as the quest for freedom did on the other end of the spectrum. The community that understands history, that can distinguish between transitory and transcendent—especially in its own life, will survive all change and restore sanity. It could be Those Catholics. . . . Thanks for five years of concern, friendship, joy, encouragement, grace, and fish. It seems to me that I've made the same confession 60 times in 60 months, but as long as you're charged to forgive seventy times seven times I have reason to hope that you'll keep coming. Thanks to God for the blessing of you . . . D.

∞

29 Sept 1972

Jovial Chauvinist—

The seeming insanity reigning in the state of matrimony suggests not the presence of the devil but the absence of the living Lord. If one or both of the parties don't recognize the need to let go of present peace, bought at the cost of repressed or dishonest feelings, and risk the discomfort of adjusting to change there will be no growth, and without growth any relationship will die. Practically, growth requires sympathy and encouragement toward the other as he tries to break free of his infantile desires for a womb-warm world. (I liked that line in a recent bulletin: "a man needs sympathy, not service.") . . . The trouble with reviving the devil is that that approach raises up something outside me to be fought, not something inside me to be understood and disciplined. There is nothing inherently evil in creation; yet almost any 'virtue' can be exploited for selfish purposes. Rather than gird oneself for battle with the forces of darkness, arrayed in red leotards and armed with pitchforks, a person would do better to discover his own potential for good and for harm without praising or condemning himself. The Original Sin was eating of the tree of the knowledge of good and evil: what's good for me; what's evil against me. Supernatural life—actually the fullness of human life—is given to those who take no thought for their own safety and convenience. Your heart knows that. . . . D.

∞

19 Oct 1972

Exhaustible Resource—

I've been reading a book one of Dan's aunts sent me as a reward for being published. (A Musketeer party and a good book—the scales are beginning to tip the other way.) The sprightly wit of Phyllis McGinley, a safely Catholic poet, has been brought to bear on the formidable, unfashionable task of rehabilitating the saints. *Saint-Watching* limns the too-good-guys in their varied humanity and goes a long way toward rescuing sanctity from small-minded hagiographers. The remarkable inconsistency of these saints' backgrounds—rich and poor, loving and unloving parents, lifelong or late holiness—restores the words 'grace' and 'free will' to respectability. How else explain a Borgia following such an un-Borgian career? But whatever their differences, they were all driven by love to give away everything they could get their hands on, preferably unfeloniously. It takes little imagination to think that one day a similar collection of saint stories will tell of the Wildman of Stony Point, who raised a cathedral on a foundation of faith and crullers. (And whose relics were themselves relics.) You, too, are driven by love, almost as recklessly as the Tijuana taxi of cringing memory. (Note: a saint, not necessarily a martyr. Take some thought for *your* body's needs; you are you, not Anthony of the Desert.) . . . Today has been one of those "even when I'm not writing I'm writing" days. No man who lives with his mother can be a contemplative. Several years ago I read a book, *Makers of the Modern Mind*, which examined the lives of a dozen men who shaped Western Culture as we know it. Significantly, all twelve men were either celibate or heedless husbands. 'Enry 'Iggins would have done well to stick to his resolution: "I will never let a woman in my life!" . . . D.

• The "Wildman of Stony Point" is Father Moran.

∞

4 Nov 1972

Imperious Impressario—

Did I tell you that one of the prayers in the book you gave me was composed by Benjamin Jenks? He is best remembered in tribal lore as the evangelist who hounded the infamous agnostic Y. Boyle Rice until he relented and became a Christian. A terse note circulated among his countless nephews and nieces, recording the triumph. It read, "Uncle Ben's Converted Rice" . . . When Charlie was here we discussed the difficulties ghetto boys face growing up virtually fatherless. Without rites of passage a boy can hardly be expected to find the courage to forgo childish wanting, the feeling that life requires constant stimulation or total cessation of sensation. Perhaps the Church should introduce schools of asceticism for adolescents, periodic two-week withdrawals from everyday life's flood of sounds, smells, sights, dreads, excitements. It would be valuable for a child of our superstimulated age to learn that he can live without, that in fact freedom lies in just such detachment. The quiet environment would have to be created by people who see discipline as liberation from, not breaking of, dead-end habits. (Sounds almost reactionary, doesn't it?) . . . D.

• "Charlie" is Will's cousin, the Rev. Charles E. Cronin.

∞

10 Dec 1972
The Summit

A-mazing Grace—

When this day is over and our church is fully church, the imperishable memory of the event will be not of Billy Jim's walls and roof and not of Bob's furniture. It will be of the space between those solid symbols, filled with the radiant faith of the man who literally created a church out of nothing. The eye will see the beauty of color, line, and form, but the heart will feel the beauty of hope fulfilled and sacrifice rewarded. The few who know the true cost of this triumph—in health, sleep, and innocence—know, too, that the church built the man. You are stronger for having discovered weaknesses, more confident for having overcome doubt, more compassionate for having been man as well as priest. P. and I have the private joy of seeing our Musketeer love reflected in the smile that declares, "It is done and won." Trumpets, drums, and cymbals sound from soul to soul in jubilation at your victory. God bless the day . . . D.

∞

22 Dec 1972

Dear A.,

How to reconcile the humble stable our thoughts are summoned to with the magnificent church our senses are surrounded by? There are children today being born who will know greater squalor and never know love. Perhaps the answer is this: in great measure the poor of the world suffer because the strong allow—compel—themselves to believe that race, caste, class, strangeness is a sign of fated inferiority. So long as our church resounds with ringing truth of Christ's gospel it will serve the poor, the weak, the forsaken better than the dollars it represents. Your preaching and our heeding will one day assure that no mother will bring forth a child in a manger . . . God bless your priestly work . . . Thanks for friendship, understanding, and care . . . A Blessed Christmas . . . D.

∞

5 Jan 1973

Habitual Haranguer—

Only a celibate would imagine that every man-woman encounter not regulated by rings or wimples is destined to end in the Nobags Motel. There is a natural reticence in most men that a woman can use to set the terms of their relationship. If she chooses not to, it may mean that she no longer values the 'freedom for' celibacy affords. In marriage there's an equivalent axiom: no one is lured away from his mate while the commitment is still intact. As long as a person believes his chosen condition is the only life for him his vocation is invulnerable . . . I've started reading a book on Joan of

Arc. P. would fill the role perfectly—completely unfazed by the pretensions of power. I'd follow her into battle, staying in her wake as she flailed angrily against the foe. . . . D.

∞

23 Jan 1973

Dear A.,

Thanks for the letter and the painful revelation. To be equally truthful, I have to admit that if you hadn't told me I wouldn't have known that I had touched off the eruption. It seemed situational rather than personal. I'm sorry you had to go through all that, but I can't say that I would act differently if we could replay the whole scene. What we have was a collision of weaknesses, which are also our strengths. I can see a problem from so many sides that I tend to see any solution as more or less workable. The difficulty is that some of the solutions involve anguish and agony and ought to be avoided for just that reason. You, on the other hand, generate tremendous spiritual energy by zeroing in on a goal and lasering your way through every obstacle to attain it. The new church is a monument to your single-mindedness. But the dark side of that moon comes into view when an opinion or feeling is promoted to a goal. Then you become blind to the relativeness of your own position, and it's not hard to sniff out treachery in others who hold even shaded allegiance to the same objective. In a sense we're both victims of our education—yours in the seminary, mine in the library. It would be ideal if each of us had an equal measure of the other's strength, but God chose to go about it otherwise. So we have to thrash things out in the space between, civilly, rationally if possible, but always charitably. I don't think you're a dunce because you don't see things my way, and I know you don't think I'm a Judas because I don't share your fervor. What matters is how a conflict ends, not who won. And we are still friends—and will be until you make admiration of the Cherubim wings a point of orthodoxy . . . The Supreme Court decision on abortion must have depressed you. It surprised me. I didn't think this court would loose that moral tiger on an already confused, suspicious, demoralized society. But the decision only articulates a negative policy: the *state* has no demonstrable right to *compel* an individual to sustain the life of a fetus. (A thorny precedent.) Now it is the job of the Church to teach, not by righteous denunciations but by active compassion that killing destroys two lives, that the sometimes frightening burden of pregnancy does not have to be borne alone . . . D.

∞

3 Feb 1973

Ms. Understood, si; Ms. Guided, no!

. . . . Jung has some interesting things to say about man's penchant for projecting his fears, wishes, illusions into the gaps between the things he knows from experiences. It's Heidegger's 'man sagt' all over again. And the sad truth is that men are most willing to kill one another over their collective imaginings, whether white supremacy, Cold War ideology, or the Will of Allah. Jung suggests that man will have to learn to live with the Unknown, 'to live with ambiguity,' as the pop existentialists have it . . . Sorry I had to blot out yesterday's easy joys with that depressing disclosure. I decided to unload on you while you were facilitating, only because it occurred to me that no time would be truly opportune. I know it's useless to urge you not to torment yourself over our problem, but try to replace worry with prayer. It'll do everyone more good. Thanks for halving our sorrow . . . P. knows; I told her in a letter last week . . . D.

• Will's "depressing disclosure" was that his brother John Jenks is being divorced from his wife Carolyn. John will receive custody of his two elder sons, Billy and Johnny, and has asked Will and his mother, Ella, to move to Mundelelein, Illinois, to live with John and the boys.

∞

9 Mar 1973

Cartoon Cultist—

Before I ride off in every direction at once I want to thank you, unpunctually, for the generous words about my tenure on the council. (Not once, but twice. A third time might have suggested the publication of banns, which would break too many hearts.) The greatest satisfaction in serving, apart from having built that church in the face of obstinate opposition, was discovering that I can function outside of books. But as much as I enjoyed the experience I don't want to be appointed to one of the three pastor's-choice seats; such a move would subject you to harsh criticism, on the grounds that the Expansion Amendment is an ad hoc arrangement. Besides, I may not be available after four or five months . . . D.

∞

16 Mar 1973

Station Master—

Jung even had some good things to say about celibacy: it can be the expression of wholeness, of the overcoming—by embracing—the opposition of masculine and feminine. That's not an endorsement of mandatory celibacy, but at least it establishes that there's nothing necessarily deficient about your life-style. Perhaps the Church should investigate the psychology of celibacy to develop a priesthood with positive commitment to full personhood as its discipline. D.

∞

24 Mar 1973

Angel's Advocate—

Last week's *Criterion* printed excerpts from a speech you may have heard on the desirability of recruiting young men for the priesthood. The speaker noted that so many priests are themselves doubtful about the future of the priesthood as they know it that they're hesitant to invite anyone to participate in the confusion. I think nothing could be more stimulating for a young man than to be a part of change, to shape the future by rediscovering what it means to be a priest. The Church doesn't need Bing Crosbys; it needs a new Ignatius, Dominic, Francis—for this age. Like the Marines, the priesthood needs tough men . . . D.

∞

15 Apr 1973

Guesticulator—

We may have to reschedule our A-day party. I've had a better offer for May 13. This morning reveille was advanced ten minutes when the postmaster himself brought around a special delivery letter (71 cents worth of stamps!) from NASA headquarters. Joe Kerwin, of Fenwick and Holy Cross, notified me that I will soon receive a formal invitation to the launching of Skylab, the 28–day orbiting space mission. Joe will be the medical member of the three-man crew. A pre-blast-off blast is part of the itinerary. Oh well, just to be asked is prestigious . . . The *Criterion* published skimmed data from a report on What Makes A Good Family. As nearly as I could understand, the standard of success was getting kids through high school without acquiring a record for juvenile delinquency—hardly a demanding requirement. It will reassure you to learn that a 'ghetto' environment—home and family friends—creates the most stable kids. What the article failed to deal with is the problem of freedom: how to become conscious of what it means to be a responsible person here and now, what it means to be me. . . . D.

∞

Easter 1973

Dear A.,

There is Easter for those who believe, who know that a thing dies only to be reborn in new forms, with new beauty. Faith sees and rejoices, and death loses its dread.

The greatest grace is the way He chose to reveal that truth, living our life, dying our death, becoming our hope. He is risen indeed.

I know this better for having known you. Your face is the Easter sunrise. In the bond, D.

∞

27 April 1973

Doggerel-dogged Dominie—

Can it be wrong to rejoice over another's misfortune if that other is Richard Nixon and the misfortune is so richly deserved? Watergate is becoming a case study in communicable paranoia. It's almost as though the campaign committee believed the highest immorality would be to leave any ploy untried. Somehow there's an analogy between Nixon's war/peace strategy and his election game-plan: better obliteration than ambiguity. (Or: sincerity as a pathological condition.) . . . Finished *The Exorcist* and enjoyed it, even though it didn't win me over to devil-dread. It was, after all, a fiction, plausible and pleasurable but not terribly profound. I suspect that in actual cases of demonic possession an exhaustive search would reveal a suggestive influence, a pretext for reorganizing a disintegrating psyche around a totally unconscious personality. The consequent evil isn't willed by some external power; it's allowed by the freedom inherent in God's creative process in which 'human nature' is potentiality, even to extreme variations from normal. I read the book with an eye measuring O'Malley's part; it's not weighty, but it does give him the Pat O'Brien role in the final death scene. And he gives absolution in Latin! . . . D.

∞

3 May 1973

Dear Father,

In answer to your question about the present condition of the Church, I can testify that where your priesthood has been felt the Faith has thrived. A life wholly—holy—given to making Christ's love present to the world is more persuasive than doctrine; it compels the heart's assent to truth. If you could retrace your steps over the past twenty-one years, you would find that you have been a Johnny Appleseed for Christ. The Word bears fruit in ten thousand lives touched by your ministry—mine among them. My prayers join yours in thanking God for the grace of your vocation, especially for that Nazareth home that taught you love. I know P. lends her voice to the Musketeer Te Deum. We are grateful for your priesthood and your friendship. A.M.A. D.

- Father Moran was ordained May 3, 1952, for which reason a "Te Deum," a hymn of praise and thanksgiving, would be sung.
- "A.M.A." stands for the Latin "Ad multos annos," meaning "To many (more) years."

∞

4 July 1973

Doctus in Doctrina—

Thomas Merton would have found the luxury incongruous, but he would have appreciated the cenobitic isolation. A moat would be redundant. No one attempts to breach the walls of our privacy. Maybe that's why the families here are so large. Without one's own, life would be empty . . . Last Sunday we went for a ride through downtown Chicago, with its proud cloud-puncturing structures. If a single skyscraper stood in the middle of a cornfield its enormity—in the opprobrious sense—would be immediately evident. But lost in the forest of high-rise Hubrishouses, even the new Sears building seems natural, built to scale. An Old Testament prophet would call down the wrath of Yahweh on the whole presumption . . . One of the nine-kid families has a girl with only one of her four limbs fully developed—a leg. Her age—nine or ten, I would guess—suggests that she may have been a Thalidomide baby. From a distance, at least, she seems happy, but her condition raises questions about the Love of God. Obviously God did not single out this innocent child for punishment by deprivation. Which must mean that His gifts of health and strength are not meant to reward the normal. Is it fair to say, then, that nothing we are given is our own but that it belongs to the whole? God loves humankind and each person only as a part of—participant in—the whole. So society must be organized to reflect that commonality. On with the Revolution . . . Pray for Mimi? She's in the hospital . . . D.

- "Cenobitic" refers to a monastic community. Will and his mother have moved into John's house in the town of Mundelein, near Chicago.
- Mimi is Will's aunt, his mother Ella's younger sister, who suffers from depression.

∞

11 July 1973

Wanderlustliking Westwarder—

I'm trying to get my mind back in harness by reading Henri Bergson, the first philosopher to attack Kantian metaphysics. He stresses the point that our minds can deal only with states and things, not with processes and tendencies. I think it's that limitation the Existentialists try to overcome . . . Even though I'm no longer a member of the parish—unless 'in pectore'—I share the joy of marking the beginning of your seventh year as pastor. If you had done nothing more than rescue me from the trash heap you would have done well. But there has been more, much more. Prayers will say thanks to the spirit. Best to your folks . . . D

• Literally, "in pectore" is Latin for "in the chest." As an idiom, it means "secretly."

25 July 1973

Mute Musketeer—

Who can account for the behavior of humankind? A month ago I would have guessed that P. would have left things to drift with the current, and yet she has penned a dozen cards and still other notes. Mirabile visu! . . . After a month—almost five weeks—at T40 Osage Rd., I haven't quite moved past the denial stage; I refuse to believe it's not merely an extended vacation—though why anyone would choose to vacation in this adult-forsaken place beggars the imagination. Day-to-day there is no noticeable falling off of acuity, perspicacity, cogency, and those other gifts of mind that make me the envy of the easily gulled. But I begin to sense a certain slackening of interest in the "Presence of what is present"—Heidegger's neologism for the ontological. With no one to becudgel with my erudition the incentive to ponder long and deeply vanishes. There are times when I foresee a disintegration of wit that will leave me little intellectual advantage over Pinky Lee. Ora pro me . . . D.

• "Mirabile visu" is Latin for "marvelous to see."

• Pinky Lee was a popular television comedian, best known for broad, slapstick humor.
• "Ora pro me" is Latin for "pray for me."

∞

30 Aug 1973

As you may have deduced from the 'loose' 10 cents at IC last Sunday, the Third Musketeer was home on leave. But our Number One Man was elsewhere, and the reunion was incomplete (though candor compels me to say that the sight of P. in all her loveliness blinded me to the possibility of fuller fellowship). It was good to be home—something like putting on street clothes after two months of wearing pajamas. The porch has lost none of its magnetism; in three hours Friday afternoon it drew about twenty people, most of whom I had wanted to see. At the Fall Festival those who were aware that I had left town were kind enough to say they missed me, if only as a familiar landmark. (Turn right at the big white house with the white-haired old man on the porch.) Twas truly grand . . . I think the time has come for priests to return to priesting. The rush to acquire all of secular society's credentials has been disastrous. We don't need priest-psychiatrists, priest-astronauts, priest-plumbers; we need priest-priests. The chancery, the schools, the philanthropic agencies should be cleared out, staffed with competent laymen or deacons, and allowed to function under the bishop's guidance. Every priest should be where the people are: in parishes (small enough for the pastor to know each parishioner as a person), in prisons, in missionary work. The other major problem, loneliness, could be alleviated by the sense of belonging small parishes create. And the people should come to understand that a priest is human, that he needs friends, someone he can talk to. If jealousies over 'favoritism' make friendships impossible the community can hardly be called Christian . . . Mailman

∞

12 Sept 1973

Rocco Gibralter—

Charlie stopped by the other day on his way to Santa Maria d P, where he was to present a proposal to the priest's senate. The revolutionary legislation would require each priest to spend some time during his first fifteen years in an inner city parish. I think the Church needs to make a public commitment to the poor, the old, the helpless, the imprisoned, the forgotten people in our affluent society. Such a move might lose a few lukewarm country club priests, but it would reinvigorate those who are scandalized by the apostolate to the Nice Folks . . . Ain't you never gonna come and see us? It won't help to visit me in the Bono boneyard. "Those soft few treads above me" may warm Danny Boy's dad, but not me . . . D.

• Santa Maria del Popolo is the church that Will and his mother attend in their new home. It had been chosen as the venue for a meeting of the northern section of the priest's senate of the archdiocese of Chicago.

∞

18 Dec 1973

Dear Pamphleteer—

Just yesterday I came across that taunt, "Physician, heal thyself," in an early chapter of Mark or Luke. Could that hint at some physical deformity? I know the Shroud of Turin gives Jesus the dimensions of a light-heavyweight boxer, but the perplexing statement raises questions . . . I'm almost embarrassed to report still another coda to the *Guideposts* piece. This morning I had a phone call from the Dana elevator, from the woman who runs the buying and selling operation. She had just read my article in *Grit* (True!), a national weekly newspaper aimed at rural readers. According to our agreement, *G'posts* is supposed to split the resale fee with me, so there should be one last squirt in the old cow's udder. Meal money for our holiday outing? . . . D.

∞

3 Jan 1974

Midnight Cowboy—

One of my co-workers gave me a slim volume on *Contemplative Prayer*, by Thomas Merton. In the introduction he speaks favorably of Heidegger and Camus, whose working through the problem of existential dread is an authentic modern expression of the contemplation of the Desert Fathers and the monastic patriarchs. Detachment from security, even of creed and liturgy, alone allows God to enter the heart in its silence—the source of creative freedom. There must be direction, purpose, meaning to life, but it will not necessarily be the accepted understanding of things—all the moreso in periods of disintegration. Questioning, self-doubt are the tools of this irregular discipline . . . Heard from Bill O'Malley, M*O*V*I*E* S*T*A*R, this week. He finally saw *The Exorcist* and pronounced it gruesome. Of himself he said, modestly, that he was gorgeous. So far I haven't read any more objective reviews. I trust the critics will be kind to him. The film has created a sensation in Chicago. Police have had to be called out to control traffic around the two theaters. It's minting money and may even outdo Larry's Godfather . . . D.

∞

9 Jan 1974

Plaguey Semi-Pelagian—

Read an illuminating piece on woman's thought processes, such as they are. The theorist suggested that a history of oppression has taught the ladies to make room for contradictory thoughts—the mostly no but partly yes that yields maybe. That allows them to hope when a man sees only catastrophe. I remember once offering P. a totally negative—and amazingly accurate—appraisal of her then-spouse's inner workings. Because she needed hope, however illusory, she deeply resented my gratuitous verdict and chilled me for long months. (I didn't advise her to quit trying; I was just meddling, with the intention of hinting that it would take something more radical than domesticity-as-usual to change the situation.) Man's yes-OR-no thinking contributes to his capacity for action—and for destruction. Woman's yes-

AND-no thinking corresponds more realistically to the ambiguity of things as they are. Women should be our theologians. . . . D.

• Pelagius denied original sin and held that, consequently, man has the freedom to do either right or wrong.

∞

22 Jan 1974

A-miable—

. . . . Merton, in *Contemplative Prayer*, makes some good points about sacrifice. He suggests that sacrifice for its own sake, with the object of sacrifice chosen by the aspiring saint, very often has the opposite effect from that intended; it creates a sense of accomplishment, self-satisfaction. Merton advises that we wait for events to demand sacrifice, usually of the familiar and comfortable, whether surroundings, life-style, ambitions, or even beliefs. Risk is the measure of sacrifice. Personally, a Lent without licorice always seemed risk enough for me . . . D

∞

15 Feb 1974

Il Duce—

It has been reliably reported that you pushed through your desired political reforms, aimed at diluting the dangerous democratic tendencies of the council. My instincts tell me that was a regressive move. Isn't it possible to attribute the dissociation of males from the life of the Church, notably in Latin countries, to the clergy's paternalistic attitudes? Admittedly, it's hard to be the chief executive in a system that doesn't allow you to campaign for—and, implicitly, against—candidates. But you can—and do—campaign for and against issues, and that ought to be an adequate safeguard against 'a handful of willful people' selling the church to Hugh Hefner. It will be interesting to see if voter participation is affected by the change . . . D

• "Il Duce" was the title of the fascist dictator Benito Mussolini, who held power as premier of Italy from 1922 to 1943.

∞

29 March 1974

Vain But in Vain—

Wednesday night's Lenten homily was delivered by a scholarly priest from the seminary. In his quiet way he had some very radical, un-Catholic things to say about Jesus and the Gospels. From computer studies of the speech patterns in the gospels, scholars have determined which of the sayings attributed to Jesus were actually spoken by him. (Some of the authentic sayings are found in fragments of apocryphal writings.) Both in style and in content the recurring thrust of the teachings is that observance counts for next to nothing; doing the Father's will is the single imperative. In an interesting aside the priest noted that Christ's word for 'Father'—'Abba'—is the Aramaic equivalent of 'Daddy.' (If Daddy is loving and forgiving, why does Mommy Church have to be such a scold?) Finally, in inviting us to the Eucharistic meal, he suggested that we think of ourselves not as the twelve at the Last Supper but as the tax-gatherers, whores, and bad persons Jesus caught so much grief over. Yet we have a closed communion, if only for one heinous offence. These bookish types will ruin things if we're not careful . . . D

∞

12 April 1974

Easter Dutiful—

Had a strange, providential experience the other day. The background needs to be filled in. Shortly after the *Guideposts* piece appeared I had a letter from a woman who related the truly woeful story of a fellow polio, a woman rescued from a nursing home by a church group but still affected with depressions. Would I write to her? I did every five or six weeks, though I hadn't written since just before or after Christmas until I sent off a card today. I sensed from what I had been—and hadn't been—told that she was in worse shape than me. So when the guys from Northwestern were here, setting up this electronic servant, I repeatedly thought of suggesting that they could get a fairer test of the equipment if it were given to Marge Pfrommer. But I decided to hold the suggestion until they were satisfied I am too naturally dexterous to need the machine. During that same interview, the head of the engineering team mentioned a girl who works in his office, even though she's paralyzed from the neck down. Again, no name was spoken. Then Wednesday afternoon the phone rang and the voice introduced herself as Marge Pfrommer, occasional target of my letters and part-time office worker at Northwestern Med School's engineering adjunct. A remarkable coincidence, at least. Marge seems to be a willow-lovely woman, understanding, courageous, buoyant. I sense she has had a much harder time of it than I have, but she's filled with hope. A grace to know her . . . When you lighted the Paschal candle you expressed your whole life in a symbol. You bear the flame that testifies to resurrection. Your faith is caught from the new fire of the Risen Lord. Blessed Eastertide, good friend . . . D.

• Actually, much of the "sip and puff" technology had first been developed on behalf of Marge Pfrommer. Will was the second or third beneficiary of the environmental control system and the electric wheelchair which he would receive in 1975. Marge was also the person who told Will about the training available through Lift, Inc., which led to his working as a computer programmer for Walgreen Company.

∞

9 May 1974

Agradable Amigo—

 . . . . Just read John Deedy's *Conscience, Freedom, and Authority*, part of the *What A Modern Catholic Believes About* ___ series. You would be appalled at what Deedy says, if only because he does not use the term Modern Catholic in the pejorative sense. Will it assuage you to learn that he is a Holy Cross man? Actually, you would find nothing new in the thesis. It's just what I've been trying to tell you for five years: many Catholics study the pronouncements of the Pope and the bishops and the theologians and then adjust their own understanding according to what seems most nearly true to their reason.

For the most part that has meant ignoring the fulminations against 'novelty,' 'subjective judgment,' and 'secularism' and heeding the pleas for peace and justice. That way lies the future, willy-nilly . . . D

∞

1 June 1974

Estimado Amigo

Earlier in the week I received my copy of the Holy Cross quarterly, an *Esquire*-sized magazine of 120 pages, all of them devoted to the Irish problem. The 'troubles' are viewed from every conceivable perspective—history, religion, economics, sociology, literature. As I made my way through the densely packed pages, my reaction shifted from anger—first with the Protestants, then with the Catholics, then with the British, then with the IRA—to sorrow to despair and finally to hope. The situation is so complex, so tangled in injustices that it can only be resolved by some new, yet unarticulated means. And in the process of creating a society of mutual tolerance and respect they may discover realities useful to the disintegrating polities of the West . . . Before and after reading the Irish issue I divided my attention—risking walleyedness—between *Death and Dying*, a manual compiled by the resident psychiatrist at a medical center, and *The Rise And Fall of the Third Reich*, the massive history of the Hitler event. You might find some pastoral value in the dying man's handbook, though the author refers to belief in immortality as a kind of denial. That seems to be the chief problem—getting people, both victim and family, to accept the approach of death. *Rise & Fall*, like all history, is a record of using others, betraying others, humiliating others, killing others. Hitler, of course, surpassed every villain before or since at those arts. As the Devil was reported to have said of Talleyand, he exceeded his orders . . . D

∞

4 June 1974

Jovial Chauvinist—

Sometimes I wonder if you don't automatically tune out anything that might unsettle those fragile Scholastic certitudes. That startling theory proposed by Sr. Superior, O.P., has been the basis of all our arguments over woman's role in the Church and in the world. What we term masculine and feminine traits are not biologically determined. For the most part, they are socially, culturally imposed in order to insure the society's continued existence—as it defines itself. (Even something as 'innate' as the male sex drive is so indeterminate that some primitive cultures have to rely on ritual dances to arouse the men to sexual activity.) In its simplest form cultural conditioning assigns roles of child-bearing and child-rearing to women and of protection and provision to men. But there have been almost infinite variations on that basic arrangement. In Neolithic times, men tended to be subservient to women, who were looked upon as divine custodians of fertility. Over the millennia infant mortality, plague, famine, war condemned women to breed as often and as long as possible. And xenophobia, ignorance, and greed kept men occupied with just staying alive. So the seeming inevitability of me-Tarzan/you-Jane arrangements came to be accepted as the divine plan, the Natural Law. But the gradual evolution of mankind has freed us from Necessity, has allowed us to use brain instead of brawn and—though infrequently—to compromise and cooperate instead of kill. Now it is not only historically unnecessary for a woman to birth as many babies as she can, it is positively irresponsible. That very escape from what seemed to be her sole reason for being has given woman time to examine the assumptions behind the model of femininity, and she has become conscious of her 'masculinity'—her ability to think within the formal contexts of science, mathematics, philosophy, etc., and to work with and over others. She has also become aware of the obsolescence of the prevailing male notion about masculinity and femininity. The man/woman sexual complement will not perish; it has too much to recommend it—physically, psychologically, spiritually. But the wide range of human activity outside the family—the work sphere—will be and ought to be open to whoever can do the job. And little girls are going to be encouraged to develop aptitudes once thought to belong exclusively to boys . . . D

13 June 1974

Gone and back, without calamity. It was a memorable experience. After twenty-three years' absence I returned to Holy Cross, scene of the happiest of my forty-two years, and I was not disappointed. The campus has changed unimaginably in the meanwhile; there were eleven buildings then; there are twenty-two now and a modest fieldhouse staked out at the top of the hill. My classmates have grown older and almost invariably more friendly. I recognized most of them without resorting to name tags, no doubt because I had studied the yearbook the day before leaving . . . Friday's schedule called for a cocktail party, class pictures, and a class dinner. Afterwards we staged a sing-along in our 'suite'—so-called because we had a two-chair sitting room in addition to a bedroom. The Musketeer medley, especially the Irish songs, seemed to be universal favorites. It kept us going till three-thirty. Six hours of sleep prepared us for the new day, with its picnic, Mass, banquet, dance, piano bar, and late, late party. . . . Sunday, just before we left, we dropped in on Jack Weimer's 11:30 Mass to catch his seven-minute homily. I considered leading a cheer when he finished. His doctrine of the Trinity really vibrated with meaning. How sad that the large Saturday crowd didn't hear it . . . Saturday afternoon we stopped at Father Pat's grave in the Jesuit cemetery. From the distance of five years his prodigious work of friendship seems incredible even to me . . . D

∞

21 July 1974

Amicus (though not a Meek Cuss)—

How good it was to be back among the Musketeers. There is something comfortable about being together, about knowing that honesty, not pleasantry, is the accepted currency. It's strange and somehow sad that we have to approach our feelings from the sidedoor. I know I hold back to keep from disturbing your equilibrium and thereby annoying P., who guards you like a mother hen against hawks and foxes. It may be that my tone says not, "This is what I feel, what I believe," but "This is what you should feel, believe." Anyhow, I'll try to remember to defang candor so we can talk without defenses up. . . . The other day Dora Smith, Aunt Mimi's apartment mate for 30 years, brought out a trunkload of stuff—luggage, clothes, jewelry, photo albums, slides, junk. She also showed me a sheaf of cartoons that I drew for Mimi; Dora wants to put them in a book something like the ones you and P. have. Her motive, though, is medicinal. The son of a friend was recently left paralyzed from the neck down after an accident, and Dora thinks my marginal triumph over adversity—the absolute absence of talent—will some-how encourage the young man to keeping trying. . . . I was deeply moved by your words on friendship at Saturday's Mass. It is good to realize that Jesus himself needed friends. The temptation is to suppose that His every com-munication was a teaching, that He didn't have to think out loud about the difficulty of making himself understood. And we impose that same burden on our priests, who are considerably more human than divine (No offense!). It's good to know that you value our friendship, that you feel you receive as well as give. Thanks for that reassurance . . . D

∞

31 July 1974

A-typical—

Sent O'Malley a detailed critique of his work in *The Exorcist* and, as a bonus, my opinion of the whole film. He may enjoy the cartoon more than the aesthetic assessment. It was a shrugging Oscar, with the caption, "So what do they know?" Second and third thoughts on the movie haven't changed my original judgment. Somehow evil seems less believable when it is explicit and grotesque. In writing about Nazi war criminals, Hannah Arendt coined the phrase, "the banality of evil," to account for nondescript functionaries like Eichmann. The spooky stuff is too remote from ordinary life. How much more frightening Kafka's *The Trial*. . . It's getting closer. The Episcopalians ordained 11 women this week, albeit uncanonically. We will be among the last, of course, but that day is not far beyond the horizon: "Bless me, Mother, for I have sinned" . . . D

∞

16 Aug 1974

Unimpeachable Pastor—

In last week's letter you noted that you sometimes are surprised by apparently honest compliments for sermons you felt had missed fire. I find that true in almost everything I do. The things that seem merely a bad compromise with necessity work out better than those that fall together easily. That happens with writing, with drawing, with IPR's (Inter-Personal Relationships). But I still try to meet my own standards. There's no other way to do it. (But even then there must be a sense of acceptance. Otherwise it can happen that failure to measure up becomes a source of self-condemnation. Not the 'golden mean,' which suggests mediocrity, but cohabiting demand and forgiveness, another instance of yes-and-no—or, more accurately, no-and-yes.). . . . D

∞

5 Sept 1974

A-droit—

Thanks for your letter. The secret to writing regularly is to have nothing to do and to dread isolation. Typing messages to the outside world gives me the comfortable illusion of being part of things. It's a rather drastic way to motivate yourself . . . I'm 75 pages into *Survival of Dogma*, by John Foster's boy, Avery. It was the gift of a friend who wants to learn the prognosis at second-hand. The structure of the work should be congenial to those who are ignorant of or turned off by traditional apologetics. Working from the existential to the revealed, Dulles simply makes the argument that man needs faith to live and that the faith expressed in the Church's symbols—the Gospels and theology—answers those needs explicitly. He ranged across the centuries and surveys seven basic theological modes in Christianity—Primitive, Patristic, Augustinian, Scholastic, Reformation, Counter-Reformation, Existentialist. None of these stirs a response in modern man, who more than anything longs for a reason to hope. So Dulles suggests that a contemporary theology has to appeal to our experience of humanity's indivisibility, and he cites Teilhard's models as approximations of what's demanded. I have trouble with his equivocal treatment of the Kingdom of God and its whereabouts, but the book prods thought. Dulles is no stylist, but he has a dry wit. Referring to the spate of books about the future, he confessed, "One can scarcely suppress a sense of envy of the endowments of people who write so voluminously about things that have not yet come into being." And he offered a good definition of mystery: a truth the mind cannot master but rather masters the mind . . . D

∞

19 Sept 1974

Dogged Dogmatist—

Why is it that you give me books that you should read? The Holy Spirit went to all the trouble of putting *Survival Of Dogma* in your hands, and you lateral it off as though the Four Horsemen of the Apocalypse were bearing down on you, intent on nailing you with heresy in hand. You'll be discouraged to know that Dulles says in scholarly language what I've been muttering at you for years: doctrinal articulations are conditioned by the mindset of their time, by the questions they seek to deal with, by the emotional state of Church authorities. He even goes so far as to say that there are sociopathological elements in pronouncements like *The Syllabus of Errors* and *Humani Generis*, to say nothing of *Humanae Vitae*. But the tone is not negative. Dulles insists that the magisterium, the Church teaching (and of necessity, the Church learning), can translate the Gospel truth into symbols that address today's problems according to today's understanding. He doesn't want to scuttle the past; he simply wants the past to serve the present. In one place he writes, "We must use the present to free us from the tyranny of the past, and we must use the past to free us of the idolatry of the present." A good book. You must read it . . . Nixon's pardon has given the theology of forgiveness a sudden prominence. No less a learned journal than *Time* gave over two pages to an essay on the need for repentance. Everybody from Billy Graham to Eugene Kennedy was given space, but no more than one line. Dr. Billy made a bald assertion that the pardon was good for the country. You may recall that he once declared that God had raised up Richard Nixon to lead us in these perilous times. If John the Baptist had been equally myopic

Judas would have had his endorsement for messiah. Ford's timing was incomprehensible, of course—hardly a reassuring augury. But politically, the pardon was inevitable. The bitterness among the paranoid Right would have polluted the public mood into the next century. D

∞

5 Oct 1974

Allah's Gardener—

.... I'm not sure what the distinction would be useful for, but in a sleepless interval the other night it occurred to me that people who are likable—congenial as long as you focus exclusively on their good points and pretend blindness to the bad—are in turn capable only of liking. The whole basis of a liking relationship is a tacit agreement to limit communication and activity to what is pleasant. The dark side of things simply doesn't exist. That attitude makes a person capable of doing great evil. In a sense it's the one-voice of insanity. . . . I would say that marriage between a likable and a lovable would be doomed at the outset; they wouldn't be covering the same area. So much for dim reflection . . . D

∞

25 Oct 1974

World Champion A.—

The search for someone to take care of me while my mother is convalescing from cataract surgery has come full circle. A chain of hot leads ended with the phone number of Lake County Community Health Service, which is simply another name for the Board of Health, the original 'we-don't-provide-that-sort-of-service-but' in the long run-around, now we have a half dozen new hot leads to pursue. I wonder if one of the cryogenic storage vaults would rent me space for six weeks. That would save everyone a lot of trouble. . . . D

∞

21 Nov 1974

A-OK?

Last night we went to visit my mother. It was my first sight of her since the surgery. I had talked with her on the phone several times, chiefly to relieve her anxieties about the hospital routine and to help her through a period of disorientation, the result of having slept at irregular times. The operation apparently took more out of Mom than we had expected. She seemed to have aged ten years and grown feeble. I think faith saved me from a sadness near depression. I am convinced that with time and love she will find new strength and joy, with clearer sight and renewed self-confidence. There is always enough for life with meaning. We will have to lighten her load, but that is no insuperable obstacle. Grace abounds . . . D

∞

1 Dec 1974

A Fortiori—

Good morning, Mr. Blank. My name is Bill Jenks. I'm with PFC Industries—no, *P-F-C*, as in Private First Class.—I wonder if I could quote you our prices on polyethylene plastic film?—Well, we have 2 mil—that's right, .002 in—4 mil and 6 mil.—Yes, I know. Most construction supply houses are interested chiefly in 4 and 6 mil.—Our prices are $10.00 a thousand—that's right, 1000 sq ft—for the 4 mil and $15.00 a thousand for the 6 mil.—Quantity? We prefer to ship at least a pallet; that would be 30 boxes of the heavier stuff to 50 of the lighter.—Delivery in 5 days—Right now we're shipping out of Minneapolis.—It would be your freight on shipments under 2500 lbs.—OK, I'll give you my number, and I hope we can do some business. Goodbye . . . That's more or less typical of my phone pitch, repeated 18 to 20 times an hour, with variations and evasions, depending on whether I want to share my extensive knowledge of plastics or conceal my vast ignorance. Friday I got hold of a guy who had nothing better to do, so he asked my advice on all his problems relating to polyethylene film. Muhammed Ali never displayed such blinding footwork. My boss and I laugh about the PFC empire—a mammoth, conglomerate comprising his phone and mine, a phone credit card, an answering service, a post office box, and a box of stationery. The operation is completely legitimate. PFC has a quality product, manufactured by a reputable processor, and we fulfill every contract to the letter. The camouflage is necessary because purchasing agents would rather deal directly with the plant instead of a manufacturer's rep. (I hope the warden will let me keep my typewriter.) . . . How's this for a metaphor on the man/woman ways of perceiving? A man's eye is a still camera with which he captures things in their simultaneous relationships. His mind studies each picture, makes comparison between one picture and another, and devises theories to account for changes. In time his theories come to govern the focus of the lens and the investigation of new pictures. Inevitably, he finds his theories out of joint with new realities, and he must create new theories to span the gaps. A woman's mind is a moving picture camera that records reality as it unfolds. Her mind seeks the rhythm of change and the feel of the present whole. She is not very adept at changing things, since she isn't interested in the why-and-how, but she does adapt to new circumstances better. (These distinctions don't follow strictly biological lines; they're not determined, only conditioned.). . . . D

• Will began selling polyethylene film for the Porter Film Co. in November 1974.

∞

5 Jan 1975

> TO FATHER MORAN,
> IN THE SPIRIT OF
> THE THREE KINGS
>
> In years gone by, at party's end
> You've left the festive hall
> Without so much as a can of beans
> Or a dime-size Super Ball.
>
> Today, be warned, there's no escape,
> Whatever excuse you use,
> Because we've planned a small surprise
> – A gift you can't refuse.

It seemed a timely thing to do,
And fitting, to say the least:
The Holy City, the Holy Year
– They summon the holy priest.

Just think! You'd enter that giant door
And stand where saints have stood.
Then, later, you'd meet Pope Paul himself
– Which would do you both some good.

A pilgrim's meant to walk the way,
But the ocean's no mirage.
So here's the fare to go by plane
– And an early "Bon Voyage."

∞

25 Mar 1975

Buon Viaggio, Amico Mio!

Or something like that. It is truly meet and just that you are leaving for Rome just after Easter. A rigorous Lent will have cleansed your palate for the soul's feast. You're naturally—supernaturally?—attuned to the sacramental, so Rome should satisfy your hunger for the holy. My prayers go with you, all the moreso if you're going to be flying Aire Italia, with a pilot who got shot down by a blowgun during Mussolini's atrocity against Abyssinia. . . . Each Easter adds a layer of new meaning, like the alluvial deposits on a delta. The liturgical floodcrest carries particles of resurrection experience and leaves them to form part of the growing mystery, the deepening sign. You could not be so alive if the Paschal mystery didn't fill your heart and leave no room for Death. Joyous Easter, immortal friend . . . D

∞

6 May 1975

Ageless A.—

. . . . The simple joy of your birthday is that you are alive—not just numbered among the living by the Census Bureau but felt and remembered as a
biophile, a lover of life, all life. At the heart of that love is a belief, deeper than
creed, that what has been given can be given away without loss, even with
gain. And the gain is the fullness of grace you make present every day of your
life. Phyllis McGinley had it right: generosity is the surest sign of sanctity,
and sanctity is the highest expression of human life. (It occurs to me that if
you were God you would be too busy giving everyone everything that you
wouldn't have time to loose the fateful lightning of your terrible swift sword.)
Anyhow, it is a happy birthday for those of us you give to. God be thanked
for it . . . If it hadn't been for the Musketeer party the weekend would have
been totally depressing. I suppose it had something to do with the realization that I was merely a visitor—and possibly with the sense of guilt over
letting the house stand vacant. At bottom it may have been a mourning for
the comfortable illusion that my life in Dana had meaning. The truth is that
I probably do more good here, where I mediate between three generations.
There would be less occasion for angst if fate had dealt a full House—work,
wife, family, good deeds, and a Lincoln Continental, but it's precisely the
dislocation that gives me a perspective on things. As you said, a person can
choose to see either the good or the bad in his own situation, and that makes
all the difference . . . D

∞

26 May 1975

Heinrich, alte freund!

I have to tell you about my latest—first, actually—success at simulating a
foreign voice. When I called Dudley Childress, the Northwestern electronics
wizard, to warn him that his creation was to be on the tube I introduced
myself as Bruce Wa Samata, of Nippon Facsimiles, Ltd. In my best Sessue
Hayakawa accent I expressed interest in Dudley's inventions, and only when

I had used up my prepared dialogue did I reveal the hoax. Dudley must have laughed for two minutes. Of course, he was a set-up because he gets a dozen calls a week from foreign doctors and engineers, and he couldn't afford to be sarcastic. The prank made both of our days . . . Your letter, with its elaborate hyperbole, set the tone for the apotheosis (as O'Malley mockingly described it) at Holy Cross. I hope I kept a safe margin of genial disbelief between me and praise. . . . Friday's euphoria began as soon as we crossed Southbridge St. and rolled onto the lowest level of the campus, around the baseball diamond, and across the north end zone of the football stadium to the robing tent. On the way we met Fr. Hart, who has been the heart of the school for 43 years. He assured me that Father Pat would be with us on that great day. (Think of the curious sequence of events that led to my doctorhood. If Father Pat hadn't persisted in friendship, you would have had no reason to nag me about writing the *Guideposts* article and there would have been no *Crossroads* coverage, no reunion recognition, no honorary degree. Leave out any link and the chain would have ended there. Thanks for your part in it, even though I don't like to encourage you in bulldozing the reluctant.) At the robing tent I met the other honoraries—and made a special overture to George, the multi-millionaire Black businessman, whose Afro-Sheen factory is only a few blocks from Charlie Cronin's rectory. The ceremony got underway with the academic procession—graduates, faculty, deans, and the five of us. John pushed me over the route and deposited me on the stage. After the "Star Spangled Banner" we sat through the presentation of 560 diplomas and the valedictory address, a fashionable harangue against the world as it is, and then Fr. Brooks got on with the important business of the day, the awarding of the honorary degrees. Eileen was first; her works have been the difference between life and death for millions of people. I would have applauded loudest for her. Then William Henry Peter, the living legend—more aptly, canard. Then George, who's given away more money than most honkeys earn. Then Mabel, whose citation abounded in Classical allusion. Finally, Judge Stevens, in the Doctor's circle for the eleventh time. (When he came over to say goodbye I wished him a '76 without honor, so he could spend the time fishing.) Mabel's address chanced to rebut the despair of the younger orator. She urged the creation of new myths for our times, little knowing that the writer of my citation had already begun the task. The recessional took us back to the disrobing tent, but I had to detour for a TV interview (Gad, the burden of celebrity!) and a surprise quiz from a newspaper man who asked me what I thought of the valedictory address. I rambled on for five minutes, and he took down every tenth word. Since Holy Cross hasn't asked for its hood back, I assume the damage wasn't irreparable. At long last I was allowed to escape the gown and make connections with a beer. A reception in an open tent on the baseball field gave me a chance to talk with people from the school and the bishop and alumni and anybody who would listen. We stayed there until early afternoon, when the publicity guy summoned me to his office for one last interview, an inane session with a disc jockey for Westinghouse broadcasting. After a brief moment at Father Pat's grave, we made a quick tour of the campus and left for Boston, under threat of traffic-clogged roads. There were none so we had two hours to kill. Our flight just beat a squall-line into Chicago; we were home by 9:30 and in bed an hour later, though sleep was delayed by a crank call . . . Thanks for the letter and the phone call. I've left instructions that I'm to be buried with that encomium in my pocket. If perchance you can take it with you, better a recommendation than cash. Cartoon when leisure returns . . . D.

L.H.D. ( )
D.H.L. ( )
A.P.D. (X)

- Rev. William J. O'Malley, S.J., raised Will's reception of the honorary degree "mockingly" to an apotheosis, or deification.
- The five recipients of honorary degrees were Eileen Mary Egan, projects supervisor of Catholic Relief Services; W. H. P. Jenks; George E. Johnson, industrialist and philanthropist; Mabel Lang, Paul Shorey Professor of Greek at Bryn Mawr College; Harold A. Stevens, presiding justice of the First Appellate Division of the New York State Supreme Court.
- "L.H.D." stands for the Latin, Litterarum Humanarum Doctor. D.H.L., for the English, Doctor of Humane Letters. A.P.D. represents Athos, Porthos and D'Artagnan, the Three Musketeers. Will put his "X" in the Musketeers' box, indicating it is more valuable than the honorary degree, whether in Latin or English.

15 June 1975

Longanimitous Listee—

. . . . It may be that my outlook has been colored by a recent jolt. A week ago I had a phone call from a girl—woman, to acknowledge our age—who lived in Park Ridge long, long ago and passed through my life as the best friend of my first love, Edie Lahrman. . . . But to make a long story incomprehensible, the phone call brought the appalling news that Edie was dead, victim of an unsuspected aneurysm. (I've told nothing of this to P. She doesn't need further fears planted in her imagination.) The day before she died I had received a long letter from her, the first spontaneous missive in more than a year. Until I met you I never knew anyone so much alive. It's hard to think of her as dead. Death always jars the mind out of its complacency . . . D

∞

26 June 1975

Avatar of Abnegation—

Edie's death has shaken her parents far more than I had supposed it would. They are Teutonic and therefore phlegmatic in most things, but this blow has nearly unhinged them. The problem, I think, traces back to the Calvinistic belief—not at all foreign to Catholic presuppositions—that good things happen to good people and bad to bad. When some evil befalls a good person we unconsciously search out a morally persuasive why, if not in the behavior of the victim, then in ourselves, who suffer loss. The view of God as micro-craftsman, with strategic purpose in the placement of every sub-atomic particle fosters the superstition that I am me because He planned it that way. That makes God responsible for my biology and man responsible for my psychology—a curious division of labor. So I can be angry at man for the hurts he inflicts but not against God for the breakdown of my body, including death. The truth, as I see it, is that creation operates by the play of chance in a medium of abundance. I happen to be me because of an almost infinite convergence of contingencies. The miracle is that creation has given man so many more potentialities than he can use that he is free to adapt to new conditions and even create conditions for himself and others. So the given—I—has no claim on itself or the world, but it has gifts to give and to enjoy—never wholly free from chance/death. That outlook at least has the virtue of muting the voice of blame and allowing self-love. It also makes every minute valuable, especially every minute of others' lives. (Opaque, no?) . . . *New Republic* has a caustic editorial about honorary degrees. The heading read: "Sweet Nothings." I may cancel my subscription . . . D

∞

3 July 1975

A-gog—

Tuesday morning Mom and I went to a memorial Mass for Edie, my teen-age love. After Mass there was a gathering in the rectory for family and friends. Edie's parents are still discomfited by the loss. There wasn't opportunity to talk with them, except in greeting and leaving. I think they would have like to have had some time with us, probably because I have so many memories of Edie's springtime . . . D

∞

8 July 1975

A-bettor of Sure Things—

Today's *Time* says the Holy Year is a staggering success. And you were there. The article says the Pope's spirits picked up perceptibly after Easter. I knew it would do the old gentleman good to see you. . . . D

∞

24 July 1975

Non-privative A—

Here's a quandary for a canon lawyer: if I marry a divorced woman I sin in the eyes of the Church, and Confession cannot restore me to good standing, except on the unreasonable condition that I give up the marriage. And yet if

I murder the woman's ex-mate I can confess that sin, with imperfect contrition, and have the Church's blessing on my marriage to the widow. (Thought: if a confessor asked about my motive and I told the truth would he—could he—grant absolution on the condition that I never marry the woman?) The original dilemma seems to penalize good conscience and reward bad conscience . . . Since I was the one to raise the question about unhappiness and its roots in lack of appreciation I should undo my own failings by speaking out. Paradoxically, what I value most in your friendship is not your words of praise—in which I hardly recognize myself—or even your gratitude but your willingness to let me be me, to say my mind and differ and at times attack your dearly-held-beliefs. (It honestly annoys me to be called 'great' or 'good' or 'exemplary' or whatever. I'd rather be told that my friendship makes a difference in the other's life. Still more I like to recognize a new sense of freedom in the other, the surest affirmation that my love has reached the heart.) You have the grace to make a friend feel he is important to your life, that he is a reason for your happiness. You see only the bright side of the moon because you are its sun. . . . The decision to sell the house left me depressed for several days. Emotion's struggle against reason . . . D

• Will and Ella are selling the Dana house.

∞

29 July 1975

A-nointed—

  On tonight's news there was a story of a man who has decided to forego thrice-weekly treatments on a kidney machine, even though he is doomed without them. Already diabetes has blinded him, and a complex of diseases has eroded his strength so drastically that he will not live another year. I know that if my other kidney, the survivor, were to fail I would refuse a transplant or a life in bondage to a mechanical flusher. It's a simple question of extraordinary means . . . Try to stay free Aug 21, 22, or 23. We expect to be down for all three days of the Fall Festival. Maybe P. will break down and buy us a bowl of chili . . . D

• Here is Will's informal health care directive, predicated on his ethical right to refuse the use of "extraordinary means" to prolong his life.

∞

9 Oct 1975

A-biding A-better—

Tuesday, if the contraption and I prove compatible through the trial run T40 Osage will become the new speed capital of the world. I have to admit to a degree of nervousness—something less than stark terror but more than palpitations. Maybe it's accumulated impatience . . . *Ascent of Man* continues to provoke. The latest chapter had to do with man, the builder. Bronowski claims building is the highest expression of the human spirit. This may be true, but the Billy Jims work with fixed, quantifiable materials. Building community, with freedom and justice, out of the infinitely variable material of us is beyond the ken of the engineer. Man the lover is the avatar of the species . . . D

• The "contraption" is Will's new battery-powered, "sip and puff"-guided wheelchair.

∞

20 Oct 1975

Apparent Amnesiac—

. . . . You've probably heard, either by word of mouth or sound of crash, that I'm powered for Go-Stop-Turn. My dodge-em car can be maneuvered out of any space a warped enemy could push me into. It would require great patience and forethought, of course, but in time the escape would come to pass. So far, no outdoor ramps. They will be built the day after the first blizzard. In the meantime, though, I'm learning to weave through life's obstacles . . . Sermon-before-last, Fr. Doyle gave the most wholesome interpretation of Christian suffering I've ever heard in a Catholic church. Unavoidable suffering—loss of anything humanly irreplaceable—can, if faced and accepted, open the heart to a world of new possibilities, new powers, resurrection. And with that new awareness comes a new life, where there is joy in being part of God's creative care for the world. There's a catch. Increased sensitivity leaves a person vulnerable to deeper suffering. But that in turn fissures the heart's rocky crust and releases new energies for loving. Life is going to hurt. Seeking safety by keeping things at a distance diminishes life rather than expands it. That's the paradox of the cross. . . . D

∞

11 Nov 1975

Avid Arranger—

I've discovered the secret of your Svengalian powers. You make a friend learn to like himself a little better because a person as good as you has said, "you're OK." There's nothing quite like the feeling. Thanks for coming and making 48 hours of aimlessness seem like Mardi Gras . . . Last Sunday we were held captive, by cowardice or civility, I'm not sure which, during what must have been the worst organized sermon ever delivered. The atrocitor, a young, bearded priest with a faint Irish brogue, wandered for 20 minutes and quit only because a two-year-old with no conditioned piety let loose a bellow that perfectly expressed the frustration of the rest of us. The experience was not altogether unprofitable. It moved me to formulate Jenks' Law of Homiletics: "The impact of the liturgy is directly proportional to the impact of the homily, which is inversely proportional to its length" . . . I'm reading *Why Am I Afraid To Tell You Who I Am?* which is not, as I had assumed, the Lone Ranger's Apologia Pro Vita Sua. The first 75 pages were no more than a survey of the literature. Every paragraph capsulized the thought of some philosopher or psychologist, most of whom I've read. He even gave Heidegger space, so he must be sound. The chapter on getting out your gut feelings was worth the price of admission. I was especially chastened by the rule against making judgments on the other's motives, a temptation that seems to grow stronger as the relationship grows closer. Apparently I assume that someone who loves me knows my needs and my weaknesses well enough to avoid hurting me. The rules for getting things out without attacking the other are valuable. I may even violate a personal principle and memorize them. (At a certain stage in a relationship there is a danger, if the process stalls and the other seems to say, "Thus far; no further,' that I will begin jabbing the other with barbed remarks just to provoke some kind of emotional response. I find myself doing that to P.) . . . D

∞

29 Nov 1975

Azygous Anomaly—

. . . . The CBS Evening News covered a Catholic gathering in Detroit. I peered expectantly into the throng, searching for your face. You were nowhere to be seen, incredibly. The shared interest of the symposium, Ordination of Women, seemed a likely magnet for your iron theology. Too late now, I think, to wire an anathema. You'll have to issue a retroactive malediction in the name of the momentarily prorogued Holy Inquisition. At least you can draw comfort from the thought that Rome moves slowly, even toward inevitable changes; so you will be twenty-five years dead before there are ordained Mothers . . . D

∞

11 Dec 1975

A-WOL—

It was one of those times when things just didn't work out. Even John Cameron Swazey would have found it hard to get together. P. and I had a half hour in the kitchen. We spent much of the time worrying over you. Actually, we alternated between worrying and laughing. The mere suggestion that you might seek oblivion in sex, booze, or drugs defies gravity. (Forgive our callousness.) We do in fact worry that you will work yourself into a frenzy with such wild imaginings. Exclude the extremes and stay within the range of the possible. Don't accuse yourself of high crimes and misdemeanors simply because you'd rather feel pleasure than pain. You're entitled to the small joys life affords—a pretty face, even a nice shape; palatable food; sleep that knits the raveled sleeve of care; leisure; the company of friends; aspirin; Pepsi (before 6:00 P.M.): It's semi-Pelagian to deny yourself those good things on the grounds that they are but the first steps on the road to degradation. Relax. Be confident of your ability to discern real occasions of sin. Be still more confident of forgiveness if you should get singed by that lake of fire—or whatever lurid temptation happens to snare you. God made us to do good, not to be good. Jesus refused the attribution of goodness for himself; "Only God is good." Who does more good than you? End of exhortation . . . D

∞

30 Dec 1975

UnAltarable—

It becomes harder and harder to get 'up' for the 50 or so notes I write in lieu of Hallmark greetings. Everyone is different—myself, most of all. And for some reason it takes a lot of work to write something suited to each person. Age seems to be robbing me of once-inexhaustible resources. (Christmas tends to bring on its own depression. I think it traces to the incongruity of lavish presents and unfeeling behavior. I'm not exempt from that contradiction, but I find myself wishing for less loot and more love.). . . . New Year's Resolve: To think kindly of the Holy Father, as long as he doesn't meddle . . . D

∞

9 Feb 1976

. . . . Forty-eight hours ago I was groping my way back to consciousness after having taken a garage floor to the head. I had insisted on loading with the lifter in order to go to the barbershop before my hair grew to my waist. So John ran the lifter into the garage, ran the car up on a block, and then ran me just short of the seat. The front tire was too low. He backed me off, still hanging from the lifter and drove the car up an improvised ramp. That cleared the frame enough to allow the lifter underneath, and I relaxed—too early, it would seem. The next thing I knew I was in the family room, watching an Abbott and Costello movie. In the meantime, I had been picked up by John, had puffed my way up the ramp, had been interviewed and instrumented by the Countryside paramedics, and had had Bill and Betty Kane here for a consultation. I remembered none of that. Yesterday I was sick and achy; today I'm only achy. Tomorrow who knows? . . . My legs and hips are sore, so I'll say adieu for now . . . D

∞

20 Feb 1976

A.1—

To dispose of the obvious question, I am nearly recovered from the bruised buttocks and sore tailbone acquired in my fall from grace. My head, found sound in a series of skull shots and a brain scan, quit aching a week ago. Only my taste and smell have failed to return. The neurologist at NU Med seemed surprised they had fled. . . . The days following my head-cracking gave me an appreciation of what it's like to get along without an active mind. My thoughts couldn't come to grips with new ideas or even with open-ended questions. And when energy permitted me fifteen minutes at the typewriter I could think neither critically or creatively. It was frightening. With time the brain began to escape to narrow confines of the indicative mood, and I was reassured that I wouldn't be permanently punchy . . . D

∞

26 Mar 1976

Amnesiac Anonym—

. . . . Forgot to answer your inquiry about the Joan of Arc statement: "Everyone in your life will be there with you." I understood it to mean no one can testify in his own behalf; only those you have loved and have not loved will be allowed to speak for or against you. Behind that image is a basic truth. God's creatures are completely interdependent; none, not even man, lives by and for himself, whether physically, esthetically, intellectually, morally, or spiritually. My life was and is the gift of other human beings, and I must give whatever I have to others, the same and different, old and new others so that their lives may become gifts to still others. Nothing else matters. That's the Kingdom . . . Thanks for your letters—what's in them and behind them . . . D

∞

1 April 1976

All-Too Ardent—

By now you should have recovered from your zealoholic hangover, sadder but no wiser. All the "How-To-Organize-Your-Life-For-Power-And-Might" books seem to have failed you or even frustrated you. It must be obvious that a clean desk is not necessarily a godly desk. If remorse accompanies exhaustion the problem could lie in the inability to accept limitations. Your spiritual horizons draw your concern into regions your legs can't reach. As compelling as the role of Savior of the World must have seemed to Jesus, He never took His message outside His homeland. In fact, the pace of His public life was rather casual. (Maybe that's why the Father sent Him before the invention of trains, planes, cars, telephone, -graph, and -vision. A public life modeled on a Presidential campaign would have killed Him long before a paid assassin could have crucified Him.) What you have to do *BEFOREHAND* is to ask yourself if the work you're going to do is pastoral, if the worry you're going to get involved in is worthy of priestly concern. So many of the demands made on you fall under the job-description 'Salving the Saved,' a ratification of already approved lifestyles. (I think it's harder to be a priest in a middle-class parish than in a desperately poor mission where necessity absorbs every energy.) Sometime, somewhere, I preached this sermon before. So it must be True if I still agree with myself. . . . A. P. *D.*

∞

7 April 1976

. . . . Over the past two or three weeks *Time* has published supposedly inside information about Nixon's disintegration during his last days in office. Why that gossip seemed pertinent has not been explained. If Nixon's actions had been sinister or psychotic there might have been some point in disclosing the events within the White House, but the man's behavior was merely pathetic, the eruption of inner chaos in a person who had believed feelings could and must be repressed. Those who share that belief will be disgusted with the display of weakness; those who realize that emotions contain some truth and must be heard will pity Nixon in his humiliation. The downfall has been compared to a Greek tragedy—but wrongly, because the hubris sprang from ignoble motives . . . D

∞

16 April 1976

Alleluia (Allegro)

I wonder if we were the last generation to live the liturgical drama of Holy Week. The events of Christ's Passion and Death seemed more real than any events in our own lives, His suffering more gruesome than anything we might endure. It's impossible to say how that immersion in ritual affected us. No doubt Freudians would say it alienated us from our own experience, but didn't it also keep us a healthy distance from neurosis? And will the void be filled with something better? . . . D

∞

12 May 1976

Albeit Albescent—

Saturday my mother and I went to Park Ridge, our pre-Dana hometown, to join the celebration of a fiftieth wedding anniversary. The recycled bride and groom were the parents of my first love, Edie, who died last June of an aneurysm. Because the occasion would have brought her back to Park Ridge for the first time in five years, it became that much more palpably evident that she wasn't there. Mom overheard someone saying that Edie had been in love with that white-haired man in the wheelchair. The speaker got it backwards, but I'm content to let that version take root . . . One day last week I heard a sociologist depart from a detached recitation of dreary data to fervent advocacy of unquantifiable values. He asserted that society has to create a loving environment for children by caring for those who care for children. His premise is that each child needs at least one adult who cares for him irrationally—without time clock, work rules, or division of labor. He cited China as a culture that affords minimal material support to its children, and yet everyone takes responsibility for children. (Maybe I liked what the guy was saying because I've said the same thing about small towns.) If the Right To Life people want to make a radical change in the attitudes of women who seek abortions they can undertake programs to make life rewarding not just for children but for those who meet their needs, physical and emotional. It can't be a government project; the bureaucrats would hamstring it from the start. Let the government give money. The church should give unconditional affective support . . . D

∞

8 July 1976

August Absentee—

 . . . . If it didn't give me an excuse to go back to Dana I doubt that I would have approved of the project EPD celebrated. That otherwise un-distinguished structure is a monument to Dana's collective ego. There was scarcely reason to memorialize Ernie again. Already his name adorns a high-way, a school, and a roadside park, all of which serve some public need. It's not as though scholars could examine Ernie's childhood environment for clues to his genius. He lived there only 18 months, and besides, there is no one, even in Dana, who claims he was a genius. The sole purpose was to re-inforce the town's tenuous link to history, at someone else's expense . . . This afternoon two of Edie's three sons came by with their grandmother, aunt, and two cousins. Both of them had their mother's facial features; the youngest son even has blonde hair and light blue eyes and her midday smile. I felt an ache after they left—so many memories stirring . . . D

• "EPD" is Ernie Pyle Day.

∞

17 July 1976

In my old age I have become leery of self-inflicted pain, so for the most part I avoided watching the Democratic convention . . . I did tune in both keynote speeches (Jordan, si; Glenn, no), the nominating speeches (Chavez, si; Kovic, si; all others, no), and the acceptance speeches (Mondale, si; Carter, no) . . . Carter disappointed me. I had hoped for a simple, fervent articulation of his vision of America, what forms he intends to create in order to make our society hospitable. But instead of radical insights he gave us banalities. I still expect to vote for Jimmy, but without enthusiasm . . . The right-to-life spokesman did nothing to advance his cause. The absurdity of his claim that Catholics have been expelled from the Democratic party must have annoyed daily communicant Daley and the thousand more papist delegates who still consider the party their home. The platform's rejection of the constitutional amendment strategy reflects political judgment, not theological. As Sen. Stevenson observed, the Supreme Court's excesses in its abortion rulings do not make counter excesses appropriate. Constitutional amendments have traditionally dealt with either extensions or restrictions of direct governmental action against individuals or with reshaping of the institutions of government. The only time an amendment was used to control individual behavior—the prohibition amendment—there was flagrant violation of the law and consequent loss of respect for government. Other strategies have to be developed, especially to protect against compulsory abortion, euthanasia, bureaucratically coerced contraception or sterilization . . . D

∞

14 Aug 1976

Amiable Auditor—

Apparently vacationing is an art form related to oratory; at least the same rule applies: a good ending makes both memorable. Just 90 minutes with you brought about an end to a two-day decline in spirits, attributable to bad weather, sluggish bowels, and lack of activity. It was therapeutic to talk about things I had been thinking about and not about things that had happened. I run out of history quickly, out of ideas never. Thanks for listening . . . D

∞

20 Aug 1976

. . . . I've been re-reading *Five Cries of Youth* for staff discussion. This week we were to go over 'the cry of the prejudiced,' who turn out to be the 'good' kids, the ones who are ready to fight for their church. Several surveys show that they tend to believe life is a matter of doing your best to please God. . . . They are Law-oriented, judging themselves and others by rules for good living. They resist the notion—the truth—that no deed is intrinsically pleasing to God—not fasting, not abstaining, not even worshipping. It may be the heresy is grounded in the idea that Creation was a once-and-for-all thing, that we are not part of an evolving creation, with a responsibility to the world, to the future, to the Spirit whose work is making new, ever-more-inclusive forms. God doesn't want to be told He's done good work, because He's not done . . .

21 Aug. Ten years ago today my father died. He was 80 and had been a total care for a year-and-a-half. I'm not able to measure the extent of his influence on my life. He was not a textbook father in either the Freudian or the Spockian sense. As the non-Catholic parent he took a passive role in our religious formation, though he did instill decency and duty. Whatever wit I have I have from him. I would not have traded him for a Joseph Kennedy . . . D

• Ella Jenks cared for both Mack and Will by herself during those eighteen months.

∞

27 Aug 1976

By chance, only a few days after I had read a *New Republic* 'Reconsiderations' essay on Graham Greene's *The Quiet American*, I found it among John's paperback books. The essayist spoke an appalling truth: Greene had written the story of our involvement in Viet Nam many years before it happened. The attitudes of the Quiet American foreshadowed the awful arrogance of Rostow, McBundy, NcNamara, and Rusk; his ardent innocence led him to commit detached atrocities in the name of Democracy. If there can be said to be a moral to the story it must be that the noblest ideology becomes inhuman when it sanctions indiscriminate violence . . . Twenty-five years ago today, I awoke and found my right arm useless. Polio had arrived to alter my plans.

Actually, I had no plans beyond returning to Holy Cross and sweating out two courses with Father Bean, the scourge of sophomores. Perhaps it was just as well that my agenda held nothing definite, like marriage or career; at least I was spared bitter disappointment. I can't say whether it's been a long or a short 25 years. When there was pain, it was long; joy, all too short—much the same as any other life. In an overall context of unluck I've been incredibly lucky. All my might-have-beens, given my physical conditions, could only have made life less. Among the good things to come my way your friendship counts as one of the best. Coincidentally, it is nine years since you interrupted my reading of *The Phenomenology of Perception* to introduce yourself as the new pastor. We have come a long way together, mostly through joys. Subtract your love, and I would shrivel with the loss of strength. Thanks—to you and Him who sent you . . . D

∞

4 Sept 1976

I may have discovered the literary corollary to the Jungian thesis that all emotional problems in people over 33 are essentially religious. My spin-off theory says that depressing novels are about people with no religion. For want of something better to read, I've been plodding through *Letting Go*, by Philip Roth. I haven't been so uncomfortable since I read *Something Happened*, another narration of a life powered by selfishness. The fundamental trait of a religious person, it seems to me, is a freedom from concern with self. It comes of seeing life as part of being, both given and giving. Phyllis McGinley called generosity the common denominator of the saints she wrote about. In some measure it's necessary to less-than-sainthood . . . Filling out the biographical information sheet for the Fenwick board of trustees, I proudly listed membership on the parish council. If you hadn't pushed and prodded, I might still cower in the face of responsibility. Sometimes Father knows best, forsooth . . . Sallfernau . . . D

∞

13 Sept 1976

Amaranthine Ami—

Nowhere is the absurdity of middle-class mores so apparent as it is in post-hijacking interviews, when the released hostages credit their abductors with courtesy and consideration. It is apparently of no consequence that the terrorists have used other human beings as disposable means to their unconditional ends. Insensitivity to being used by others suggests a latent—more probably active—capacity for using others. I wonder how many radical leftists who condemned American inhumanities in Viet Nam have been equally zealous in pronouncing anathemas on the wanton violence, actual or threatened, of 'Liberation' groups? The conduct of revolutionaries in seizing power gives strong portents of their behavior after coming to power. Who in his right mind would want to live under an IRA, PLO, or Yippy government? (My blood pressure must have soared 50 points as I wrote this paragraph . . . D

∞

21 Sept 1976

Affective Affirmer—

At times I wonder if you don't credit me with any and every mind-marking phrase you chance upon. I don't recall having crafted 'migrants in inner space,' and I'm fairly sure you reduced the Three Musketeers to 3M. Have I become the Moses of your private Pentateuch, attributed author of every inspired word? (Obviously plagiarism, even popularly inverted, was not a matter for litigation in ancient times.) . . . In late August I wrote my friend Father Hart, HC's memory bank and loving presence, and told him about my twenty-fifth anniversary. I asked him to offer thanks from the altar for all the blessing Holy Cross had brought into my life. He graciously assented, but he also showed my letter to Father Brooks, the President of the school. Father Brooks wrote a beautiful letter in which he intimated that he saw the power of the Risen Christ in my life. It's just that kind of caring that makes Holy Cross a community even before a prestigious liberal arts college . . . D

• See Will's letter of September 11, 1976, answering Father Brooks's letter and also his letter of August 20, 1976, to Father Hart.

∞

25 Sept 1976

Angsted-About-Adequacy—

If you can feel inadequate as a priest then Genghis Khan must have entertained feelings of inadequacy as looter-sacker-ravisher-laywaster. Strange, how self-perception becomes distorted by accumulated trifles. We tend to lose our grip on the fact that no one person can bring about the Kingdom. Even Christ felt obliged to found a church to carry on His work. And He didn't reach everybody, either face-to-face or heart-to-heart, but there's no indication that he agonized over that limitation. Because the good you do usually surfaces in times and places out of sight—and probably in ways not immediately recognizable as your creation—you are made aware of only a miniscule fraction of the good you sow. That's why it's not enough just to have friends. You need friends who can let you know, verbally, affectively, honestly, that you're adequate. Jesus didn't go it alone, and I think it's fair to assume that his friends reassured him with smaller daily truths than the declaration, "You are the Christ, the Son of the Living God." The mail's delay make our responses out-of-sync with the other's needs, but 'unneeded' reassurances have a residual effect. It's never untimely to show love, and it's never unfitting to draw on past expressions of love for support through a present crisis. (The fireman-to-the-rescue style of loving doesn't work. By the time the fireman is alert to the problem it's usually beyond his fixing.) What you need is a friend like Father Moran, whose words and deeds are laden with praise and encouragement FOR no specific reason, except that he is a loving friend . . . Maybe you could isolate those letters of mine that contain some heartening lines, and then in times of self-doubt you can re-read both of them, confident that the love is perpetually renewable. . . . Hold fast to this thought: adequacy is within reach . . . D

∞

1 Oct 1976

Your letters carry magic. They can turn a rock into a cork, and not just by transposing 'r' and 'c.' I think I'd rather have your panegyrics published post-humously (post-my-humousing). My cause would be irresistible. Thanks more for the meaning than for the message. . . . I wonder about Kennedy's (Eugene) suggestion: give voice to the small things that are bothering you. Giving voice is inarguable; it's that or madness. But usually the small things that bring you down are loaded with history and deeper significance. Conc. Ex.: yesterday I was on a high no kinky chemist could induce. Your letter, the sunshine, a witty lecture by Robert Hutchins, praise for something I'd written, the steaks for tonight's CCD party, even a good bowel movement—all fueled my moon shot. Then the loss of a 59-cent razor-cleaning brush sent me into subterranean depths. It may have been that the high was superficial, that to every season of mania there must be one of depression. But the brush's disappearance triggered a disproportionate reaction because it confronted me with graver problems. With age, my mother has become increasingly disorganized, and the inevitable delays and doing-without create continual frustration. What depresses me is guilt over my annoyance with my mother, who deserves at least a minute's patience after 25 years of unstinting care. So small things are not simple things—and they're small only compared to death and dandruff . . . The Chancellor Hutchins talk was a sly satire on the mindless 'philosophies' of Dale Carnegie, Norman Vincent Peale, and other pundits. He held forth on the work of Dr. Sucherkandel, of Addle, Austria, whose central thought is that the purpose of life is sheer survival and unconsciousness, achieved by reducing all activity to habit, which is the surest way to that end. (Repetition isn't necessarily dehumanizing, so long as it's recognized as appropriate to the occasion.) The mock scholarship of Dr. Sucherkandel—a German pun, I imagine—was riddled with wit, much of it cerebral. I had forgotten how delightful it can be to indulge my taste for intellectual snobbery. . . . DEE

- "Conc. Ex." means concrete example, which Father Moran would frequently request during discussions with Will.
- "CCD" stands for Confraternity of Christian Doctrine, the religious education program for Catholic youngsters enrolled in non-parochial schools.

∞

30 Dec 1976

Somehow I came on a possible insight into your periodic downcasts. We have been conditioned to divide labor according to sex. A man's work is supposed to involve him in planning, sustained thought, single-minded concentration on the task, and a sense of accomplishment. A woman's work is defined by the exigencies of child-rearing: constant monitoring, improvised solutions or healings, repetitive chores, unconditional concern, deferred satisfaction. It's just that total demand the libbers want to halve with men. For the most part priesthood follows the 'feminine' pattern. But administering a parish is 'masculine' business, and it could be frustration of 'masc' by 'fem' that leaves you feeling inadequate—unmanly? The truth is that all of us are both. Acceptance of that truth is the first step to creativity . . . D

∞

7 Jan 1977

Academy Aware Alcoholic—

A book review in *Time* quoted Simone Weil, described as 'a secular saint': "It is not those who love a Cause that serve it best; it is those who love the life the Cause makes possible." I misunderstood that at first, possibly because 'for everyone' is only implied after "possible." Substitute Church for Cause and you make the statement still more provocative. As it stands, it's a safeguard against totalitarian attitudes, much like "By their fruits you shall know them." A Cause gets caught up in its own ideology or metaphysics, and it becomes more concerned with being true to itself than to the people's needs. An ossified structure will shatter when logic and necessity collide . . . My sense of smell may be making a come-back. A whiff of smoke from John's cigarette alerts the old olfactory sensors. Why couldn't it have been perfume or at least garlic? . . . D

∞

3 Feb 1977

This time your Italian friend—not Frank, Paul—has gone the whole way into absurdity. Of the 3764 ridiculous reasons he could have picked to disqualify women from priesthood he fixed on the silliest. Must we ride the Natural Law down the Great Ka-Chung! of history. Obviously a God-made-man would have to be one sex or the other. A hermaphrodite would hardly stand a chance in any culture, least of all a Semitic one. And a woman would have been stoned for presumption the minute she stood up in the synagogue to read. It has nothing to do with Nature and everything to do with History, which is man's handiwork. (Maybe somebody thought the Church should appeal to young people's taste for the irrational by contriving a doctrine that flies in the face of good sense) . . . Patrick Moynihan, erstwhile Kennedy advisor, recent UN ambassador, and present senator from NY, has written a trenchant critique of Liberalism and its failure. He contends Liberals have concentrated exclusively on gaining freedom from social institutions, whether government, business, religion, or political; but they don't concern themselves with what Moynihan calls, awkwardly, the subsystems that make society livable. (Conc. Exs: Liberals want to do away with the churches' tax-exempt status; they fight state aid of any kind to church-related schools; they insist pornography is protected by freedom of the press; they reject the notion that an individual should forgo any of his privileges or pleasures for the common good.) They have no interest in fostering or preserving groups, the middle ground between each and all. Belonging is what gives life meaning, and the only freedom worth having is freedom-for, not freedom-from. And belonging implies taking responsibility for—something Liberals assign to government. Not surprisingly, it was the self-serving dominance of groups—the Church, the aristocracy, the crown—that gave birth to Liberalism, and if groups are going to make a come-back they'll have to be democratic and non-ideological. We need 'subsystems' that serve and respond to that change. Neither Liberals nor Conservatives seem to care for the idea . . . During the past week or so, I had occasion to ponder the heresy of self-reliance and its sorry consequences. If a person comes to believe that his strengths alone make things happen his way, what is left when his strengths are taken away, either by age or accident or, worse, opposition? Defeat and despair, a loss of belief in self, are consequences that undermine old age, especially. True courage, it seems to me, is not braving down a hostile world but assuming the world is hospitable, ready to help. You are a man of courage; so, I hope, am I . . . D

2 April 1977

A propos,

Just thought of an epigram, worthy of Wilde or Shaw, to answer those well-meaning friends who sometimes encourage me to write a book: "I'd rather have ten people asking why I haven't written a book than ten thousand asking why I had" . . . The DRE's firing is 'irrevocable,' according to the firer. What a time for the spaghetti-spined shepherd to stiffen! There was a prickly confrontation last week, when the pastor and one of the associates appeared before the RelEd board. They dismissed the avalanche of mail supporting the DRE as 'expected,' however that explains things. I would love to have been there, with the chance to role-play the Grand Inquisitor. Anyhow, I've reached an equally irrevocable decision: no more ministry to Santa Maria's youth, as much as I love them. (And as much as I enjoy the escapes into friendship.) . . . D

• "DRE" stands for Director of Religious Education at Santa Maria del Popolo.

∞

26 April 1977

Had a letter from O'Malley last week. His next project will be a book titled, *Why in God's Name Would Any Intelligent Human Being Want To Ally Himself With An Organized Church?* Its audience will be today's kids, who have a hard time seeing Jesus in some of the Yahoos who speak for His Church. I may buy 1000 copies for the youth of Santa Maria . . . D

∞

30 April 1977

Dear Father,

There may have been moments, while the Spirit dozed, when you questioned your priestliness, but imagination can hardly suggest a more fitting marriage of personality and vocation, no doubt because Christ is at the center of both. I sometimes puzzle over the meaning of *to be;* yet its sense comes clear in the simple truth that you *are* a priest. When I think of you I think 'priest'; when I think of priest I think 'Father.' You are wholly His, fully being. That is your joy and your beauty. Ad multos annos, good friend. Bill

• Written to acknowledge the twenty-fifth anniversary of Father Moran's ordination.

∞

5 May 1977

Ageless Ancient—

In Confucian China you would now be entitled to be heard. Anyone with fewer than fifty years was counted an apprentice human, hardly detached enough to see things whole. That practice may have given rise to the saying, "Damn clever, these Chinese." But Christianity has never venerated the Wise Man. Its heroes have been more wild than wise—Francis of Assisi, Francis Xavier, Dorothy Day, Peter and Paul, and you. Love seizes a life and thrusts it, without caution, into the world, where it reels from one need to the next, with no thought for equilibrium. So it means nothing that you are 50. Christ will keep you impetuous until you blunder into eternity. I love you for your lifelong headlong rush. Happy Birthday, reckless friend. D

∞

31 Aug 1977

Sesquipedalian Sacker—

A mushrooming thought on presumed detachment brought me back to St. Teresa's quote: "Never assume you possess a virtue until you have been tempted by the opposite vice." It's so easy to congratulate ourselves on strengths when their exercise is optional. I deceive myself that I am patient, kind, all the qualities Paul ascribes to love. Yet I sometimes have matricidal urges when my mother, who has only given me 26 years of total care, betrays the imperfections of age. I think it's dishonesty about our own ability to deal with deprivation that allows us to believe, for example, the poor have only themselves to blame. Better to count everything a gift, recallable, and judge not . . . D

∞

17 Oct 1977

Whether the kids are taking away anything from CCD or not, my time is well spent. Thinking through what I 'know' in order to make it clear to 12-year-olds brings me to new understanding. Truly, qui docit discit . . . Somehow my total recall of time, place, and apparel failed me two months ago, when our friendship marked its tenth anniversary. It was a joyful, sorrowful, and glorious decade, and I know I would be less if there had not been our loving and being loved. The God who made such things possible is a good God, and you are the best of His goodness. Thanks for the gift . . . D

- Will resumed teaching CCD classes when he and his mother began attending St. Mary's Church in Fremont Center, Illinois. Ella found their former church, Santa Maria del Popolo, too big and impersonal, and it is clear from earlier letters that Will found the direction of its religious education program wanting.
- "Qui docit discit" is Latin for "he who teaches, learns."

∞

25 Feb 1978

Abba's Associate—

Is it canonically required that a poem to The Father use the rhyme scheme ABBA? . . . If you grow rapt over the mere thought of my typing and drawing with my mouth, you will be ecstatic over my latest oral undertaking. Last week I finally got a new aluminum stick to replace the one that broke. But it was too big at both ends, where the rubber hose and the rubber eraser are supposed to fit. I gave the stick to my faithful lieutenant, the 12-year-old boy across the street, but his filing didn't meet specs. So I had John buy me a file at the Savage and had Charlie fix the stick in the C-clamps that hold my razor. Then away I went, gripping the file's plastic handle in my teeth. The top end worked down to a perfect fit, but the small end fell victim to my zeal for symmetry. It now needs a millimeter's padding to hold the eraser. But I have a new tool and a new trade. . . . D

- "Abba" is Hebrew for "Father."
- "Savage" refers to The Railroad Salvage store on the corner that carried all sorts of odds and ends.

∞

23 March 1978

Almost Abe—

Nancy opened my birthday cards and held them up for me to read. So I repaid the kindness by reading the greetings aloud. When I credited Abe Lincoln with the quote about friendship, Nancy's face lighted with recognition. I suspect she thinks Honest Abe himself sent that card. And at that, she was not too far wrong . . . Long thanks for the typewriter ribbons. They're the right kind, and they should last me until 22 Sept 1979. P. was probably thinking of the Arab proverb, "If you have two pennies, buy bread with one but spend the other on hyacinths." For me, though, typewriter ribbons are more spiritual than material. They are my soul's vocal cords. . . . The other day my friend Fran Bates, with whom I theologize, threw out a provocative thought, taken from an unremembered spiritual writer: the highest quality of the fully mature person is the ability to suffer. Both of us were repulsed by the idea, probably because we confined it to the narrow category of self-inflicted punishment, Dominic Savio-style. But on further reflection I've come to agree with that assessment. When the situation makes a creative response impossible and the only choice is between destruction and suffering we must choose suffering (not mere resignation.) . . . D

∞

4 July 1978

Away Awhile—

.... Done with Hans, endlich! OBAC ranks with *Courage To Be* as the most important book I've read. It's not so much that Hans gave me a whole new perspective on faith in Jesus as that he articulated and substantiated what I've come to believe. Even his Christology, built on the carefully established humanity of the pre-Paschal Jesus, didn't seem radical. Whether or not his program for reforming the Church follows from his scholarship will have to be debated among theologians, but the agenda will be his. A summary of Küng-think: Faith is a commitment grounded in basic trust of reality as supporting. The God revealed in Jesus' life, death, and resurrection is experienced as a Person (is in fact the God of the OT) whose cause is man's well-being here and now, in the always-coming Kingdom. That understanding places believing man under obligation to serve God not in Himself but in His cause, man; not in law, which is God's only insofar as it is good for man; not in past 'nature' but in present need. The post-Paschal Christing of this Jesus affirms, despite the rejection of Crucifixion, his proclamation and life. What does it mean to be a Christian, a follower of Jesus-raised-to-Christhood? We must live as he lived, trusting the Father and serving His Creation, especially the poor, the weak, the losers; we must suffer as he suffered, accepting the hostility of the self-serving and the sometimes forsakenness and deprivation of existence. Our constitutions and institutions must reflect discipleship; our morality must be worked out in relation—therefore relative—to the present requirements of society; our worship must recall the life-death-and-resurrection of our Lord, Jesus. (It took him 601 pages to say that?) . . . Relax and re-create yourself. Vaya con dios . . . D

• "OBAC" stands for Hans Kung's *On Being A Christian.*

∞

11 Oct 1978

All-out Allgaueran—

It was the best of our fall frolics, perhaps because so badly needed by at least two of us. All care dissolves in laughter, love's laughter. Now to live the nettled days till next time . . . If I didn't tell you at the Pie Palace, I should have let you know that you were the friend who bullied me into letting myself be loved by people outside my family and small circle of friends. Thanks to you—I overcame the fear of being loved, of accepting myself as I am. There's no fuller liberation . . . D

∞

21 Oct 1978

Alles Fur Arbeiten—

Can you read on the horizontal? I assume you went at it immoderately again this year and now lie abed, repenting your zeal. All for thee, sweet lucre, all for thee . . . John promised to save his copy of an article on time-management objectives so I could forward it to you. The writer attacked a problem that could be dubbed Moran's Syndrome. It's described in one sentence: We ask ourselves, "Am I doing this right?" when we should be asking, "Am I right doing this at all?" Elsewhere he proposes a method of speed-reading that Evelyn Wood would never add to her curriculum. You can handle 50,000 words at a glance by deciding none of them is worth reading. With the time saved you can pore over Hans at a leisurely pace . . . The cardinals' surprise can only be good for the Church. I have no illusions that JP II's theology will be much in advance of your own, but any loosening of the fine Italian hand's grip on the tiller has to steer us away from the straits. The Polish experience could have inspired the apotheosis of the Polish Gestalt, and his call for collegiality could mask a plan to Polskify the world. But hope tells me otherwise . . . In reading an article on child abuse I came upon what might be a useful argument against abortion, something more persuasive than the warcry, "Abortion is murder." Frightened teenage girls have carried babies to term, only to kill them or leave them to die, 'as a kind of belated abortion.' For me, that is strong evidence an open abortion policy does in fact breed attitudes receptive to infanticide and euthanasia . . . D.

- "Alles Fur Arbeiten" is German for "Everyone for the job." It's cruller-time at St. Joseph Church so the parishioners will have turned out to make and sell the baked goods to raise cash during the Parke County Covered Bridge Festival.
- "Hans" is Hans Küng.
- "The cardinals' surprise" was the election of John Paul II as pope.

∞

10 Nov 1978

All-out Anthemizer—

Sunday, at Charlie Cronin's annual salt-and-pepper party, John and I talked with Jim Murphy about Mom's condition. Jim, husband of cousin Lou, specializes in the problems of aging at the mental health center in Lafayette. His advice was useful, if only because he made us appreciate how frightening her confusion is to Mom. Empathy lessens anger and relaxes frustration. Jim said disorientation, a feeling comparable to waking suddenly in a dark room requires patient re-orientation to the where and when. It's important always to use the same terms, terms the disoriented person is familiar with. It helps . . . D

∞

26 Nov 1978

Amos Alonzo Stagnant—

. . . . It snowed last night, but not enough to keep Charlie home. A snow day would have helped. Willard couldn't make it. So I went without washing and settled for dressing and chairing. Mom is now exhausted and confused, and we are just starting four days without John, who's California-bound. To heap woe upon woe, fate picked this time to sap my battery, possibly because it hadn't been watered for months. Any one of those afflictions could have been borne—maybe any two. But unrelieved helplessness creates depression.

It makes a strenuous exertion of will to see beyond the immediate situation, to hope. If there is one thing to keep in mind it is that there is no one thing to be blamed for depression, no single defeat but a series of setbacks undermining the sense of control . . . Understanding self and other helps . . . D

∞

11 Dec 1978

Abbreviated Adventist—

. . . . Today I was filling out a passport application, and one of the blanks asked for "Distinguishing Marks." I thought 'big blue eyes' might sound vain. So I wasted 10 minutes trying to come up with something. Then it came to me: Quadriplegia! That tends to mark me as distinctive if not distinguished. Getting a passport raises another problem: How do I prove I'm me? The only valid identification is either a passport (Catch 22), a driver's license, or a government ID, none of which occupies a place in my portfolio. A Blue Cross card serves as my only link to the Real World. Maybe I should list my occupation as 'hermit' . . . Yesterday I had a letter from the cochairman of the HC Silver Anniversary gift committee, a form letter meant to dispose everyone to heroic surrender of goods and property when the mendicant team makes its spread-eagle appeal. In making their pitch the guys asserted, with some truth, that '54 has been in a class by itself, in giving, doing, caring and then this: "Will Jenks typifies this spirit and commitment, though we like to think he is more representative than exceptional." More than parchment or bowl, I value this designation as eponym . . . Thanks for the note and the love that flows from it. You are forgiven much (doctrine) because you have loved much . . . D.

∞

20 Dec 1978

A.—

Christmas seems to be the time when we revisit the distant regions of family and friendship and expect those close to us to understand. So, briefly . . . Hans would have us take the Christmas out of Christ, since the Nativity stories no longer serve Matt and Luke's purposes. And O'Mal insists Jesus is not the 'holy infant, so tender and mild' but 'The Lion of Judah,' dangerous to approach. Hallmark has a 'contract' out on both trouble-makers . . . Till the issue is resolved, rejoice that He has come . . . D.

∞

18 May 1979

Anti-Avantist—

. . . . *New Republic* reviewed a book about my hero, Heidegger. The reviewer was himself an Aficionado of Der Grosser Dinker. (The Great Thinker, in pidgin Deutsch.) He, too, found *Being and Time* an almost-religious work, except for H's insistence of 'self-sponsored' heroism. I think Jesus lived 'authentically,' to use Heidegger's term, and communicated Himself as Truth. The Church has made that Truth conventional rather than existential, but the Gospel and Hans Kung have rallied a few of us to Dasein (Being there). Alas, Martin was not without flaw. He made public statements supporting the Nazis shortly after Hitler's rise to power and never recanted when the monstrous evil of the Third Reich became incontrovertible . . . As Tillich would say, we must have the Courage To Be. So Be, bravely . . . D.

∞

2 Aug 1979

Avid Anagogist—

Last week I got a book in the mail: *Jesus: An Experiment in Christology* by Schillebeeckx. A letter arrived the next day, confirming my suspicion. The donor was Fr. Brooks, President of Holy Cross and still-active Prof. of Christology. I had written him about Hans [Kung] last summer and asked for a different perspective. Hence, Schillebeeckx. After 53 pages I can already detect a difference. Hans calls post-paschal theology relative and dismisses it; Ed tries to find out what the early Christians may have meant . . . D.

∞

14 Aug 1979

a.k.a. A.—

. . . . Typically, what I happen to be reading—Schillebeeckx's *Experiment in Christology*—is the answer to everybody's problem, including the defection of the clergy. . . . If the Church is to be served by a celibate clergy it must offer satisfactions larger than conjugal intimacy; it must do work important enough to justify the gift of self. So the Church has to subject itself to constant scrutiny, and the point of reference must be the Gospel, Jesus himself. But He can't be the Jesus of seminary theology, who seemed to license everything the Church did. Like Hans [Kung], Schlbx says Jesus reveals that God's cause is man, so our cause must be man. That truth alone could provide a critique of the Church's relevance and the pertinence of some of its ministries. Is God's cause served by closing ghetto schools, by keeping silence in the face of an unjust war, by creating a bureaucracy of its own, by equating observance with service? Too much is done from habit, and so the Church seems dead, even to those caught up in its activities. The Church needs Jesus—more than Jesus needs the Church. As for making celibacy attractive, good luck. It's suffering, and it has to be made worth the hurt . . . We've been friends a dozen years now. Thanks for lifts, laughs, joys, encouragements, trust, love . . . D.

∞

24 Nov 1979

Already-Albumed Artist—

Charlie Cronin offered some interesting assessments of JP II in recent conversations. He admired the Pope's forceful personality and his unyielding demands for justice among and within nations, but he found his stringent demands for conformity within the Church showed a parochial rather than Catholic understanding of the Church. Until he learns to live with pluralism, wholesome child of freedom, he will alienate more seriously questing Catholics than he will fascinate. Those views aren't new to me; what is new is the realization that they are being voiced by the clergy, and, in Charlie's case, the non-controversial clergy. The remedy lies with the bishops, in their insistence on dialectic collegiality . . . D.

∞

25 Dec 1980

All-out Adventist—

This must be a Christmas card, since it's being written on Christmas Day, in lieu of Mass. The wind-chill stands at -33, ideal weather for pneumonia for me or a heart-attack for John, lugging me up St. Mary's double-run of stairs . . . I can't recall feeling so futile as I've felt the past week. As Christmas moved closer and closer it seemed things were more and more out of control. Gluttony and Sloth took command of my will. I ate every cookie within 50 light years of the Great Black Hole in my face. And at night, after supper, I simply sat before the typewriter, as though faithful vigil would be rewarded by spontaneous Selectricity. This is perhaps the eighth or ninth card I've written since I finished my past-due Classletter. It would be easy to claim fatigue, but the truth is that dejection begets a weariness of escape. I suppose it's not feasible to maintain as many friendships in my new life as a workingman as it was in my long leisure. I begin to appreciate your angst whenever you feel there is too much world and not enough you, though for you the sense of inadequacy must be more profound, because caring-for is your vocation. I finally worked my way through, relying on prayer . . . Father Brooks sent me a book of short pieces by fellow Jesuit, Francis Sweeney. To write with such clarity and simplicity I'd have to rework something for a month. In a litany on Boston he wrote, "Boston is Jack Kennedy saying, 'I'm glad to be back where words are pronounced as they are spelled.'" During Viet Nam he ended a piece on his passion for singing national anthems with, "Oh, my country, I cannot sing your anthem now" . . . Must haste. Our guests are arriving . . . D.

∞

30 June 1981
or 1 July—not sure

At the moment I am mighty unhappy with your friend, God. He loosed some fateful lightning yesterday and blew out my tube and my electronic control box, including my phone. So I can't make calls to get things fixed, chiefly my tube. All of Walgreens is waiting for me to complete my latest—which is to say, very late—program, the culmination of a dozen or so programs creating drug label data. I made the labels in five fashionable styles. Or will, if I ever get my tube back . . . Uh I uh was uh on the uh radio uh this afternoon, and uh if I do uh say so my-uh self, I uh was uh articulate, uh even uh glib. The program, on a small FM station in Highland Park, not far from the Botanic Gardens, was a half-hour interview about LIFT, the outfit that trained me. One of the partners did most of the talking. I was 'living proof.' I doubt I'll be asked on *Meet The Press* . . . D.

∞

30 Nov 1988

Apprentice Archangel—

Even better news: In the Sunday bulletin from St. Mary's Student Chapel, Ann Arbor, MI, the catechumen count was 28. The Church is seen as rich in grace and relevant to today's world even in that citadel of secular learning. Wherever young people take life seriously, the faith will thrive. It's only among the morally lazy that the Church is ignored. As the Pauline experience illustrated, antagonism toward Christ can turn inside out once the Hound of Heaven seizes the soul. . . . Today's mail brought the original of the letter I hope to send along in Xeroxed copy. As you will see, 'my' chair is in English literature. Apparently someone thought to check my Latin grades, to spare me the embarrassment of misfitting the chair of Classical Languages. I will go to my grave wondering why this happened to me. Lincoln was twice quoted—by Adlai—with saying, "As the fellow said when they rode him out of town on a rail, 'If it weren't for the honor involved I'd just as soon walk.'" (That must be my favorite—or at least most useful—quote. I've recalled it again and again.) . . . D.

∞

21 Jan 1989

Armed For Armageddon –

   Tonight is Book Group night. Here. Book: *Fathers and Sons*, Turgenev. Menu: beef Burgundy a la Jenks. Heinz, the German-Catholic intellectual will be rejoining us after an extended absence. Since the paperback edition is only 208 pages, no one will have an excuse for not having read it. So all should go well. . . . It's now Sunday evening, just after the Super Bowl. The Book Group met, meated, metaphysicked. Though the story itself didn't trigger the best discussion, we spent the last hour pondering the possibility of innocence or even of a definition of innocence. With Heinz's guidance we settled on a range of meaning, between 'intending no harm and intending as much good as feasible.' Merely avoiding the inflicting of harm is not enough. There must be willingness to risk guilt while seeking the other's good. Innocence is not an end; it is a consequence of the means chosen. . . . Hold fast . . . D.

∞

The Holy Cross Community

Letters from Will Jenks

to

Rev. Raymond J. Swords, S.J.
upon the death of
Rev. Patrick J. Cummings, S.J.

Rev. Francis J. Hart, S.J.

Rev. John E. Brooks, S.J.

∞

Reverend Raymond J. Swords, S.J.
upon the death of
Reverend Patrick J. Cummings, S.J.

The Reverend Raymond J. Swords, S.J., was president of Holy Cross and rector of the Jesuit community at the time of this letter. Rev. Patrick Joseph Cummings, S. J., professor of English and Latin at Holy Cross when Will was a student, was born in North Adams, Massachusetts, on March 19, 1894. He studied two years at Holy Cross, during which time he was elected president of the class of 1918. In August of 1916 he entered the Society of Jesus at St. Andrew-on-Hudson, Pough-keepsie, New York. After finishing philosophy at Woodstock College in Maryland, he spent his regency at Brooklyn Preparatory High School as a teacher and as moderator of athletics. Completing his theology studies at Weston, Massachusetts, he was ordained as a Jesuit priest on June 22, 1929. He later became dean of men and moderator of athletics at Boston College until 1936 when he came to Holy Cross where he spent the rest of his life. He died in the Holy Cross infirmary July 7, 1969, after a "saintly borne, long illness," shortly after writing his last letter to Will. A brother Jesuit at the college, Rev. Richard J. Dowling, S. J., wrote of the long hours Father Cummings spent counseling the many youths who sought him out after class as well as in the confessional. Father Dowling noted the "apostle-ship of letter writing . . . with his spiritual children through the years of their manhood. He had a pleasant smile, a ready wit [and] a Christ-like sympathy for the afflicted."

∞

Dana, Indiana
10 July, 1969

Dear Father Swords:

Because Father Pat Cummings has no family I am writing to you to let it be known what his life meant to at least one Holy Cross man. The recollection of his enduring kindness makes mourning give way to thanksgiving and quiet joy. Perhaps that in itself is a tribute to the man and his way.

During my freshman year at Holy Cross (1950–1951) Father Cummings was teacher, confessor and friend, and when, in the following summer, I was stricken with polio, my first thought was to notify him. His response was to inundate me with mail. Every day of that first year he wrote to me, assuring the urgency of his prayers and encouraging an acceptance of God's will after the affliction had been fought to the limit. I showed little courage in facing my fate, but I would have showed none at all if Father had not prodded and prayed me toward manhood.

In the next seventeen years a letter arrived every other day—more than three thousand in all. When I learned to type with a stick in my teeth, a regular if lop-sided correspondence grew up. We discussed and argued politics, literature, philosophy, and everything to do with Holy Cross. Unfailingly there was a word of advice or approval, some expression of concern for my spiritual welfare. Father's constant theme was simply this: God asks only that you never quit trying to love him. I think his own loving perseverance taught me that truth even more forcefully than his words. If I have not quit, it is chiefly because of the grace of his friendship.

Reducing even a part of a man's life to two paragraphs would be a desecration of his memory if there were nothing more to survive. But the good men do is not interred with their bones; it is carried forward by those who have been touched by that goodness. I hope to be counted among the many people, most of them Holy Cross men, who live more truly in Christ through the personal and priestly love of Father Pat Cummings. God be thanked for his life.

In Christ,
William Jenks, ex-'54

∞

Reverend Francis J. Hart, S.J.

Selections Written 8 August 1963–18 January 1986

The Reverend Francis J. Hart, S.J., was the student counselor at Holy Cross when Will arrived as a first-year student in the class of 1954. Born on December 3, 1899, in Haverhill, Massachusetts, Father Hart graduated from St. James High School in the same city. He completed his freshman year at Holy Cross before entering the Society of Jesus novitiate at St. Andrew-on-Hudson, Poughkeepsie, New York, in September, 1918. He was ordained on June 16, 1931, at Weston, Massachusetts. Following a year's tertianship of additional reflection, study and prayer (1931–32), he spent his entire priestly career at Holy Cross until his death on February 3, 1986. In addition to teaching Latin, he served as student counselor, moderator of intramural sports and associate college chaplain during more than five decades of service to his college and his students. His whole life honored his Lord.

The first letter reproduced below is dated August 8, 1963. Although this is the earliest letter from Will to Father Hart that has been recovered from the college archives, Will states in the opening paragraph that he has previously written yearly accounts of his "doings" which have always found "a ready ear—or, in this instance, eye—for a word from one of your boys. So here is the word from Bill Jenks." To Father Hart he always signed off as "Bill."

∾

8 Aug 1963

Dear Father Hart,

As I recall, last year I waited almost until school had begun before I annoyed you with the yearly account of my doings. This year I mean to be more considerate. I will annoy you now, when you have a few moments of relative leisure to throw away on such trifles. Truthfully, I know full well that you always have a ready ear—or, in this instance, eye—for a word from one of your boys. So here is the word from Bill Jenks.

The past twelve months offered virtually the same possibilities that each of the 10 preceding years have presented. I managed to get through another winter—a particularly cruel one—without falling victim to anything worse than the sniffles, and I extended my no-doctor, no-hospital streak still further. So it was another profitable year for Blue Cross.

Socially, life was not quite overwhelming. I did get to see most of the home games of the local high school basketball team, and on Saturday night I did go to the Dana Theatre. But I had only one overnight furlough from Dana, a three-day Christmas holiday with my brother in Indianapolis.

Because none of my relatives got married, said a First Mass, or entered the Convent, I could find no excuse to visit Chicago this summer. Sometime this fall, though, we plan to trek northward to the Big City to inspect my older brother's new house. As soon as he is settled we may commute between here and there.

As usual, I spent most of my time reading and the rest of it writing (although for the first time in five years I was not asked to put together a few paragraphs to awaken class interest in the Alumni Fund drive.) In February I took on a tutoring job; I pretended to explain algebra to a high school freshman. (Doc McBrien forgive me.) Later he asked for help in Latin, in which, as Father Izzo will assure you, I am not at all adept. Still, we struggled through. For the past few weeks I have been working with a high-spirited twelve-year-old whose reading habits require policing. It is not that he reads bad books; it's just that he reads few books, and those poorly. I'm making him use the sports page for his exercise. In that way neither of us is bored. I'm afraid my approach would scandalize a professional teacher.

I've kept in touch with most of my old Crusader friends, and I even added the now Father Bill O'Malley to my list of correspondents. He and Dave Driscoll and Father Pete McCord maintain a select alumni unit at Woodstock. No Holy Cross men have passed this way since Dave Driscoll's surprise invasion last summer but in February Doctor Bill Kane phoned from Chicago to say that only car trouble had kept him from dropping down to Dana on his way back to the University of Minnesota from NYC. Bill, a bone doctor, is going to teach and do research in his field at UMinn. With all of my classmates I mourned the untimely death of Bob Luddy, a fellow inmate of Campion. I pray that God will provide for his widow and seven children. . . .

The school publications proved interesting (*The Crusader*) and bewildering (*The Purple*). The newspaper's attitude seems to reflect the feeling of discontent that afflicts every college today. At times the editorials, features, and letters to the editor are provocative; at other times they are merely amusing; occasionally, though, they are offensive. I would like to see the school grow in academic stature, but I would hate to have the traditional spirit of friendliness and courtesy sacrificed to achieve that growth. The magazine apparently has become a private joke between three or four would-be intellectuals. It seldom bothered me that I didn't understand the poetry; but now it worries me that I can't fathom some of the prose. I feel as though I might have slept while the English language was abolished.

For all of my enthusiasm for the old school I am deeply indebted to you, who have supplied me with the material to feed my great appetite for things Crusader. The papers, booklets, and magazines you send along not only keep me informed of happenings on the Hill but give me the assurance that the College's Hart (pun intended) is still beating strong and that all's well. There are no words to say thanks for what you have done for me and for so many others. There are only prayers that God will continue to bless your generous service. God bless you, Father . . . Yours in Christ, Bill Jenks, ex'54

• Woodstock, Maryland, was the site of a Jesuit seminary at the time Will wrote this letter.

∞

13 Aug 1971

Dear Father Hart,

. . . . I wish I could rhapsodize over Nature's handiwork here in Indiana, but the truth is she's too busy growing corn to create myriad patterns of beauty. If you are partial to green you would be enchanted by mile after mile of corn or soybeans. Otherwise you might find the Hoosier landscape monotonous . . . Our new church creeps closer and closer toward realization. The architect promises to offer the plans to bidders later this month. We should be underway before the first of October. I got involved in overseeing the transplanting of a garage from the building site to the rear of the new rectory. Father assured me it would take only a few phone calls to arrange the move. That was over a month ago. . . . If you read my latest classletter you may have noticed the signature I affixed. That's my newest triumph. I've learned to write and draw with the pen in my mouth. The result is indistinguishable from the writing and drawing I once did with my hand . . . Keep me in your prayers. You are in mine . . . In Christ, Bill Jenks

∞

10 Oct 1971

Dear Father Hart,

Autumn has been a moody damsel today. Even her smiles have given off a faint chill. It matters little to her that we craved the blessing of her warmth for our Covered Bridge Festival, the one chance the parish has to separate city folks from their money. The Festival, a 10-day, $1 million exploiting of Parke County's thirty-eight covered bridges, attracts 250,000 people to these parts, some of whom invest a dollar in a bag of crullers from St. Joseph's stand. Last year we netted $4000. It's imperative that we do as well this year . . . From the day he read my *Crossroads* letter about Father Pat Cummings my pastor and friend, Father Moran, urged me to write a more detailed account of that enduring friendship. To appease him I did just that. But he continued to goad me to submit it for publication. Eventually I yielded on that point and sent the piece to *Guideposts*, a small interdenominational magazine devoted to 'inspirational' stories. After three months of correspondence with an editor I finally got a check for $100. No publication date has been set . . . Thanks for your prayers. You have ours . . . Bill Jenks

∞

15 Dec 1972

Dear Father Hart,

The more Christ, the more Christmas, and so you will know all the joy the feast inspires: " . . . is born a savior, who is Christ, the Lord." Through faith the event will be new again, full of wonder at the ways of God. It will be a Blessed Christmas for you . . . Last Sunday we dedicated the new church. The stained glass, the altar, and the altar furniture arrived 48 hours before the Bishop stepped off the procession. In its sudden wholeness, the church stunned even those who had been through the entire gestation period. The interior space, embraced by brick walls and beam-and-plank ceiling, glows with a golden light rising from the carpet, and the warm tones of wood create aureoles around the altar and the interlocking chairs. Very nearly Heaven, more than one awed admirer remarked. A gratifying day . . . Bill

∞

16 Jan 1973

Dear Father Hart,

Jim Pierce told me that the *Crossroads* article will lead off with your face-tious allusion to my drawings as theftworthy works of art. I'm afraid that constitutes trading on a famous name to capture reader interest. Anytime your name appears in an HC publication 20,000 eyes are drawn to that page. . . . Last Wednesday I closed out a five-year stint on the parish council. The meeting ran till eleven-thirty, and so my farewell address was greeted with yawns, attributable to the hour rather than the oratory (Hora, non ora), I try to tell myself. What I will do without the council is a far more urgent problem than what the council will do without me . . . From time to time I've been tutoring high school freshmen in algebra—hubris of the highest order. The text book is written for kids who teethed on the New Math. Last week we graphed inequalities, but only after careful exegesis of the text. That sort of thing was unknown in Doc McBrien's College Algebra class an eon ago . . . Bill

∞

10 May 1973

Dear Father Hart,

For a time I had hoped we would meet at Joe Kerwin's space launch. The *Crossroads* article jogged Joe's memory and inspired him to send me an invitation to the blastoff. (Joe was a year ahead of me at Fenwick H.S., as well as at H.C.) Both my brothers offered to accompany me to Florida, but after careful thought I decided that the risk of delays or postponements made the odds too chancy for this close-to-the-vest farm boy. The invitation and a phone call were thrill enough . . . Your letters, cards, clippings, and prayers are graces for my days . . . Thanks. Bill

• Dr. Kerwin, who received his M.D. from Northwestern University, was a flight surgeon in the Navy. He was the physician member of the astronaut team aboard Space Lab.

∞

4 June 1973

Dear Father Hart,

On learning that you didn't attend the launch of Kerwin & Co.'s space trailer I was gladder still that native thrift had dissuaded me from betting the price of a plane ticket on NASA's efficiency. . . . Now for news I had been hoping would never need telling: my mother and I will be leaving Dana in two weeks to make our home with my brother and two of his sons in Mundelein, IL, 40 Osage Drive. My brother's wife divorced him recently, complaining, with some justice, that he devoted too much time in attention to his work. We are hopeful of an eventual reconciliation, but in the meantime those boys will need a home. So Gram got the job. We're keeping the house in Dana for visits or a possible return. I hate to leave the town and the parish but it has to be done. All of us make a claim on your prayers . . . Thanks for the letters, the clippings, the kindness. Bill

∞

2 July 1973

Dear Father Hart,

. . . . Our new house suits our needs admirably. It has four bedrooms, a modern kitchen, a large family room, a living room, and two bathrooms—all on ground level. The man who built it lived in it for 17 years before selling it to my brother. He used the best materials, including acres of wood paneling—a reflection of his Norwegian upbringing. It's easily the finest house I've ever lived in, and it poses few housekeeping problems for my mother. (My heart, though, refused to vacate the big white house in Dana, with its high ceilings and wide front porch.) . . . The surrounding area boasts the two chief perquisites of suburban living, open space and privacy. We are segregated from the larger community—the town itself—by farmland and from the neighboring houses by hedges. Thanks largely to those dubious assets I have lived here ten days without speaking to a stranger older than fourteen. I'll have to re-read *Seeds of Contemplation* . . . With 200 miles between me and the farm I find myself worrying about what I should be worrying about. Drought? Flood? Corn Borer? Chinch bug? Milkweed? Thistle? I'm not sure that the crop will suffer from my lack of focused anxiety, but I'd feel better about the whole thing if I were close enough to ride out to look over the Jenks corn and beans. The same man will do the farm work on shares. I can conduct my end of the business by mail. . . . Your letters are like visits from an old friend. Thanks . . . Bill

∞

29 July 1973

Dear Father Hart,

. . . . The experiment is going well. My mother has adjusted to the responsibility of cooking for five or six and caring for two teen-age boys. The push-button labor-savers relieve her of daily drudgery, and my brother and the boys look after the more onerous chores. Physically, there is less to do here than there was in Dana. Unfortunately, there is also less to do socially. Though many of her friends live in the Chicago area, most of them don't care to chance driving out here on the expressways. So the extended family is her world. It remains to be seen if that is enough . . . Bill

∞

26 Oct 1973

Dear Father Hart,

. . . . The tremors and shockwaves centered in Washington rock the country so mercilessly that people long for an end to it all. I doubt that Nixon will ever again govern with moral authority. After the firing of Cox and the resignation of Richardson sentiment for impeachment flamed highest in middle-class neighborhoods and suburbs—the bedrock of Nixon's support. Unless the President's behavior becomes dangerously irrational I think impeachment would be calamitous. But this second term is not going to be the tranquil interlude Middle America thought it was buying. . . . I'm saving one page from the Homecoming program for next Saturday, when Bill Kane, Jack Rutherford, and Paul Rollins have promised to take me to the Northwestern-Minnesota game. In the account of Homecomings past it told that the first prize for the

1952 display was won by Charlie Millard and Paul 'Cookie' Rollins. He should be amused by his belated fame . . . Your prayers beget prayers of thanks for such constancy. May God bless that boundless heart . . . Bill

∞

21 Nov 1973

Dear Father Hart,

The day before Thanksgiving, and I can smell the turkey thawing in the kitchen. How our forefathers would have marveled at our everything-but-predigested meals. Even on the farm no one raises his own turkey or pumpkins or prepares his own mincemeat. In my lifetime that way of life has vanished; farmers are merely businessmen who work in edible commodities . . . A cousin, Father Connie Cronin, (God rest his soul), once suggested a theme for an Irish Thanksgiving. After having visited the modest Cronin home place in County Kerry, he admonished us, only half-jokingly, "get down on your knees and thank God your grandfather didn't miss the boat." If all 12 brothers and sisters had stayed in Ireland there would've been little to share but poverty . . . On Nov 3 Dr. Bill Kane, Jack Rutherford, and Paul Rollins—all '54 men—drove out and picked me up and took me to the Northwestern-Minnesota game. Bill is head of orthopedics at NU Med and previously taught at UMinn Med, and so he cheered for both teams, who responded by scoring 13 touchdowns. Minnesota won, 52–43. Afterwards we went back to Bill's home in Kenilworth and had dinner with Mesdames Kane, Rollins, and Rutherford. ('Mesdames' is an arcane word whose use, in the twentieth century, has been restricted to the society column of the Dana News.) It was a great day, blessed with sunshine and laughter . . . If our CCD program is an accurate barometer of the Church's future, Cardinal Cooke can think about leasing St. Patrick's to the NY Philharmonic or the Museum of Modern Art. Only four youngsters, of the eligible 200 or more, show up for the meetings, and one of them is less than ardent in her enthusiasm for the Church. But small beginnings can lead to small triumphs and more . . . So God is to be thanked—for the harvest and for such friends as you . . . Bill

∞

26 June 1974

Dear Father Hart,

Almost three weeks after the event I still find it hard to believe that I was able to return to that happy small hill I had left 23 years ago. And it seems still more incredible, as the best of blessings always do, that I was able to see you again, though the thought of revisiting H. C. without visiting its most valued treasure defies the right order of things. What pleased me most was finding you full of youthful vigor. How you withstood fatigue of mind and body through all those hours of standing, moving about, and greeting 1000 changed faces and remembering their names surpasses understanding. If Reunioning were an Olympic event you would be the Jim Thorpe of the sport . . . Bill

∞

4 July 1974

Dear Father Hart,

Now there is sorrow. We have had a death in the family. My Aunt Mimi, my mother's sister, died here yesterday morning. She had been staying with us for three months while we tried to persuade her, with words and love, that the self-scourging of her depressed states was the unfounded hostility of her only enemy, herself. She was, in fact, a generous, loving woman, who lived wholly for others, especially her nieces and nephews. But through some distorted working of her mind she fell into self-loathing, and not our arguments nor the long, tedious probing of the doctors could free her of that evil. And so she threw off her tormenting fate; she took her own life. Even in the midst of horror there are mercies. The boys weren't home when we—my mother and I—found the body. They had stayed overnight with their mother. By another timely coincidence my brother John called about quite a different matter just as we were trying to summon enough calm to call him. (I later tried to dial my cousin, Father Charlie, and my neck muscles were so taut I misdialed three times and finally had to signal the operator for help.) The police disposed of their grim business in an hour and by that time my brother had arrived from his office. The rest of the day was taken up with planning the funeral, notifying the family, and comforting one another. None of us had a good night. Only by an act of faith will we be able, eventually, to come to terms with this horrible event. I know your prayers will be with us, because you are a friend in times of sorrow as well as in times of joy and because you are a priest in all things. Thanks for sharing my grief. Bill

∞

1 Aug 1974

Dear Father Hart,

I hope there will be space left, after thanks are recalled, for a short paragraph of news and crop reports. Your Niagara generosity floods out all thoughts but gratitude. My mind is on your healing words of sympathy following my aunt's death, when both my mother and I looked for the understanding of friends. That dark event still haunts us, but less so than it would have if we had had to bear it alone. Thanks, too, for the Mass remembrance on the fifth anniversary of Father Pat's death. That date was pressed even deeper in memory when I paused at his grave and scanned his tombstone. You revived other memories of Father Pat with Palgrave's *Golden Treasury*. Twenty-three years ago I would've been sworn that we had been made to memorize the entire volume, but in leafing through what I discover is that the number of lines assimilated, though prodigious, falls short of the book's total. I lingered over favorites like "Invictus," "Toys," "When I Was One and Twenty," and "Hound of Heaven." Somehow I appreciate them more now than when I was compelled to read them. (Maybe education should be postponed until a person is emotionally mature. Or does education contribute to maturing?) I value the anthology for its past and future evocations and for the link it provides with two great and good men . . . Bill

• Francis Turner Palgrave (1824–1897), a graduate of Balliol College, Oxford, and later professor of poetry at Oxford, selected and arranged with notes *The Golden Treasury (of the Best Songs and Lyrical Poems in the English Language)*, first published in 1861.

∞

2 June 1975

Dear Father Hart,

. . . . I believe something of that day in May will be part of me forever. If a theologian wanted to understand the workings of grace, the mystery of God's love, he could do worse than meditate on my recent experience. I have been told, rather dramatically, that what seemed from the inside an almost trivial life is to some eyes an especially rich life. And suddenly it is, not because newspaper and TV reporters are curious about me but because people recognize that love can be miracle, even resurrection for someone who should have been given up for dead. And all that is asked of any of us is that we let ourselves be loved . . . If we had had to do without either sunshine or Father Hart I would have chosen to defy a blizzard rather than miss you. Your presence was a blessing on the day and on the deed, and it reminded me of those who were present in my heart—Father Pat, whose indestructible love, centered on one struggling friend, came to flower in full view of millions who have read about him; my own father, who tolerated my youthful insolence and gently rebuked my noisy certitude; my uncle Roy, who engaged my mind in lively debate and who put aside his equal affection for all his nephews and nieces in order to leave me the means to live comfortably; my aunt Mimi, who could not believe she was lovable and who loved beyond prudence . . . My mother remembers the day of her first meeting with Father Hart, who has been Holy Cross in her experience. A red carpet, the Marine Band, and an armful of roses would have pleased her less than your greeting. Like me, she found a warmth in your embrace, relaxing and reassuring as a tropical sunrise. And your kiss told her, as no formal proclamation could have, that the gift she really renews daily is recognized as the cornerstone of my life. . . . Love and thanks, Bill

• The "means to live comfortably" refers to the quarter share in the farm which Roy willed to Will.

∞

16 October 1975

Dear Father Hart,

I've entered into a new era—with a bang! Several bangs, in fact. Last Tuesday I went downtown to the Northwestern Medical Center, where I crashed and skidded around a large empty room in my new self-aimed electric wheelchair. The steering, starting, and stopping are controlled by inhaling or exhaling into a plastic tube. A hard puff activates an electronic switch that turns on a small battery-operated motor on each rear wheel. That sends me forward, on a more or less straight course. A hard sip stops the chair. Another hard sip propels me backward; then a hard puff cuts off the power and stops me. A soft puff turns the chair to the right, either on the move or in place; a soft sip turns left. And if all that seems confusing in print you can imagine how much more bewildering it is when you're backing into a wall and can't remember how to stop. After four hours of huffing and puffing I was pronounced ready for the road—or the labyrinthine traffic routes of this house. So far I have maimed no one, and the property damage has been minimal. It will take time to program my brain for automatic reaction but I have only to survive mistakes in the meantime . . . Mom's fine. So is Bill

∞

18 December 1975

Dear Father Hart,

What a thrill it was to read the clippings of your grand opening. The picture of you and Ron Perry standing at center court captured the meaning of the event beautifully: calling at long last the thousands of us who are proud to be called your boys had found a way to say thanks. I'm sure mine were not the only tears that rose out of the deep wellsprings of love . . . Your heart will have room for Him, as it has room for His. My mother joins her loving prayers and thanks to mine. Blessed Christmas . . . Bill

• The Hart Recreation Center at Holy Cross provides various indoor athletic venues.

∞

18 February 1976

Dear Father Hart,

My absence has been extended by 10 days, thanks to contusions incurred in a collision with a concrete floor. The mismatch took place a week ago Saturday, when my brother was trying to load me into the car with the hydraulic lift. Somehow he tipped the front end of the lift beyond its base, and the laws of physics took hold. The next thing I remember I was sitting in front of the TV, watching an Abbott and Costello movie. Two hours had passed, during which time I had been examined by the paramedics and by Dr. Bill Kane, whom John had phoned in panic. I vaguely remember Bill's presence in our living room, but I have no recollection of questions asked or answers offered. Anyhow, consciousness returned gradually—and with it, the realization that my bottom and legs were aching. The next week was a prolonged agony. Comfort eluded my every grasp. Saturday—and again Monday afternoon—took me downtown to Northwestern U. Med Center for skull X-rays and a brain scan. Both indicated that my Irish cranium had sustained no deep wounds. So now I'm waiting for the seat of my woes to heal . . . Bill

• This is the accident in which Will temporarily lost his sense of smell and taste.

∞

12 March 1976

Dear Father Hart,

Last Sunday I tried to spare myself disappointment by suppressing the hope of seeing you at the HC club brunch. At bottom, though, I honestly wished to increase my surprise should you have been in Father Brooks' entourage. So there was a twinge of regret when I saw you were not among the Worcester contingent. Except for that vagrant wish the day held only delight. . . . A concelebrated Mass drew 60 or 70 people, and the social hour increased the crowd by 30 or 40. During the mingling a young lady came over and introduced herself as Marylou Millard, daughter of classmate Charlie. She was in Chicago for the spring break, and so she decided to attend an

HC function. A poised, personable damsel. When Bill Kane returned with my tomato juice he met Ms. Millard and in the course of the conversation mentioned that he works at Northwestern U. I corrected that piece of information and said that Bill was an orthopaedist at N U Med School. Marylou asked if he was a doctor—"a real doctor, an M.D., there are so many artificial doctors!" . . . Bill

∞

16 June 1976

Dear Father Hart,

Wes Christenson—or to credit the actual packager, Pamela O'Keefe—sent me a full press kit on the '76 commencement. I must confess Jimmy Breslin's address suited the occasion perfectly, except for the gratuitous remarks about tenure. The valedictorian must have attended a different school from the barren, cold Holy Cross last year's spokesman assailed. Judge Garrity's honorary degree brought recognition to the college that formed him. Just this week the Supreme Court upheld his decision in the Boston busing case, and last week's *New Republic* ran a two-and-a-half page editorial detailing his impeccable reasoning in reaching that decision. A proud day for Holy Cross. I'm sure Mother Theresa's unobtrusive saintliness gave the day a beauty discerning eyes delivered reverently to memory . . . Bill

∞

12 August 1976

Dear Father Hart,

On my return from vacation—at a lake resort just 25 miles from Dana—I found your letter dated July 31. In it you told about offering Mass the preceding Wednesday for Dana's farmers. When we visited our crops and saw they were verdantly robust we asked how plentiful the rain had been. Our rain-gauge watcher told us a two-and-a-half inch rain the Thursday before—the day after you begged that blessing from St. Joseph the Worker—had come just in time to get the corn through the ear-filling stage. Barring blight or frost, the crop is certain to be ample. Thanks for being a pluvial partner (non-profiting) in the Jenks' farm . . . Among the developments that took place during my Hoosier hiatus was the packing-it-in of the Porter Film Co., my place of business for almost two years. For the past six months our hopes for survival hinged on obtaining poly film from an extruder in Dallas, where resins—the makings of the product—are reputedly abundant and cheap. The working arrangement never happened, so my boss decided the market held only heartbreak for the uncompetitive and he folded our tent. . . . Bill

∞

20 August 1976

Dear Father Hart,

    . . . . On Aug 27 it will be twenty-five years since polio took me out of the game. I rarely think of what might have been. What has been has been life enough. I doubt that a more normal existence would have forced me to live my faith quite so arduously. For 18 of those years I had my friend Father Pat to help me through. The first ten years held most of the rough times, and he got me through them all. And always there have been your prayers and letters and clippings and love. God must have guided me to Holy Cross, knowing that no other school could answer the needs of my lifetime. Think of it! I spent one year on campus, and my failure to return created deep and lasting friendships and a bond with the school few of its graduates could claim. Any other college would have dropped me from its records and its memory. Would you someday offer a Mass of thanksgiving for the blessings the last quarter-century has brought me? Thanks—for that and much else . . . Bill

∞

6 January 1977

Dear Father Hart,

    We are in the midst of protracted negotiations to buy a cousin's one-eighth share of the farm. That's the last fraction not owned by my mother, my brother or me. Early this week we received an appraisal and, by a reckoning outside my understanding this guy priced the 260 acres at $423,000. All this time I was rich and never knew it. . . . Bill

∞

31 January 1977

Dear Father Hart,

Last Sunday I received a phone call from the Jesuit retreat house in Barrington that warned me of an intruder, unnamed, intent on disrupting my afternoon. The mystery guest was Father Bill O'Malley, whom I hadn't seen in almost 26 years. I distinctly recall our last meeting, in front of the chapel. Bill announced that he was going to be a Jesuit; I revealed I was going to be a Hoosier. He asserted he had chosen the better part. . . . We had 30 minutes together, and the laughter ceased only when he gave me his blessing. It resumed immediately, because he added a guarantee against demonic possession. . . . Bill

• Father O'Malley was the technical advisor for *The Exorcist*. He also acted the role of the young priest in the film.

∞

26 February 1977

Dear Father Hart,

Home one week, and I'm still shivering. That's the price a tropics explorer has to pay. Besides it was sublime while it lasted. Except for the one day Hawaiian winter, when the mercury plummeted to 75 degrees and an intermittent mist bedewed the air, the weather followed the script. The sun stood faithful sentinel over the island, the breeze rushed into minister whenever sweat seeped through untoiling brows. Away from Honolulu there were subtle variations on the fair-and-warm. Valleys on the leeward side of the mountains were filled with rainbows, as humid air tumbled over the tops and fixed in tiny droplets in the lush shade. In at least one mountain pass the winds poured through the fissure at wig-lifting speed. The contrast in surfs was less nuanced. The Pacific that surged rhythmically over our beach behaved peacefully; not so on the other side, where the surfing championships are held. There waves war with each other, then link arms to assault the shore. Since the floor is coral a bobbing human throws himself into the arms of Aku every time the ocean lifts him on its crests. (Aku is the local deity, or so I surmised.) Hawaii's fauna and flora could be catalogued in two volumes. Fauna would take fewer pages than "The Irish Popes"; there are no snakes, no flies, no mosquitoes, and no platypi. Flora would fill a single volume that the Russian weightlifting team couldn't budge. Surprisingly, many of the plants were brought from other tropical regions. Even the pineapple isn't indigenous to the islands. To a Midwesterner, used to the quiet reds of the rose and the pale purple of the lilac, the jungle flowers seemed intemperate, ostentatious, licentious. The tiger's paw, the queen's powder puff, the bird of paradise—all look even more exotic than their names. And the tangle of green leaves was a perfect metaphor for anarchy. In the presence of such prodigal growth a Puritan would fear for his soul. It was beautiful . . . The doings worth telling had to include our visit to Ernie Pyle's grave, which still attracts those who served in WW II . . . Bill

∞

6 April 1977

Dear Father Hart,

It seems Nature is incapable of marching directly into spring. She must dance along the path, pirouetting coyly, retreating in a flutter, rushing ahead only to draw back, tantalizing with sudden outbursts of sedate stroll. Let the feminists rant. Nature is a woman, capricious, seductive, imperious, tender, unfeeling, and irresistible. (The foregoing was summoned from the shallows of my soul by the sight of snow lying on just-greened grass.) . . . Just this week I had a long-awaited phone call from a polyethylene manufacturer in Dallas. So I'm back in business, selling poly. This time I'm working on commission, 3 percent, instead of for wages. If I can sell a truckload of the stuff I'll get almost $300. Maybe you could ask Father Brooks if he needs one million and a quarter square feet of plastic wrapping, in clear or black, for a presently unimagined project . . . Blessed Easter, good friend, and our love . . . Bill

∞

19 July 1977

Dear Father Hart,

I liked Father Sweeney's work, especially the America piece on his boyhood summers. The setting was different from our Indiana farm, but the
feeling was much the same, even to the ritual sniffing as we crossed the state
line: "smell that good Indiana air." We slept in a tent, away from the house;
it and the sounds and smells were distinctly rural—fox hounds baying in
distant woods, weaned calves and their anxious mothers bawling and moan-
ing antiphonally, cicadas droning like Buddhist monks, overalls carrying
memories of the day's whereabouts, barns, woods, strawstack. What a gift
to be able to evoke the past with all its textures . . . As advertised, we made
the long trek to Lee's Summit, Mo, for a glimpse of our cousins' surroundings. . . . Cousin Walter, son of my father's twin sister, is 20 years older than
John, so it has only been recently that we have come to know each other.
Twenty years seems less a gap at 45 than it does at 15. Walter has retired from
the mill and grain elevator business, and now he devotes almost full time
to maintaining his camper and houseboat, both of which he has stamped
with his own native ingenuity. At 66 he has the strength and agility of most
men half his years. . . . Two weeks ago Bill Kane's wife, Betty, and Audrey
Rutherford, came out for an afternoon picnic. I doubt that the British Royal
family packs such a basket for its summer outings. But we spent too much
time eating and too little talking. . . . Bill

∞

11 May 1978

Dear Father Hart,

Last Saturday I put one more worry behind me; I delivered a five-minute
after-dinner stammer at St. Joseph Church, Rockville. The speech was merely
a pretext to bring me back to Indiana for a weekend. John hauled me as far
as Kentland, Indiana, something more than halfway between Mundelein
and Dana. There my friend Madelyn Saxton picked me up and took me
the rest of the way. That afternoon Madelyn pushed me around town to
visit whoever happened to be outside. Then we went to five-thirty Mass at

the church I built. After Mass the famous 'multi-celebrational' design was invoked to convert part of the nave into an extension of the Nazareth social room. Tables, fully clothed, candled, and flowered, gave the space almost believable pretensions to grandeur. About 50 people, most of whom I knew, sat down to a spaghetti dinner. All the while everyone was forking down the pasta I was thinking of Father Luke O'Connor, the saintly man who taught Apologetics right after Kimball's Tuesday midday meal, spaghetti. By ten after one the Italian soporific had worked its magic. Snoring rattled the windows. Whether it was the speaker or the spaghetti, a somnolence fell over my audience. Perhaps the only canon of elocution I observed was to resist the urge to hurry and get it over with. People were kind afterwards, though their kindness simply convinced me my performance merited pity, not praise. It's back to ghost-writing for me . . . I haven't written since Willard came, providentially, into our lives. For at least ten weeks I had petitioned every public agency involved in home health care for someone to take over my daily ablutions, for wages. Everyone referred me to someone else who in turn referred me to someone else, until I had made the full circle, to no good end. Then I asked Father Marcy to publish my plight. Three days after the help wanted notice appeared in the bulletin, Willard applied for the job. He's a 67-year-old retired man, onetime farmer, and polio victim himself. Despite muscle weakness on his right side, Willard hefts me about when hefting is needed, and he usually has me at my desk by nine o'clock. Mom is relieved, grateful, and almost carefree . . . Bill

∞

2 September 1978

Dear Father Hart,

John's presence on Mount St. James simplified the problem the alumni office tossed my way a few weeks ago, when Father George O'Brien, Director of Development and '54 man, notified me of my having won the Joe Perrotta award as outstanding class secretary for 1978. The Revere bowl is to be presented at the alumni lunch 30 September, homecoming. Next June's 25th reunion and the Big Gift have first claim on my purse, so I saved airfare by asking John to accept the trophy and speak the speech, I pray, trippingly

on the tongue. Maybe he'll get a free meal and a couple of football tickets
for his exertions . . . A follow-up on Jenks family lore: My daily-care man
and friend, Willard, is a coin collector, and he gave me a coin catalogue that
includes colonial coinage. The first money minted in America was designated
the "New England" pence and shilling. The book attests, "Joseph Jenks made
the punches for the first coin at his ironworks in Saugus, Massachusetts."
From the three crude discs pictured it's evident Joe was more blacksmith
than artist. . . . Bill

∽

13 November 1978

Dear Father Hart,

In a future that daily looks more and more distant I have the promise of
a new career. Several weeks ago I was chanting the woes of the polyethylene
market to a fellow polio, and when I finished she gave me the name of a
non-profit corporation that trains disabled people to be computer programmers. Within a week I had undergone an aptitude test and an interview
and, despite the puncturing of ego inflicted by the test (my first timed test
in 27 years), had qualified for the program. Now it's a matter of waiting for
an opening. (The in-home learning program requires cooperation of the
sponsoring company, which must sign a contract before the schooling can
go forward. After six month's initiation into the mysteries of computercraft,
I'll work for the sponsoring company in my 'office' here at home. 'Office':
the south half of my bedroom.) . . . Bill

∽

16 February 1979

Dear Father Hart,

The past two weeks, this time of my mother's hospitalization, seem to
stretch back to the dawn of creation . . . At the most elemental level, in the
mending of the break and the healing of the incision, Mom is doing well.
No complications have interfered with the body's repair work. But mentally

and emotionally, she has suffered serious losses. At times her confusion seems total; she recognizes no one and responds inappropriately to conversation. Even more disheartening, she resists the nurses' efforts to move her, feed her, and give her water . . . A period of rehabilitation at a skilled health care facility has been suggested. Sunday John, Jim, Jim's wife Carol, and I intend to tour two or three such centers. . . . I'm getting along OK . . . Bill

• Ella had sustained a fracture of her hip, hastening a decline which led to her death April 9, 1979, at age 78.

∞

9 May 1979

Dear Father Hart,

. . . . Today is Mother's Day, our first without mom. I found myself wishing I had told her more often that I loved her. At the Sign of Peace there were only three of us—John, Charlie and I. And we felt the absence . . . Bill

∞

25 June 1979

Dear Father Hart,

Mom came to mind almost before I registered in Hogan. Dr. Charles Kickham, '23, was there, and when Pat McCarthy introduced us I reminded him of a story my mother read in one of his classletters. She laughed every time we recalled the punchline "Bury me between Martha and Ethel, but a little closer to Martha." Dr. Kickham said it was in fact his dying father's wish. Throughout the weekend I unconsciously hoarded memories to share with Mom. Holy Cross and my Purple friends were a large part of her life . . . Father Jack Weimer, Jack O'Grady, and I, who had covenanted to be Wheeler roommates for sophomore year, resumed our friendship on the first sighting. . . . You sent me a copy of the clippings from the Worcester telegram, perhaps to keep me humble. The picture distorted my face almost as grotesquely as the interview twisted my words. . . . As Bill Kane "former hockey star and coach at Holy Cross," remarked, "When you read something you know is wrong it makes you wary of articles you only think may be wrong." . . . As a final embarrassment, one of our classmates talked to the captain of our airplane back to Chicago and informed him there were two celebrities on board, "Will Jenks, a remarkable man, who. . . . etc., and Dr. Bill Kane, his Holy Cross classmate and personal physician." Hockey coach and personal physician to Will Jenks! What prouder boasts? . . . Bill

∞

22 July 1979

Dear Father Hart,

A month ago Father Pat would've celebrated his 50th anniversary as a priest, and a week later my mother and father would have had their Golden Wedding anniversary. Those two events, so important to my life, took place just seven days apart. The ordination: 22 June 1929; the nuptials, 29 June 1929 . . . Bill

∞

6 September 1979

Dear Father Hart,

This morning, after a 4-month void, I heard more about my career as a computer programmer. When all the details are smoothed out I'll train for eventual employment with Walgreens, a large national chain of drugstores. I'll be paid as I learn, under one of those Federal boondoggles. Anything will be better than trying to sell polyethylene film . . . My friend Willard, the man who took care me for a year, until he was hospitalized for lack of oxygen in his blood, died this week. He was an old polio himself, badly crippled in an arm and a leg, and that was a bond between us. He was also an old farmer and that gave us much in common. He had a slow, diffident matter, which made him easy company in the morning, and he could laugh at his old physical and mental shortcomings. A typical farmer, he figured out ways to work around his handicap. Because his curled fingers couldn't button my shirt he borrowed an old button hook and did the job with it. Willard Tonyan, dear friend, faithful morning man, true Christian. Rest in Peace . . . Bill

- It is probable that Will's commonality with Willard provides Will with the key to his own problems a decade later. Will, whose memory and analytical skills were so keen, was unlikely to ignore the significance of "an old polio" dying for "lack of oxygen in his blood."

∞

5 October 1979

Dear Father Hart,

Chicago has never seen such a day, and such a 24 hours. Not Napoleon, not Grant, not Patton could have taken this city as decisively as John Paul did last night and today. By sheer force of love he moved through streets and neighborhoods filled with unresisting Chicagoans. The same people would take up weapons—guns, ball bats, bricks—against an armed invader, but they were overpowered by this open-armed man. As the pope remarked, Chicago is the second Polish city; they are more than one million, most of them still living in Polish enclaves. His motorcade from O'Hareski to Holy Name Cathedral passed through the northwest side, heavily Polish, and this morning's Mass at 5 Holy Martyrs gave more than equal time to the Poles of the southwest side. (Why Chicago keeps on electing Irish mayors baffles me. Either the Blacks or the Polish could easily outvote the Irish wards.) The Mass in Grant Park supposedly attracted one million and a quarter people, many of them stood in the cool lakefront breeze for eight hours before the two-hour liturgy and hour-long evacuation. But no one complained—at least not for publication. There were several delightful personal touches during the pope's encounters with the crowds. At Holy Name Cathedral he went into a side courtyard to greet the overflow crowd. When the shouting subsided the pope said, "Good evening." That provoked more cheering, then he blessed the people. With a smile he said, "Goodnight," and left. But he did it so nicely everyone felt the moment had been special. Later that night, when he finally arrived at the Cardinal's residence, he climbed out onto a balcony to bless the throng. Finally, he closed his eyes, tilted his head, and put his prayer-clasped hands along side his cheek, in the child's mime of sleep. Laughter and applause sent him off to bed. Tonight, Friday, he repeated the balcony appearance, though this time he had a microphone. After taking on the role of a song-leader for a simple "Alleluia" refrain he advised the still larger swarm to "go home; go sleep," and exited, smiling and waving. John Paul charmed everyone but the unregenerate Madelyn Murray O'Hair. The TV reporters and commentators loved him. They were as excited as the masses of spectators. Even the bishops snapped photographs and waved wildly in farewell. Possibly in the long run the Church will come to remember this visit for the pope's intransigent stance on issues like celibacy, and all-male priesthood, birth-control, and divorce, but for the moment the man's personality has driven everything else from memory . . . 6 October. Yesterday was also significant for another reason. I began my schooling in computer programming. . . . The course is structured on televised instructions and detailed explanations in workbooks. From time to time a tutor, a young man proficient in the art, will test me and deconfuse me, and by April Fools' Day I should be ready to take on jobs for Walgreens . . . Bill

∞

29 November 1979

Dear Father Hart,

God is good. He has made man in his image and likeness—loving and caring, today's children are taught. My generation didn't find that appealing doctrine in our catechism, but we learned from the loving and caring of good men and women. No one has given more luminous proof of that truth than you, beloved friend. Your reckless generosity with life's most precious gift, yourself, discloses God in His graciousness as Aquinas himself could not. But the telling argument is made by your enduring power in the Spirit, even as your physical powers are diminishing. God is your strength at 80, no less than at 40, because your love is His. All of us who have known your love thank Him for your long years and your beautiful heart. Happy birthday, holy man-of-God. I could wish you nothing God has not anticipated. You are graced to be grace, blessed to be blessing. I love you as grace, blessing, gift, good, and friend . . . Computering occupies eight of my working—or waking—hours. With time the strange procedures have become familiar if not natural. Right now I'm trying to make sense out of the Walgreen program. Their language differs from the language the textbook teaches. The contradiction would be like traveling in Portugal after having studied Spanish . . . Bill

∞

20 December 1979

Dear Father Hart,

If God will grant you good health I'll ask nothing more for Christmas. A nun once counseled us pliable children to do God the honor of asking for valuable things. Her theology probably can't stand sharp scrutiny but I embrace it anyhow, since it serves my present needs. What I need, good friend, is valuable beyond counting—a well and hearty Father Hart. So I will ask that only, and leave it to the gracious God to answer. In the meanwhile, heed the words of a famous orator: "Let yourself be loved." Pax Christi tecum, nunc at semper . . . Bill

∞

6 April 1980, Easter Sunday

Dear Father Hart,

Last week my brother John and I went to Dana for a memorial Mass for Agnes Bussing, my mom's best friend. She died quite unexpectedly of cancer, 50 weeks after her friend and bridge partner passed into eternal life. For some reason, I was more deeply shaken by Agnes' death than by Mom's. Perhaps Agnes reminded me of the time when Mom still enjoyed life. Our families were Dana's only Catholics for much of the time I lived there, so we shared that small ghetto. . . . As of last Tuesday I began drawing wages for my work on the computer. In the last three weeks of my novitiate I gained modest confidence in my abilities as a speaker of COBOL, THE sacred language of the craft. Even more heartening, I finally had a 'tube' to work on—the TV-like instrument whose screen offers the programmer's immortal logic in words of light, there to be edited quickly and quietly, without immense buildup of paper. Bill

∞

22 June 1980

Dear Father Hart,

Friday marked the end of seven years at 40 Osage. By biblical reckoning I should be entitled to a wife or a goat or my freedom. Instead, I got an extra cookie for dessert. Even now I wonder if we made the right decision for Mom. She probably would have worn out more quickly in Dana because the burden was hers alone. But there she had friends, especially Agnes, fellow Irish Catholic and bridge partner. Here she had only occasional meetings with family and old friends. Who can say which choice would have been better for her? I do think our coming here was better for the boys. They learned to love through patience, understanding, taking responsibility. They will be—are, in fact—good men for the experience . . . Work leaves me with little time and less energy for writing in my native language. I log on every day at eight-thirty on my terminal (lighted screen with keyboard) in my room. Every other week I travel to Walgreens by van—to huddle with younger but wiser programmers and analysts, who scrutinize my program or offer advice . . . Soon I hope to have transportation of my own for more timely trips . . . Bill

∞

9 October 1980

Dear Father Hart,

Thanks for the loving words about my visit and my single 'testimony' (not homily, because Rome has forbidden preaching by laymen, even us eloquent fellows.) It was a soul-swelling pilgrimage, not to the shrine of Memory but to the abbey of Life . . . Your book, *As Bread That Is Broken*, arrived this week. I can understand why you value it. In the early pages at least, Father van Breemen insists that God loves us, accepts us just as we are. So does Father Hart. What theology, what preaching makes God so real? "By this will men know you are my disciples, that you love one another." All thanks for the book; greater thanks for the long love you have loved me with. . . . I carry the memory of OUR Mass in the innermost vault of my heart. I'm sure God allowed my amendment of your intentions to include your saintly mother who is important in my life through her loving son . . . Bill

∞

17 January 1981

Dear Father Hart,

Work takes the larger part of my time and almost all my energy. Reading and writing, which used to fill my days, now struggle for room on the margin. I did read Father Sweeney's book, *It Will Take A Lifetime*, a gift from Father Brooks. Until then I'd had congratulated myself that envy was the one Deadly Sin I had escaped. Father Sweeney's supple style found me coveting his easy mastery of the written word. At one point he told that if he sought to write like anyone, that anyone would be E.B. White, essayist for *The New Yorker*. I detected a similarity from the first, though White is merely 'civilized' and Father Sweeney is committed, Christian Catholic, Jesuit . . . Bill

∞

26 August 1981

Dear Father Hart,

As you remembered, lovingly in your letter, 27 August is the 30th anniversary of my polio. Who can say how my life would have turned out if that Monday had passed uneventfully for me? For that matter, who can say how your life would have turned out if you had been idle all the hours you have given to writing, clipping, stamping, sealing, and mailing things to Dana and Mundelein? I only know that love has brought me back more than arms and legs; it has taught me to see the way God makes his grace available in everyday life. The Sacraments teach us the same thing, but their meaning comes clearer with the study of faint signs, the kind we too often miss along The Way. Your constancy—and Father Pat's—has reminded me again and again that good renews itself endlessly. To the unbeliever, my life must seem cursed; to me and to those who see through faith, it must seem blessed . . . Today was payday, my first as a full-time Walgreens employee. Until 1 August

I worked as a contract programmer, doing Walgreens work but getting paid by LIFT Inc., the non-profit organization that oversaw my training and negotiated a contract with Walgreens. Three weeks ago I was summoned to the boss' office and was invited to join The Big W, with a $2000 raise and immediate insurance coverage. Ordinarily there is a three-month wait. That 'fringe' is worth $1200 a year since my Blue Cross had just jumped to $93 a month. To celebrate the late blooming of this amaranthine weed, I had 14 of my co-workers to a cookout at our house. A borrowed volleyball set entertained the young people during the minutes away from the food and drink. I made a brief speech of thanks to all who had helped and accepted me during the long acclimation . . . Bill

∞

3 April 1982

Dear Father Hart,

   Last night found me in Evanston, a near-in suburb, at a lasagna and litera-ture gathering. A friend of Dana days, now married to a lawyer, created the idea and the group and included me and two young friends from Walgreens. All of us read the same book, bring a side-dish or a cask of rum and surround a table for an evening of scintillating conversation. The book this time was Flannery O'Connor's, *The Violent Bear It Away*. There were two distinct factions in the assessment of the work, believers and non-believers. The non-believers saw the story as ugly, pointless; the believers saw it as pointed though ugly. Toward the tail-end of the evening the talk turned to personal decisions to abandon the Church or forgo God. At that point I fell back into a kind of silent psalm: where would I go if not to the Lord when things go wrong? Who would I thank for the grace springing from the rubble of hopes? I hesitated to ask the newly godless how they choose when to do and when to suffer, how do they pray? But the questions bothered me past our goodbyes. And they bother me still. Perhaps in my pride I expected someone to ask me if religion had helped me in my obvious difficulty, my radical disabling. No one did, maybe out of fear that I'd make my famous speech. . . . Bill

∞

18 December 1984

Dear Father Hart,

There are some people who are so close to Christ it seems awkward to write of this Holy Season, of His Birth, of Peace and Joy and Love. Has there been a day of your life when you were not more aware in heart and mind of God's gift to us in his Son than the rest of us are at our Christmas? And we only wish the Peace He brought; you make it real. All the more so with Joy and Love. I will remember what you have taught me when I pray my thanks at Christmas Mass. In His Love, Bill

∞

6 April 1985

Dear Father Hart,

Holy Saturday, as it was called in the Old Dispensation. It raises memories of three-hour rites with blessings over new fire, new water, Paschal candles, food, and sacramentals of every sort. My brothers and I joined a friend in serving as altar boys for Holy Week liturgies—though the word was unknown to us then—at a novitiate for the Sisters of Mercy. Saturday was the back-breaker. One of us had to be the walking bookstand for a 10 pound Missal, through a dozen "Flectamus genua's" and a dozen "Levate's" and endless incensings and sprinklings. All of this began at 6 in the morning. Our only reward, outside of Heaven's smile, was the breakfast the nuns set for us. Remarkably, the women understood that teenage boys can eat their way through the Kansas wheat harvest in one sitting. They cooked eggs, made toast, poured milk after the manner of the General Motors assembly line, and it seemed to please them as much as it sated us . . . Bill

• "Flectamus genua" is Latin for "We bend our knees"; "Levate" is Latin for "Arise."

∞

11 Nov 1985

Dear Father Hart,

Veterans' Day. Armistice Day when I was young. That was my dad's war, WWI. He served in France but never at the front. As a boy, he thrilled to the Civil War stories the remnant of Company C., 18th Indiana, recounted at the general store in Bono, a half-mile from the farm. His father, dim-sighted, stayed home, though he was 18 when the Blue-Gray war broke out. Most of his aunts married men who had seen friends and neighbors cut down. Strangely, they gloried in their memories. And my father forever embraced the romantic notion that war was always the highest experience available to man. Viet Nam had only begun to work its evil when he died. I'm afraid we would have waged generational warfare over the nobility of that bloodletting. But I ramble . . . Bill

∞

27 Nov 1985

Dear Father Hart,

As I begin this birthday laud I'm listening to the Vienna Philharmonic performing Beethoven's Fourth Symphony. Overpowering as it is, the music doesn't delight my soul as Mozart's does. Where Beethoven is massive, Mozart is delicate; when Beethoven is complex, Mozart is simple. There is a purity that resonates through the more classical form and somehow fills the heart with light. And it is just such purity that I find beautiful in you. You simply love—or love simply, without theology, art, elaborate gift. Your notes, cards, clippings, your prayers keep you in my life, in hundreds of lives, and renew the feeling that one good man cares about me and that is all that matters, for only the assurance that we are loved brings peace to the soul. The life you have chosen gives fullest freedom to love without reckoning the cost in time or substance. So to rejoice in you is to rejoice in Christ and His priesthood, and what could be higher affirmation than that? The litany of praise could go on until it is time again to celebrate your having been born. I will still my voice and sing silently in prayer, thanking God for you, for your friendship. Happy Birthday, Grace-among-us. In Christ, Bill

∞

18 Jan 1986

Dear Father Hart,

Your note and a letter from Father Brooks told me what I dreaded to hear—that you are in the hospital, just as you had feared in your closing words of the letter I received earlier in the week. A phone call to Father George O'Brien brought to light several worrisome matters you failed to mention, chiefly your alarming weight loss over the past few months. I can only hope, in prayer, that you will be spared surgery. It's not that I think you couldn't make it through the ordeal; it's just that nobody who already suffers the daily aches of arthritis should be subjected to further woes. Whatever the doctors decide, know that my prayers ask God's kindness on your body . . . Bill

• This is the last of the 169 extant letters Will sent to Father Hart, who died, February 3, 1986, after fifty-four years teaching and counseling at Holy Cross.

∞

Reverend John E. Brooks, S.J.

Selections Written 11 September 1976–23 July 1989

The Reverend John E. Brooks, S. J., '49, was the twenty-ninth president of the College of the Holy Cross. He followed a unique path to this post. Upon graduation from Boston Latin School, he attended Holy Cross for a few months in 1942 before serving in the European theater of operations with the U.S. Army until 1945. He then returned to Holy Cross and received his bachelor's degree in 1949. Following a year of graduate study in geophysics at Penn State, he entered the Society of Jesus in 1950. After teaching math and physics as a scholastic at Holy Cross, he was ordained a Jesuit priest in 1959. He received his doctorate in sacred theology from the Gregorian University in Rome in 1963 and returned to Holy Cross to teach religion. Father Brooks was named dean and vice president of the College in 1968 and inaugurated as president in 1970. He wanted Holy Cross "to be the best Jesuit undergraduate liberal arts college it can possibly be." His vision, his articulation of that vision, his managerial skills and leadership, and his dedication to his religious vows served him and ultimately the College of the Holy Cross magnificently throughout the twenty-four years of his presidential tenure. As president emeritus, he has remained active on behalf of the College alumni association as well as serving as a director on the boards of various theological, biotechnical, educational, medical and athletic organizations.

∞

11 Sept 1976

Dear Father Brooks,

I know you intended your letter to be a personal message, but even as I read it for its sustenance of love I recognized it as the very kind of blessing Holy Cross has brought into my life. For me, at least, the Christian/Catholic/Jesuit character of the school, which you have fought so relentlessly to preserve, is epitomized in Holy Cross' twenty-five year ministry to 'the least of My brethren.' A scoffer might dismiss the monumental charities of Father Pat and Father Hart as peculiar to the nature of those men, not to the nature of the school. But how would he account for the priestly concern of the college president, full-time game warden for that most endangered species, the small Catholic liberal arts college? Because your years as president will be remembered, gratefully, for your epic achievement in taming a budget gone berserk, it may go unnoticed that your more profound influence has been spiritual. I wish there were a time capsule to preserve that letter, so that history might know the whole man . . . If you see the power of the Resurrected Christ at work in me it is because His love, experienced as the support of family and friends, overcame Death's victory in my life. I now read the miracle accounts in a Resurrection context, having found the key in Christ's own Socratic query: "Which is easier to say: take up your bed and walk; or, your sins are forgiven?" There is tremendous guilt attached to being less than perfect. It's in loving acceptance that we discover the abundant possibilities for new life. . . . Will

∞

[Fall of 1978]

Dear Father Brooks,

If I hadn't been convinced that you lead Holy Cross with a wisdom unavailable to wholly secular schoolmasters, the President's Council Newsletter would have won me to that opinion. As impressive as your presidential answers and assessments were, your Apologia for the Jesuit character of Holy Cross revealed the deeper dimension of your understanding, a faith that is at once knowledge and vocation. When disillusionment with curricula that were too rationalistic, too quantifying, too Greek swept the campuses in the 60's academicians for the most part either bitterly resisted or surrendered to the kids and ephemeral relevance. Only those schools already grounded in the Gospel were able to make a creative response. Holy Cross had the good fortune to come under the direction of a Jesuit professor of Christology, and that perspective, more than fiscal sleight-of-hand, has given the school its present strength and its future stature. Given the choice between an ample endowment and a Fr. Brooks, I would insist on a Fr. Brooks. Money simply can't buy what you bring to your work . . . In Christ, Will

∞

27 April 1979

Dear Father Brooks,

Your gracious, consoling letter arrived hardly twelve hours after my mother's death, but already expressions of sympathy had come to assume a seemingly ritual form. Against that drone of sincere antiphons your words sounded with the rich timbre of simplicity and clarity, words of blessing and promise. They gave all of us hope and strength. One of the more perceptive members of the family remarked, in honest awe, "he's quite a man." And you are—a man of God, of The Word. Thank you for that work of mercy. For the family, too, Will

∞

15 July 1984

Dear Father Brooks,

When "Brooks' Folly" came into view for the first time my mind ran down the index of History's other admirable follies. The marked—and now remarked—difference between Fulton's/Seward's/Ziegfeld's and yours is that theirs were the highest rung on their ladders. Your wrought-irony, handsome as it is—elegant frame for a surpassing work of art, will stand as a minor monument to your presidency. You will be remembered as a Julius II for the landscape, the Kantor, the organ, and the fence but as John XXIII for the windows you have opened to let in breath and light, Breath and Light. Because we are a sacramental people, whose modes of understanding transcend the intellectual, the entire campus will body forth the splendors of the Brooks years. Only a puritan could fail to sense the meaning you intend for Holy Cross. Only one thing remains: somewhere there must be a plaque noting that you did it all while wearing CEFM around your neck. Diffuse and deflect praise as you will, you cannot flee the awe and gratitude of all Crusaderdom, even for your 'Folly' . . . In Jesus, the Celebrator, Will

• "Brooks' Folly" was what detractors called the wrought-iron fence which replaced an ordinary chain-link fence at the periphery of the campus.

∞

17 Dec 1985

Dear Father Brooks,

. . . . In late November my almost forgotten career as a tutor afforded me an unimaginable reward. A young woman I had guided through algebra—and accompanied through a stormy adolescence—sent me home from her wedding reception with thanks for my love, which, she said, had been important to her. I can think of no words that got so directly to the heart. In my joy, I resolved to do the same to those who have loved me. Your love has been important to me, good friend, not because you are an important man but because you are a loving man, a living disciple of Jesus, the revelation of God's love. Your Yes to my life, my return to life, gives me the courage to face the truth of the Cross. That has been my freedom and my peace. It is a great gift, and I thank you for it. In Him Who took flesh, Will

∞

4 Feb 1986

Dear Father Brooks,

As President of our College, you not only speak for Holy Cross, you listen for Holy Cross. So I ask you to hear and accept these words of sympathy for our loss in the death of Father Francis J. Hart, S.J., priest, teacher, friend to more than 50 years of Holy Cross men and women. The loss falls most heavily on you, because it will be your part to comfort those of us who mourn and to remind us that we are a Resurrection people.

How can we mourn the quiet, merciful death of an 86-year-old man whose life was rich in the things of God, a saint whose simplicity taught us more tellingly than erudition, a smiling pilgrim who has made his way at last to the dwelling place of God? We mourn, of course, for ourselves, for the College. If we did not mourn we would surrender our past, the memory of those loves that made us strong in faith and in purpose, and without that past we would drift with every current. Father Hart was not the whole of Holy Cross' love, but for many he came to embody that love, as memory crystallized in myth and symbol. It is unlikely that one person will ever again become the center of our recollection, and so we feel the soul of Holy Cross is somehow less.

But if we mourn we must also call to mind that we share the truth of Resurrection. What Father Hart brought to our lives did not die with his last breath. It remains among us, within us, and it will glimmer in unexpected places, wherever we carry the spirit of Holy Cross. We must remind ourselves that Holy Cross was his past, too, that it was a grace to him just as he was a grace to us. And Holy Cross lives. In the Resurrected Christ, Will

∞

21 July 1986

Dear Father Brooks,

Some forgotten lapse kept me from making known my thanks for your Remarks reminding us that the President of Holy Cross has more to account for than numbers. It took unblinking courage to reaffirm the College's Jesuit bearings in the face of upper-bracket infatuation with the Reagan ideology. Upholding justice, not only in the annual report but in your daily dealings with the rich and powerful, calls for an Ignatian toughness of soul. If the eschatological moment forces a choice between the demands of justice and the comforts of the ruling class, Holy Cross will suffer, even to the cross it makes its own. How much harder to risk the life of the College than one's own and at the same time to resist the temptation to cheap martyrdom. To put it tautologically, our chief strength is our chief . . . As you may have sensed, I have begun to sample Liberation Theology, Jon Sobrino's *Christology At The Crossroads,* specifically. My reticence in reading in L.T. seems all the more inexplicable now that I've found the ideas and themes to be much like the patchwork system I put together out of books, thoughts, prayers, yes, sufferings. Of course, even in its embryonic stage L.T. has greater coherence, greater depth than my scattershot notions, but it is heartening to discover I was not distilling a private stock of heresy. My sole reservation—besides the eschatological—with Sobrino's work is his haste in excommunicating everyone who doesn't take the next boat to Brazil to liberate the oppressed poor. I realize it's not enough simply to feel sorry for the Third World or even to send a check. But to repeat the question yet another time, What must we do? Actually, it's invigorating to have one's life called into question on terms more compelling than the Baltimore Catechism. (Could you recommend further readings in L.T.? I came to Sobrino by chance.) . . . In Jesus, God's Firstborn, Will

∞

11 April 1987

Dear Father Brooks,

How paradoxical, that in the first year of the New Age of Virtue our football team should attract more attention than it had during two decades of venial decadence. As only a Liberated mind could perceive, an imaginative coach and a shrewd publicist can create more excitement than a herd of thick-necked line-backers. And to the pure of heart, even the soul-sold must bow in brief reverence: in an NCAA basketball game from the Far West the announcer caught Tom Heinsohn using a two-syllable word not taken from Al McGuire's *Crayola Colorbook for Hiplip Omniscients*, so he chided our Chrysostum, "Oh, sure, Heinsohn, you can use those fancy words because you went to a high-class college like Holy Cross." That was more satisfying than having a team in the grab-bag 64. . . . A John Fowles short story, "Poor Koko," poses a problem Liberal Arts education seems ordained to deal with. An intellectual menaced by a young anarchist/criminal watches in horror as he gratuitously burns the work of four years' scholarship. Then, on reflection the victim surmises the hatred is aimed precisely at his mastery of words, this age's priestcraft. Populists of the Left and the Right harbor resentment of those who use their learning to serve the powerful, to maintain wealth, to subvert justice. Reading that, I recalled an annual encounter at the county fair; my brother and I invariably entertain ourselves at the Anti-Lawyer Party booth, where angry men and pamphlets argue the perfidy of the legal profession. In other times the Jesuits excited a like frothing in the paranoid. But there is a glint of truth to the grievances of the unlearned. Too few college graduates understand their education as a public good, as a resource in the service of the less blessed. I think Holy Cross, in its Catholic dimension, at least counters the pull of private possession with the summons to Christian discipleship, but in our pluralist society we must find secular grounds for correcting the perversion. Where better than our College to undertake that work? . . . Until soon, In the Paschal Mystery, Will

- "Chrysostom" literally means "golden mouth," but is used here to indicate "someone who speaks well."
- Thomas W. Heinsohn, '56, a basketball star for the Holy Cross Crusaders and the Boston Celtics, became a television sports commentator for college and professional games.

16 Dec 1988

Dear Father John,

When I read your eulogy of Edward Bennett Williams, I was stunned to learn that you consider him the most Christlike man you have known. Stunned but not scandalized, because you risked misunderstanding among those who worship the effete if not effeminate Christ of mawkish art. The Jesus you saw in Ed Williams is the brother I have come to know through the dialectic between his story and my life. He was tough-minded, demanding, fearless, confident, present in power. I'm sure Jesus is as pleased with the comparison as Ed Williams is . . . Today is Beethoven's birthday, and Chicago's fine arts FM station has played his music all day. His genius made present 218 years later reminds me of the trap anti-abortionists use to ridicule the sentimental argument for aborting a fetus doomed to less-than-perfect gifts of mind and body: Would you abort the fifth child of a tubercular mother and syphilitic father, a man destined to live the last half of his life in deafness? A yes answer earned the retort, "You have just killed Beethoven." As improbable as genius out of squalor may seem, it scarcely compares with divinity out of humanity. Yet several billion people in the course of history have believed it to be so, have staked their lives on its truth. Christmas takes its meaning from Easter, of course, but every birth since Bethlehem has held greater hope and promise because God has made flesh the medium of His fullest revelation. That good news is repeated faithfully in lives like yours. All the joy of the feast to you, good friend. Yours in Jesus, God's Surprise, Will

∞

23 Jul 1989

Dear Father John,

All manner of things has kept me from writing this or anything more stirring than 'Pay to the order of.' But the wait may have been worth it. In the meantime, I saw *Dead Poets Society* and found it at once charming and disturbing. From the outset the scent of suicide lingered in the air, so it came as no surprise when the father-oppressed prepster did away with himself. The plot has been recycled every five years, and this version differed from its cousins only in resisting the standard Hollywood ending, with the remorseful adults acknowledging the moral superiority of the kids and their mentor in solipsism. Banality was avoided at the cost of honesty, though. The argument for 'Carpe diem' never confronted its antipodal truth: life is long and resurrection, always at hand. If the school had been Jesuit instead of secular, the students would have been taught not just how to discover one's own voice but how to find the Christ within each of us—the man for others. How much better to have a Christologist at the helm rather than a romantic poet. Will

∞

Northwestern University Rehabilitation Engineering Program

Letters from Will Jenks

to

Margaret (Marge) Pfrommer

Professor Dudley S. Childress, Ph.D.

∞

Margaret (Marge) Pfrommer

Selections Written 2 April 1974–2 July 1974

Margaret Pfrommer, also a polio quadriplegic, worked as a receptionist at the Northwestern University Rehabilitation Engineering Program (NUREP). Born in 1937, she contracted polio in her mid-teens, but unfortunately did not have the benefit of home-based supportive resources comparable to those available to Will. By her mid-twenties, she was living in a nursing home primarily for the elderly in River Forest, Illinois. Members of the Lutheran church on the nearby campus of Concordia College became acquainted with her and believed she deserved a chance at a fuller and better life. Working with the faculty and staff of the college, the congregation moved Marge into her own home and cared for her until her death in 1998.

During a visit to the original Rehabilitation Institute of Chicago on East Ohio Street, it was recommended that Marge meet Dr. Dudley Childress and his team of rehabilitation engineers. She became the inspiration for much of their subsequent research and was the first patient to use the "sip and puff" environmental control system and battery-powered wheelchair they developed. Like Will, Marge used a thin rod for typing. She ultimately worked for over twenty-five years as secretary-receptionist for NUREP. She was transported to work five days a week in a specially equipped van driven by a River Forest neighbor who worked near the rehabilitation center. Very importantly, she continued to serve as test-person for new rehabilitative technologies and as a role model for other rehabilitation engineering programs.

Will was independently aware of her existence and had corresponded with her for several months before discovering that she worked at NUREP. She is the person who initially recommended that Will contact Lift, Inc., the nonprofit organization which provided the technical training that led to his employment as a computer programmer for Walgreen Company.

∞

2 April 1974

Dear Marge,

   All the clichés are true. It is a small world. The best is yet to come. Great minds run in the same channel. Feed a cold and starve a fever. It's fun to phone . . . That litany celebrates the crossing of our stars under the beneficent influence of the Giant Star, Dudley—in the Northwestern galaxy. If I weren't a convinced skeptic I could almost believe in ESP, since your name was palpably present, though unspoken, during Dudley's visit here. I suppose our common fate reduces the improbability of the coincidence, but it still seems a fortuitous boon . . . Shortly after our conversation it suddenly came to me why my voice was blurred. Before I talked to you I had spent three hours talking with a friend from the distant days of my youth. Not merely talking but pontificating on an encyclopedic array of topics, from mass transit to designated pinch hitters. That would account for the weary vocal chords. Three hours of filibustering, at heightened volume, is the limit of my speaking endurance. (My other limits: five beers; a double feature with one cartoon; two-and-a-half televised football games; four innings of baseball; six hours of typing; ten minutes of preaching— listening to; ten hours of reading or ten pages of Heidegger, whichever comes first; 23 hours of lascivious fantasizing; three bushels of popcorn; 27 seconds of Nixon.) . . . Rather than dredge up memories of Acapulco I'll enclose a four-page account I wrote for the other members of the expedition. My brother, a marketing director with Bell & Howell, took me along as the other half of his vacation-for-two, a perquisite offered to worthy B&H management people. A great experience, if only because it afforded a respite from Chicago's depressing winter . . . I'm in the middle of writing an article about microfilm systems, and if it's acceptable to my collaborator I may find unsteady employment—a distressing prospect. The guy who is auditioning me read my Acapulco piece and somehow imagined that I could write propaganda for his division of B&H. So he sent me six pages of rambling comments dictated into a tape recorder at three in the morning. For the most part I ignored his efforts . . . Pass along my greetings to Dudley, John S., Bill Kane, and Johnny Pont . . . I like the sound of your voice and the buoyancy of your spirit . . . Bill

• Johnny Pont was the coach of the Northwestern football team.

∞

2 July 1974

Dear Margaret,

It pains me to have to resort to conventional stationery, but I just discovered my supply of recipe cards has run out . . . If I had to sort out my feelings after your party I'd put a tag on delight, admiration, and shame. My delight was in the people, whose playfulness revealed assured affection. My admiration was for the team's work, the giving of their gifts for the good of the unimportant and powerless. (There was something symbolic, almost sacramental in your giving them absurd presents. It expressed the need/unneed to say thanks, despite a poverty of means.) And my shame was with myself for ever having accepted the praise of friends on my triumph over adversity. When I beheld the strength you have summoned out of nothing and the courage it took even to survive, I feel guilty at having made so little of my prodigious potentialities. That is literally true. You are David against a Goliath fate. And I am craven Saul. . . . Friday my mother, my aunt, and I are going to Dana, home of Ernie Pyle, for two weeks. I'm excited at the thought of seeing old friends again—from a young protégé who's running for county prosecutor to the two retarded boys across the street. I may even run the risk of a 1941–style haircut at the Friendly Philosopher's barber shop. For $1.50 and no tip it's almost worth the gamble . . . Did you encounter the same reaction among those you told about our finally meeting? The first thing I was asked was "What does she look like?" I described you as honestly as I know how: large, expressive eyes, a sunrise smile, lovely reddish blonde hair, and not-too-tall-to-wear-heels-to-a-dance. That answer seemed to trigger other, more curious questions. I finally had to explain that unless Dudley creates an even more sophisticated technology our relationship is destined to be Platonic and long-range. I think there are people who would pair off the Venus di Milo with the Discus Thrower. . . . Go slow rounding corners and remember to look both ways at intersections . . . Hi to everyone . . .

∞

Professor Dudley S. Childress, Ph.D.
Northwestern University Rehabilitation Engineering Program

Selections Written 10 May 1974–3 November 1985

Professor Dudley S. Childress, "the Giant Star . . . in the Northwestern galaxy" [WHPJ to Marge Pfrommer, 2 April 1974], was born and raised in Harrisonville, Missouri, thirty miles south of Kansas City. He received his bachelor of science degree in electrical engineering from the University of Missouri in Columbia, and his Ph.D. in the same field from Northwestern University where he continues to teach and create rehabilitation devices for the disabled. When he met Will in the 1970s, Dr. Childress was professor in the departments of Electrical Engineering and Orthopaedic Surgery; he is now professor of Physical Medicine and Rehabilitation and Biomedical Engineering. In addition to his inventive leadership in advancing the "sip and puff" system for environmental control, he has received worldwide acclaim for developing artificial limbs that are controlled by transcutaneous electric signals transmitted from the remaining muscles of an amputated limb.

Will and Dudley shared "tastes and opinions" [WHPJ to the Kanes, 5 April 1974] and formed a mutual admiration society.

∞

10 May 1974

TO: Dudley & Co.
FROM: Your Six Million Dollar Man
ABOUT: Locating A Six Million Dollar Woman

The status of the great experiment can be reported in a few words: I like it. It affords me greater safety, convenience, pleasure, and—hardly less important to me—a feeling of independence. With the addition of the call-buzzer and the plastic tubing (Thanks, John), my sense of security has been so markedly enhanced that I've abandoned my night-night prayers. Until a permanent route can be fixed, the plastic tubing will continue to be strung casually from table to chest to picture hook—something like a Corsican telegraph line. So far I haven't had occasion to summon aid against nocturnal invaders, but I have come to tune in WFMT on awakening—a little Bach before breakfast. The telephone hook-up is the most valuable of the features. At times my haste in answering creates problems, but for the most part it's a boon to me and my mother.

A few curious phenomena: Once I answered the phone without turning off the typewriter. Remembering the protocol, I resisted the urge to puff and instead turned the machine off at the switch. For reasons not apparent to the electronically illiterate, the phone connection cut out. The same thing happens with the lamp. Another oddity occurred during a power failure. Though the juice withdrew while I was typing, its return triggered the call-buzzer, next in the sequence of red lights. Finally, a bolt of lightning during a phone conversation severed the connection, though I'm not sure the box was the locus of the villainy.

I haven't forgotten my promise to send pictures and negatives of your technically augmented prototype at work and play. I'm merely waiting until I get a haircut.

Vast thanks to all. Further details furnished on request. Bill

• The "great experiment" is the environmental control system developed at NUREP which Will runs by sipping and puffing on a straw. By allowing him to control lighting, typewriter, radio, phone, etc., the technology greatly increases Will's self-reliance.

∞

24 Oct 1975

Dear Dudley,

I wish the accompanying check had three more zeroes to underwrite the good work you and your co-conspirators do. The technologies you focus on the physics of every problem seem magical to the Neolithic mind, but the honest compassion that allows you to see the human problems implicit in your work eases my Luddite anxieties and makes me grateful for minds still in touch with their heart.

Unsippable thanks to everyone—you, John, Jay, Ed, Terry, Ted, Mark, Fran, Greg, David, Nancy, and the subversive-in-Residence, Ms. Pfrommer, and anyone I may have unwittingly slighted (Carole, posthumously)—for new freedom and dignity. Irreversibly, Bill

• Will is now using the "sip and puff" battery-powered wheelchair developed by the Northwestern team.

∞

28 Sept 1976

Dear Dudley,

. . . . The recent improvements to the chair—passing gear and balloon front tires—have answered my felt (as in 'panic' and 'rattled') needs. With the added speed and comfort I wouldn't hesitate to enter the Pike's Peak hill climb . . . I wish I could find a doctor with John's telepathic powers. He listens to a recitation of the symptoms, asks a few probing questions, then affects a long-distance cure. The AMA might question the efficacy of over-the-phone appendectomies, but it condones an all-purpose two-aspirin ano-dyne, and John is more discriminating than that . . . There's not a book I can recommend, though Graham Greene's 20-year-old *Quiet American* read like an allegory on our later Viet Nam obsessions. For my Youth Ministry work, I examined Merton Strommen's *Five Cries Of Youth*, a creative extrapolation of various surveys of young people, churched and not. Contrary to the claims of the Counterculture, kids who belong to a church tend to be more sensi-tive to social issues and more diligent about working for solutions . . . Too infrequently I think of my great good fortune in having this miraculous chair. Some people see God's love in the workings of nature. I prefer to look on the gifts He has endowed man with. Nature, after all, is uncaring about its mistakes. Man, at his best, discovers new ways to adapt conditions to salvage otherwise wasted lives. All of you are helping bring about what Teilhard calls The Divine Milieu. It is at least as worthy of a psalm as the splendors of Creation . . . Bill

∞

AN UNSOLICITED TESTIMONIAL FROM A
PLEASED-PUFFER-AND-SATISFIED-SIPPER

When Dr. Dudley Childress and John Strysik were installing the magic box that gave me control of a whole new environment (phone, radio, emergency buzzer, reading light, and gismo-of-your-choice switch), they mentioned that the Northwestern University Rehabilitation Engineering Program was working on an electric wheelchair for quadriplegics. Maybe because I had made too complete an adjustment to polio's mischief against my limbs I couldn't put myself in the driver's seat. My imagination was locked in to the necessity of plotting moves with human push-power. But with the possibility of self-propulsion planted in my mind I gradually came to realize how often I wanted to be elsewhere, and I became impatient for mobility.

By the time the prototype was ready I was ready—or I thought I was. After a four-hour novitiate on the NU Rehab Engineering obstacle course, my confidence was shaken, but that first taste of freedom lured me past doubt. So the chair and I were vanned home and turned loose in a real-life labyrinth of furniture, doorways, and pedestrians.

My debut as a driver happened to coincide with a night game in the World Series. To the consternation of out-of-work shovers I made my way to the family room and took up a position in front of the tube. An early-inning uprising sent one team ahead by five runs. It also sent everyone else to distant parts of the house. Still thinking in the old mode, I found myself wishing I could hitch a ride to my typewriter. Then it hit me: I could get there on my own. What's more, I could have the best of both worlds. By tuning in the radio account of the game at odd intervals I could learn whether a promising rally warranted my attention; in the meantime I could go on typing. It happened almost according to script. I typed until the eighth inning, when a sudden eruption put the Red Sox and me back in the ball game. For the first time in 24 years I was in control of my destination, if not my destiny.

Liberation has its practical benefits, among them the creation of free time. My job as a polyethylene film salesman demanded no more than five hours a day, but the phone vigil, my first line of defense against the wrath of my boss, the people at the factory, or mere customers, kept me nailed down, day and night, to my work area, within reach of the puff-n-sip phone activator. With the powered chair I could now range as far as five ring-a-lings from my desk, and a 15-minute phone call would take only 15 minutes of my time—and none of anyone else's. Writing, too, became less troublesome. A quick trip to my reading stand could retrieve a stray quote or fact for newsnotes, lesson plans, letters. Even reading, with over-forty eyes, became easier, as hard sips—reverse—brought print into focus. I can look forward to an unspectacled old age, provided I can move backward unobstructed.

Construction of a ramp from frontdoor to driveway gave me easy access to the outside world, though in Towner subdivision that hardly puts me within puffing distance of the centers of culture and commerce. But it does let me escape whenever the walls begin to pinch. The latest modification of the original equipment allows the driver to summon more speed while underway and so there is no longer a need to compromise between indoor and outdoor speeds. Mobility offers one other inestimable boon: it aids and abets the summer sunner in seeking shade before his subcutaneous tissue is well-done.

For a person delivered even partially from stuckness, there is a temptation to rhapsodize over the technology that made it possible, but what the practical mind wants is economic justification for underwriting the research behind the puff-n-sip chair or for subsidizing its purchase in cases of hardship. Obviously, in each case the return on investment would be different. Those quadriplegics who already carry a marketable skill in their head—doctor, lawyer, engineer, writer—would move immediately into productive work. Those who can be educated for available jobs would find the doors of a useful future open to them, and they would eventually repay society. The unfortunate few who suffer intellectual as well as physical handicaps would seem a poor risk. But there is a chance that the gift of unhoped-for freedom would spark a desire to participate in human affairs in some way. Even by an accountant's standards it is possible to consider $2700 for a chair a prudent outlay. Assuming a chair-life of ten years, the cost breaks down to less than $1.00 a day, less than a half-hour's wages for an attendant. An electric wheelchair may not make a quadriplegic completely care-free, but it would certainly free care for more than 30 minutes a day. What cannot be estimated is the social good that would come of delivering otherwise healthy quadriplegics from confinement in nursing homes, where chances of transcending their handicaps are infinitesimal.

Arguing on different terms, I would suggest that the character of a society can be seen in its efforts to restore human dignity where fate has visited indignity. The consequences of such caring may not be reflected in the Gross

National Product, but they are recognized in the faces of those who have been helped. A quadriplegic who can smile is a symbol of reassurance to anyone paralyzed by life's risks. For that benefit alone the puff-n-sip chair should be counted a good, beyond price.

∞

21 Dec 1977

Dear Dudley, John, Margaret, Fran, Bonnie, Lenny, Ed, and Everyone Else Who Probably Wears An NU Rehab Eng Lab Jacket,

I send you greetings and thanks from the third most remote outpost equipped with your dignity-restoring technologies. (The Georgia chicken keeper and the Far West rancher outrank me in remoteness.) I can think of no group of people whose daily gifts of memory, imagination, concentration, persistence—thought and sweat—have done more to rescue lives from pointlessness. If Heaven were to reward you in full measure you would have wealth undreamed of by either Nieman or Marcus. Failing that, Heaven must at least give you Joy and Peace . . . Bill

∞

3 Nov 1985

Dear Dudley, John, Margaret, Bonnie, et al,

Halloween sent me back, unbelievably, a decade to the still-resonant meeting with Madame Sadat. It was ten years ago, too, that my chair was new, and I can no longer remember what it was like to be cast in stone. Of the several divisions of my life—able-bodied/quadriplegic, idler/worker, Hoosier/Chicagoan—one of the most significant is stationary/motorized. So much of what I do assumes an ability to move from place to place. It is a rare day when I am not made aware of the miracle you worked, and if thinking thanks seldom gets past a smile Heavenward, please know that everyone who marvels at your invention is required to celebrate your genius and your kindness. Thanks for every sip, every puff . . . Love, Bill

∞

Holy Cross Classmates

Letters from Will Jenks

to

Rev. John C. Weimer

*Elizabeth K. (Betty) Kane
and William J. (Bill) Kane*

∞

Reverend John C. Weimer

Selections Written 11 October 1982–12 October 1988

Monsignor John C. Weimer, '54, was born October 13, 1932, and educated in parochial elementary and secondary schools in Buffalo, New York. Upon graduating from Holy Cross, he returned to Buffalo and entered Christ the King Seminary. He was ordained in 1958. Father Weimer first taught at Bishop Turner High School and, later, homiletics at the seminary. He now serves as director of Catholic campus ministry for the Newman Center at Buffalo State College and as director of continuing formation of priests for the Diocese of Buffalo. He was appointed domestic prelate in 1993 by John Paul II.

Jack Weimer and Will became good friends during their freshman year at Holy Cross and, before Will's polio prevented him from returning to the college, they had intended to room together during their sophomore year.

∞

11 Oct 1982

Dear John,

The rhyme is neat but false. 50 is NOT nifty. It's mildly depressing, especially when you think of the things a 50-year-old is ontologically precluded from doing, like sustaining an impure thought for 30 seconds or trimming the eyebrows with anything lighter than hedge shears. As compensation, of course, there is Wisdom, out of favor even in the Orient. (Ignore the curmudgeonly tone. I'm schooling myself to follow Dylan Thomas' advice: "Do not go gentle into that good night.") In the Church and the Mafia 50 marks the beginning of reliability, though you have probably forfeited fair repute with your anarchy and light blue suit. A recent review of Graham Greene's latest identifies his idée fixe as Power vs. Glory, the first, invariably strong and corrupt, the second, weak and faithful. That inverted Manicheanism hardly gives play to Power-Glory tension of the kind you embody. There must be the risk of office—quite opposed to the grace of office—if Power is not to go to the self-aggrandizing by default. Innocence in children and the simple-minded has its appeal, but in men and women called to serve it becomes a temptation to withhold. From the first days of your priesthood you have known what to yield and what to keep. No now-forgotten martyr, our Johannes, but a present force for vital change. The term 'survivor' has come into fashion. I find it loathsome. Talleyrand was a 'survivor'; he served four widely disparate regimes but himself most of all. You serve Him who prayed to be spared the cup but drank it when the time came. He was a 'transcender'; so are you, old friend. Happy Birthday . . . If it weren't for the reading group I belong to, I would have made the slide to dronehood without twist or bump. Our book-look meetings attract a dozen people intent on staying alive in the margins not overrun by job, family, and Sodality. We are lawyers (4), teachers (4), computer-types (3), and counselor, and we pointedly avoid Truly Great Books. Instead we choose *Winter of Our Discontent, Henderson the Rain King, The Violent Bear It Away, Angel of Light,* and *The Movie-Goer.* Somehow the exchange finds its way to religious belief, disbelief, and unbelief. It's amazing how feeble the grounds for abandoning belief. If the same people made consumer choices based on equally puerile understanding their relatives would ask the court to appoint a guardian, lest they do themselves harm. My favorite of the five books? Walker Percy's modest venture along Kierkegaardian paths . . . The World Series and Sloth have caused this to be several days in the making. So I haste away, leaving prayers and greetings, and love to be distributed as you see fit. In Jesu, Will

∞

Rev. John C. Weimer delivered the following remarks as part of his homily at the special Mass celebrated by the class of 1954 during their 1984 Reunion. These words provide the basis for Will's thoughts in his October 12, 1984, and October 8, 1985, letters to Father Weimer.

. . . . I dare raise an issue with you today that might at first seem out of place on such a light and joyful occasion. Last year a group of men older even than we published a pastoral letter entitled, "The Promise of Peace: God's Challenge and

Our Response." In it they identified the nuclear arms race as one of the greatest moral issues ever faced by humankind.

The deployment of new weapons with first strike capability has destabilized the nuclear stand off and the counterforce strategy we are now promoting has escalated the possibility of forcing the Russians into a "use 'em or lose 'em" posture. Finally, with delivery time now approaching fifteen minutes we must depend ever more totally on computer technology to decide if an attack is in progress. The situation is grave. It is not just a continuation of the same old stand off we have lived through since Russia developed its own arsenal of nuclear weapons or when Dick Cavallaro was at Guantanamo during the Cuban missile crisis.

But why address the issue now and here? The reasons are two. The first is George Fargis's remark that he is concerned about the possibility (probability) of a nuclear holocaust during his children's lifetime. Your love for your children and grandchildren is evident on every page of our report. Eric Erickson suggests that the penultimate developmental stage of adult life is generativity, responsibility for a new generation of adults. This generativity shows itself in the need to create products of value and to participate in collective enterprises that advance human welfare and contribute to the coming generations of society.

In short, we are at the stage in our lives when we can look beyond our personal accomplishments and take greater responsibility for the common good.

The second reason I address this issue is because you are men and women committed to Gospel values, especially the sanctity of human life, and because you are people of vision and competence. Most of you have served in the Armed Forces, some have made a career of it. Everett Ashe says that he learned firsthand how difficult it is to negotiate the brotherhood of man as a member of an industrial advisory group to NATO. You are moulders of opinion, knowledgeable about government and capable of having an influence in your community. If anyone can, you can influence the public debate on the nuclear arms issue.

Our Gospel reading today challenges us to engage in that debate. To be salt for the earth, to be light for the world, we need to do more than give public witness to private morality, like honesty or marital fidelity. Surely we need to continue to give witness by our personal struggle to live out our lives after the pattern of Christ. But we are far too sophisticated to believe that matters of public import lay outside Christ's preaching of the Kingdom of God. That kingdom is frustrated by the ideologies, the systems and the structures that lock us into a frightening confrontation. The very future of God's creation is at risk. We dare not remain ignorant or silent before that risk.

What I ask you to commit yourself to is not an easy task. The issue is complicated, but not so complicated that it will not yield itself to serious study and concern. How you will come down on the issues does not concern me.

Surely, the Bishops' Pastoral with its profound reflection on the Catholic Christian tradition on war and peace is the place to begin.

But the important, no, the essential thing, is that we become part of the process. We are called to take up the dialogue in the pews, schools and homes, in factories and offices, in government and military circles. We must learn to share our diverse visions in an atmosphere of mutual respect and of mature dialogue. If our dialogue degenerates to hostile debate we risk repressing the Holy Spirit and frustrating our growth to greater moral maturity. Finally we will fail to defuse the frightful situation that faces us and threatens our children and grandchildren.

We must become peacemakers. God is at work in us, Paul tells us, reconciling the world to God's self. We must be the instruments of God's peace. We owe it to our brothers whom we remember today, to our children and grandchildren and to the God who gave us this earth, this life, this precious company of friends and lovers.

∞

12 Oct 1984

Dear Peacenik,

Reverberations of your Reunion homily refuse to drop below the level at which the mind can give full attention to the untroubling lullabies of Uncle Ron. To be honest, I haven't found an altogether compelling position to make my own. Still less have I fixed on a modest strategy to act on my eventual convictions. But you have made it impossible for me to let the issue lie. In part, this opening is report; in part, Birthday tribute. Over the years I have pieced together impressions and filled in the spaces with faith in the man I knew. Now I speak from the center of a soul shaken awake by your priestly voice. If you were to do nothing more with your life than stir a handful of people to give time and thought and work to history's greatest peril your worth would outweigh the life-mass of all the check-writers and civic-dutifuls on the honoris causa roster. . . . Unlike Israel's prophets, you speak with passionate reason, as to brothers and sisters, with the authority of a pure heart and a clear mind. With a life so full, I doubt that you bother to imagine other Jack-Weimerhoods. The one you have chosen surpasses all imaginings. God's great blessings on your yesterdays, today and tomorrows.

Help me with my study of disarmament. I'm looking for books that examine the history of previous negotiations to limit nuclear weapons, with an eye to learning workable openings to the next round of talks. I happen to believe Russia will agree to arrangements that serve their interests. Climate, warm or cool, makes little difference to them. For the most part, they turn the thermostat up or down to make us shiver, sweat, or relax. The present chill owes at least as much to their determination to exploit the anxieties of Europe's anti-nuke movements. An alternate reading of Kremlin thinking sees the Red funk as a chess-player's made at an opponent's insistence on taking back a careless move: deployment of the SS20's went unanswered; then the opponent says he really meant to counter that move, as though this were a walk-through scrimmage. But given a realistic trade-off, they would haggle to an acceptable accommodation. Even a xenophobic totalitarian society must recognize advantage in reducing its defense budget. A pre-packaged deal seems doomed. So the question arises: what has drawn the Russians to the bargaining table? A detailed account of previous successes and failures would contribute to informed opinion, which serves the cause better than slogans. I might even write a letter to the editor of *The Mundelein Herald*.

Your governor—may he one day be your President and mine—found a lever long enough to nudge the abortion debate into motion, even to overcoming the inertia of the *Chicago Catholic*. For years—the Cody years—our undistinguished weekly shrieked 'Murder!' and elaborated on the theme. Last week the new editor broke through to reasonableness and agreed with Cuomo, Father Whelan, S.J., and—mirabille dictu!—Jerry Falwell in forgoing the Amendment strategy in favor of creating a livable society: Not a coerced birth but a convinced choice for life. The pious fire-eaters have yet to be heard from. Their furor will top a million megatons. At least the monolith has been broken. We can get on with more Christian responsibilities. For my part, I think Cuomo's argument is incomplete. A Catholic public official can use his influence to set state policy on matters of legitimate concern: public funding and parental rights. In no other case that I'm aware of has the court moved from prohibition to claim on the treasury. (Certainly not in the case of church-related schools). Let those who advocate abortion contribute to needy unmothers through a private foundation. And the inconsistency surrounding the parents' authorization for all other non-emergency surgery has to be resolved. Apart from those desiderata, we must work for justice and freedom-for, to make the world hospitable and sex less casual. . . . In Him Who is in us, Will

∞

8 Oct 1985

Dear Johann,

I think of you most often when I read some thoughtful piece on disarmament. So far I've come upon nothing to put me in either camp, Hawk or Dove. Perhaps the most useful undertaking I've heard of is the New York City Bar's study of Russian negotiating over the years, which promises they've made and kept or made and broken. (Lou Craco is on the No-Bomb squad.) Until we can assure mutuality of intent toward limited objectives it's pointless to clamor for cutbacks. I have made an irrevocable judgment on Star Wars: SDI will be the biggest digression since the Passamaquoddy project . . . A summer *Harper's* offered an essay on Man The Gardener, proposing a secular view of Nature. Throw a little Teilhardian disinfectant over it and it would suit a Curial colloquium. In the long spiral of evolution one level's adaptation to conditions created the conditions for the emergence of the next level. But with man the process became reflexive; man can choose his conditions, more, can create conditions. So culture is nature taking charge of itself. Hence, Man The Gardener. I think Jesus fits into this schema of his teaching that every person must be free to love, to raise conditions for his patch of being. As his disciple, you teach that same freedom, as much with your life as with your words. If you have given the whole of your existence to the Jesus project it must merit thought and, with grace, liberation. . . . Happy Birthday, good man . . . Little to tell. The working man thanks God he was not caught up in this daily scrabbling earlier, else he would be lost to Mammon . . . Shop around for a workshop out this way. I hunger for more than chit-chat. Will

∞

15 Dec 1985

Dear Vater Hans,

Even if I had husbanded my time better I would need no more than a minute to cover the past two months. You must have heard of Dick Gralton's swift surrender to cancer. And of Phil McGrath's death, with the final failure of his three-year-old heart and lungs. . . . It's not as though I'm waiting for an apt thought to gift-wrap. Unlike King Midas, who gave everyone on his list a gold muffler, I am making do with simple words—and borrowed words, at that. Three weeks ago a young woman I tutored in algebra and inspirited through empty times sent me away from her wedding reception with thanks for my love. She set my soul to tingling by telling me my love had been important to her. Right then I knew what I must do. So I tell you, no less truly, that your love has been important to me—from the first, when I needed tolerance, through the long struggle, when I needed reassurance, into the late years, when I have needed affirmation. I thank God for you, good friend, and rejoice in the grace of your friendship. In the God who took flesh, Will

∞

10 Oct 1987

Frater Johannes,

. . . . I can wrap up a year's worth of days with the log entry, "Sailing as before." Doctors/hospitals and I have kept a healthy distance from each other. In early July my brother and I drove, in my air-less van, to Kansas City, to visit two of his sons and their wives. Eleven hours on Interstate highways is as long as I care to detach myself from human society. On oath I could not have vouched for the presence of a single Iowan besides the privateer who operates an Amoco station in a town renowned for its bleu cheese. KC is a likable town, easy to traverse and pleasant to browse. Even the 96° readings were made comfortable by a brisk, dry wind. Later in the month we vacationed in Dana, for a high school Reunion. There the heat was unmitigated misery. On the consolation of memory, past July days warmed further by the tin roof of the haymow, made breathing less oppressive. Amazingly, the turnout was large and congenial. As the Methodists are wont to say, we fellowshipped heartily.

What's to become of our Church? The Big Guy is sitting on the safety valve to generate more heat, but the seams won't hold much longer. The twin heresies of women priests and married priests hold promise of salutary, even graced correction of centuries of masculine theology, thought- and thing-oriented. Pastoral theology, given new dimensions by the feminine understanding of the personal, could animate a new sense of service to balance the paternal duty of disciplining. Those are not tangential issues. In Christ, Will

∞

12 Oct 1988

Dear Jack:

As nearly as I can reckon, I'm taking time out from writing 1981 Christmas cards to wish you a Happy Fifty-first Birthday. . . . As if to confirm my mental disarray, I pulled this from the typewriter five days ago and digressed or diddled till today, 17 Oct. You are a bit older by now and presumably a lot wiser. . . . The life choice you have made gives force to your words, especially for the young, who sniff out hypocrisy wherever it lurks. While I cringe at medallists who worship Christ, Energizer, I pray that he will be your energy as the body's resources dwindle. Many years and rich, great friend. . . . I wish Dukakis inspired enough faith to make his defeat catastrophic. Maybe Bush will be overwhelmed by the Spirit and discover the truth about our condition . . . If not sooner, June . . . In Him who first walked the Way, Will

• In his October 11, 1982, letter to Fr. John Weimer, Will indicates that John is celebrating his fiftieth birthday; in view of this, Will's first sentence of this letter makes no sense, unless he's claiming complete loss of his sense of time due to his "mental disarray." Could this be one of Will's first realizations of his transient states of confusion?

• "While I cringe at medallists who worship Christ, Energizer . . . " This is perhaps Will's opinion of Olympic athletes who credit the Almighty for their gold, silver or bronze rewards.

• "If not sooner, June . . . " is a reminder of the 35th Class Reunion in 1989.

∞

Elizabeth K. (Betty) Kane and William J. (Bill) Kane

Selections Written 7 March 1965–27 June 1989

My wife, Elizabeth Knoll Kane, became Will's friend in her own right after I introduced them to each other in 1972. Betty, born February 8, 1934, in Saint Cloud, Minnesota, was the second of three daughters followed by two sons. She received her bachelor of science in nursing degree in 1955 from the College of Saint Catherine in Saint Paul, Minnesota. After working for a time as a staff nurse, she became a nursing instructor at Saint Mary's Hospital in Minneapolis. We began dating in the summer of 1959 and were married June 25, 1960. Five children, three girls and two boys, were born to us over the next seven years and today we enjoy six grandchildren. Although our permanent family home now is in a suburb of Minneapolis, Minnesota, we lived in the suburbs north of Chicago from 1971 to 1978.

I was born in the Flatbush section of Brooklyn on February 22, 1933, the first of the two sons of Margaret Redmond and William Aloysius Kane. I was fortunate to grow up surrounded by a large extended family, including my four grandparents, a dozen aunts and uncles and numerous first cousins, all of whom lived nearby in Brooklyn or Queens. We gathered often for family celebrations. Upon graduation from Queen of All Saints grade school I won a scholarship to Saint Francis Xavier High School, a Jesuit school in Manhattan. While there I participated in Junior R.O.T.C., and well remember the uniforms and drills. I also ran track and cross-country, sang in the diocesan choir (first, soprano, and later, alto), and played baseball and basketball for parish teams.

My active life was interrupted by polio in mid-August 1949. I spent the next ten weeks in Saint Charles Hospital, which caused me to miss classes for the entire first semester of my senior year. When I returned to high school after the New

Year, the faculty allowed me to earn full credit for the semester by passing the final examinations. I crammed and was successful. My personal experience with polio, including getting to know the doctor who cared for me, Dr. Herbert C. Fett, Jr., stimulated my interest in orthopaedics, both the clinical and basic science aspects of the field.

Holy Cross College, where Will Jenks and I met as first-year students in the class of 1954, was a singular experience. I took great pride in the college and its message, matured both intellectually and emotionally and enjoyed the camaraderie of faculty as well as classmates. After graduating from Holy Cross, I went on to Columbia University's College of Physicians and Surgeons, where I received the doctor of medicine (M.D.) degree in 1958. Then, after twenty-five years on the East Coast, I moved westward to the University of Minnesota where I completed my orthopaedic surgical training and also received a doctor of philosophy (Ph.D.) degree in 1965.

My academic interests in teaching, research and clinical orthopaedics led me to join the orthopaedic faculties of the University of Minnesota and, later, Northwestern University. The many advances within orthopaedics and associated specialties over the course of the last half-century convince me that I have experienced a golden period of progress in medicine. I am extremely optimistic that this progress will continue in the next half-century.

∞

7 March 1965

Dear Bill,

Is it possible that you took me off your Christmas card list because last Nov. 3 I opted for the twentieth century? That sort of reprisal is hardly worthy of Robert Welch, let alone Dr. Kane. For my part, I am so tolerant of dissent that I sent a box of Mr. Welch's taffy to Barry [Goldwater] as a consolation prize. That ought to shake the eye teeth of some conservatives.

I must confess that you caught me in the solar plexus when you assaulted me with your paleolithic political views. Where in the world did you pick up those mouldy notions about individual freedom? I suspect that you've been rummaging in Bill Buckley's Old Curiositie Shoppe, *National Review* or, worse, in the AMA's hornbook of maxims for myopics. It would be less unseemly for a liberally educated man to subscribe to *Batman Comics* or, in a case of total regression, *Playboy*. If you would care to be purged of the demon that possesses you, you should read Teilhard de Chardin's *The Future of Man*. The reading of it requires an open mind, a sturdy heart, and a patient eye, but the book repays the effort with a sense of the shape of man's destiny. Teilhard insists that you are swimming against the tide. (Cf. p. 197, "Bill Kane and his ilk are swimming against the tide.") When the force of the great seer's thoughts has surged through your brain and has flushed out all the noxious nonsense you will be fit to dwell in the Great Society, with liberty and justice for all. (Friends, if gratitude for your conversion so completely overwhelms you that you feel compelled to send a small donation to aid our cause, just mail a check or money order—please, no stamps—to: Brother Al Truistic, The-Four-Square-Gospel-And-Total-Immersion-Tabernacle, Omega Point, Arkansas.)

Except for scribbled anti-obituaries on a few Christmas cards, I have heard nothing from the world beyond the Wabash. (An anti-obituary, you will be relieved to learn, is a notice that, appearances notwithstanding, an erstwhile friend is still taking his embalming fluid orally.) It would seem that the world is too much with them.

My own doings are little more than a denial of non-being. For the past few months, I have been a fixed blip on Heaven's radar screen. I did go AWOL to Indianapolis for three days during the Christmas holidays, but my hosts, my brother Jim and his wife, saw to it that I kept my eligibility for a box of Yuletide goodies from the Baptists. It is an apt commentary on life in Dana that the Council is considering permitting the town's Catholics to omit the phrase "Lead us not into Temptation" from the Lord's Prayer, on the grounds that it is irrelevant to our situation.

After seven straight humiliating failures as a mentor of meager minds, I finally scored a success this winter. The payload I put into orbit was a high school junior who accurately if belatedly diagnosed his predicament as a congenital grammar-asthenia. (I mix my metaphors in an Oster blender.) The lad had limped through freshman algebra and Latin, leaning on this bent reed, and, undaunted, he chose to brave fate again. This time I was working on more familiar terrain, and by sheer force of will, power of intellect, and prowess of larynx I bullied the fellow into a 'B.' He might have had the benefit of an authentic miracle, an 'A,' if he had had wit enough to dispute his priggish teacher's bad judgment in a punctuation exercise. I suppose that my pedagogical style will now become as widely admired as the Socratic method. The secret is to scream a lot.

Aside from *The Future of Man,* the most interesting book I've read in the past six months was *The Book of Mormon,* by Joseph Smith, a distant cousin of mine. Cousin Joe's home-made scriptures are at once imaginative and naïve. It's remarkable that an unschooled man, even one steeped in the Bible as deeply as Joe obviously was, could invent a fantastic if tedious parody of revelation as he did. But a modern reader, aware however tangentially of the findings of biblical scholars, can find a dozen flagrant incongruities in the first few chapters. I'm afraid I won't make Heaven through my link with the last of the prophets.

I know I'm keeping you from the latest issue of *The Bone-Setters Gazette,* with its feature story on funny femurs, and so I'll flee the scene as though someone had goosed me with his Babinsky stick. You know, I trust, that if you should ever wander so far off course that you find yourself in the vicinity of Dana, you and whoever is foolhardy enough to accompany you will be welcome at the Jenks hostelry. Give my best to any of the Yeti who cross your path. Yours for one ghost, one vote, Mayor Daley

• I confess to being to the right of Will on the political spectrum, but I never felt I was so far from his views as he implies.

∞

20 Oct 1966

To: A Hawk
From: A Dove
About: The Prospect of Vultures

The loss of Bill Coakley, one of the Campion Hall crew, makes the Viet Nam exertion seem unnecessarily costly. The right and wrong of it can be debated endlessly, but who can rejoice in Coakley's sacrifice? And he at least chose to put his life at the disposal of Messiah McNamara, with his curious creed, "Greater love hath no man than to lay down the life of a friend." (An archaic word. The modern equivalent is employee, either freeman or serf.) My hopes are not so much for halting the war abruptly as for restoring decency immediately. Air power should be restricted to tactical support of ground troops, without the use of napalm. Crop-killing and food-flushing ought to be stopped. South Vietnamese troops should be responsible for all offensive action, and American forces should merely secure newly won territory. Civilian volunteers, especially pacifists and anti-war demonstrators, should be encouraged to serve as hostage-teachers in the controlled areas. . . .

All I know about any of the brethren is what I've read in the *Alumnus*. I stay informed about the situation at HC through publications forwarded by Father Hart and through letters from Father Cummings. The place has changed radically since the Class of '54 fled. Cars, girls, booze, and freedom are now standard equipment. Today's swingers would think our ascetic way of life was blatantly masochistic.

If a convention or a wrong turn brings you this way, stop in. I might be able to re-educate you in forty-eight hours. Best to anyone. Yours for self-determination, Lurleen Wallace

• Bill Coakley, '54, was a U.S. Navy carrier pilot assigned to Johnson's White House as a naval attaché when he requested to return to active duty at sea. He was later killed while flying a mission over Vietnam.

∞

24 May 1971

Dear Bill,

Congratulations to NU Med School on landing its first-round draft choice. It has strengthened itself in a key position and should be ready to challenge the Phineas Ducksong School of Chiropractic and Acupuncture for pre-eminence in the healing arts, at least on its own block . . . There's nothing momentous happening in Dana—again. I've been asked to run for the town board on the Democrat ticket. A chorus of moans was said to have issued from the Jenks plot in the Bono cemetery when I accepted. There's little danger that I'll be elected. The Democrats won't trust me and the Republicans won't forgive me . . . One, two, or seven Kanes will be welcome in Dana anytime. It's a four-hour drive, including a pit-stop in Kentland. I await your signal . . . You have my prayers that your new work will satisfy your personal and professional needs. Will

∞

18 May 1972

Dear Bill, Betty, Kathy, Billy, Steve, Patty, and Annie,

It's not that I've been debating with myself for a month about whether or not I'm glad you came to Dana. It's just that I've been devoting all my time to writing campaign speeches for the Cookie Monster. (What kind of a President would make everybody pay his taxes in cookies?) Anyhow, even though you came two weeks too soon to see Indiana at its loveliest it was good of you to make the long drive to let me meet six of you for the first time. I like the six 'new' Kanes at least as well as I like the 'old' one. . . . This Sunday, if the weather's nice, a cousin of mine is going to take five Jenkses for a boat ride up the Wabash river. I'm going to stuff the football inside my shirt, so I'll float just in case we are torpedoed by an enemy submarine. I've got my mother looking for the wooden whistle that came with the sailor suit my aunt gave me for my fourth birthday—way back in the olden days . . . I made a novena to St. Unodomo, patron of double-mortgaged suburbanites. Satisfaction guaranteed or your 'Ave's cheerfully refunded. (Is that how to pluralize 'Ave'?) . . . My rustic awkwardness prevented us from enjoying the sherry together. It won't go unsipped. Mea culpa and thanks . . . My mother sends her best to all of you . . . Adios, amigos. Will

- The "five Jenkses" are Ella, Will, and Jim, Carol and Karen from Indianapolis. The "cousin" is Walter Collins and his wife Florence. Walter trailed his pontoon boat over land to Dana from Lee's Summit, Missouri, for a visit with Will and his mother. Will's Aunt Mimi gave him the sailor suit with a whistle.
- When the Kane family moved to a second suburban home we still hadn't sold the first, hence Will's prayers to "St. Unodomo" (One House).
- "Ave" stands for "Ave Maria" (Hail Mary).

∞

5 April 1974

Dear Bill, Betty, KBSP&A,

I'm now electronically engineered to do everything but scratch wherever it itches. That will no doubt be the next scientific breakthrough, a boon to .00000000025 of mankind. With the present set-up, similar to Dr. Strangelove's magic box, I can turn the radio off and on, switch my typewriter on/off, and handle incoming and outgoing phone calls. The phone attachment offers the most immediate benefit; it frees my mother from having to match the receiver to my ear, dial, and, eventually, hang up. My ear welcomes the change, too. It has grown lumpy from pressing against the eely receiver. I'm not sure, though, that I'm the ideal subject for the experiment. The device seems to have been designed for a totally immobile, bedfast patient. My fantastic adeptness with stick, clothes pin, and pen gives me flexibility undreamed of by trees, pillars, and Northwestern defensive backs. It's something equivalent to being lower-middle-class: I really don't qualify for the programs meant for the less fortunate. But I agreed to try it, chiefly to see if any of the features could be adapted to my needs . . . Dudley—a thoroughly amiable man, with tastes and opinions close to my own (a prince of a fellow, therefore)—put my thoughts on an electric wheelchair, which would allow me to flee Dirty Sally and rendezvous with Cronkite as I choose . . . Hi to all. And thanks for this latest intervention in my behalf. I couldn't advertise for better friends . . . Will

• The "magic box" is the environmental control system developed by Dr. Dudley S. Childress and the Northwestern University Rehabilitation Engineering Program. Interestingly, Will doesn't think he's the "ideal subject" because he is not "a totally immobile, bedfast patient."

∞

4 May 1974

Dear KBSP&A,

Because you are all fans of Dana, I know you will want to read about its 100th birthday party, which will be held late this summer. Notice that I wrote one of the articles on the front page. I used the name Bill instead of Will because that's what people there have always called me. At Holy Cross I was called Will. And in China I was called Wun Dum Nut . . . Be good. Stay out of jail. No roller skating on the roof . . . Your old, old friend, Will

∞

22 July 1974

Dear Betty and Unidentified Classmate,

Just returned from two glorious weeks in Dana. The porch was rarely empty, and at times it was filled to overflowing. Our visit even managed to coincide with an ice cream social at the Fire House. So what if I didn't win the 200 lb. market-weight hog they raffled off? I got to sit between the tenor and the second baritone when the barbershop quartet sang. Everybody was real kind about welcoming us home, and a few even bragged on the piece I done for the *Centennial News*—all about the old-time threshing ring . . . On the hottest day of the sultry fortnight two friends and I drove over to Champaign, Ill., in an unconditioned car, and we ate dinner at a fancy restaurant—candles on the table and like that there. After sopping up the last drop of gravy we went on back to Danville to see *The Exorcist*. Whoo-ee! Like to scare a body out of a year's growth. (Actually, I found it tricked-up and tawdry. To be taken seriously, the film would have had to be done with restraint. The real terror lies in possibility, not in fantasy. Bill O'Malley was good in every scene but one, when he was given an inane line. Sitting at the piano during a cocktail party, he was made to say, "My idea of Heaven is me at the piano and the audience always wants more." His big scene with the dying devil-wrencher came off powerfully, even though some yahoo in a 495 cc Ford Shrieker chose that moment to simulate sexual arousal with all eight raging cylinders. O'Mal is the only person on the screen at the end, and he walks bravely into the Georgetown twilight.)

Part of my indifference to *The Exorcist's* fabricated horror may have traced back to an all-too-real horror we experienced here only ten days before. My aunt, the tormented woman for whom Bill arranged appointments took her own life after three-and-a-half months of total resistance to our pleas to seek help. My mother and I found her body hanging from the wooden swing frame in the backyard. Mercifully, the boys weren't home; they were staying overnight with their mother . . .

I know you don't need any urging to enjoy your month in Minnesota. Send me your address and I'll mail you an update on the crops and late bulletins on Chicago's political aberrations. Vaya Con Dios. Will

- Will's two dinner companions were Madelyn Saxton and Father Lawrence Moran.
- Rev. William J. O'Malley, S.J., ex '53, acted the part of the young priest and also provided technical advice on exorcism for the director of *The Exorcist*.

∞

30 April 1975

Dear Bill,

. . . . I don't know how to ask subtly, so I'll just ask straight out: is there any chance that you will be going to Worcester in three weeks? If you can swing it, I thought it would be that much more enjoyable to have you on the same flight and in the same room in Hogan. . . . Hello to everyone. Take time to ponder the meaning of it all . . . Will

∞

3 Nov 1975

Dear Bill,

In the event Dudley hasn't notified your office of my change of title, please ask your secretary to address all correspondence to :
His Ineffable Highness,
  W. Abdullah Jenks,
  Caliph of the Nile,
  Emir of Aswan,
  Grand Vizier of Thebes,
  & Close Personal Friend
  of Jehan Sadat

It hardly needs saying that I made a terrific impression during my 90 seconds in the limelight. Actually, I spent my allotted time doing Immelmann's and barrel rolls while Dr. Compere narrated. Chuck Percy engaged me in a brief but inane conversation, and Nancy Kissinger pointedly ignored me. Madame Sadat seemed truly interested in what is being done to rehabilitate the LH&B. . . . The goatless cart—smaller version of the horseless carriage—surpasses all my expectations. As I become more adept at dodging walls I find confidence flowering into style. Even John no longer accuses me of working for Urban Renewal. A week ago carpenters put in a sloping, curving ramp from the front door to the driveway. Jean Claude would find the run challenging. But for me, it's the Freedom Highway. To give some measure of the radical change the chair has made in my life I would have to clock the hours recaptured from un-drutheredness. Now I can be where I want to be when I want to be. The capability is so new that it's not yet patterned on my brain . . . I've already sent Dudley and the Engineers a note of thanks for their sorcery in my behalf. The control system may be a prototype, but the entire product was custom-made for my specific requirements, including comfort. But to go back further on the chain of causality, I must embarrass you with new thanks. I don't know what criteria would have been used to find a worthy candidate for testing the craft, but I'm glad I had so persuasive an advocate arguing my case. You've been instrumental in so many of the life-ripening happenings of recent years. The best of them, though, has been the sameness of your friendship, despite my celebrity. Hi to all. Will

- Dr. Clinton L. Compere was a Northwestern University professor of orthopaedic surgery; Charles Percy represented Illinois in the U.S. Senate; Nancy Kissinger was the wife of Secretary of State Henry Kissinger; Jehan Sadat was the wife of Egyptian leader Anwar Sadat. Will demonstrated his electric wheelchair steered by sips and puffs for these celebrities at the Rehabilitation Institute of Chicago.
- "LH&B" stands for the Lame, Halt and Blind.
- "Jean Claude" Killy, the famed skier, is presented as the paragon of mobility.

7 Feb 1977

Dear Betty,

If it's too late to celebrate your birthday, it's not too late to celebrate our friendship. Just last night I heard Uta Hagen argue that liberation is not primarily a political issue; it's a personal decision. I think you give force to that view. You chose to be a friend, quite apart from any role as the wife of a friend. I'm glad you set out on your own to discover what kind of friendship might spring up between us. That took imagination, independence, even courage. However alert and aware we are, we may never ambush Truth, but we should enjoy the chase . . . Thanks for daring to be yourself . . . Love, Will

∞

10 Feb 1977

Dear Bill,

Life's real miracles are not pulled off at Lourdes; they're done in kindness to those who need help, by those who make up for what is missing in another life with the gift of their own strength, time, concern. If I could walk I might not believe there are friends ready to lift a heavy burden. Thanks for the good time, the good talk, and the good friend . . . Will

∞

28 Feb 1977

Dear Betty,

Long thanks for feeding me, and twice-long thanks for doing it so deftly that I felt not at all conspicuous. Sensitivity expresses itself in understated deeds. Not least, thanks for letting me meet Frank. He is everything you said—friendly, witty, bright, concerned, involved, unafraid. I may register to vote in Chicago's First Ward to insure my voting for him, dead or alive, when he runs for President. It pleased me when he said he understood you and I are good friends, though it did take me off guard. In the past brothers of my female friends have invariably followed up that sort of opening with a punch in the nose. There are some compensations to being deLothario-ized. I'm glad you count me a friend, even to your brother . . . Thanks for Sunday and all the days you've made Sunday. Love, Will

• "Frank" was Betty's brother, Franklin J. Knoll, who at the time was serving in the Minnesota senate. He had come to Chicago for a meeting and had a weekend meal at our home together with Will.

∞

1 Nov 1978

Dear Betty and Repatriates,

. . . . 40 Osage houses one potential tepid scoop. With luck I will soon be launched on a new, high-paying, glamorous career as a computer programmer. Hardly a week ago I was talking to Margaret Pfrommer, fellow polio and employee of NU Rehab Engineering, and I was cursing the gods who toy with the lives of polyethylene salesmen. Margaret asked me if I knew Charlie Schmidt, of Lift, Inc. My 'no' got a quick retort, "You should." So now I do. Monday I went to his office in Northbrook and submitted my ego to an aptitude test that left me feeling inept. But I must have passed, because Mr. Schmidt and his partner in this non-profit venture, Bill Warner, interviewed me for an hour. As soon as they sign the right company to a one-man-year contract, I'll begin learning that esoteric stuff like GARBAGE-IN/GARBAGE-OUT. The program will happen chiefly in the home, where they'll set up a terminal connected to the computer of my sponsor company. In four to six months, I'll be gainfully employed in a 40-hour-a-week job, and poly be damned!

Best love to Julie Andrews, Pele, Huck Finn, Linda Carter, and Tinker Bell. And to their mother, Princess Sky Blue Waters. Eventually, Will

• In the summer of 1978 we moved the Kane family back to Edina, Minnesota, and into a house less than fifty yards from the one we had left in 1971. I chose to continue practicing medicine in Chicago, commuting to and from the Twin Cities on Friday afternoon and early Monday morning. When our five children's college educations had been paid for, I returned to the Twin Cities to practice.

∞

5 Feb 1981

Dear Betty,

I intend to escort this card with an article from *New Republic*. It may give direction to the rest of your life. As Fairlie points out, Liberalism has emptied its center of values in its centrifugal espousal of rights. And Conservatism has simply built a Doric façade for the Temple of Mammon. What is needed is a system of values reflecting, expressing the good of communities—families, neighborhoods, churches, those groups that take responsibility for their members. But Fairlie makes it fairly clear that the new moral structure must have an intellectual base. It must be reasonable because reasoned. I honestly believe the creators of the social bond will be women, who can both feel and think. It's important that the new moral consensus resonate to the fears and needs experienced in today's reality. Men tend to read reports, abstract and quantified, and propose rational absolutions, invariably based on artificial structures. Women, I think, have not allowed education to cripple their sense of what strengths are or could be available to society, what kind of support society can give to organic communities that nurture those strengths. Honest to Mondale, the coincidence of reading that article and thinking of your birthday set off that mental pandemonium. Because you have the most acute moral sense—not moralistic indignation—of all my friends, you should put it to use, not just to give your life fuller meaning but to create a world of order and freedom, where belonging implies both limits and possibilities. That's a strange birthday wish, but there you have it. Happy Birthday, earnest friend . . . All's well here. My morning person, Claudia, was heavensent. She is kind and thoughtful and unfailingly cheerful. And she thanks me for letting her take care of me . . . Love to all the Kanes, especially you, valued confidante . . . Bill

∞

6 Feb 1983

Dear Betty,

If you read Father Brooks' Report on the State of the College and of the World you must have felt confirmed in your belief that Minnesota is exempt from History's travails. My President worries that we are out-Darking the

Dark Ages, not just in Chicago but in the entire West. Minnesota, obviously, stands apart from the madding crowd and its villainies. Why? It would be worth knowing. My guess is that the Germans and Scandinavians who settled Minnesota came from societies disposed to work, order, and social responsibility for the unfortunate. Only a rebel would know alienation. Those of us from oppressed homelands, like Ireland or Alabama, seized the doctrine of rugged individualism and made it our own. And our rebels win sympathy, even approval. What has all this to do with you and your birthday? It's not to congratulate you on your good sense in having been born a Minnesotan. Maybe it's to call you to search out the wisdom underlying your native ways, to see if it carries over to the general condition. When Reagan's Tinkertoy ideology collapses there must be sanity to hold off chaos. I think the liberal answer can no longer rely on wishes, dreams, imaginings but must draw on working models of honest, humane government. (Suddenly I have a numbing sensation, born of the dread that honest, humane government is possible only when the governed govern their own appetites for public largesse. Is that Minnesota's secret, untransferrable to the larger domain? Even that would be worth knowing, to set the bounds of reality.) You can intuit the meaning I will give my prayer. You know, of course, that I love you and want only good for you. But I also want good from you. Put your mind to discovering your luck and take the good news as far as your voice will reach . . . Hi to all the Kanes . . . Love, Will

∞

9 Nov 1983

Dear Betty,

How good that you gave it a go. A renowned surgeon told me there is every reason to think you will be free of the pain that has dogged you for so long. In full health you can place new energy at the service of Fritz Mondale or Jesse Jackson, whichever candidate finally wins you over. Even if you concede the election to Reagan and merely enjoy the days without Excedrin we—the we who love you—will be glad for you . . . Having looked over the Democratic candidates, I can't pretend to any excitement for the crowd of them. With a single exception they seem to be decent enough, but none of them gives evidence of having unlearned the dogmas of bypassed Liberalism. It's a time to take tough stands on issues affecting Democrats: UNIONS, BLACKS, TEACHERS, GOVERNMENT EMPLOYEES. Unless their demands are moderate it will do scant good to correct the tax inequities created by the fast-shufflers now dealing. Who will have the courage, to say nothing of the wisdom? . . . Knit quickly and shake your head gently . . . Love, Will

• To treat chronic neck pain caused by a herniated disc, Betty successfully underwent surgery to remove the disc and fuse the adjacent vertebrae.

∞

5 Feb 1984

Dear Betty,

Christopher Dawson, once the pre-eminent Catholic historian, wrote a paper on the Esquimaux in support of a thesis that mankind can adapt to even the harshest conditions. Had he waited till this year he could have made his point by citing the hardihood of Minnesotans. This winter will be remembered as the final resting place of stories about the really savage winters we old folks recall whenever young whipper-snappers complain about frost-nipped ears. More significantly, it will be remembered as the time Betty Kane uttered a discouraging word about God's colony. That momentary angst broke down the final obstacle to intimacy; I had suggested that you—and all native Minnesotans—were superior beings from a far galaxy. Now I know you are merely superior beings who use the hardly habitable climate as a defense against the mongrel hordes. Another remark of yours has stayed with me. You told me how hard it was, even at the low ebb of postop helplessness, to ask for help. It was kind of you to say you remembered the key thought of My Famous Speech: Let yourself be loved. I think that's even more true of generous, nurturing women. There's a real danger you will come to believe you are loved for what you do, not who you are. And should age or illness keep you from doing for others, you would find little to value in yourself. Those of us who love you do so and say so out of joy that there is a Betty Kane, that God has surprised and delighted us with a way-of-being we find beautiful. Blessings on the day you were born and on all your days since . . . My knee has been free of pain for six weeks. Life is better that way. If the cold would take early retirement I would be content with my fate . . . Sameness reigns here . . . Love to all; best love to you. Will

∞

17 Feb 1985

Dear Betty,

. . . . Perhaps more than any previous birthday this one will have found you thrown back on the elemental faith that grounds your working beliefs. Certainly society seems to have rejected—and even its most fervent apostles seem to have abandoned—the Liberal doctrine of social responsibility for the outsider. At times, the sudden disintegration of the Liberal polity carries intimations of Greek tragedy. Thebes prospered and fell into decay in much the same way. If we must search out hardier truths for the next building up of justice we must look to the freedoms and attachments we value most and turn them into principles of future engagement. I'm confident you haven't lost heart. You have what Tillich called 'the courage to be,' a readiness to take part in life, whatever the moment. I wish we could talk as we once did. It would cheer both of us. Failing that, we must keep each other in our prayers, to draw strength from our friendship . . . Hi to all your family . . . Love, Will

∞

12 May 1985

Dear Betty,

When Bill told me of your mother's death, I knew without measuring how deeply you would grieve, not because you were not at her bedside but because she will not be there as mother and friend. Faith has its consolations, and yet it cannot soften the ache of joys not shared, of worries not lightened. You will find, though, that your mother is with you, is within you, in your

ways of loving. Nothing can part you from that intimacy. I will pray that
you will quickly sense her presence more than her absence, that you will take
strength from the truth that she is proud of you . . . Love, Will

∞

27 Jun 1985

Dear Betty,

Bill told me several weeks ago that you had 'picked up a little something'
for me at The Antipodes. I guessed a boomerang. If I had put my Jesuit-
quickened wits to work on the mystery, I would have roamed the vast terrain
of the subjunctive and never stumbled upon so luxurious a something. Except
for the extravagance, the sheepskin seems exactly right: you are a nurse—still,
always—as well as my friend, and you know that a sheepskin is the surest
protection against pressure sores. What better gift for Will? How did you
intuit that I've grown concerned about skin breakdowns? Ever since I saw a
TV segment on post-polio syndrome, I promote every tingle to gangrene and
every rash to an ischemic ulcer. So now, thanks—goodly thanks—to you I
am spared one of those worries . . . Saturday John and I will travel to Dana
for a four-day visit. . . . The chief reason for the trip is a farewell party for my
friend Father Moran, who has been transferred to Terre Haute after 18 years
in our parish. We'll see other lifelong friends, including one woman we've
bade a final goodbye three or four times. In September she'll be 92. My idea
of fun . . . Love to everyone, first of all to yourself . . . Will

• Will learned of "post-polio syndrome" shortly after this constellation of symptoms
  received its name; he acknowledged the exaggerated effect of this knowledge on his
  imagination.

∞

8 Feb 1986

Dear Betty,

The loss of a dear friend—most recently, Father Hart—brings other friendships into sharper focus, as the mind ransacks memory for treasured moments. That heightened appreciation carries over, if only for a brief time, to recollections of pasts shared with what the love-probers now call 'significant others.' I think back on times when you and I danced soul-to-soul, disclosing our deepest beliefs without the protective categories of theology. For the most part, those exchanges enjoyed an intimacy of two, and yet our concerns were furthest from private—justice, freedom, morality, politics. I miss those talks, not just because we agreed on so many values but because we wrestled with the Gospel question, "What must we do?" I need reminding that it is not enough merely to hold right opinions, that it is necessary to act on convictions. I like to think we were good for each other, as a counterforce to privatization of feeling. Even though we have limited occasion to continue that renewing rite, I find the fond memory of those good times still at work against the inertia of hopelessness, and I thank you for that living gift, that present love. Happy birthday, partner-in-conscience . . . It has been a quiet two months in Lake Woisme . . . Best love, good friend. Will

• "Lake Woisme" is Will's answer to Garrison Keillor's imaginary Minnesota town, Lake Woebegon, regularly featured in Keillor's monologues beginning, "It has been a quiet week in Lake Woebegon," on the weekly radio show *Prairie Home Companion*.

∞

22 Dec 1986

Dear Bill and Betty, Three Crusaders and Two Serious Scholars,

Last Thursday, Young John dropped me off at the shopping center, and two hours later his dad picked me up. In the interval, I was a free-wheeling mallie, zipping from store to store, parting with cash and taking on cargo, and generally discommoding clerks and fellow materialists. I exploited the spirit of the season and involved strangers in scrutinizing price tags and piloting elevators. Several innocent bystanders came up to tell me it delighted them to see me go about my business. And it felt good. God bless NU Rehab Engineering and my link to them . . . Betty, I meant to save a Harper's essay on salvaging the Democratic party. It was a transcript of our conversations. Alas, there was no acknowledgement, so we will not be invited to head up a new Brain Trust . . . Whatever good each of you needs in '87 is yours, if Heaven heeds my prayers. Whole thanks for your friendship . . . Will

• The Kane children, Kathleen, '84, Billy, '85, and Anne, '89, are graduates of Holy Cross. Steve is a 1987 graduate of St. John's University (Minnesota), and Patricia, a 1988 graduate of the College of St. Benedict (Minnesota).

∞

7 Feb 1987

Dear Betty,

Arturo Toscanini, asked to comment on the work of Bruno Walter, is reported to have said, "He loved the beautiful parts too much." I suspect that's true of too many of us. We sleepwalk through the drudgery of weekday chores and leave a wake-up call for the weekend. But those chosen comas place an unsupportable burden on the excitement demanded of playtime. The next thrill must outdo the last, not merely vary the tempo. It's telling, I think, that you like the music of Bach, because his work calls for close attention to the building of modestly lyrical, rather than indulgently opulent, passages. Your loving/living follows that habit. You give no less attention to small things than to large; the whole of your time for others is 'quality time.' (Did we talk about the reconstructed feminist who now believes—O rank heresy!—that simply being with the children imparts a sense of security. Mom's in the kitchen; all's right with the world.) Time and attention are the two prime elements of love, as most women know and few men discover—and then only after reading it in a book, as I did. So it can be said, in all truth, that you have loved life in every minute of your days and years. Out of carefully polished pieces you have fashioned a mosaic of lustrous beauty, the Betty we celebrate more often than birthdays. But Happy Birthday, too, dear friend. . . . There will be prayers for your hopes, and there will be love . . . Will

∞

6 Feb 1988

Dear Betty,

It's shameful that I rouse myself to write only for birthdays and offering condolences—in some cases, offering condolences on a birthday. You are not alone in this withholding of Will. With few exceptions, my network of friends has come to expect annual signals that all is well with them and me. Age has persuaded me to a kind of silence, almost to your attitude about the news. There is the danger of Quietism, of course, but I think you are right in believing we get a better perspective on today from a point outside the daily churning of events. You are the true radical, dear friend. You go to the root of things with your Bible search for durable truths, the wisdom we can trust. Sensing life's longer rhythms, you recognize the meaninglessness of the frantic din so many try to dance to and identify the important choices confronting us. Still, we must ask "What am I to do?" Let me know how you translate the eternal into the contingent, the private into the public. How do the rest of us raise ourselves to Minnesotas? I honestly need to know your thoughts. Apart from you I have few friends who look beneath the surface. Which is to say, I value the life we celebrate on your day and pray there will be greater yet to come. Happy Birth, treasured friend . . . Little has changed here. Next week I will mark the third anniversary of my last professional encounter with a doctor. Both my insurance and I are elated . . . Love, Will

∞

20 Feb 1988

Dear Bill,

Having finished with today's farm business—the reams of paperwork Cargill requires to ransom NPE (No Price Entered) corn and beans, I now have an expanse of leisure in which to turn loose thoughts on your 55 years of Bill Kanehood. Seeing a self to celebrate goes against the latest intellectual trend, Deconstruction, which displaces an identifiable 'I' with a locus of contingent historical forces. But how is it these forces are orchestrated in unlikely ways to create great good or monstrous evil? I refuse to believe you just happened. The play of chance may have taken us a long way toward our species, but it can't account for the will to excel, still less, the willingness to teach. And though you talk of entrepreneurial medicine you talk with greater feeling of the excitement of surgery and the courage of woefully afflicted patients. You could just as easily have chosen to practice bone carpentry. Instead, you are a saint of Medicine, wholly human, wholly physician, doctor to the bone. Because none of us can be all things we tend to overvalue those who are different and admirably so, but I can imagine no better Bill Kane. May Minnesota deserve you. At least one Minnesotan does. Happy Birthday, good friend . . . Love, Will

∞

21 June 1988

Dear Bill and Betty,

Before I get to the thanks for last Friday's glad reunion, I want to apologize for having put you through the discomfort of my tidal blushing. That was no coy dalliance; that was honest dread that I wouldn't know how to handle the situation. And I made a fairly strong argument for lack of grace by handling the invitation so badly. But it finally came to me that it's not my part to decide what I'm not worthy of, if only because that implies I know what love I am worthy of, and love is gratuitous, all out of proportion to merit. So, let it be or not. I'll stagger along this Way, the path I would be on whatever the distractions . . . Apart from the jab to the solar plexus, the Fig Leaf evening gave me more delight than Toast 'n' Jelly Days in Lake Woebegon. The chef made only a small contribution to the savor. It was the banter and the agape that rolled over the soul's palate exciting the whole range of appetites—except those deemed base, vicious, lascivious, or immoral. I overdrank and over-talked, surely the two excesses that guarantee a good time for me. Yet again, thanks to both of you for carrying the gift in such festive wrapping. Your friendship is another undeserved blessing, more incongruous than any chair. God be thanked for that grace . . . Love, Will

• The Fig Leaf was the restaurant where Will learned of the gift to Holy Cross to establish the William H. P. Jenks Chair in English Literature.

∞

17 Feb 1989

Dear Bill,

The Church, in its ancient wisdom, withholds its halo until the wearer is safely beyond temptation—thoroughly dead. I suppose somewhere in history there has been a deathbed perversion. And even if there is no case to support the principle, it seems reasonable, even humane, since it fosters no tainted motives. Our own Father Hart, on his apotheosis in the naming of the Center, ruefully observed, "I guess now I'll have to behave the rest of the way." By contrast, the most a birthday greeting says is 'so far, so good,' leaving room for violent shifts of whim, perhaps a late-inning spasm of resentment against Jesuit training or Irish cuisine. Up to this point, though, your life has been altogether admirable. You wear renown lightly, love your work for reasons prior to money, and find time for friends who can do nothing for you, whether by way of repute, gain, or amusement. There are bodies made stronger, bones made straighter, through your doctoring, and there are hearts made happier by your befriending. What more could be said of a man? You might have been other; you could not have been more. Happy Birthday, great and good friend . . . Health update: pulse regular, temperature normal, breathing deep, nose cold, hair glossy, tongue pink, eye sparkling, ankles trim, eyebrows bushy. A-OK, thank you . . . Van update: placed order Friday for Ford 350 minibus, with front and back heat and a/c, windowed extended roof, assorted baubles, bangles, and beads. Delivery is set for mid-April. If we have it by mid-May John and I will drive to the Reunion, then stay on in New England for a few days, with stops at Jenks shrines in Saugus, Pawtucket, Old Lime, and St. Johnsbury. Count on a cool summer. Last summer had to cancel travel plans because my van had no a/c. . . . Best to your spouse and off-spring. Stay well . . . Yours for Quayle-under-glass, Will

∞

27 June 1989

Dear Bill and Betty,

My one regret of Reunion weekend was my failure to use part of my mike-time to thank the class for recognizing your generosity, your love in taking and taking care of me at three previous Reunions. The brass plate raises the HC chair from nostalgia piece to imaginative plaque. It says the thanks I feel, and it pleases me that your loving care was evident to the rest of '54. I know the two of you love me; you know that I love you. The chair honors the beauty of that love. God bless whoever thought of it, and God bless you, dear friends . . . Will

∞

Bibliography

Brown, Stuart, et al. *One Hundred Twentieth-Century Philosophers.* Routledge, 1998.

Farme, David. *The Oxford Dictionary of Saints.* Oxford University Press, 2003.

Gould, Tony. *A Summer Plague.* Yale University Press, 1995.

Halstead, Lauro and Naomi Naierman. *Managing Post-Polio.* ABI Professional Publications, 1998.

Hastings, Adam, et al. Editors. *The Oxford Companion to Christian Thought.* Oxford University Press, 2000.

Holroyd, Michael. *Works on Paper.* Counterpoint, 2002.

Jenks, John. *The Orra Mack Jenks Branch of the Welcome Jenks Family Tree.* John M. Jenks, 1993.

Jenks, John. *The Dominick Conway Clan with the Cronin Branch.* John M. Jenks, 1994.

Johnson, Paul. *The American People.* Harper Collins, 1998.

Kelly, Michael. *The Hound of Heaven.* Peter Reilly, 1916.

Kezys, Algimantas and John Quinn. *I fled Him down the nights and down the days.* Loyola University Press, 1970.

Kübler-Ross, Elizabeth. *On Death and Dying.* Macmillan Publishing Co., 1969.

Kuzniewski, Anthony. *Thy Honored Name.* Catholic University of America Press, 1999.

McBrien, Richard. *Lives of the Popes.* Harper Collins, 1997.

McDaniel, Thomas and Frederick Robbins, Editors. *Polio.* University of Rochester Press, 1997.

McGreal, Ian. Editor. *Great Thinkers of the Western World.* Harper Collins, 1992.

Musser, Donald and Joseph Price. Editors. *A New Handbook of Christian Theologians.* Abingdon Press, 1996.

Paul, John. *A History of Poliomyelitis.* Yale University Press, 1971.

Seavey, Nina, et al. *A Paralyzing Fear.* TV Books, 1998.

Shannon, James. *Reluctant Dissenter.* Crossroad Publishing, 1998.

The author became one of Will Jenks' classmates and friends during their freshman year, 1950–51, at Holy Cross College. The next summer, Will was rendered permanently quadriplegic by polio. Bill Kane went on to medical school at Columbia University and took his orthopaedic training at the University of Minnesota. He began his practice and teaching there and later at Northwestern University Medical School where he introduced Will to the rehabilitation engineers working at the Rehabilitation Institute of Chicago. They were able to facilitate Will's amazing return to a mainstream life.

PHOTO BY CHARLES E. CUDD, 2003

To order additional copies of *Let Yourself Be Loved:*

Web: www.amazon.com (after January 15, 2004)

Phone: 1-800-901-3480

Fax: Copy and fill out the form below with credit card information. Fax to 651-603-9263.

Mail: Copy and fill out the form below. Mail with check or credit card information to:

Syren Book Company
C/O BookMobile
2402 University Avenue West
Saint Paul, Minnesota 55114

Order Form

Copies	Title / Author	Price	Totals	
	Let Yourself Be Loved / Kane	$19.00	$	
	Subtotal		$	
	7% sales tax (MN only)		$	
	Shipping and handling, first copy		$	4.00
	Shipping and handling, ___ add'l copies @$1.00 ea.		$	
	TOTAL TO REMIT		$	

Payment Information:

__ Check Enclosed __ Visa/Mastercard		
Card number:	Expiration date:	
Name on card:		
Billing address:		
City:	State:	Zip:
Signature :	Date:	

Shipping Information:

__ Same as billing address __ Other (enter below)		
Name:		
Address:		
City:	State:	Zip: